MW00377820

New Americanists

A Series Edited by Donald E. Pease

José Martí's "Our America"

From National to Hemispheric Cultural Studies

Edited by Jeffrey Belnap and Raúl Fernández

Duke University Press Durham & London

1998

Printed in the United States of America on acid-free paper ∞
Designed by C. H. Westmoreland
Typeset in Sabon with Scala Sans Bold display by Keystone Typesetting, Inc.

Library of Congress Cataloging-in-Publication Data

José Martí's "Our America": From National to Hemispheric
Cultural Studies / edited by Jeffrey Belnap and Raúl Fernández.
p. cm. — (New Americanists)
Includes index.
ISBN 0-8223-2133-5 (cloth : alk. paper). —
ISBN 0-8223-2265-X (pbk. : alk. paper)
1. Martí, José, 1853–1895 — Views on United States.
2. United States — Politics and government — 19th century.
3. Latin America — Politics and government — 1830–1948.
4. United States — Relations — Latin America. 5. Latin
America — Relations — United States. 6. Martí, José, 1853–
1895. Our America. I. Belnap, Jeffrey Grant.
II. Fernandez, Raul A., 1945- . III. Series.
E1783.M38J68 1999
303.48'27308 — dc21 98-23367

Contents

Acknowledgments

This collection owes its existence to contributions from many sources. The 1992–93 Minority Discourse Initiative, convened by Valerie Smith at the University of California Humanities Research Institute, was the intellectual environment in which the significance of José Martí for U.S. cultural studies first became clear to us. The UCHRI, centered at UC Irvine, also generously supported the subsequent conference "'Our America' and the Gilded Age: José Martí's Chronicles of Imperial Critique," the occasion that first brought the contributors together in January of 1995. Mark Rose, former director of the UCHRI, gave important strategic and moral impetus to the proposal's early stages; the subsequent Institute director, Pat O'Brien, saw the conference through to its conclusion. Members of the UCHRI administration, Debra Massey Sánchez and Christine Aschan, provided unwaveringly competent and genuine support. Important support was provided by the Office of Research and Graduate Studies, the Office of the Associate Vice Chancellor for Academic Affairs, the Department of Spanish and Portuguese, the Latin American Studies Program, the Educational Opportunity Program, the Program in Comparative Culture, and the Chicano/Latino Studies Program, all at the University of California at Irvine.

Nancy Page Fernandez not only acted as conference manager but she was a constant sounding board for ideas concerning the shape the subsequent volume should take. Karen Marie Belnap undertook the arduous job of copyediting the entire manuscript, a task that also made several key contributions to the architecture of the final volume. Edna Mejia's peerless clerical expertise in both English and Spanish allowed for the final preparation of the manuscript for publication.

At various times in the process of putting together the conference and, later, this volume, the suggestions and help of a number of individuals were crucial for its success. Running the usual risk of leaving someone out, we wish to express our special indebtedness to Gilbert Gonzalez, Manuel Gomez, Manuel Hernandez Trujillo,

George Lipsitz, Lillian Manzor, Amy Kaplan, Donald Pease, Silvia Pedraza, Gerald Poyo, Marta Sanchez, Valerie Smith, Doris Sommer, and Steven Topik. We are also grateful to all the authors whose work is included in this anthology for a wonderful opportunity to work together.

We wish to express our gratitude for the steady support that Reynolds Smith of Duke University Press gave to our project. Our thanks go as well to the readers of the manuscript who provided invaluable insights, to Charles Purrenhage for a wonderful job of copyediting, and to the entire staff of Duke University Press.

Jeffrey Belnap and Raúl Fernández

Jeffrey Belnap and Raúl Fernández

Introduction: The Architectonics of José Martí's "Our Americanism"

The conference at the University of California Humanities Research Institute from which this collection grew took as its point of departure a conviction that the cultural criticism of José Martí (1853–95) constitutes an important—and largely underexamined—perspective on the culture of the Gilded Age during the emerging stages of U.S. transoceanic imperialism. Although Martí's status as Latin America's first modernist poet, as a lucid prose stylist, and as the architect of Cuba's independence from Spain have secured for his major essays and poems canonical status in Latin America, U.S. students of American culture have neglected the enormous body of journalistic prose Martí wrote while a U.S. correspondent for several Latin American newspapers. Written between 1881 and 1895, when Martí lived mainly in New York City, this body of articles kept the readership of newspapers in Venezuela, Mexico, Guatemala, and Argentina abreast of an array of developments in the United States. Speaking from something approaching an anthropological viewpoint, from which he relies upon (or constructs) a communitarian identity between himself and his Latin American readership, Martí analyzes a variety of phenomena: race relations in the age of Jim Crow; the Native American genocide; the injustices of indentured Asian labor; Washington's political and economic imperialism; labor movements during the rise of monopoly capitalism; the lives and works of U.S. political and literary figures; and the public spectacles and amusements of popular culture. Although the ostensive purpose of these texts was to keep readers informed of events and trends in the United States, they also constitute, when considered as a whole, a telling critique of both U.S. culture in the Gilded Age and the U.S. imperial project. Our objective in bringing the work of U.S. Americanists together with that of scholars more closely associated with the Latin American and Caribbean traditions is to introduce a body of work of considerable proportions into the general reexamination of the borders, parameters, and purposes of "American Studies," a reexamination that the emerging field of cultural studies has aggressively undertaken.

Martí came to live in the United States during the last decade and a half of his life as the result of political exile from his native Cuba. The child of Spanish parents who had emigrated to Cuba before he was born, Martí was first initiated into nationalist sentiments in the school of Rafael María de Mendive, a *criollo* intellectual and educator whose twin commitments to Cuba's independence from Spain and to the abolition of chattel slavery helped the precocious Martí to articulate his early dissatisfaction with his parents' parochial loyalism. The sentiments given voice in Mendive's school produced their first political effects in Martí's life during the Ten Years' War (1868–78), one of Cuba's unsuccessful wars of independence. Arrested and convicted at age sixteen for writing a letter expressing nationalist sentiment, Martí spent six months of a six-year sentence at hard labor. Exiled to Spain as an alternative to imprisonment, he thereafter returned to his native land only for brief periods.

Living for extended periods in Spain, Mexico, Guatemala, Venezuela, and finally the United States, Martí spent the rest of his life as a political exile and revolutionary, dedicating himself, especially during the years he spent in the United States, to overthrowing the Spanish authority that tyrannized the land to which he was forbidden to return. This activism became particularly intense after the foundation of the Cuban Revolutionary Party in 1892, the democratically governed organization—led by Martí—that orchestrated the revolution. This increased activity built to its final crescendo in early 1895, when a well-planned invasion and uprising began. Martí insisted on participating in the vanguard of the military invasion, even though companions had urged him to stay behind so that his exceptional organizational and oratorical skills could be used to sustain the war from abroad. Unfortunately for the subsequent course of Cuban history, Martí was killed in a skirmish with Spanish troops at Dos Ríos on May 19, 1895, two months after his arrival in Cuba. The man who most certainly would have been the first head of state of an independent Cuba died at age forty-two.

While the essay by Oscar Martí that concludes this collection discusses in detail the complex relationship between Martí's life and the history of his reception both inside and outside Cuba, it is not difficult to intuit, even from this cursory sketch, how easy it has been to beatify the revolutionary poet within the nationalist discourses of the Cuban state. The motifs that structure the narrative—"conversion" as a young boy, imprisonment by tyrannical authority, wandering in exile, the foundation of a vibrant community, a self-sacrificing death at a young age in spite of the pleadings of trusted friends—are the classical stuff of which hagiographies are made. And the fact that the extraordinary events of his life actually took place renders the quasi-religious aura associated with his accomplishments even more powerful. As Oscar Martí's analysis helps us readily grasp, the complex history of the reception of Martí's work both inside and outside Cuba has been overdetermined by his status as the martyred "apostle" of the Cuban nation (a title that has been attached to his name with the utmost seriousness for a good portion of the twentieth century). The situation has become particularly complex since 1959 when Cubans loyal to the Marxist revolution and those in exile have all claimed Martí as their intellectual ancestor, the former seeing him as a protosocialist and the latter as a democratic liberal. The recriminations and counterclaims generated by the postrevolutionary struggle over the "true" Martí are efficiently encapsulated in a pair of ideofacts: at the same time that Fidel Castro claims Martí as the intellectual father of the 1959 Cuban Revolution, the anti-Castro radio station that broadcasts from Florida to Cuba bears the name "Radio Martí." Since Martí has been installed as a national icon in Cuba's ideological apparatus—first during its period as a corrupt client state of the neo-imperial United States, then as a shifting personification for opposing sides of an ideological battle over the same geopolitical terrain—it is not difficult to imagine why his cultural criticism devoted to subjects peripheral to nationalist politics has attracted relatively little attention.

The purpose of this collection is certainly not to trivialize the importance of Cuba in Martí's thought or to suggest that his "real" significance lies beyond the parameters of the project for his homeland's liberation: achieving independence from Spain and ensuring that the new Cuban state would be governed according to the principles of justice were always his paramount concerns. The collective objective of the collection is, rather, to explore the tension in

Martí's work between national and transnational perspectives, a tension that makes his analysis of the Western Hemisphere's different national formations and their intrahemispheric relations extremely significant for reconfiguring the way we think about "America." His overlapping identities as a revolutionary activist and as a transnational journalist taught him to see the struggle for Cuban independence as part of an elaborate geopolitical puzzle: the "national" cultural or political event is always seen as a local inflection of a transnational phenomenon that can be read according to a hemispheric dialectic of similarity and difference. And a strong reading of Martí—one like those suggested in several of the essays included here—would see a precursor of the new American cultural studies in Marti's persistent rearticulations of the triangulated cultural and political relationships between Europe and its various lines of imperial descent in America.

Martí was probably as well equipped as anyone in his generation to negotiate comparatively the tension between the national and transnational forces at work in the Americas. Even before arriving to live in New York City, extended experience as an exile in various Latin American countries provided him with a comparative perspective on the politics and social dynamics of the various kinds of Latin American nation-states. Supplementing his understanding of Euro-African societies like his native Cuba with experience in Euro-Indian societies like Mexico and Guatemala, Martí's exile exposed him to the differing ethno-cultural complexities that imperialism had bequeathed to America. Furthermore, his travels disabused him of any naive faith that the shift from colonial to postcolonial status would in and of itself necessarily produce a just society. Close observation of governmental operations in Mexico, Guatemala, and Venezuela underscored for him both the fragility of just institutions in the former colonies and the ease with which a veneer of democratic rhetoric could screen tyranny. When Martí arrived in the United States in 1881 to take up more-or-less permanent residence, he brought to the Anglo half of Europe's colonized America a sociopolitical sensibility particularly well suited to appreciating the interplay between an aggressive internal racism and a misused governmental authority, themes that would become central to his writings on the United States.

The touchstone of Martí's mature thought, and the starting point for integrating his theoretical take on hemispheric relations into contemporary cultural debates, can be located in his most widely read essay, "Our America" [Nuestra América]. Published in newspapers in New York and Mexico City in January 1891, the text relies on the premise that there is a fundamental geocultural distinction between those American societies produced respectively by Iberian and British imperialisms. Having now passed into the critical lexicon, the terms "Our America" and the "Other America" (or the "America that is not ours") carry with them something more than Martí's assertion of a cultural difference between the regions occupied by the Anglo-Protestant British and those colonized by Latin-Catholic Iberians: the words are also infused with his powerful critique of the United States and its political, economic, and cultural imperialism. Notwithstanding the fact that in Martí's day Puerto Rico, Cuba, Panama, the Philippines, Guam, and Hawaii were still yet to be incorporated within the sphere of U.S. control, his close attention to hemispheric history and to contemporary political and economic events taught him that the completion of "manifest destiny" through the annexation and colonization of one-half of Mexico's territory would not sate the expansionist quest for markets and land. The principal objective of "Our America" in 1891 was to awaken the inhabitants of Our America to the fact that the United States—the country that Martí allegorizes as "the giant with seven-league boots"—stood poised ready to expand "overseas." And subsequent events clearly vindicate Martí's judgment, for the United States would soon annex Hawaii (after complying with its legitimate government's overthrow), assume control of former Spanish possessions in the Caribbean and the Pacific, and expand into Panama.

One of the important features of Martí's hemispheric thought is that the referential limit between "Our America" and the "Other America" is *not* the line that extends along the northern littoral of the Gulf of Mexico and up the Rio Grande. Foreshadowing much contemporary thought on the historical dynamics of Latino culture in the United States, Martí's journalistic texts are attuned to the way in which the territorial ambitions of the United States had already in Martí's day led to the annexation of large numbers of Latinos and threatened to continue doing so. Writing as he was between the Mexican-American and Spanish-American Wars, he was acutely aware that the imperial competition for resources and markets was pitting the traditional colonial powers, Spain, Britain, and France, against fledgling transoceanic imperialists, Germany and the United States. Sensing correctly the "natural" direction U.S. ambitions would take, he was particularly anxious that the fate of the former Mexicans not befall the Cubans and Puerto Ricans. As an analyst of U.S. political culture, he worked to inform his readers in Latin America of the shifting ideological climate that was reconfiguring U.S. self-understanding. Going beyond continental manifest destiny, the role of the United States was being popularly redefined as that of a hemispheric (and even global) benefactor of economic "progress" and "democracy"—a rhetoric that is still very much with us. The subsequent subsumption of the Cuban War of Independence within the Spanish-American War and the fate of Puerto Ricans and their passports both attest to Martí's sagacity.

But in addition to foregrounding the effects of the denaturalization and renaturalization that juridically subsumed Our America's geography and people into the America-that-is-not-ours, Martí's status as an exile in the racist United States gave rise to a sensibility that stands near the beginnings of the U.S. tradition of Latino culture *in exile*. Further disturbing the fictional purity of the Anglo-American state, Martí's U.S. writing belongs to that tradition of exile representation which counterpoises the lived experience of being "left alone" in the Anglo United States with the reconstructed collective memories of homelands which lie elsewhere. This tradition has flourished since Martí's day, especially during the post–World War II age of global population shifts that have seen millions of people from Our America move northward. This massive migration—made up to a significant extent of refugees fleeing economic devastation substantially caused or exacerbated by U.S.-based corporations and financial institutions—has added tens of millions of "newcomers" to the already substantial Latino population of the United States. While nineteenth-century annexationism extended the Other America's geographical control southward and juridically redefined its population, twentieth-century migration has seen the reassertion of Our America's *cultural* claims to the same space. And although there are certainly profound differences among the various Caribbean, Central American, and South American cultural formations flourishing in exile in the United States,

Martí's writing from inside what he called the "entrails of the monster" helps us provisionally to give theoretical shape to their historical and contemporary affinities.

Writing across the Line: Culture, Geography, and the "Latino Outsider"

While all of the essays included in this volume are informed by Martí's sense of the shifting limits and complex interplay between culture and geography, their specific interests and disciplinary approaches are heterogeneous. The papers' protocols include specific studies of Martí's commentaries on U.S. cultural figures and events, historical approaches that relate Martí's experience as an exiled Latino intellectual to other aspects of nineteenth-century American cultural histories, as well as theoretical studies of twentieth-century cultural phenomena that adopt a broadly "Martían" perspective. Using Martí's journalistic commentaries on U.S. culture as points of departure, the first four papers take up the question of his status as an "outsider." Identifying in Martí's commentary on fin-de-siècle U.S. cultural phenomena many of the same tensions that animate contemporary debates about minoritarian and exiled subject positions, the essays by Donald Pease, Susana Rotker, Doris Sommer, and Susan Gillman find in Martí's treatment of his U.S. subject matter important resources for reconsidering nineteenth-century American cultural history. Moreover, they also take up Martí as an important tool for engaging the contemporary cultural debates that such a reconsideration necessarily carries with it.

The first essay, Donald Pease's "José Martí, Alexis de Tocqueville, and the Politics of Displacement," follows a comparative protocol that reads the differences between the meanings of "American democracy" in Martí's late essays and in the work of his long-canonized predecessor. Beyond simply setting the image of a reactionary Tocqueville against that of a progressive Martí, Pease accounts for the contrasting ideological functions of the two "outsiders" in terms of their respective relationships, both to the nineteenth-century state formation in general and to the ways in which they have been (or might be) used in our contemporary cultural environment. As an agent of the forces of reaction in France, the author of *Democracy in America* is intent on promulgating a positive image of the limited democratic institutions of the United States so that such an image might ratify the preservation of hierarchical privileges in postrevolutionary France. In other words, democracy is good to the extent that it limits the democratic project, a position that accounts not only for the popularity of Tocqueville in the Second Republic but also for his continued use by the forces of conservatism in the United States. In spite of a lapse of more than fifty years, and notwithstanding the ways in which intervening transformations remade Jacksonian America into the Gilded Age, Martí sees in the United States the same preservation of privilege masked in the same democratic rhetoric. The difference in Martí, of course, is that rather than take up the example of the United States as a model for managing popular social forces with a veneer of democratic rhetoric, he would critique this ideological formation in order to reclaim the promise of the democratic ideal. What is particularly compelling about Pease's reading is that in addition to teasing out Martí's revisionist account of how imperial annexation and monopolistic greed had "broken the foundation" of U.S. democracy, Pease finds in Martí a founding voice in the tradition of U.S. multicultural history. Suspended, as Martí is, between the annexationist demands of a U.S. nation-state that would annex his American identity to its own project and a claim on a Cuban nation that does not yet exist, his writing becomes a site of resistance where the homogenizing effect of a "democratic" state apparatus is held at a distance in the name of a yet unfulfilled promise of transnational American democracy.

Pease analyzes Martí's negotiations of the threat of geographical and cultural annexation in order to reconstruct Martí as a key figure in the minoritarian cultural history of the United States. In a parallel, yet somewhat more specific vein, Susana Rotker's "The (Political) Exile Gaze in Martí's Writing on the United States" takes as its objective a careful consideration of what it might mean to be a "writer in exile." Drawing a powerful parallel between the condition of exile and the fissure that inhabits language itself, Rotker initiates her periodizing commentary on the evolution of Martí's U.S. journalism by situating him within a contemporary point of discussion in postcolonial cultural studies: the cultural dynamics of the exiled voice. Reworking both Edward Said's account of the contrapuntal perspective immanent in a bicultural subject-in-exile and Homi Bhabha's Lacan-inspired notion of the colonizing gaze,

Rotker asserts that Marti's residence within a space saturated with U.S. cultural authority generated an ongoing project of self-differentiation through writing. Moving from Martí's early articles on Coney Island and Jesse James to his later chronicles devoted to Peter Cooper, the Charleston earthquake, and the trial of the Chicago anarchists, Rotker's reading of Martí's journalistic commentary reveals the traces of a project of self-construction through dis-identification with the United States. At the same time that Martí's dis-identification becomes constitutive of his exiled self, these journalistic accounts of North American otherness construct a communitarian identity with his Latin American readers, an act of recollection that reclaims the self as a fragment of an extended Our American community.

Martí's positive evaluations of Walt Whitman and Helen Hunt Jackson, two U.S. literary figures that Martí introduced to Latin American readers in 1887, serve as the respective points of interest for Doris Sommer and Susan Gillman. Sommer and Gillman are both attentive to the ways in which the "border crossing" inherent in Martí's assimilative reception of these North American writers might become productive for understanding the constitutive traversals that govern our hemisphere's North–South relations in general. Glossing in its title Borges's well-known short story "Pierre Menard, Author of the *Quixote*" (a narrative account of the theoretical instability of the dividing line between the concepts of "writing" and "reading"), Sommer's essay "José Martí, Author of Walt Whitman" begins by alluding to Latin America's multiple and conflicting readings of the North American poet, readings that are equivalent to authorial rewritings. Seduced by Whitman's self-representation as a Pan-American democrat whose "I" belongs to the entire hemisphere, Martí claimed the potential for cross-cultural, multilinguistic utopia implicit in Whitman's text, blind to Whitman's anti-Latino imperialism and racism. Particularly important for Sommer, as she moves virtuosically from Martí's subsumption within the erotic embrace of Whitman's pan-hemispheric phantasm to subsequent attempts by others to construct (or to resist the construction of) a transnational American community, is the way that the Pan-American project always threatens to efface the North–South power differential; such an effacement would hide a crushing imperialism beneath the guise of mutual interest and artificial intimacy. Recognizing that the age of NAFTA and anti-immigrant legislation is rendering the cross-border embrace ever more precarious, Sommer makes of the ambiguity generated by the seductive threat of Whitman's lusty persona—a seduction to which Martí himself temporarily succumbed—a powerful trope for marking a site of resistance in which a Pan-Latino, Our American community might be held apart and maintained.

Sommer uses Martí's reading of Whitman to articulate the ambiguity inherent in locating what she calls the "boundaries of American belonging," boundaries she problematizes within the metaphoric space suggested by the threat of Whitman's face-to-face speech act and his crushing, Anglo-American embrace. To this concern with the shifting boundaries between Anglo- and Latin America Susan Gillman adds the complicating category of transnational ethnicity—that is, the potential for collective identification that extends across the hemisphere's borders and languages in the name of "race." Gillman's essay "*Ramona* in 'Our America'" situates Martí's engagement with Helen Hunt Jackson's Indian-reform novel—as a translator and as a critic—within the broader context of the pan-hemispheric tradition of race-reform fiction, a tradition that includes Avellaneda's *Sab,* Matto de Turner's *Birds without a Nest,* as well as (of course) Stowe's *Uncle Tom's Cabin.* Gillman's multitiered analysis of Martí's participation in this (largely women's) tradition begins by underscoring the fact that Martí never mentioned Jackson's tale of the unfortunate *mestiza* Ramona (set in postannexation California) without also mentioning Harriet Beecher Stowe's novel in the same breath. For Gillman, this habitual gesture betrays an ever present correspondence in Martí's thought between the oppression of Africans and that of Native Americans—in spite of the fact that the U.S. reformist movements that spawned these fictions were historically and politically distant from each other. But at the same time that Gillman locates within Martí's habitual linkage of Stowe and Jackson (in what she calls a "composite figure") a single critical attitude directed toward the multiple faces of U.S. racism, she likewise links his interest in the U.S. race-reform tradition to his own concerns about the politics of race in Our America. For Gillman, Martí's border-crossing assimilation of Jackson's and Stowe's sentimental reform fiction can be ascribed to his struggle against the anti-African racism plaguing the struggle for Cuban independence, as well as to his recognition that the *mestizaje* personified in *Ramona*'s title character is the privileged category of Our America's cultural being. Indeed, Gillman ascribes Martí's particular sensitivity to the complexities of African and Native American hybridization to his homeland's geography. For Cuba lies at the intersection of Our America's two principal transnational cultural formations: the geocultural system we have come to know as the Black Atlantic and the complex region of interactions among the Spanish, Native American, and English peoples (extending from the Caribbean to California) that we have come to call the Latino Borderlands.

Annexationist Designs and the End(s) of Manifest Destiny

Taking as a common methodological entry point analyses of specific instances of Martí's writings about U.S. culture, the papers included in Part I explore the significance of Martí's status as a Latino outsider whose reading constituencies have homelands outside the United States. Shifting their emphases away from the specifics of Martí's cultural reportage to his more generalized critique of U.S. imperialism, the essays in Part II undertake a shared comparative project that articulates powerful affinities between Martí's exile-subject position and that of his contemporary, the *californiana* novelist María Amparo Ruiz de Burton. Having recently entered the mainstream of U.S. Latino cultural studies, Ruiz de Burton's novels *Who Would Have Thought It?* (1872, reprint 1995) and *The Squatter and the Don* (1885, reprint 1993) reflect the critical engagement of a woman annexed and minoritized by the Treaty of Guadalupe Hidalgo (1848), the document that forcibly remade Mexicans into U.S. Latinos at the close of the Mexican-American War. Exploring the commonalities in the Cuban patriot's journalism and the ex-Mexican's oppositional fiction, the essays by Rosaura Sánchez, Beatrice Pita, and José David Saldívar not only refine our specific understandings of Martí and Ruiz de Burton, but they likewise articulate elective affinities between the twin lineages of exile and annexation that constitute U.S. Latino culture's genealogy. And although these essays carefully note important differences between the two writers, they nevertheless see Martí and Ruiz de Burton as fellow travelers in a world characterized by the closely related phenomena of a declining Spanish imperialism and a rising Anglo-U.S. hegemony.

Rosaura Sánchez's essay "Dismantling the Colossus: Martí and Ruiz de Burton on the Formulation of Anglo América" continues the work of interpretive elaboration that she (in collaboration with Beatrice Pita) initiated in the critical introductions to the Arte Público Press editions of the author's rediscovered novels. Sánchez opens her comparative study of Martí and Ruiz de Burton by situating them within the ongoing tradition of opposition to U.S. expansionism, a gesture that draws a line of continuity between their critique of the U.S. empire during turn-of-the-century monopoly capitalism and oppositional voices raised during the present neo-imperial age of NAFTA and "free trade." Specifically articulating parallel lines of thought developed in Martí's journalistic texts and in Ruiz de Burton's first novel (*Who Would Have Thought It?*), Sánchez discloses the ways in which being racialized as Latino outsiders in the United States generated a shared sensitivity to Anglo-American racism. Both Martí and Ruiz de Burton were attuned not only to the ways in which the U.S. colossus's white supremacist ideology effaced the economic, legal, and social rights of non-Anglos, but also to the fact that this ideology justified an imperial foreign policy that masked the interests of a predatory multinational capitalism in terms that wrote the Anglo-American "race" into world history as the harbinger of progress and modernity. (Indeed, one of the incisive features of her collaborative reading of *Who Would Have Thought It?* is that the triumph of Anglo modernity is predicated on the imperial appropriation of non-Anglo wealth.) And while Sánchez sees a severe limitation in Martí's and Ruiz de Burton's inability to locate the fundamental problem of North–South relations in the capitalist relations of production themselves, she nevertheless finds in their work important critical resources that might be useful for articulating a transnational, pan-Latino cultural identity, a hemispheric solidarity necessary to consolidate opposition to the advances of transnational capitalism in our own day.

Like Rosaura Sánchez, Beatrice Pita is also interested in the ways in which the class and cultural identity common to Martí and Ruiz de Burton generated their respective critical responses to the United States. But while the organizational axis of Sánchez's analysis leads her ultimately to underscore the affinities between the two writers, Pita is interested in probing the differences between them. And although Pita's essay "Engendering Critique: Race, Class, and Gender in Ruiz de Burton and Martí" takes the two writers' shared identity as Latino outsiders as its point of departure, she is particularly interested in the ways in which the contrasts between their levels of social integration, their gender, and their readerships inflect their critical responses. While Martí's primary roles as foreign journalist and revolutionary activist left him at the fringes of Anglo society, Ruiz de Burton's marriage to a high-ranking U.S. military officer gave her (at least partial) access to the elite U.S. social and political world; while Martí's traditional gender conceptions left him possessed of an utterly conventional sense of women's "proper" social location, Ruiz de Burton's status as an ambitious, highly capable woman—and yet one who was legally and socially aggrieved—focused her critique of U.S. society through the lens of gender; and while Martí's journalistic and literary texts were written primarily with a Latin American readership in mind, Ruiz de Burton's novels are written within the English-language sentimental tradition of romance fiction—a tradition that she simultaneously inhabits and ironizes as she addresses her critique of racist social relations and monopoly capitalism to the class of readers who are those systems' principal beneficiaries. Moreover, in spite of the fact that Pita's closing pages return to the writers' common denunciation of the United States as a juggernaut that crushes anyone standing in its way, the essay's subtle calibration of the differences between the two reminds us once again of the ways in which the minoritarian and anti-imperial projects are always already shot through with the complexities of social location generated by differences in class and gender.

José David Saldívar's project in "Nuestra América's Borders: Remapping American Cultural Studies" incorporates a reading of Ruiz de Burton's *The Squatter and the Don* into a vast cognitive map of the displacements constitutive of the Latino Borderlands, concentrating especially on Our America at the turn of the nineteenth century. Ruiz de Burton's narration of the violations of Latino rights in the former Alta California marks one side of a geocultural space that extends from the San Francisco and San Diego of the robber barons, through the Southwest, reaching finally into Martí's Caribbean. Saldívar's account couples his reading of Ruiz de Burton's novel with a detailed consideration of the late nineteenth-century ethnographic project of John Gregory Bourke, the Indian fighter turned anthropologist whose work on the Southwest and the lower Rio Grande Valley betrays the violent operations of Victorian anthropology's imperializing gaze. While Martí's Cuba constitutes this elongated triangle's farthest extension, his "Our America" counters Bourke's text with a theoretical rejoinder, reclaiming the Latino Borderlands as the northernmost extension of an Our American formation whose civilization eludes Bourke's apprehension. What is particularly compelling about Saldívar's text is that, in addition to charting the overlapping claims laid on this triangular space at the end of the nineteenth century, he interrogates the academic discourse that makes such a charting possible at the end of our own. Prefacing his readings with an autobiographical account of his own academic production within U.S. institutions, Saldívar chronicles the triangular trajectory of his movement from South Texas public schools, first to the Puritan "origins" of Yale and then to the northern California university that bears a robber baron's name. This outline, a not-quite not-homologous institutional triangle, superimposed over the nineteenth-century Borderland that Saldívar expertly maps, functions as a powerful image of the theoretical difficulties immanent in contemporary Borderland cultural studies.

Martí's Prescriptive Map of Our America

While the first two sets of essays concentrate heavily on Martí's analyses of the United States, the essays included in Part III shift their emphases away from Martí's interest in affairs internal to the expanding U.S. borders to his concern with pan-hemispheric cultural and political relations. Rather than dealing with Martí's journalistic representations of the United States, these essays concentrate on his analyses of Latin America's cultural politics — analyses that, nevertheless, are always already informed by his heightened awareness of the threat that the United States poses to Our America's political and cultural integrity. Examining Martí's criticism of Latin America's ruling classes and Martí's relationship to Caribbean social politics, the essays by Enrico Mario Santí, Jeffrey Belnap, Brenda Plummer, and Ada Ferrer help us grasp his comparative take on the American nation-states. For Martí, the hemisphere's countries are parallel sociopolitical formations: national-bourgeois rule — culturally mimetic of Europe — similarly inflected national amalgamations of European colonists, minoritized Native Americans, diasporic Africans and Asians, as well as peoples of mixed race. Yet at the same time that Martí sees North, Central, and South American societies as similar in terms of the hierarchies of race that structure their social relations, he also repeatedly emphasizes the need for Latin Americans to differentiate themselves, not only from Europe but more especially from the United States. Urging Our America's ruling classes to abandon the residue of colonial mentality that keeps them disoriented within systems of Eurocentric ideals and isolated from the complex realities of their own societies, Martí simultaneously emphasizes the need for Our America's peoples to articulate identity formations that cross ethnic as well as national dividing lines. Only when Our America's nation-states are unified—both nationally and transnationally—will they be able collectively to oppose the cultural, economic, and political threat posed to their sovereignty by the rise of the United States.

Enrico Mario Santí and Jeffrey Belnap explore different aspects of the context and content of Martí's "Our America," focusing on the relationship between the text's analysis of the U.S. threat and Martí's concomitant diagnosis of the cultural pathologies afflicting Latin America's ruling classes. Santí's objective is to contextualize the canonical essay, drawing attention to the political circumstances surrounding its production. For Santí, the key to grasping the significance of Martí's essay lies in understanding that it was written in the wake of the U.S.-sponsored Pan-American Conference: this eight-month gathering brought representatives of the various American nations to Washington in order to discuss a U.S. proposal that would have "unified" the American markets under a single trade agreement. Santí's collation of Martí's journalistic texts, correspondence, and public addresses proximate to the conference demonstrates that, although from one perspective Martí's activism among the delegates was successful (in that he was able to orchestrate a general rejection of the U.S. proposals), his experience was also profoundly disillusioning. For Martí was unable to gain formal support for the Cuban cause from the independent Latin American nations' delegates. Suggesting that the national representatives capitulated to pressure from the United States to stay out of Cuban affairs so that it could orchestrate the island's annexation, Santí argues in " 'Our America,' the Gilded Age, and the Crisis of Latinamericanism" that the canonical essay (written in the months following the conference) needs to be read as a critique of the neocolonial mentality that left the representative Latin American elites unable to unite behind the Cuban cause. Furthermore, Santí suggests that the history of the text's reception includes a general blindness to Martí's critique of Latin America's ruling classes, a blindness symptomatic of what he calls the "ideology of Latinamericanism." For Santí, this ideological discourse of supposed Latin American unity counterfactually presumes that the Our American solidarity for which Martí's essay calls has already been achieved.

While Santí focuses on the immediate context within which "Our America" was written, Jeffrey Belnap's objective, in "Headbands, Hemp Sandals, and Headdresses: The Dialectics of Dress and Self-Conception in Martí's 'Our America,'" is to read Martí's critical examination of the negative social effects of Our America's miseducated ruling classes, underscoring at the same time Martí's prescriptions for their decolonization. Belnap's first step is to reconstruct Martí's critique of Our America's neocolonial educational institutions, systems whose curricula engineer the intelligentsia's sense of self according to Eurocentric schemata. Not only does the education system produce a bourgeoisie unable to disenthrall itself from its fascination with Europe and its café culture, it also simultaneously leaves that class unable to govern Our American societies with any degree of competency. (Moreover, says Martí, the ruling class's inability to respond effectively to the threat posed by the United States is owing to the same miseducation.) Martí's solution to the negative effects of this elite enclave within the system of cultural reproduction is to redesign the American university, replacing the Eurocentric curriculum with an American one—a curriculum that he suggests should be rooted in Our America's "natural," pre-Columbian cultures. Belnap, as the title of his essay suggests, is particularly interested in Martí's metaphors of dress, images Martí uses to articulate the tension between the pathological self-understanding produced by Eurocentric education and what he sees as a socially responsible alignment with America's objective cultural circumstances. By representing the distinction between colonized and decolonized minds in terms of the difference between figures dressed up in amalgamations of foreign costumes and figures who self-consciously claim traditional indigenous dress, Martí does more than suggest that the sense of self is socially produced within educational institutions; he also holds that the American subjectivity produced in such institutions needs to be performed as a reclamation of America's "natural" cultures—regardless of the particular "facts" of biological descent. On the one hand, Belnap sees (in Martí's call for an abandonment of "artificial" European identity and a return to a "natural" American one) a participation in the naturalistic ideology endemic to nineteenth-century nationalism; he nevertheless argues that Martí's insistence that the largely Euroamerican ruling class learn, through their education, to identity with the native peoples their ancestors invaded and victimized could be an important institutional step toward social justice in America's multiethnic states.

The essays by Brenda Plummer and Ada Ferrer move us from Martí's critique of the neocolonial cosmopolitanism that deforms the perspective of Latin America's ruling elite to the interface between Martí's theoretical Our Americanism and two specific Caribbean contexts: fin-de-siècle Haiti and revolutionary Cuba. Plummer's comparative study, "Firmin and Martí at the Intersection of Pan-Americanism and Pan-Africanism," articulates a parallel between Martí's thought and that of the Haitian scholar and statesman Anténor Firmin. Starting at the meeting between the two intellectual activists near the Dominican-Haitian border at Cap Haitien in 1893, Plummer sets up a contrast between the respective ways in which Martí and Firmin negotiated among the conflicting claims made upon them by the discourses of nationalism, cosmopolitanism, and racial identity. Martí's call for the unification of Latin American nations against the threat of the United States was coupled with a persistent insistence that the Cuban independence movement had been damaged by anti-African racism (hence his strategic insistence in "Our America" that races, in fact, do not exist). For Martí, to consider race as an issue was antipatriotic. Although Firmin was likewise very interested in promoting the Caribbean polities' international solidarity in order to combat the imperial powers more effectively, his take on the political culture of the nation-state is always already referenced to his native Haiti—the *African* American nation that was also Latin America's first independent state. Not only does Plummer subtly analyze the significance this difference makes for Firmin's version of Pan-Americanism, but she likewise provides us with an excellent introduction to the intellectual work of an American thinker whose potential for stimulating a reconsideration of the boundaries of American Studies may be on a par with that of Martí.

In "The Silence of Patriots: Race and Nationalism in Martí's Cuba," Ada Ferrer's fascinating objective is to demonstrate unequivocally the powerful—albeit temporary—effect that Martí's antiracist nationalism had on the discourse of Cuban unity during the War of Independence itself. After first tracing the ways in which racism had debilitated the independence struggle's early stages, she then reminds us that when he was alive Martí had systematically insisted in both his public and private discourse that racial distinctions were antithetical to the nationalist project. She then goes on to suggest one aspect of the actual effects of Martí's discourse: the archival sources from which we can reconstruct the rebellion's history reveal a systematic and very uncharacteristic exclusion of racial categories from the Cuban insurgents' official interactions. Ferrer's search of autobiographical accounts and military records dating from the war reveals an almost complete absence of racial categories for establishing personal identity. (Indeed, she suggests that the occasional use of race as an identity marker seems to have been a lapse into a prewar habit.) More than this finding, though, Ferrer provides evidence that the occasional enunciations of racist attitude among the insurgents were coded as unpatriotic. Particularly poignant is Ferrer's account of the way that the end of the war brought a concomitant end to this officially sanctioned effacement of racism. While the heat of the insurgency kept prescriptions (like Martí's) for a color-blind Cuba alive, the problematic independence and a resumption of the rhythms of everyday social relations saw a reinstitutionalization of racist hierarchies.

Using not only Martí's writings on race but also the complex discourse of race in the movement to which Martí dedicated his life, Ferrer reveals how the "silence of patriots" became "emblematic of the ways in which the struggles between racism and antiracism defined Cuban nationalism."

"Our Americanism" in the Age of "Globalization": Contemporary Frontiers

Nation-states and their institutions make a habit of attempting to regulate and solidify the ever shifting limits between culture and geography, seeking to establish an "organic" concordance between the way people imagine their worlds and the geographical terrain states try to claim—irrevocably, of course—as their "natural" domain. Many of the essays we have discussed thus far interrogate a rising U.S. hegemony's "organicist" claims to cultural and geographical superiority. Instead of turn-of-the-century affairs, the final set of essays in this collection turn their attention toward the twentieth century, concentrating especially on the ways in which Martí's thought runs parallel to the current reexamination of what it means to study the hemisphere's cultures. We find in the contemporary academy a new awareness that the conceptual borders traditionally regulating the study of America have been ideologically coterminous with the Anglo institutions of the United States. Rather than studying America as if it were a "natural" organism coequal with the U.S. nation-state, New Americanists struggle to reimagine the hemisphere's cultures as dynamic systems that traverse and dialectically interact with the various national formations. Although the essays representative of this new take on hemispheric cultural dynamics are different from one another in their respective disciplinary origins (as well as in their theoretical frames), they register a revivification of a Martían perspective within U.S.-based, English-language scholarship.

David Noble's objective in "The Anglo-Protestant Monopolization of 'America'" is to trace precisely the way in which an "exceptionalist" nationalism, one that wrote the U.S. state formation into world history as its natural apotheosis, perpetuated itself in the institutionalization of American Studies. Intermingling theoretical and autobiographical elements in his text, Noble is likewise interested in characterizing his personal history within this traditionally Anglocentric discipline as a sustained retreat from its American exceptionalist doctrine, a retreat that culminates at the end of his long career in a perspective not too distant from Martí's "Our Americanism." Noble's analysis draws a line of continuity between the nationalist historical discourse in the nineteenth century and the foundation of American Studies in the present one. Extending from Bancroft, Parkman, and Motley to Perry Miller's "American Civilization" program, this intellectual tradition saw the United States as the higher—indeed, the ultimate—realization of the European civilization that it sublated. Furthermore, this tradition simultaneously left non–Northern European Americans (both within and without the borders of the United States) outside the scheme of historical significance. Noble sees his own work in the 1950s and 1960s, and the work of his colleague William Appleman Williams, as representative of the gradual realization by some U.S. Americanists that their disciplinary production had left them blind to the vast diversity of America's cultural systems. For Noble, this process of reeducation reached a kind of denouement in 1983 with the publication of Benedict Anderson's *Imagined Communities,* a book that suggests (among other things) that the doctrine of American exceptionalism is merely a local variant of the nationalist ideology of the transnational bourgeoisie. The significance of Martí's "Our America" for Noble is that it constitutes an exemplary gesture of resistance to Anglo-America's monopolizing threat, as well as a text whose call for a many-voiced America anticipates by a century the present generation's "new" way of thinking.

Noble's essay might be called a genealogical critique of the tradition that produced him, an account of the emergence of a critical voice directed against the academic discourse that the U.S. nation-state institutionalized in order to ratify its own claims to transcendent authority. Brook Thomas's project, in "Frederick Jackson Turner, José Martí, and Finding a Home on the Range," is to disrupt the primacy of the nation-state as an analytic category by introducing the notion of the "frontier" as a more productive conceptual frame for the study of cultural interaction and change. Suggesting that the emergent category of "border studies" in the contemporary academic environment carries with it promising as well as problematic features, Thomas takes up and reconfigures Turner's seminal 1893 "frontier thesis" as a starting point for questioning what it might mean to interrogate the cultural dynamics that emerge within zones that are both "at the edge of" and "in between" political and cultural limits. Martí's contemporary, Turner argued that the existence of a frontier at the western limit of the United States (defined as a "zone at the edge" rather than a quasi-militaristic "limit between") was U.S. history's formative feature. This frontier was a space where the violent social conflicts characteristic of European history could work themselves out diachronically, through successive stages of migration, displacement, and change. Although Thomas critically acknowledges the Eurocentric and teleological nationalism that is very much a part of Turner's intellectual equipment, he nevertheless finds a useful tool in Turner's articulation of the frontier's importance as a liminal space where old identities are abandoned and new ones assumed. At the same time that Thomas finds in Turner's frontier an important corollary to contemporary notions of the Borderlands as sites of transformation, he also recognizes that the ratification of liminality and border identity can easily romanticize the homelessness and material oppression that accompany cultural displacement and marginalization. For Thomas, Martí's "Our Americanism" acts as an important corrective to this romanticizing tendency, reminding us that (as in Turner's day) there are, strictly speaking, no "empty frontiers"—no innocent spaces where new identities can freely remake themselves, independent of the violent inscriptions of racialized social hierarchies.

While Noble provides a critique of the naturalistic nationalism promulgated through the U.S. state apparatus, and Thomas asks whether the interstitial spaces "at the edges" of national formations are perhaps more significant than the states themselves, George Lipsitz compels us to consider a third nuance: Is "national culture," under the conditions of transnational capitalism, perhaps becoming completely noncontinuous with the territorial state? Lipsitz's essay, "Their America and Ours: Intercultural Communication in the Context of 'Our America,'" uses the memory of Martí to explore the significance of certain strains in contemporary Latino musical culture, a set of migratory cultural phenomena typical of the transnational dynamics of the present age. Lipsitz begins with a Benjaminian query about the material difference between Martí's fin-de-siècle world and our own. Although in the contemporary context both the North–South power differential and a persistent U.S. hegemony remain in place, the ideologies that facilitate the exercise of power have changed. Martí responded to the twin rhetorics of the imperializing mission and the sovereign nation; the present age requires that we respond to ideologies suggesting that the nation-state is becoming universally weak, and that the prosperity of all is expedited through the unrestrained, cross-border circulation of products and information. Giving the lie, however, to this globalizing phantasmagoria, Lipsitz points to contemporary research that paints a horrific picture of the increase in human misery that this "globalization" of telecommunicational capital is generating. Charting the transformations of diasporic Dominican music in the United States (as well as newly urbanized musical culture in Peru) as specific popular resources for living within these new conditions, he also suggests that effective responses to the newly globalized "giant with seven-league boots" require strategies that link national political action to transnational communicative strategies.

Lipsitz begins his analysis of the cross-border dynamics of the Americas' populations, and of the mutability of their cultural formations, by underscoring the need to proceed carefully: as we struggle to integrate Martí's analysis of the late nineteenth-century Americas, we would do well to remember that our own time is characterized by very different ideological and technological conditions. Oscar Martí's closing essay on the complexity of Martí's reception implicitly seconds this point, chronicling the ways in which the pathos of José Martí's political life and the richness of his texts have lent themselves to conflicting political interpretations. "José Martí and the Heroic Image" initially reminds us that snippets of the apostolic hero's eloquence and anecdotal excerpts from his life story have served as ideological fodder—for even when still alive, Martí struggled to manage the overdetermining effects of his conflicting public images as poet, politician, and soldier. Oscar Martí goes on to review the ways in which Cuba's twentieth-century political history has been punctuated with conflicting, often contradictory versions of this "heroic image." Certainly Martí's "Our Americanism" is a vital resource that can help a new American studies to awaken more thoroughly from its long, Anglocentric dream. But reading Oscar Martí sounds a cautionary note, for the history of Martí's reception has been fraught with narrow appropriations that have fallen far short of Martí's hemispheric vision of the Americas.

Perhaps it is precisely the value of this collection that when the essays are considered together as a whole, they both open up a view on the architectonics of that hemispheric vision and foreclose the project of any who would read Martí's work too narrowly. Not only does the collection give us access to Martí's analyses of specific phenomena in both halves of the Americas, it likewise helps us grasp the ways in which Martí saw these discrete phenomena within a larger critical framework. "Our Americanism" is this framework's name. The formal retreat of European imperialism left kindred state formations in its wake, nation-states ruled for the most part by the elite descendants of European invaders who, at the end of the nineteenth century, struggled to manage ethnically diverse populations by wielding the ubiquitous nationalist ideology of the bourgeois age. For Martí, the challenge this newly born state system faced, of course, was that the hegemony of Europe was being replaced by the rise of the United States. Martí's "Our Americanist" call (published almost simultaneously in New York City and Mexico City) was for the Americas' Iberian half to bind together in order to use their kindred cultural identities and economic strength to combat this new hegemony.

In rethinking the significance of Martí within a new technological and cultural environment—an environment whose ideology increasingly proclaims the obsolescence of the national border and the universal benefit of "free trade"—it is perhaps most important to underscore once more the place of the *nation-state* in Martí's "Our Americanist" perspective. Unlike a simplistic nineteenth-century nationalist, Martí strategically wielded the naturalistic nationalism of his day in order to negotiate the complexities of the hemisphere's geopolitical dynamics. From twin vocations as a national activist and a transnational journalist, he learned to read national events in relation to transnational forces; he also saw Our America's nation-states as strategic actors—agents whose resources needed to be unified in a multinational consortium in order to protect their populations from the economic and political bullying of the United States. As American Studies, newly demystified, retreats from organic nationalism, it is important that the demystification of the nation-state does not become confused with a belief that states have somehow become insignificant international actors, because the same gigantic bully still strives to push around the same countries' grandchildren and great-grandchildren. The thematic that these essays persistently recapitulate is that those who work within the New American cultural studies, supported within the same "monster's entrails," ought to interrogate the significance of this continuity. The example of Martí's "Our Americanism" is a necessary starting point for any attempt to pursue such an interrogation.

I.

Writing across the Line: Culture, Geography, and the "Latino Outsider"

Donald E. Pease

José Martí, Alexis de Tocqueville, and the Politics of Displacement

Couldn't they just as well displace our geographical latitude, our entire Island, with its mountain, plains, rivers and trees, carry us with the wind to another location less persecuted by cyclones and colonial governments? — José de Diego, "El desplazamiento"[1]

Imperialism, led by the USA, presents the struggling peoples of the earth and all those calling for peace, democracy and socialism with the ultimatum: accept theft or death. The oppressed and exploited of the earth maintain their defiance: liberty from theft. But the biggest weapon wielded and daily actually unleashed by imperialism against that collective defiance is the cultural bomb. — Ngugi Wa Thiong'o, *Decolonizing the Mind*[2]

Both Alexis de Tocqueville and José Martí turned their prolonged stays in the United States into occasions to discover and record their understandings of America and democracy. Each writer constructed a knowledge about American democracy within a context informed by the possibilities for social change that such knowledge might afford his native land. In referring their lived experience of American democracy to the structures of belief prevailing in France and Cuba at the time of their respective compositions, however, Tocqueville and Martí constructed contradictory understandings of its fate and purpose that are not wholly attributable to the different historical conditions of their composition. The incompatibilities in their motives for writing and in their works' intended audiences also disclose radically different attitudes toward the Americas and democracy.

José Martí's revolutionary opposition to Spanish colonial rule in Cuba led to his imprisonment at age sixteen in a hard-labor camp, deportation to Spain a year later in 1870 and, from 1881 to 1895, political expulsion to the ghettos of New York. Between 1881 and his death on a Cuban battlefield on May 19, 1895, Martí transformed this site of exile into a nodal point of political activism on behalf of the Cuban revolutionary movement in particular and liberationist causes in general. His newspaper columns would play a significant role in the development of minoritarian cultural histories that provided support for emergent Hispanic communities that refused the melting pot's terms of cultural assimilation.[3]

In addition to his work within and between these communities, Martí also invested his considerable energies in workers' causes in the Northern as well as the Southern Hemisphere. His essays and speeches were instrumental, for example, in determining the sociopolitical significance of the Haymarket Square riot in Chicago and in the proposal of specific remedies for the exploitation of laborers in sugar and tobacco plantations throughout the Americas. During his fifteen years of political exile he would leave New York City only to further anti-Spanish and anti-imperialist separatist movements and to clarify—through such activities as participation in the International Monetary and Pan-American Conferences—the differences between the socioeconomic needs of the South and "El Norte."

The literary personae Martí invented for his essays, poetry, translations, fiction, journalism, political oratory, and history were addressed to political exiles in the United States, Cuban nationals, fellow revolutionaries in North and South America, as well as to those citizens in the North who found that the political ambitions of what he called "imperial Rome"—Martí's favored name for the United States of the Gilded Age—were incommensurate with their understanding of "Nuestra América." By way of the remarkable anti-imperialist manifesto published under that title in *El Partido Liberal,* on January 30, 1891,[4] Martí decisively separated the condition of becoming a Cuban (or any other non-U.S.-based) American from the uncritical stance of simply "being American" as the normative basis for dwelling in the Americas.

Martí described the composite formation "Our America" as, like himself, displaced from the processes through which a national democracy could be linked to a person. While living in New York, Martí believed that he inhabited a nation that had become an empire and a national culture that had colonized the lifeworlds of its citizens in the name of democracy. Martí, who had become a political refugee as a consequence of a related form of nationalism, associated himself thereafter with transnational American democracy, which he represented as a condition of permanent exile.

Unlike Martí who construed himself their agent, Alexis de Tocqueville experienced the emergence of democratic forces as a form of social estrangement. As a loyal French monarchist, Tocqueville owed his seat in the July monarchy to the votes of country landowners who counted him as a hereditary member of their territorial aristocracy. Tocqueville addressed *Democracy in America,* in the last instance, to the governmental bureaucrats who granted him leave from his official duties. Tocqueville accepted temporary leave from his office as an assistant French magistrate with the understanding that the information he gathered during his trip to America concerning governmental rule in general and prison reform in particular would become instrumental in regularizing democratic institutions in France. In fulfilling this mandate, Tocqueville accumulated a mass of details about democratic institutions in the United States that he painstakingly related to what he understood to be the central theme of *Democracy in America;* namely, the art of governmental rule.[5]

A member of the French aristocracy that had been superseded with the revolutionary overthrow of the feudal order in France, Tocqueville characterized the emergence of democratic forces as a potential danger to the dominance of the French ruling elite. Prominent among his intended addressees, that class read *Democracy in America* as a defensive weapon useful in that historical moment's war of cultural positioning. After Tocqueville had become a magistrate, he was commissioned to travel to America as an official of the French state. In his efforts to discover in the United States a form of democratic rule, Tocqueville devised a complex rhetorical strategy that enabled him to recover the persona of the French aristocrat as an analytic perspective required to formulate the differences between democracy in France and America.

In enunciating the social and cultural conditions surrounding America's distinctive form of democracy, Tocqueville habitually assumed an aristocratic attitude toward American democratic ideas and customs. Writing from this subjective standpoint authorized Tocqueville's signature detachment from the political phenomena that he described and, at key moments, turned his exposition of the American political economy into a reflection on the generalized crisis that had emerged in France after it had undergone the loss of institutions that had formerly legitimated the feudal order.

Writing thus became a kind of transferential process whereby

Tocqueville translated the social position lost after the French Revolution into the literary standpoint through which he practiced his historic movement throughout the United States. In codifying Americans' contradictory attitudes toward freedom and equality by way of formulaic phrases such as the "tyranny of the majority" and "salutary servitude," Tocqueville's political analyses disclosed an anxious desire to recover the aristocratic tradition in the displaced form of the historical perspective from which he discerned what was significantly absent from American democracy.

As a representative of a superseded feudal tradition that he construed American history as exceptional in lacking, Tocqueville also thereby added to Jacksonian America the class position that French democracy had replaced. This class supplementation was conveyed in the analytic distinction Tocqueville adduced between political and civil society. The difference between civil society and political society was sustained, Tocqueville reflected, by the irresolvable conflict between "private interests" and "public liberty." Given this contrast and American individualists' "natural" predisposition to gratify their individual interests, political society depended upon a residual feature of feudal society; namely, respect for liberty in its aristocratic aspect, as a precondition necessary for its emergence.[6]

Paradoxical as it may seem, Tocqueville believed that the democratic individual's love of political liberty "presupposed the presence of a kind of virtue of which the proud independence of feudalism was an anticipation."[7] Claude Lefort has recently traced Tocqueville's unworked-through attachments to the aristocratic tradition by examining the paradoxical status of American "individualism." American individualism, under Tocqueville's description, oscillated from an "abstract" subjectivity whose resolutely private interests alienated it from any meaningful political form to a social subjectivity so "lost in the crowd" of prevailing opinions as to be void of any subjective point of view. In Tocqueville's representations of his dilemma, the American individual, had been, on the one hand, "released from the old networks of personal dependency and granted the freedom to think and act in accordance with his own norms"; on the other hand, that individual had been "isolated and impoverished and at the same time trapped by the image of his fellows, now that agglutination with them provides a means of escaping the threat of the dissolution of his identity."[8]

Writing from the standpoint of an aristocracy whose political estate the French Revolution had overthrown produced in Tocqueville a historical "knowledge" about the need for a political society that was missing from America. But Tocqueville's production of this "knowledge" depended upon his reanimation of the aristocrat's love of liberty that French democracy lacked. Understood as an intermediate realm between the state that would simply reduce the public to a manifestation of its sovereign power and the civil society where diverse private interests emerged, political society alone, Tocqueville concluded, could organize these interests into a representative formation capable of exercising supervisory power over the government. In representing its emergence out of this gap between the utterly apolitical private individual and the public individual utterly submissive to the rule of social opinion, Tocqueville reasserted the need for liberty as the political virtue required to mediate between the individual and the social power that the state would otherwise incorporate.[9]

One way to calculate the difference between Martí's project and Tocqueville has to do with the usages to which their works have subsequently been put. The recent culture wars have conscripted the disparate circumstances and purposes of *Democracy in America* and *Our America* into the service of political polarization. In reducing the dimensions of their projects to a dualism that opposes Martí's multicultural values to Tocqueville's monoculturalism, the contemporary political sphere has undergone a related diminution.[10] The restriction of their projects to the terms of this controversy has of itself effected a cultural homogeneity that occludes their asymmetrical relations to political power.

In a sense, both Tocqueville and Martí possess multicultural credentials, but neither is wholly identifiable with the multicultural project. Tocqueville's understanding of political society presupposed multiple interest groups, and Martí's pluralized affinities enlisted the "love of liberty" as a universalizing political force. But while Martí and Tocqueville shared the belief that identity formations take place at the site where the state articulated individuals to the national culture, Martí resisted the hegemony that Tocqueville forged at this juncture. Tocqueville described political society's resistance to the centralized state as analogous with the French aristocracy's historical antagonism to the monarchy. He nevertheless presupposed the state's power to link the heterogeneous interests constituting political society with a coherent national imago. But

Martí did not refer the various political formations constituting "Our America" as having a single national core, nor did he represent the participants in his Pan-American project as "interest groups" consolidated in an effort to establish a multiculture. Martí opposed intranational understandings of political identity in all of its forms.

He criticized the "multicultural" values of formal equality and social tolerance as ethical universals that liberal pluralists had erected to efface economic inequalities and social disempowerment. Elevating differentiation into a systematic principle of political formation, Martí rejected consolidated practices and meanings and turned dissociation and relinkage into the motive forces for his project's powers of transnational identification. In separating this transnational political formation from the national cultures that could not represent it, Martí dispatched the means whereby this formation and those cultures became unrecognizable to one another. In his elucidation of these political incompatibilities, Martí also supplied mechanisms for exposing the ideological procedures whereby such disparities might be disavowed.

That Martí does not at present exert such an effect can be explained in part by the inequivalence of their positioning in contemporary culture. While Martí and Tocqueville have been invoked to construct a narrative of oppositional binaries in the debate over the multiculture, *Democracy in America* has supplied the terms regulating its exchanges. In restricting the range of available positions to the interest groups currently populating U.S. political society, the culture wars have also corroborated Tocqueville's strictly nationalist understanding of political formations. *Democracy in America*'s capacity to subordinate a periphery to a center has been thereby extended to include *Our America* among its margins.

To underscore what has been occluded by way of this usage of Tocqueville to eclipse Martí's different understanding of political formations, the remainder of my essay will bring into focus Martí's and Tocqueville's different attitudes toward displacement. My discussion will be divided into sections turning on the differences in Martí's and Tocqueville's attitudes toward the displacement they shared. The first section discusses displacement as a psychological strategy that Tocqueville practiced in an effort to reconstitute French national identity. The second describes Martí's *Our America* as a radicalization of displacement into a two-tiered political process that severed linkages to national identity and mobilized a range of political identifications. The final section reads a section of *Democracy in America* against the grain as an incomplete displacement of Martí's form of American democracy.

1

Intellectually, I can approve of democratic institutions, but I am an aristocrat by instinct. I passionately love liberty, legality, the respect for rights; but not democracy. That is the essence of my personality. — Alexis de Tocqueville, "Mon Instinct, Mes Opinions"[11]

Throughout his stay in the United States Tocqueville was haunted by the fear that a change in political conditions in France might turn his official state visit into a form of political exile. This fear suffuses the nostalgia that constitutes the work's pervasive tone, a tone that perhaps originated with the following observations about the "French of America" recorded in Tocqueville's *Journey to America:*

> The French of America are to France as the Americans are to the English. They have preserved the greater part of the original traits of the national character, and they have added more morality and simplicity. They, like them, have broken free from a crowd of prejudices and false points of departure which cause and will cause all the miseries of Europe. In a word, they have in them all that is needed to cause a great memory of France in the New World.[12]

The key phrase in this passage appears at the conclusion where the "great memory of France in the New World" provides the rhetorical leverage to break from the "crowd" of unwanted attitudes, predispositions, and false starts that had migrated with the Old World French. America functions here as a secure space for a political experiment whereby the French can safely detach the unruly elements in their native habitude but without threatening the coherence of their "national character."

The agents responsible for this excision of the "crowd of prejudices" are not the French citizens, whose participation in revolutionary processes represented a "crowd" Tocqueville wanted to control, but the French of America. The French differed from other Americans, according to the mythology upon which Tocqueville draws here, in remaining primarily attached to the French national memory. By way of this memory, a troubling portion of the past was displaced to another location, where the events evoking negative associations lacked historical referents. As a consequence of this memory work, emigration to the United States not only effected a significant transformation in the France they remembered but also proved itself able to void the French national character itself of a "crowd" of unruly predispositions.

Unlike the French of France who were presumably as yet deprived of the anamnestic effects that emigration facilitated, the French of America liberated themselves as well from the related democratic tyranny of opinion that characteristically afflicted, Tocqueville observed, American democracy. In the same passage in which they remind him of the monumental difference between the French and the French of America, these travelers reveal to Tocqueville the political changes he could effect by arousing in his French readers political attitudes continuous with the processes through which France was remembered in America. In *Democracy in America,* Tocqueville would deploy the influential memory of French travelers by himself becoming one of them to reconceptualize American democracy as if it were the recollective process within the French national character.

Tocqueville assumed that character in the act of writing *Democracy in America.* In writing about American political culture as if he were a living embodiment of aristocratic liberty, Tocqueville reconstituted the aristocratic psyche that had been debilitated in the democratic process. Tocqueville struggled thereby to recover, albeit in the displaced form of his literary style, from the loss of status the aristocracy had undergone in France. Writing the book performed the work of displacing the trauma of class conflict onto a place lacking the feudal tradition's class stratification. By "working through" such residual class anxieties, Tocqueville turned the feudal tradition that he associated with the displacement he feared into a backdrop against which he could project what American democracy lacked. In his travels across a landscape lacking a feudal past, Tocqueville evacuated memories of France's democratic revolution from his haunted psyche. What became of that past in America, Tocqueville implies, is what will have become, or—put into the more optative mood that Tocqueville's official commission would recommend—what should have happened during the revolutionary moment in France.[13]

In the years he was at work on *Democracy in America,* Tocqueville understood unmanageable democratic forces to be a potential threat to the dominance of the French ruling class. Counting members of the French elite among his principal addressees, he promoted an understanding of *Democracy in America* as a defensive weapon in their war of cultural positioning. No matter what political forces threatened its status, *Democracy in America* was designed to restore the ruling class's image of masterful self-possession. By directing the French elite's aspiration to regulate democratic forces toward his description of actually existing institutions in the United States, Tocqueville elided any meaningful distinction between the French national imaginary whose specular designs he was productively regulating and the American political formation he claimed *Democracy in America* represented. The basic unit of symbolic exchange underwriting Tocqueville's book was at once circular and reciprocal. Tocqueville would deliver to America a coherent image of its national identity. Only metaleptically, however, after a reading of Tocqueville's classic, could American readers acquire their self-image. And, insofar as that self-image was itself the gratification of a desire to be recognized by the French ruling class, only in a relentlessly displaced form. America, according to the tacit symbolic economy through which Tocqueville negotiated his cultural authority, was France's democratic ideal coming from the New World future.

In *Democracy in America,* Tocqueville was less interested in establishing an accurate historical record than in associating his representations of American democracy with the needs of French governance, particularly those pertaining to the maintenance of France's dominance among European powers. *Democracy in America* turned American democratic formations into a French chronotope, a memory of France displaced onto nonsynchronic shores. By way of an anamnestic reading of *Democracy in America,* this more orderly recollection of France's past could be understood as having mysteriously migrated to America.

The last half-century of comment on *Democracy in America* by U.S. cultural historians bears significant witness to the fact that the purveyors of the official national history depended upon Tocqueville's magisterial representations for their authentication.[14] What is perhaps less evident in this commentary is its collective repression of what Jacques Ranciere has recently described as Tocqueville's imperial designs on a U.S. national polity that he had remade in the image of France's cultural imaginary. "What Tocqueville is looking for in America," Ranciere observes, "is good democracy, reasonable democracy, for he comes from the land of bad, unreasonable democracy. . . . America is the place where democracy is at the same time opaque to itself and transparent for the sovereign observer."[15] The sovereign observer to whom Ranciere refers is Alexis de Tocqueville, who reconstituted America's democratic regime as the likeness France desired and who thereafter passed this mirroring reflection onto the sovereign French state.

Throughout his suggestive reading, Ranciere effectively redescribes the America represented within Tocqueville's *Democracy in America* as a kind of French dependency. Ranciere proposes that Tocqueville's book should be understood as a simulacrum. According to this reading, France rediscovered in Tocqueville's masterwork a mirror image of its own democracy that had become alienated from itself by the Reign of Terror and the Atlantic Ocean. Having reduced the heterogeneous elements of U.S. culture to sociopolitical dimensions answerable to France's urgent contemporary needs, Tocqueville effectively incorporated America within the empire of French memory, as an additional unit of wealth in his symbolic patrimony and as an informal possession within France's cultural empire.

Situated between the French Revolution and Tocqueville's publication of *The Old Regime and the French Revolution* in 1856, *Democracy in America* furnished the French people with an image of the Old Regime's passion for a centralized form of governance that could be translated to the political needs of the Second Empire. Through the mediation of *Democracy in America,* a monolithic image of postrevolutionary France was addressed as well to the citizens of the Second Empire: "If I am asked how this portion of the old regime was able to be transferred in one whole piece and incorporated into the new society, I will answer that if centralization did not perish in the Revolution, this is because it was itself the beginning and the cause of the Revolution."[16]

Tocqueville's official stay in America taught him how to disavow the difference between America's nascent imperialism as it was evidenced in the Americanist doctrine of manifest destiny and the "democratic" institutions of France's Second Empire. In his preface to the 1848 (and 12th) edition of *Democracy in America,* writing at a time when what he referred to as "revolutionary" democratic sentiments had undergone renewal throughout Europe, Tocqueville underscored the fundamental lesson he learned in the writing of *Democracy in America* as the power to discriminate between democratic liberty and what he called democratic "tyranny":

While all the nations have been ravaged by war or torn by civil strife, the American people alone in the civilized world have remained pacific. Almost the whole of Europe has been convulsed by revolution. America has not even suffered from riots. There the republic so far from disturbing them has preserved all rights. Private property is better guaranteed there than in any land on earth. For sixty years the principle of sovereignty of all the people, which we have introduced but yesterday, has prevailed unchallenged. It is put into practice in the most direct, unlimited, absolute way. For sixty years that people who has made it the common fount of all the laws has increased in population, territory, and wealth; and let it be noted, throughout that period it has been not only the most prosperous but the most stable of all the peoples of the world.[17]

This remarkable passage attests to Tocqueville's ability to adapt his persona—in the extensive form of this preface to his literary property—to the highly volatile political circumstances of mid-nineteenth-century Europe. In his nearly forty years of public life, Tocqueville would survive by turns the French Revolution, the Reign of Terror, and the Napoleonic dictatorship. In 1848, Tocqueville found in the United States a symbolic property whose cultural value derived less from its actual political institutions than from his demonstrated capacity to transmute the heterogeneous political forces at work in the early American republic into a representative order answerable to France's political needs. In fashioning an artifact fully responsive to the changing circumstances of the French political landscape, Tocqueville simply ignored the highly contestatory political forces that American democracy had in fact released.

Tocqueville entered the United States a half-century before Martí and at a moment in the nation's history before the doctrine of manifest destiny had been fashioned into an instrument of extraterritorial rule. Among the several discoveries he found pertinent to his commission, Tocqueville would number among the most valuable the Jackson administration's ability to effect the generalized transference of the citizenry's volatile political passions onto their collective desire for westward expansion.[18] Competing historical accounts of the time period Tocqueville "covered" in his masterwork have also correlated the stability of the American polity with the resituation of aggressive drives onto an elusive and ever expanding frontier. In 1848, the year Tocqueville wrote the lines just cited from his preface, a boundary dispute between the United States and Mexico precipitated the so-called Mexican-American War. When conjoined with the national policy of westward expansion, the ideal of democracy subsequently mutated into a belief in national popular sovereignty that depended on the power to acquire new territories.

Instead of diagnosing the doctrine of manifest destiny as an ideological motive for the aggressive forces he had found at the core of democratic tyranny, Tocqueville, in a startling exercise of revisionist history, differentiated the American frontiersman's Indian policies from those of the "Spaniards." Unlike the Spaniards, whom Tocqueville describes as having "let their dogs loose on the Indians as if they were wild beasts" and who pillaged the New World like a city taken by storm without discrimination or mercy, "the conduct of the United States toward the natives was inspired by the most chaste affection for legal formalities."[19] Moreover, unlike the "United States Americans," the Spaniards—even though they fostered "genocide and atrocities"—"did not succeed in exterminating the Indian race and could not even prevent them from sharing their rights." Ascribing the chief difference between the two forms of imperialism, Tocqueville referred to the "fact" that Americans acquired native territories "quietly, legally, and philanthropically, without spilling blood and without violating a single one of the great principles of morality."[20]

Tocqueville's description of Spanish imperialism as the least "enlightened" of the several varieties of this enterprise at work in the Americas was strategic and designed to prove the superior status of French imperialism.[21] As a consequence of this revisionist account, Tocqueville constructed an ideological legitimation of American expansionism that turned on the difference between American and Spanish imperialism. As he traversed the historical border separating the democracies in France and America, Tocqueville also participated in constructing their geopolitical boundaries. In associating the borders of "America" with the territorial borders of the United States, Tocqueville depended upon an image of imperial Spain as the Other of both North America and France. Tocqueville maintained the specular relation between French and American democracy in part through their shared opposition to Spain. As the empire that both France and the United States excluded from democracy, Spain, in Tocqueville's account, secured their imaginary national boundaries. This representation presupposed an understanding of the "North" as a kind of unmarked term that encoded a history of colonial relations within "Northern domination of the South."

Implying that American expansionism required France's approval, Tocqueville invoked French colonialist traditions as a kind of imperial standard. With these criteria in mind, Tocqueville condemned the Spaniards for their atrocities; but on the other hand, he cited as their chief failure the fact that the Spanish "did not succeed in exterminating the Indian race." This ambivalence betrayed Tocqueville's preference for imperialism after the French model. The Maximilian empire in Mexico would depend upon just such discriminations to legitimate intervention in what the French called "Latin America," an intervention to be distinguished from both Hispanic and North American imperialism.[22]

2

The colony continued to live on in the republic;
and our America is gradually rescuing itself from its past mistakes.
—José Martí, "Nuestra América"[23]

The French democracy that Tocqueville was summoning into existence from the other side of the Atlantic was nevertheless organized in part through its difference from the Cuban and Latin American democratic formations in whose development Martí's work *Our America* would later play a crucial role. In defining the goal of "Our America" in terms of political independence from both Spain and the United States, Martí revealed the ways in which Tocqueville's criticism of Spanish imperialism masked the colonial histories of France and the United States. In *The Dialectics of Our America,* José David Saldívar explains how *Our America* teaches a history lesson almost the reverse of *Democracy in America.* In confronting the United States' "imperial history, its imperial ethic and imperial psychology," Saldívar observes, Martí "reads the grammar of imperialism and dramatizes U.S. domination of weaker economies."[24] Read by way of the dialectical logic Saldívar proposes, Tocqueville's conceptual appropriation of American democracy might be understood as having enacted a form of symbolic violence continuous with imperial rule.

Throughout *Our America,* Martí takes Tocqueville at his word by explicitly associating the genealogical line that eventuated in the official policy of American imperialism with Tocqueville's France. Instead of surrendering American histories of democratic freedoms to these two powers, however, Martí constructed an alternative site for an understanding of American democracy, a paradoxical space between empire and what Martí described as the "broken foundation." Unlike Tocqueville, who conflated them, Martí drove a wedge between the imperial will to annex and democratic aspirations to liberty, solidarity, and social justice. Martí thereby redescribed the political exile's temptation to become Americanized within the U.S. imperium in terms that identified citizenship with acquisitive drives and a cultural assimilation indistinguishable from territorial annexation. The construal of Cuban Americans as second-class citizens on the domestic sphere, Martí explained, was a direct consequence of U.S. foreign policy. Dependency in the one sphere authorized subordination in the other. And the illusion of democratic inclusion for the Cuban American masked this policy of internal colonialism.

Tocqueville's desire to link political society to the centralized state also diverged significantly from Martí's project in *Our America.* While his political writings depended for their formulations on the European political tradition that Tocqueville had extended, Martí was also sensitive to the ways in which that tradition had subverted non-European democratic traditions. The different Americas Martí convoked in his political manifesto derived their historical cogency and revolutionary force out of a radicalization of Tocqueville's strategies of displacement. After Martí emigrated to the United States in forced exile from Cuba, he began to formulate the social and economic principles that would provide the Pan-American revolutionary movement he organized there with an intellectual basis.

As a political exile, Martí was alienated from U.S. civil society as well as from the Cuban political authorities responsible for his deportation. Unlike Tocqueville, who struggled to displace such experiences from his memory, Martí transferred this redoubled lack of position into the basis for a general critique of "imperial nationalisms." In place of representing a national identity, Martí hollowed out an enunciative site between nationalism and whatever provisional identificatory processes linked him to the various exile communities that would grant him temporary shelter throughout his lifetime. Rather than demanding a return to *his* native land or constructing a single imagined community, Martí constellated multiple knowledges around what he termed "Our America," a political formation that those knowledges also reproduced.

He configured this project at sites where political refugees, migrant populations, nomads, expellees, and the dispossessed intersected with international trade agreements and the nationalist ideologies of race and ethnicity constructed to regulate the movements of such people. Martí's most remarkable political achievement was the ease and proficiency with which his revolutionary project bridged the gulf separating South from North America. "Our America" was the outcome of Martí's linking these knowledges with various political formations. The relay of practices that resulted was the outcome of his having learned how to address the political and economic needs of thousands of political émigrés, how to organize the Cuban proletariat in Tampa as well as exploited workers in New York and Chicago, how to unite Cubans in exile with patriots on the island, how to advocate independence from Spain while opposing annexation to the United States. Overall, Martí harnessed his political aptitude to the project of dismantling the various nationalisms that would impede the emergence of this irrecuperably relational process of becoming American but without being *an* American.

Martí was neither a subject nor a citizen that either the United States or Cuba would recognize as a bearer of human rights. Instead of accepting the attenuation of powers inherent to this lack of status, however, Martí deployed his literary powers to recharacterize Cuba and the United States as under the control of an antidemocratic power. If "annexation" named the process whereby the United States "naturalized" its subjects, the national identities that resulted, as Martí concluded the syllogism, could not in fact be differentiated from colonial subjugation. In describing the U.S. political relation with the Southern Hemisphere as shared in terms of annexation, Martí established a political rationale for his subsequent politics of displacement as the strategy best suited to subvert the intranational as well as the international operations of annexation.

Rather than complying with the powers that had forced him into exile, Martí differentiated his project from the nationalist ideologies that might have otherwise wholly assimilated them. A Cuban American in political exile within the United States, Martí transformed displacement from an imposed condition into a strategic force in resisting hegemony. As a geopolitical strategy, displacement operated in two separate but overlapping registers: it effected a generalized negation of linkages to national communities, and it also produced the power to identify with a broad range of political coalitions.

Martí discovered these separate strategic usages while undergoing the painful experiences that accompanied his condition as a displaced Cuban exile. Exiled in New York at the historical moment in which the annexation of Cuba was under discussion in the U.S. Congress, Martí believed the foreign policy of annexation to be more or less interchangeable in its motivations with the domestic policy of assimilation. Arguing that the metaphor of the "melting pot" domesticated in quite literal terms the U.S. foreign policy of imperial aggression, Martí discriminated that imperial drive from the cultural ideals that had dissimulated it. Representing the assimilationist drive as itself non-American, Martí detached that drive's force from the literary and political works that had been characterized as representatively American. Having thereby set up a distinction between his political condition as a Cuban American and the processes of Americanization he associated with imperialism, Martí proposed an alternative understanding of becoming American.

In distinguishing democratic from nationalist identifications, Martí effected a different relation to political exile as a condition situating him between the U.S. imperium and the emergent Pan-American democracies. In effecting his delinkage from the condition of national belonging, Martí reversed the direction of the state's regulatory power which was responsible for his status as a politically displaced person. He shifted his orientation to displacement—from a condition the state had imposed to a strategy through which he could practice the ongoing delinkage from the state's restrictions. With this reversal, Martí represented the displaced person as a figure within the social order who had been produced wholly out of the state's sovereign power to displace its subjects from the national culture to which they would otherwise be linked. As the bearer of this state power, Martí construed his power to reperform displacement as continuous with the sovereign power by whose force the state had produced him—as a displaced person. But this very shift transmuted his status from that of a figure subject to the state of displacement to a figure identical with the power of displacement.

Having transformed himself from the passive agent who was subjected to this power into the subject of it, Martí displaced the linkages identifying him with the position of the displaced person. He represented displacement as the state's sovereign power that could be reperformed as the power to displace the state into a power that the state had indirectly granted him—as his chosen means to displace state power. Consequently, the state power whose sovereign force formerly had precedence over his status within the political order now appeared to have itself been the effect of its "subject's" relation to the sovereign power of displacement.

Martí's writings deployed this distinction to disseminate a comparable internal distance within his readers that encouraged their understanding of democratic citizenship and subject formation as interlinked processes. Martí also encouraged an attitude toward social conflict that required various, and highly provisional, models of organization for its redress. As Martí's strategy crossed national borders, the displacement that had enacted the generalized negation of nationalist linkages became affirmative and multiplied into powers of identification across an uneven field of minoritarian communities and political coalitions. When communicated to his multiple readerships, Martí's strategies of internal and external displacement effected the political condition of not being wholly integrated within any political and cultural system.

This strategic estrangement enabled Martí's readers comparably to distinguish imperial from democratic processes and to understand the latter as composed of heterogeneous communities whose members, though not identical, were similar in their openness to "nonassimilated others."[25] Existing between emergent American social movements and an antiannexational attitude toward nationalism, Martí's displacement strategies effectively turned the assimilationalist drive against itself. His construal of the process of becoming American as the social correlative to anti-imperialism would subsequently elevate the non–North American into the primary rather than subordinated agent of this dynamic process.

Martí described the composite formation "Our America" as, like himself, exiled from the processes through which a national democracy could be linked to a person. This description accrued political value by way of its having redefined the possessive pronoun "Our" in *Our America* as a collectively shared willingness to be dispossessed of acquisitive drives. In this manifesto, Martí designated the territorial borders of the United States as the site where "Our America" had been displaced by empire. In distinguishing imperial from democratic formations, Martí derived political authorization for his project by speaking for Pan-American democracies at the site of their displacement.

Published during the heyday of imperial democracy, *Our America* regrounded at this site the emergent democratic movements that Martí was helping to organize throughout the Americas. Unlike Tocqueville's master narrative, Martí's *Our America* did not foster a belief in national identity. It provided the imaginative resources required to refuse imaginary identification with national communities. In place of a coherent image of an Americanist nation-state or of the citizen-subject who might be annexed to its imaginary community, Martí positioned a political apparatus designed to disarticulate citizens and subjects throughout the Americas from their national identifications with authoritarian political regimes.

In a companion text to *Nuestra América* that Martí entitled *Madre América* and delivered in 1889 as a talk before the Spanish American Literary Society of New York, he vividly distinguished his understanding of American democracy from Tocqueville's representations in *Democracy in America*.[26] This discrimination involved Martí in the construction of a critical genealogy that situated U.S. commerce with France at the origin of imperial democracy. The following passage engages intertextual relations with Tocqueville's *Democracy in America* in order to foreground, as the absent cause of its history, the imperial ambitions that Tocqueville had earlier displaced onto Spanish imperialism:

> The people that was to refuse help to others accepted help itself from France. The freedom that triumphed was like the people itself, haughty

and sectarian, with French cuffs and velvet hangings, more concerned with its own local circumstances than with those of humanity, a freedom which hung, selfishly and unjustly, over the shoulders of a slave race, which before a century had passed shook off the litter it was carrying on to the ground; and then emerged, axe in hand, the woodcutter with pious eyes from amidst the clamor and dust raised by the chains that fell from a million free men. Amidst the broken foundations in the tremendous convulsion strode victory, greedy and arrogant. The factors that made up the nation reappeared, accentuated by war; and beside the corpse of the gentleman, lying dead on top of his slaves, the pilgrim struggled for predominance in the republic and in the universe, the pilgrim who had not accepted any master over himself or servant underneath or any other conquests than those made by the seed in the earth and love in the hearts of men. Came the cunning and rapacious adventurer, accustomed to acquiring possessions, and driving through the forest, with no other law than his own wish or other limit than that made by his arm, a salutary and fearsome companion to the leopard and the eagle.[27]

In this incompatible account of the historical formation of the "new Americans" in the South, Martí displaced several of the key dramatis personae—the rustic woodcutter, the adventurer, the gentleman—from their places within Tocqueville's mise-en-scène. But then Martí restores the history of class conflict that Tocqueville had displaced from his account of American democracy, repositioning these figures within a line of imperial succession that originated with the French aristocracy's attitude of mastery toward American colonials ("French cuffs and velvet hangings") and continued throughout the United States' colonialist policies toward the Americas to the south ("came the cunning and rapacious adventurer"). Thus resituated, the freedom in which these figures purport to believe is described as having in fact been galvanized by a will to power—an imperial will that had refashioned freedom into a mask for rapacity.

In designating France's feudal tradition as a historical precedent for Tocqueville's representations of American democracy, Martí implied that U.S. imperial policies did not constitute exceptions to feudalism, as Tocqueville had maintained, but instead derived their legitimacy from that tradition. The range of connotations that Martí cannily encoded throughout this passage associated the colonial exploits of "haughty and sectarian" French aristocrats in the

North with those of the Spanish *conquistadores,* who had described themselves as "salutary and fearsome companion[s] to the leopard and the eagle." With the addition of this Hispanic accent to U.S. political history, Martí refused to credit Tocqueville's basis for distinguishing among forms of imperialism.

In refusing to acknowledge the difference between the Spanish imperialists who chose "the leopard and the eagle" and the French imperialists who adopted "French cuffs and velvet hangings" as their defining emblems, Martí also rejected the nationalist contexts in which these distinctions were hierarchically ranked. Martí grounded his refusal to discriminate among imperialisms in their crucial difference from a democratic movement that he represented as having been produced out of the power to establish such distinctions.

Martí identified the figure effecting this relentlessly negative relation to imperialism as "the pilgrim who had not accepted any master over himself or servant underneath or any other conquests than those made by the seed in the earth and love in the hearts of men." This figure emerged *at* the site of political difference between historically repetitive efforts of imperial appropriation, but also *as* the residuum of what those actions could not wholly incorporate: "beside the corpse of the gentleman, lying dead on top of his slaves, the pilgrim struggled for predominance in the republic and in the universe."

In this passage the pilgrim exercised the ongoing motion of displacement that metonymy performs in the field of rhetoric. But the pilgrim exercised this strictly negative activity in order to effect a political distinction between imperialism and what it could not subsume. Emerging at the site that the "broken foundation" had opened onto, the democratic formation with which Martí affiliated the pilgrim's resistance operated an ongoing disjuncture between imperial incursions and a coming democracy. What Martí called the "coming of democracy" expressed itself at the site of and as the force of this resistance. Bereft of any institutional form other than the pilgrim's power to resist what had taken place in its name, American democracy, Martí believed, always took place as a future prospect rather than an already accomplished political society. The future of democracy happened through the performance of actions like the pilgrim's.

In the following passage from *Nuestra América,* Martí's rhetoric enacts this uncanny temporal relation between democratic formations and the political performatives through which they realized their worldly effects:

> Nations must live by self-criticism because criticism is health; but this has to be done with one single breast and one single mind. Stoop to the level of the unfortunate and pick them up in your arms! With fire in our hearts, let us thaw out clotted America! Make the natural blood of the country flow bubbling and tumbling through its veins! Standing upright, with the merry eyes of workers, the new Americans are greeting each other from country to country! Native statesmen are coming to the fore from the direct study of Nature. They are reading to apply their reading, not merely to copy.[28]

Throughout this passage, Martí's rhetoric reverses the direction of the temporality organizing the relations between cause and effect. The agents responsible for the ethical imperative "Nations must live by self-criticism" do not emerge until the paragraph's penultimate sentence, where they are assigned the ontological status of a future prospect: "Native statesmen are coming to the fore." The urgency discernible in the speaker's apostrophes refers to the present need for these statesmen to provide these examples of statesmanlike speech acts. As they enact the struggle to call these figures from the future into the present, however, the speaker's enunciations also make the statesman's presence felt *in* the speech he is enunciating but also *as* the force taking the speaker up in the act of enunciating these democracy-evoking words.

Deriving his authority from the native statesmen evoked within his enunciation, Martí's subjectivity does not seem separable from the phrases he is enunciating, but appears instead provoked into existence in response to the need to accomplish the political imperatives he declares. In a relentlessly circular mode of address, Martí's rhetorical figures effect a pervasive metalepsis whereby the agents that the passage has assigned to an uncertain future, as what its apostrophes might possibly call forth, apparently "cause" the statements evoking them.

This shift in the relation between the cause of agency and its effects refers to all the speech agents represented in this passage. In the transition from the commanding order "Make the natural blood of the country flow bubbling and tumbling through its veins!" for example, to the ecstatic observation "Standing upright, with the merry eyes of workers, the new Americans are greeting each other from country to country!" the agents responsible for the greeting in the latter phrase could have performed it only after having been warmed in the "blood" of the prior apostrophe, "Make the warm blood of the country flow!" That enthusiastic enunciation in its turn would appear to have been the effect of the greeting it will have also caused. Having been caused by the preceding imperative(s), the "new Americans" recover their agency by enacting as a greeting the warm-bloodedness that called them forth. In reperforming the performatives that evoked them into existence, these new Americans become the retroactive agents of the stirring speech acts that provoked them into action.

In its individual phrases as well as its overall trajectory, the passage materializes an anterior future that is radically different from the present yet seems to have the capacity to realize an alternative to the present *now.* The "one single breast and one single mind" that Martí has designated as the agent responsible for the immanent national critique does not preexist the passage nor is it reducible to the figures that the passage represents. This democratic formation addressed in the passage "is" in the final instance the outcome of a *reading* of the inspiring democratic speech acts that the passage enacts. Like the future democracy they call forth, these performatives can be accomplished only by way of their having already been taken up by reading formations that would reperform that future in the reading of these words. But as the action taking place in the passage indicates, the act of reading also entails being taken up by these speech acts that require these future readers for their accomplishment "now."

Such passages as these reveal Martí's effort to turn displacement into a literary as well as a social force. In encouraging the reading formations that his writing addressed to find in his writing ways of imagining and thereafter accomplishing as yet unrealized democratic futures, Martí wrote as if he himself were evoked by his readers' future needs.[29] Writing in the gap between the democracies his works evoked and the present distortions of an imperializing will, Martí imaginatively associated his projected readers, their political formations and intertextual networks, with the democratic forces internally shaping his acts of writing. Martí did not simply aspire to realize that imagination differently, but also to become other than identifiable in the present political formation by way of a literary act that was (like himself) in need of alternative formulations.

The literary imagination became thereafter a material, as opposed to strictly formal, linkage that associated him with a different order of becoming American.[30] As the anticipatory realization of a democratic formation that Martí believed to be internal to the performative resources shaping the literary imagination, Martí's discourse, in its most extensive sense, became a historical force enacting the emergence and transmission of a coming American democracy.

In refusing to separate literature as a social practice from the material social conditions to which its forces could become applicable, Martí constructed a meaningful alternative to the social totalities that nationalism and imperialism had supervised. In becoming American by way of a literary formation that was becoming other than Americanist, Martí turned this double articulation — for American democracy but against U.S. imperialism — into a transnational and inter-American political resource that he could address to his native Cuba as well as to other emergent democracies. Martí's writings produced the strategic means for disarticulating a radically democratic reading formation from a cultural imperialism that had invoked national literary traditions in order to authorize its acts of political appropriation.

3

I admit that I saw in America more than America.
— Alexis de Tocqueville, *Democracy in America*[31]

I lived in the monster and know its entrails: and my sling is that of David. — José Martí, "A la raíz"[32]

The subject position Martí constructed for himself in *Our America* displaced him from within any already existing American political formation and recirculated this displacement throughout the ensemble of political entities with which he had articulated his project. The political location for the "becoming America" that his writing calls forth takes place at this imaginary border — within subjects and between political formations — where he distinguished the never-ending process of becoming American from the Americanization which negated that process. In the process of enunciating this border, Martí discriminated his new Americans from Northern Europeans who, like Tocqueville, traveled to America in order to effect the generalized transference of unfinished European business onto the emergent democratic formations such acts of transference would displace.

Martí also described the state formation reproductive of U.S. citizen-subjects as indistinguishable from the acquisitive drives migrating from Northern European spaces such as Tocqueville's France. He designated the democratic revolution that Tocqueville had written *Democracy in America* to displace from the French national memory as the ongoing process responsible for the emergence of democracy throughout the Americas. Martí finally situated "Our America" in the space between Tocqueville's *Democracy in America* and these emergent democratic forces. Martí's project involved dismantling the structures of selective displacement undergirding Tocqueville's nationalizing memory.

At the beginning of this essay, I remarked the hegemonic usage to which Tocqueville has recently been put in identifying emergent democratic formations with the preconstituted subject positions through which the state links its citizen-subjects to national cultures. I cannot conclude, however, without providing an example of an instance in which a figure that Martí associated with the coming American democracy erupted from within Tocqueville's *Democracy in America* and disrupted the hegemony it had effected.

Tocqueville's journey to America involved, as we have seen, his recuperating the French national memory's capacity to displace the memory of the French democratic revolution by linking its figures to preexisting positions within the French national culture and removing the crowd of disturbing associations left over from the crisis. In the following passage, though, Tocqueville encounters a figure within the American democratic order who resisted this strategy of displacement. Indeed, at this internal limit to the great memory of France in the New World, Tocqueville recovers the memory of the trauma he had written *Democracy in America* to forget: "The Negro of the United States has lost even the remembrance of his country; the language which his forefathers spoke is never heard around him; he abjured their religion and forgot their customs when he ceased to belong to Africa, without acquiring any claim to European privileges."[33]

Throughout *Democracy in America,* Tocqueville had displaced the scene of what he called the "democratic revolution" by finding that America lacked the social stratification required to generate a democratic revolution. It was the very absence of class antagonism that had permitted Tocqueville to recover the aristocratic standpoint through which he perceived himself as what America was lacking. In adding the class position missing from the antebellum United States, Tocqueville displaced the trauma of the democratic revolution that threatened the French aristocracy with cultural dispossession. In the "Negro of the United States," Tocqueville encountered a figure crucial to the reproduction of the class system he claimed America lacked.

As a figure that Tocqueville had constituted wholly out of signs of cultural amnesia, the "Negro" represented Tocqueville's need to forget. But Tocqueville's representation of the "Negro's" cultural amnesia has only recalled traumatic scenes from the French Revolution. These scenes, moreover, have entered his field of perception by way of the structures of representation he had designed to displace them. Not only that, but all this seems to have taken place in the space of unrepresented class antagonism that lay between democratic freedoms and the aristocratic privileges to which they were opposed.

The elision of the slave trade from this description—Tocqueville forgot how the Southern plantocracy had involved the state as the agency responsible for the cultural dispossession of the "Negro of the United States"—disclosed two aspects of the trauma that Tocqueville could not altogether remember to forget. The very terms Tocqueville used to describe the social estate of the "Negro of the United States" recalled scenes from the Revolution that he also feared reencountering upon his return to France. By way of such expressions as "abjured" and "forgot," Tocqueville granted to the "Negro" the "European privileges" that in the same passage he also claimed they were without. Insofar as such catchwords could be enunciated by both of the conflicting parties in the French Revolution, they in turn recalled that primal antagonism. On the one hand, the "abjuring" of cultural relations recalled the democratic "mob"; on the other, the scene provided a vivid description of the state of cultural dispossession that Tocqueville associated with the revolution's effect on the aristocracy. In the "Negro of the United States," he had rediscovered at once the terrible cause of the Revolution as well as the terrifying effect on the French aristocracy.

Overall, Tocqueville would appear to have encountered the selfsame trauma that he had traveled to America to avert — and by way of the very structure that had been designed to facilitate its displacement. The scene recalled the Revolution as an event that had in France already happened as well as a democratic revolution that had not yet taken place — in America. Disconnected from the past, the future of the "Negro of the United States" had to entail a democratic revolution that Tocqueville had declared could not happen here.

Tocqueville had previously associated his memory work with the project of recovering the coherence of the French national identity. But Tocqueville could not remember the "Negro" back into the French identity without recalling the "crowd" of traumatic associations he had described the French as traveling to America to forget. Because he was unable to link this scene to the French memory without reactivating recollections of the democratic revolution, this scene constituted the limits of the narrative through which Tocqueville had deployed official memory to consolidate the national identity.

Unlike Tocqueville, Martí read U.S. history as a figure who, like Tocqueville's "Negro," was permanently displaced from within the space to which he could never "democratically" belong. As a consequence of this countermemory, Martí evoked an American democracy that has not yet come.[34]

Notes

1 José de Diego, "El desplazamiento," in *Obras completas* (San Juan: Instituto de Cultura Puertorriqueña, 1966), pp. 25–26.

2 Ngugi Wa Thiong'o, *Decolonizing the Mind* (Nairobi and London: Heinemann, 1986), p. 3.

3 In this usage "Hispanic" refers to native-born U.S. citizens — Chicanos, Mexican Americans, Nuyoricans, and mainland Puerto Ricans — as well as Latin American immigrants of all national and racial combinations.

4 See José Martí, "Nuestra América," in *Obras completas* (Havana: Editorial Nacional de Cuba, 1963), pp. 15–23.

5 In her *Headless History: Nineteenth Century French Historiography of the French Revolution* (Ithaca: Cornell University Press, 1990), Linda Orr has remarked incisively concerning Tocqueville's politics of displacement that "it would be easy to say that the 'only essential difference' between the 'then' (Old Regime) and 'now' (Empire) of the text is the Revolution—and this would be true, except that the Revolution would be seen as an imperceptible step toward the Empire or the displacement between two historical objects (Old Regime and Empire) that are almost identical" (p. 100). Whereas Orr concentrates her analysis in the Old Regime and the French Revolution, I would argue that *Democracy in America* did the work of displacing the difference between the Old Regime and Empire, thereby rendering the two events all but indistinguishable.

6 When Tocqueville claimed America as a French cultural possession, he was inaugurating a venerable culture tradition whose legatees include Camus, Sartre, Malraux and, most recently, Jean Baudrillard. Jean-Phillipe Mathy has provided an illuminating account of this tradition in *Extreme-Occident: French Intellectuals and America* (Chicago: University of Chicago Press, 1993).

7 Blandine Kriegel, in *The State and the Rule of Law* (Princeton: Princeton University Press, 1995), p. 157, cites George Lefebvre as the source of this quote.

8 Claude Lefort formulated this dualism in *Democracy and Political Theory* (Cambridge: Polity Press, 1988), p. 180.

9 Lefort goes even further than Tocqueville when he constructs a genealogy that explains the emergence of democracy in terms of the complete loss of the feudal order's transcendental guarantees. In passages such as the following, Lefort suggests that Tocqueville reexperienced the trauma of the Revolution in the gap between the abstract individual and the "crowd": "When social power is divorced from the person of the prince, freed from the transcendental agency which made the prince the guarantor of order and of the permanence of the body politic, and denied the nourishment of the duration which made it almost natural, this power appears to be the power society exercises over itself. When society no longer recognizes the existence of anything external to it, social power knows no bounds. It is a product of society, but at the same time it has the vocation to produce society; the boundaries of personal existence mean nothing to it because it purports to be the agent of all" (ibid., p. 167).

10 Throughout the so-called quincentenary celebration of Columbus's expedition to the Americas, Martí has been invoked as a kind of Anti-Columbus. The centenary celebration of Martí's martyrdom has fostered a renewed interest in histories of the Americas previously subjugated to a colonialist model of the "Discovery." Philip F. Foner's editions of Martí's *Our America* (New York: Monthly Review Press, 1977) and *Inside the Monster: Writings on the United States and American Imperialism* by José Martí (New York: Monthly Review Press, 1975) have played a key role in the Martí renaissance among U.S.-based Americanists.

11 Alexis de Tocqueville, *Œuvres completes,* vol. 33: *Ecrits et discourses politiques* (Paris: Gallimard, 1985), p. 87.

12 Alexis de Tocqueville, *Journey to America,* ed. J. P. Mayer, trans. George Lawrence (New Haven: Yale University Press, 1960), pp. 189–90.

13 As the prominent citation of *Democracy in America* in the Republican Party's 1994 "Contract with America" starkly attests, Tocqueville occupies a central place in the "representative" political tradition of the United States. Newt Gingrich gives Tocqueville his featured role in official U.S. history in the following sentence, which redacts the "Contract with America": "From the Jamestown colony and the Pilgrims, through de Tocqueville's *Democracy in America,* up to the Norman Rockwell paintings of the 1940's and 1950's, there was a clear sense of what it meant to be an American." See Gingrich, *To Renew America* (New York: HarperCollins, 1995), p. 7. The entire book, particularly Gingrich's recollections of his stay in Orléans, can be read as in intertextual dialogue with Tocqueville's *Democracy in America.* The pertinence of Tocqueville's travels both to Jacksonian America in the nineteenth century and to the political aspirations of Republican Party office seekers in the twenty-first discloses the transhistorical value of his official mission. Alexis de Tocqueville journeyed to America to ascertain the regulatory ideal of a people that "while all the nations of Europe have been devastated by war or torn by civil strife . . . remained at peace" (Tocqueville, "Author's Preface to the Twelfth Edition," *Democracy in America,* ed. J. P. Mayer, trans. George W. Lawrence [Garden City, N.Y.: Doubleday, 1969], p. xiv). The United States, in Tocqueville's masterful survey of its institutions, had become a paragon of the socially regulative ideal of "law and order" that constituted the political imaginary of post–Cold War Republicans as well as postrevolutionary French bureaucrats. The unitary image of the United States that Tocqueville constructed in

his masterwork was put into service in the latter half of the nineteenth century as France's elusive political ideal of an integrated democratic community. But the framework of Tocqueville's project was also transferable, as evidenced by the Republican Party platform, and is able to support homologous ideological work across history.

14 Among the many works responsible for the central place Tocqueville holds in U.S. cultural history, I would cite Louis Hartz's *The Liberal Tradition in America: An Interpretation of American Political Thought since the Revolution* (New York: Harcourt Brace, 1955) and Robert A. Nisbet's *The Sociological Tradition* (New York: Basic Books, 1966) as landmark works in this reading tradition. For a different reading of Tocqueville, and of Americanist political history, see Claude Lefort's close reading of *Democracy in America* in *Democracy and Political Theory,* pp. 183–209.

15 See Jacques Ranciere, "Discovering New Worlds: Politics of Travel and Metaphors of Space," in *Traveller's Tales: Narratives of Home and Displacement,* ed. Jon Bird et al. (London and New York: Routledge, 1994), p. 35.

16 Alexis de Tocqueville, *The Old Regime and the French Revolution,* trans. Stuart Gilbert (New York: Doubleday, 1955), p. 60.

17 Tocqueville, "Author's Preface to the Twelfth Edition," p. xiv.

18 In his *Politics and Remembrance: Republican Themes in Machiavelli, Burke and Tocqueville* (Princeton: Princeton University Press, 1985), Bruce James Smith argues persuasively (pp. 189–93) for an understanding of Tocqueville's reading of "democratic values" as a cover for aristocratic sentiments. "He understood the distemper of the aristocratic affections, that its origin lay in a great sense of loss. He, too, had drunk from the bitter cup of revolution," writes Smith. Such distemper could be abated only by giving up the rage for the great memory of aristocracy that democracy afforded. Only *Democracy in America,* Tocqueville argued, provided a historical generality pervasive enough in its temporal range and regulatable enough as a political institution to displace the violence of the French Revolution from aristocratic memory. If Tocqueville, in Smith's reading, aspired to efface the memory of the revolution from the French past, Martí construed democracy in America as an event still to come.

19 Tocqueville, *Democracy in America,* p. 339.

20 Ibid.

21 George Mariscal has demonstrated the several ways in which monolithic constructions such as Tocqueville's had worked in the service of producing a Eurocentric hegemony. See Mariscal, "Can Cultural

Studies Speak Spanish?" in *English Studies/Cultural Studies: Institutionalizing Dissent,* ed. Isaiah Smithson and Nancy Ruff (Urbana: University of Illinois Press, 1994), pp. 59–75.

22 Ernesto Laclau elaborates on this observation in his exchange with Judith Butler in *Diacritics* 27, no. 4 (Spring 1997): 10–11.

23 In Martí, *Obras completas,* vol. 6, p. 19.

24 José David Saldívar, *The Dialectics of Our America: Genealogy, Cultural Critique, and Literary History* (Durham: Duke University Press, 1991), p. 9.

25 I borrow this phrase from Iris Marion Young's essay "The Ideal of Community and the Politics of Difference," in *Feminism/Postmodernism,* ed. Linda Nicholson (New York: Routledge, 1990), p. 319.

26 Martí, "Madre América," in *Obras completas,* vol. 6, pp. 133–40.

27 Ibid., pp. 135–36.

28 Martí, "Nuestra América," pp. 20–21.

29 I am using the term "reading formation" in the sense proposed by Tony Bennett in "Texts in History: The Determinations of Readings and Their Texts": as "a set of discursive and inter-textual determinations operating on material and institutional supports, which bear in upon a text not just externally from the outside in but internally shaping it—in the historically specific forms in which it is available as a text to be read—from the inside out" (*Post-Structuralism and the Question of History,* ed. Derek Attridge et al. [Cambridge: Cambridge University Press, 1987], p. 72).

30 In keeping with Martí's mandate to found an alternative to the America of empire, Benigno Sanchez-Eppler has discovered a homoerotic tradition for Martí. See Sanchez-Eppler's "Call My Son Ismaael: Exiled Paternity and Father/Son Eroticism in Reinaldo Arenas and José Martí," *Differences* 6, no. 1 (1994): 69–128. In this essay Sanchez-Eppler associates *Ismaelillo,* the poem that the "founding father" of revolutionary Cuban nationalism addressed to his estranged son, with the poetry of Reinaldo Arenas, a Cuban poet whose homosexuality resulted in exile from Castro's Cuba. By way of a moving reading of *Ismaelillo,* Sanchez-Eppler describes it as a complex national allegory wherein Martí's only means of coming to terms with his exile in America was the construction of a poetic persona whose longing for reunification with his estranged son was likewise expressive of the desire for an intergenerational homoerotic liaison. Having thus refashioned the figure that Fidel Castro had acknowledged as the founder of the Cuban Revolution into a gay father, Sanchez-Eppler invoked the authority of this reading of Martí in order to deny to Castro

retroactively José Martí's authorization for the exclusion of gays from "Our America."

31 Tocqueville, *Democracy in America,* p. 19.

32 Letter to Manuel Mercado, May 18, 1895, in *Obras completas,* vol. 4, p. 170.

33 Tocqueville, *Democracy in America,* p. 317.

34 Throughout *Our America,* Martí deployed rather crude racial stereotypes to describe the Northern Europeans whose racism he had elsewhere found instrumental in the cultural subordination of the peoples of the South. But in characterizing the Swedes and Germans, for example, as incarnations of a free-floating violence that originated in Northern Europe but that they displaced (once these Northern immigrants became fully assimilated) onto their relations with Latino Americans, Martí did not exactly continue the circulation of the North's symbolic violence. Instead, he identified the Northern Europeans' displaced aggression both as the basis for experiencing their displacing violence and as the precondition for the coming of an alternative politics.

Susana Rotker

The (Political) Exile Gaze in Martí's Writing on the United States

The thought of dying. From the book
My eyes flee already, searching on high
For a greater book: but I want
Neither rest in an enslaved land, nor in this
Land in which I was not born: the rain itself
Seems like a scourge, and foreign
Are its trees to me. Yes, I am moved
By my horror of the cold: Oh, fatherland, just
Like my heart, my body belongs to you!

[El pensamiento de morir. Del libro
Huyen los ojos ya, buscando en lo alto
Otro libro mayor: pero no quiero
Ni en tierra esclava reposar, ni en esta
Tierra en que no nací: la lluvia misma
Azote me parece, y extranjeros
Sus árboles me son. Sí, me conmueve
Mi horror al frío: ¡oh patria, así
Como mi corazón, mi cuerpo es tuyo!]

—José Martí, from "Lluvia de junio"[1]

To read José Martí's *Escenas norteamericanas* from the point of view of exile, of exile considered as a fissure of writing, a fissure of being, a fissure of one's worldview, implies the task of reconsidering at least two critical conventions. One is the interpretation of Martí's esthetics as only a condensation of an age's sensibility (reflecting the schism brought about by the arrival of modernity); and the other, the very notion of the writer in exile.

The experience of exile is not a mere anecdotal detail in Martí's case. As we know, he was deported from Cuba to Spain when he was only eighteen years of age, a fact that began a cycle of displacement that would end only with his death twenty-four years later.

Leaving aside Martí's stay in Spain (the colonial power), Martí's experience of exile in the American continent is divided in two very clear phases, the first of which is marked by his life in various countries of Latin America. This phase is characterized by such a degree of direct engagement with local politics that it does not seem possible to speak convincingly of Martí's life "in exile," at least not if exile is understood in the sense of *being outside* (the word "exile" is derived from *ex*—outside of—and from the Latin *salire* [to leap, spring, or bound]).[2]

In 1881, Martí begins his lengthy period of exile in the United States. He no longer lives the fragile fiction of belonging that he experienced in Latin America. The fragility of that fiction is found in the fact that Martí's exiled condition ensures that his stays in Mexico, Guatemala, or Venezuela (between six months and two years) are brief ones. In the United States, in contrast, he does not try to *participate* as an immigrant who wants to *belong:* exile and belonging are no longer opposite, but instead form a dialectical tension stemming from his otherness in a country and language foreign to him, and from the effort that he makes to reconstruct his identity and a sense of home. On the one hand, he is an activist for Cuban independence; on the other, by means of his chronicles on the United States, Martí casts his anchor in the language and attempts to become familiar with the strange; that is to say, he endeavors to apprehend the Other in order to apprehend himself. He does this obsessively for more than a decade. As a correspondent in Latin American newspapers, he explains repeatedly the nature of the society in which he finds himself to be moored and alienated at the same time.

1

In the writing of exile there are permanent tensions that are not resolved: inside/outside, presence/absence, memory/forgetting, expropriation/appropriation, present/past, lived/imagined/written. There is in exile writing the double gesture of recuperating nationality by reterritorializing it in one's memory and by making the strange familiar. These actions represent a double gesture that is, in the final account, unequivocal: it speaks for the desire to reconstruct the home.

According to María Moliner's *Diccionario de uso del español,* the word *patria* (fatherland) comes from *padre* (to beseech, to perpetrate); the word is defined as native land, native soil, the relation of a country to the natives.[3] Father and fatherland, Cuba and José Martí. Given this plain and perfect formula that equates its two extremes to the founder of a nation, how to think about the fissure that is both palpable and visible, of two-thirds of a life lived in exile? I do not mean to say that tradition (in the sense of "culture" and the invention of nations ascribed to it by Hobsbawm)[4] ignores Martí's epic outside of Cuba; I mean, rather, that tradition does *not* consider Martí's exile experience as a fissure in his writing. This fact is curious, because in the nineteenth century the definition of the past and of the identity of the individual depended on that whole represented by nation/state; thus, the exile was seen as someone who had been divested of identity.[5] In the case of Martí, literary tradition speaks of exile as redemption: exile is remembered as if it were the vehicle necessary to construct an independent nation, or the fact that would allow for the triumphal return of the prophet. Martí, founding father: in this pairing, the tradition that contains Martí is revealed to be similar to the one that narrates the lives of Moses, Mohammed, or Jesus.[6]

How to read Martí today, without being snared by his condition of eminent personage? And, at the same time, how not to take into account that his extraordinary newspaper chronicles—a sort of an experimental laboratory for modernist writing—were written when Martí was a tattered exile, not the icon of a colonized *patria*? Martí was, to those who read him in *La Nación* (Buenos Aires), *La Opinión Nacional* (Caracas), *La Opinión Pública* (Montevideo), *La República* (Tegucigalpa), *El Partido Liberal* (Mexico), and *La América* (New York), only a newspaper correspondent, a talented chronicler. Cuba, as state, was only a history that had yet to be written.

Before considering specific examples of exile-writing in Martí's North American chronicles, I would like to pause—albeit briefly—on the relation between the writer and exile, the terms of which have been recently redefined by Edward Said, the Palestine critic who, like Martí in his own time, lives and writes in New York. Basically, Said conceives the writer as a marginal individual in a foreign society and considers the advantages and disadvantages of this position; for Said, the writer's marginality implies primarily the impossibility of resorting to institutions in the traditional manner.[7] The exile-writer, he suggests, cannot appeal to armies or states for support; the exile has only a context that keeps him or her inside and outside at the same time.[8]

In Martí's case, Said's proposition becomes relative: Martí invents devices that make marginality into a category operating according to other criteria. Martí is part of an army in exile, or at least he devotes more than a decade to achieving its creation. In a historical moment marked by the consolidation of national states, widespread industrialization, and a questioning of the hemispheric project, Martí is Latin America's diplomatic agent, committed to the notion of continental unity. Martí also articulates strategies in his writing that bind him again to a sort of home, as shall be seen. Or perhaps all these developments are just variants of a deep sense of despair before the reality of exile, born of a feeling of desperation that impels him to re-create his "broken history." What makes it difficult to read Martí from this perspective is that, over time, he truly was able to reconstruct his history. The expression of his desire for home became home.

In his last book, *Representations of the Intellectual,* Said accentuates his elegy for the intellectual in exile (as if he were interpreting the word "exile" through its other Latin root: to exult, exaltation), with the result that he generally transforms (and more than ever) his own particular situation. In that book, the exiled intellectual is seen as occupying a privileged place: not belonging ensures the distancing of the gaze[9] and the denial of concessions to the institutions that the true intellectual, according to Theodor Adorno's proposition in *Minima Moralia,* should exercise.[10] Said's criteria would be valid for the purposes of this study if we thought of Martí as a writer trying to make his way in the United States (much like Said himself) or in what we still call the First World: his gaze would remain at the periphery and, hence, free. But this idealization of "freedom" is difficult to accept, since identity depends on and is the very realization of the state-dictated "nonbeing" of the person who is outside of, or occupies, the border.[11] Exile is dismemberment, reduction, and the need for recomposition, as well as the interruption of the mechanism forming the political and cultural spheres.[12] Exile is the internalization of the fissure, the crossing and recrossing of the border; it is astonishment, bewilderment, constant confrontation, and comparison. It is the mythifying nostalgia of the lost home's locus and the desire for a return, even if that return is possible only by means of the word. It is all this, together with a revision of the ties (implicit for the many who have never left their geography) that define social coherence: e.g., the value of tradition; the legitimacy of the familiar; the supremacy of what is known, or of nationalism. Exile is the reformulation of the coordinates of human solidarity and of the empathy felt toward one's neighbor: it is contamination.[13] Seen from the point of view of the one who does not desire insertion into the new place, exile does not spell out the "privilege" of an objective, distant, and free gaze.

Said's position has several facets, which somehow contain the most contemporary notions about writing in exile. One is summarized in Said's citing of George Steiner's introduction to his book *Extraterritorial,* where Steiner states: "It seems proper that those who create art in a civilization of quasi-barbarism, which has made so many homeless, should themselves be poets unhoused and wanderers across languages. Eccentric, aloof, nostalgic, deliberately untimely. . . . "[14] This sentiment is well suited to the modern conceptualization of the *poète maudit* who, like Don Quixote, tilts at windmills, or even to the image of the modernist poet resisting the vacuity of depersonalized and materialistic bourgeois society. Another facet is that of the inventor of national romances who tries from a distance to recuperate the totality of a lost land. It is, somehow, the scene of Eric Auerbach, a Jewish intellectual exiled in Istanbul during World War II. There, while the world he knew exploded in a thousand pieces, this formidable scholar (re)created Western culture, once removed. The result was *Mimesis,* a book impossible to conceive without the gaze that distance allows.[15] Here Auerbach tried to recompose, by means of the word, a world that threatened to vanish as much from his memory as from history; without secondary sources, he risked being inexact, but it would have been worse to risk the consequences of exile by resigning himself to silence and thus lose the texts, the traditions, the continuities that weave the web of identity. Loss of memory and loss of identity: one writes in order to recuperate and, at the same time, to ward off extinction.[16]

This second image remits us once again to the intelligence that the gaze acquires with distance. It represents the alternative of assuming one's foreign condition before culture, as in the case of Julia Kristeva, whose novelty within the currents of thought in Western

Europe has everything to do with her consciousness of being a foreigner;[17] or the similar case of the breakthrough that Franz Kafka, a Czech Jew writing in German, achieved in relation to the literary system of his time.[18] In his writing, Martí produced fissures in the literary system, but his texts did not represent a transformation in how U.S. culture thinks itself; rather, it affected how Latin American culture — the one that marks his origin — conceives itself. There cannot be a wider gap between the situations described, perhaps because, in the final analysis, Auerbach, Adorno, Kristeva — the writers that Western critical thought takes into account — remit their work to the great tradition of Western culture. Edward Said himself, though he has produced important works on the Palestine problem, has made a name for himself by compelling the West to examine its own critical thinking. Martí's "positioning" compels us to rethink Said's ideas from different angles.

Clearly, "positioning" is not a minor factor. It defines not only exile but also the context of the gaze. As both the product of a society still subjected to colonialism and the instrument of a nationalist project, as well as a major witness of the Gilded Age and of U.S. imperialism, Martí's North American chronicles would allow us to elaborate, moreover, on the interesting propositions that Homi Bhabha develops in relation to *the gaze and colonialist discourse* which he conceives from the site of enunciation of the colonizer (see note 9 below). Bhabha describes the gaze projected on the Other from the point that defines the "lack of the other"; one could shade this description with what Said so lucidly qualifies as the contrapuntal perception of the exile, alluding instead to the exile's tendency to compare, or to the plurality of views that people who know at least two cultures possess.[19] The confrontation with the Other — in this case, not the marginal or the colonized, but the site of power — allows, as in the Lacanian mirror stage, a redefinition of one's identity by means of differentiation (recognizing the reflected image by what is different about it). The site of power is displaced in Martí's *Escenas norteamericanas.* The gaze is projected onto New York (a relative model and, at the same time, a threat), not onto the relation of colonial immediacy that Spain represented for Cuba. Perhaps this displacement determines other forms of empathy in the texts that constitute the collection.

While Martí articulates his discourse in relation to the society in which he finds himself (living "in the belly of the beast" [en las entrañas del monstruo]), he does not seek that society's ear. Latin America is his interlocutor, his global "us," and his point of reference. Latin America is present in a thousand ways in each chronicle, beginning with the letter-like heading addressed to the director of the journal and following with the very texture of the representation. Martí's work, even the one that refers to the United States, is a perpetual reflection on being, or on the imperative of being Latin American.

2

How to think of José Martí as an exile? One key is found in the "Carta a Bartolomé Mitre y Vedia," written at the beginning of Martí's collaboration as a correspondent for *La Nación* (Buenos Aires). There he alludes to a previous letter by the editor as a "ray of light *from my own sun*" [rayo *de mi propio sol;* my emphasis]: "nor does it seem to me that I'm writing to a new friend, but rather to a friend of old, high-minded and the owner of warm heart" [ni me parece que estoy escribiendo a una nueva amistad, sino a amigo antiguo, de corazón caliente y mente alta]. In his reply, Martí draws clear distinctions between "nuestra América" [our America]—i.e., Latin America—and "aquí" [here]—the United States. He contrasts the "here," a place where there is an "exclusive, vehement, and anxious love for material fortune" [amor exclusivo, vehemente y desasosegado de la fortuna material], with "the younger and more generously restless lands of our America" [las tierras más jóvenes y más generosamente inquietas de nuestra América].[20] Martí constructs his fatherland upon this model: a personal dialogue with Latin America, with the urban center as its theme. The "here" is temporal and it is also Other. It is seen with the curiosity derived from the discovery of modernity: the reification of commercial goods, the creation of a new public space, the confrontation with multiple and strange beings, the experience of displacement and disunity[21]—all characteristics shared by the experience of exile. To write chronicles was the way to earn a living—a fact lamented by the modernists—but also the way to shape that experience of being a witness, of trying to produce for the Latin American reader a sort of revelation and re-creation of the native land (or of

Latin America as total source of belonging) by means of memory and writing.

Exile, as we know, is the loss of home, that is, of the ontological myth that reconciles time and space; exile is the loss of that place of residence brimming with metaphorical qualities, as was seen by Bachelard.[22] A strategy for recovering home in *Escenas norteamericanas* consists in using a national language, a brand of Spanish for the whole of Latin America, as if the continent were a coherent linguistic space. Thus, for Martí, language would be the agent of communal intelligibility, with a clear aim: to re-create "us," Latin America, by means of journalism. Home and identity are affirmed through the creation of a metaphor for the "us" and the "them." Writing is, at the same time, an allegory for its own otherness. His notebook shows that as early as 1871, and from the beginning of his exile period, Martí was already developing the dichotomy: the United States ("them" but at the same time "here") is postulated as the empire of the practical, of cold calculation, of prosperity and corruption, in opposition to the "us," or the territory of the heart, of the imagination and the new (21:15–16). Martí's global perspective on identity and belonging generally ignores the marked differences between nations and the specificities of Latin American politics. The dichotomy undergoes further refinements to become the warp and woof of one of his most famous texts, *Nuestra América* (1891); the dichotomy will also, with the arrival of the twentieth century, become the foundation of José Enrique Rodó's *Ariel.*

"Us" and "them": Martí displaces his own condition by creating a rhetoric of belonging, a formidable political machine much more dynamic and complex than the marginal person's own nostalgia. He builds a sort of collective ethos for Latin America from the place of exile and confronted by exile, from and confronted by the continental giant.

A double scene results from writing: the allegorical space that affirms "I am" (a sovereign subjectivity that finds itself at home in modernist esthetics) along with the reformulation of the world, cast in a recognizable and familiar manner that limits the absolute otherness of that "I am."[23] The North American chronicles are defined by an encounter between rationalization and subjectivity, between technique and emotion, between myth and the encroachment of everyday life, between disenchantment and faith. While the chronicles speak of the desire for unceasing and cosmopolitan novelty and fragmentation, they reveal the desire for the reconciliation of contradictions and the restitution of the loose fragments of reality, of self and otherness. In the chronicles, writing becomes a sounding board that gathers all of Western culture and mixes it with a search for the indigenous, for the new, and, at the same time, with what Martí recognizes as the most valid aspects of tradition.

In this writing, a sensibility that evolved from the experience of the nineteenth century's end — evident in the breakdown of certainties, the amazement before the new and the multiple — coexists with the exile's sense of instability and astonishment. So perfect is this union that it is almost superfluous to assert that modernism and exile are equivalent in Martí's chronicles. In spite of that fact, both sides of the equation are usually not taken into account in literary analysis, as if we were not dealing with a process of wreckage and survival, in which the exile is trying desperately to bring together what is rent asunder. But that, too, is the writing of exile: the figure of breakdown and the gesture intended to bring about a transformation by means of connecting labor (itself a figure).

In the hundreds of chronicles that Martí wrote in New York, he was able to assemble a sort of unity out of fragmentation in a space of condensation. In other words, he achieved a single representation that itself fuses several associative chains, and that unique site of representation marks the point of intersection of those chains. These associative chains are formed by means of symbol and analogy; Martí's prose, as well as his poetry, weaves a system of correspondences between the writer's internal states and objective reality.[24]

3

How does all this affect Martí's view of the United States? It is not necessary to go to the *Versos sencillos* in search of nostalgic palm trees, or resort to the seemingly infinite letters and speeches that deal with the Cuban situation, because in his numerous *Escenas norteamericanas* the theme of exile is always present.

Bewilderment, subjectivity, the need to recompose what is fragmented are all present in the chronicles; but also astonishment and simultaneity. Are these not the vectors that constitute one of the earliest chronicles from New York, titled "Coney Island" (1881)? Astonishment is the word that is most often repeated in that account: astonishment before the multitude of people, astonishment before the unending process of transformation:

> [W]hat astonishes there is the size, the quantity, the sudden outcome of human activity . . . those roads that, seen from the distance of two miles, are not roads but long carpets composed of heads . . . that overwhelming and unyielding expansiveness, firm and frenzied, and that naturalness in the expression of the marvelous. [lo que asombra allí es el tamaño, la cantidad, el resultado súbito de la actividad humana . . . esos caminos que a dos millas de distancia no son caminos, sino largas alfombras de cabezas . . . esa expansividad anonadadora e incontrastable, firme y frenética, y esa naturalidad en lo maravilloso.] (9:125)

What is the source of this gaze? In "Coney Island" Martí states: "Those people consume quantity; we consume class" [Aquellas gentes comen cantidad; nosotros clase] (9:127). This is the beginning of his exile in New York, and the weave of his writing clearly verbalizes the territorialization and the border: us, them, and not I-as-Other. The following year, in the aforementioned letter to the editor of *La Nación,* Martí exercises the caution of the foreigner. He lays out his plan:

> to cast the eyes, free of prejudice, on every field, and set the ear to the various winds, and after having filled our judgment with different opinions and impressions, to let them boil, allowing them to release their essence—*being careful not to put forward an antagonistic judgment if it has not been pronounced first by mouth that belongs to the land*—so that my mouth does not appear to be reckless. . . . For my part, I contribute nothing more than my love for expansion—and the horror I feel for the imprisonment of the human spirit [poner los ojos limpios de prejuicios en todos los campos, y el oído a los diversos vientos, y luego de bien henchido el juicio de pareceres distintos e impresiones, dejarlos hervir, y dar de sí la esencia—*cuidando de no adelantar juicio enemigo sin que haya sido antes pronunciado por boca de la tierra,*—porque no parezca mi boca temeraria. . . . De mí, no pongo más que mi amor a la expansión—y mi horror al encarcelamiento del espíritu humano.] (9:17; my emphasis)

If on the one hand the refusal to focus his gaze on the negative is a characteristic of Martí's esthetics (perhaps as a reaction to literary realism), his strategy at the beginning of exile is well established. In the case of negative criticism, he will only repeat what the inhabitants of the land themselves have said; his love for expansion will add the literary dimension to his journalistic writing. Now, if it can be said that in exile language acquires the power of the territory, of localization, in the case of Martí—and much more than in the case of any other modernist writer—that writing will significantly recuperate its origin in the conceptualism of the Spanish Golden Age, and he will revive archaic usages, Góngora's hyperbaton, Calderón's Baroque style, Baltasar Gracián's conceptual and lexical wit, along with the tendency that favors the aphoristic sentence or impersonal constructions that begin with neologisms from existing words.[25]

Martí assures us that he merely allows his judgment to be filled up by different opinions, and that he then lets the mix boil so as to release its essence. The modus operandi announced by the displaced writer produces notable appropriations. In his chronicle "Jesse James, gran bandido" (1882), he extracts from the excitement and skepticism of the masses, and from the mediocrity of some paid assassins, a story cut in the Renaissance mold, yet set in the Deep South of the United States. Jesse James is transformed into an epic, quixotic knight. The text reflects the geography and North American context with allusions to New York, Missouri, Kansas, Grant, and Sheridan, but another reality seeps into the tale until it permeates all of it: Martí invokes the Duke of Alba, Pizarro, and Flandes, and from there he develops the story, through an exaltation of bravery that diminishes the bumbling judges, toward the motifs of the thieving knight, the bullfight, the reddened ring, the ladies of Spain who throw their fans into the air, the bullfighter, the Spanish shawls. This kind of cultural association extrapolates a simple and ephemeral local news item into the sphere of the literary epic: a character who is also an "Other" in the society where he lives is transformed, by association and opposition, into the Latin American epos.

Martí is living his first years of exile in New York. In the process of consolidating the new space occupied by his self, the fragility of his situation is still evident. In 1883, he cries out with pain upon hearing the news of Peter Cooper's death:[26] "This country he leaves behind is that of his children. I have not been born in this land—and neither did he know about me—yet I loved him as if he were my own father. If I had chanced upon him on my way, I would have kissed his hand" [Este que deja es un pueblo de hijos. Yo no he nacido en esta tierra—ni él supo jamás de mí,—y yo lo amaba como a un padre. Si lo hubiera hallado en mi camino, le hubiera besado la mano] (13:48).

Martí's exile in the United States can be looked at in three clearly differentiated stages. The first, from which I have already cited several texts, was from 1881 to 1884. During this stage, several masterful pieces stand out which show the dazzled spectator, struggling with the enigma of time and space, searching for harmonies and the conciliation of opposites, as his portrait of Emerson and his chronicle on the inauguration of the Brooklyn Bridge make evident. There is a second stage, taking place between 1884 and 1892, which is marked by the critical radicalization of Martí and the slow break with the canons that we still use to think about exile today: bewilderment, nostalgia, and marginalization. This period begins after his protests over the disadvantageous terms of the commercial treaty between Mexico and the United States (deemed to be too favorable for the United States), and it gains definition in 1886, when he perceives the possibility that U.S. expansionists might end up purchasing Cuba from Spain. This is the year in which he tightens the bonds of solidarity with the tobacco workers in Florida, a year also marked by Martí's disheartenment upon hearing about workers' strikes and the death sentence received by the anarchists in Chicago. His radicalization progresses. In 1889 he writes about North American greed; this is the moment in which he writes "El Congreso de Washington," "Madre América," and *La edad de oro*. Then, in 1891, comes the International Monetary Conference and the writing of *Nuestra América*. Full radicalization marks the turn toward the third and last stage of exile, for which a reading of *Escenas norteamericanas* is no longer relevant, since Martí breaks off his collaboration with Latin American newspapers. In 1892, he founds the Cuban Revolutionary Party (Partido Revolucionario Cubano), and in April 1895 he sets off on his final journey to Cuba.

Let us pause to consider the second stage, the one marked by Martí's progressive questioning. His text on General Grant (1885) is different in tone from the ones preceding it, but Martí still attempts to maintain a sense of equilibrium: "He might have been guilty; but his sin will always be less than his greatness" [Culpable pudo ser; mas su pecado será siempre menor que su grandeza] (13:43). In his marvelous chronicle concerning the Charleston earthquake of 1886, the perfect order of its beginning—the one with the description of the little white houses and the prosperity that resulted from the supremacy of the whites over the blacks—is going to be destroyed by Nature unbound. Unlike his counterparts in such North American newspapers as the *Sun,* the *New York Times,* the *Baltimore Sun,* or the *Tribune* (September 1886), Martí is not concerned with material losses. What he *is* interested in is the explosion that rises from deep within the earth to upset the well-trimmed hedges of civilization, and the sound of that "terrifying drum [which] calls for battle from the bowels of the earth" [tambor espantoso (que) llama en las entrañas de la tierra a la batalla] (13:68). The clamor of the drum disrupts the order of the representation: the "arrogant whites" humbly join their voices to the hymns sung by the blacks (13:70), and

> from the mucky memory of the poor blacks an estranged nature was rising to their faces: it was the nature of a burdened race, it was the Africa of parents and grandparents, it was that sign of propriety that nature imposes on each one! . . . Each race brings its mandate to Earth, and each race must be given right of way if we do not mean to obstruct the harmony of the universe. [de la empañada memoria de los pobres negros iba surgiendo a su rostro una naturaleza extraña: ¡era la raza comprimida, era el Africa de los padres y de los abuelos, era ese signo de propiedad que cada naturaleza pone a su hombre (!) . . . Trae cada raza al mundo su mandato, y hay que dejar la vía libre a cada raza, si no se ha de estorbar la armonía del universo.] (13:72)

Martí has begun to conceive of other alliances in the heart of the society he inhabits. At this stage, he realizes—and he gives intimations of this development of his thought in "Terremoto de Charleston"—that, for the continent that had declared itself to be a mix of races, syncretic, and the product of a melting pot, the moment has arrived to begin to flow with its own voice: a voice whose identity is nourished by the appropriation of all cultures and all pasts. The voice of the continent is legitimized—like the mixing of races—when the languages that compose it recognize their unity in shared experience, a shared history and an originating nature.

That same year, 1886, in the first note that he writes about the Chicago anarchists, he joins in the condemnation of their actions. This is significant because Martí represents the anarchists as a version of the Other, one that disrupts the established order with its irrational backwardness: he places emphasis on the foreign expression of these people who do not understand the workings of democracy.[27] The anarchists come from a European "there." Indeed, "Three of them did not even understand the language in which they were being condemned" [Tres de ellos ni entendían siquiera la lengua en que los condenaban], he writes, expressing the scorn felt by one exile before another who has not known how to conform to the codes of the nation.[28] These new arrivals do not understand the North American "here." Hence, in this place "where the most wretched is free to express the words in his mouth . . . and can cast with his hand the vote that enacts the law" [donde el más infeliz tiene en la boca la palabra libre . . . y en la mano el voto que hace la ley], writes Martí, "they recommended the barbaric remedies imagined in countries where the downtrodden have neither voice nor vote" [A]consejaban los bárbaros remedios imaginados en los países donde los que padecen no tienen palabra ni voto].[29] It is not the case that Martí is idealizing the "here–United States," which he defines in the same text with references to selfishness and the plight of the poor. But he is horrified by violence and by the contempt for, or incomprehension of, a system that for him (mindful of the Cuban colonial experience or even of his desired extended Latin American family of nations) represents admirable values: the electoral process and legal freedoms that exist in the United States.

While it is true that Martí is not deceived by the relationship of democracy to inequality and to the period's currents of annexationism, it is important to point out the impression that the democratic system made on him as a Latin American. Pertinent here is the attitude expressed by *La Nación* of Buenos Aires upon receiving Martí's description of the presidential elections of 1888. The editor gave Martí's report the title "Narraciones fantásticas," and he cautioned his readers:

> Martí has wanted to give us proof of the creative power of his privileged imagination by sending us a fantasy. . . . Only to . . . a fresh and original writer like him would it occur to portray a people, in today's day and age, thus given over to the ridiculous electoral process. [Martí ha querido darnos una prueba del poder creador de su privilegiada imaginación, enviándonos una fantasía. . . . Solamente al . . . escritor original y siempre nuevo, podría ocurrírsele pintar a un pueblo, en los días adelantados que alcanzamos, entregado a las ridículas funciones electorales.] (13:337)

In a new reference to the anarchists, months after having written his dazzling paean to Walt Whitman, Martí's point of view has turned around: the anarchist, though he is clearly a European, is not a foreign being that must be ostracized even by means of language; rather, he is the victim of a social system that is cruel and unjust vis-à-vis the poor. Martí never becomes an apologist for terrorism, but now he has cast his lot with the working classes, while the Other has become the system itself. The year is 1888 and his gaze is aligned with "the exhausted masses, which suffer each day with increasing pain" [La masa fatigada, que sufre cada día dolores crecientes];[30] his position is no longer that of a dazzled spectator, but one marked by solidarity and a critical identification with social struggle. Thus, he states that "in order to measure the full depth of man's despair *it is necessary to live in exile from one's fatherland or from humanity*" [para medir todo lo profundo de la desesperación del hombre . . . *es necesario vivir desterrado de la patria o de la humanidad*].[31]

In this pronouncement, one is able to read empathy as a mark of exile. Empathy is the process of approach to the Other, and the formation of knowledge; it represents a sort of dialogue that enables one to think about the Other and about the self as parts of a whole, or, as Emmanuel Levinas would say, that allows us to take into account "the proximity of one's neighbor."[32] Empathy is a form of care and knowledge that is not imposed as a form of power on the Other; it is a process of understanding in solidarity. In the concrete case of exile, it is also "a space which would facilitate a vigorous negotiation between the limits of the self and the beginnings of the other."[33]

That dialectical process of political radicalization and the progressive deepening of the sense of empathy, of breaking, is also an intensification of Martí's willful solidarity with Latin America. Since Latin America is his fatherland, Cuba, by deduction, is the center of what was lost, the home that in 1895 it was necessary to regain. Exile taught Martí to understand the pain of others and to measure his own pain, to measure above all the "depth of man's despair." The fissure that runs deep in Martí's writing makes it extraordinarily rich, to be sure. But exile has not proved to be, in his case, a mere sentimental myth, nor a gaze that reproduces or passively absorbs the framework of neocolonial power, nor the privileged (and comfortable) expression of an intellectual living at the margins.

Notes

This essay and the quotations from Martí's various texts have been translated by Jorge Hernández Martín, professor of Spanish and Portuguese at Dartmouth College.

1 Unfinished poem, written in New York, found among Martí's posthumous papers.

2 In Mexico (1875–76), Martí supports President Sebastián Lerdo de Tejada Díaz and is forced out of the country by Porfirio Díaz's military coup; in Guatemala (1877–78) his departure is related to Justo Rufino Barrios's politics. He returns to Cuba and is again deported to Spain in 1879. After a brief stay in France, he travels to New York in 1880, where he collaborates with The Hour, is made the president of the Comité Cubano Revolucionario, and becomes involved with Calixto García's expedition, part of what is known as the Guerra Chiquita (Little War). At the beginning of 1881 he arrives in Caracas and writes for *La Opinión Nacional* and *Revista Venezolana;* six months later, Antonio Guzmán Blanco's government forces him to leave the country, in reaction to an article Martí writes in support of the poet Cecilio Acosta.

3 María Moliner, *Diccionario de uso del español* (Madrid: Gredos, 1984).

4 E. J. Hobsbawm, *The Invention of Tradition* (Cambridge: Cambridge University Press, 1983).

5 E. Kedouri, *Nationalism* (London: Hutchinson University Library, 1960), p. 70.

6 Edward Said, "Secular Criticism," in Said, *The World, the Text, and the Critic* (Cambridge: Harvard University Press, 1983), p. 6.

7 Ibid., 7. See also Edward Said, "The Mind of Winter: Reflections on a Life in Exile," *Harper's* (September 1984): 49–55 and *Representations of the Intellectual: The 1993 Reith Lectures* (New York: Pantheon Books, 1994).

8 Said, "The Mind of Winter," p. 7.

9 In the exile's gaze, there is a subtle subversion of power. Normally, the observing subject exercises power over the observed (the object), imposing upon it his or her rules of the ideological game. However,

when the subject of the gaze is the exile, what is revealed is not only the *object* of his gaze but the very rules of the game. As a matter of fact, the exile who looks and comments on what is seen has in turn been cast out and silenced by the structure of power; in the act of looking/writing, the exile re-creates and structures the mechanisms of appropriation of that structure from a different place, imbuing them (or not) with his or her own sense of meaning. In every instance, the exile's gaze is an agent of displacement. (I acknowledge here the valuable contributions made by Tomás Eloy Martínez and Margo Persin, whose comments improved this text.)

10 Theodor Adorno, *Minima Moralia* [1951], trans. J. Chamorro Mielke (Madrid: Taurus, 1987), pp. 38–39. Adorno allows himself to be tempted and presumes that "for the man who no longer has a homeland, writing becomes a place to live." But, right away, he regains his habitual intransigence: not even writing should be a place in which to live, since the intellectual must cultivate a sense of alertness and oppose laxness and self-pity. He or she should oppose, most of all, the dulling warmth of comfort. Finally, according to Adorno, it is part of morality not to feel at home even at home.

11 Gayatri Spivak, "Strategy, Identity, Writing," *Melbourne Journal of Politics* 18 (1986–87): 47; reprinted in *The Postcolonial Critic*, ed. G. Spivak and S. Harasym (New York: Routledge, 1990).

12 Nikos Papastergiadis, *Modernity as Exile: The Stranger in John Berger's Writing* (Manchester: Manchester University Press, 1993), p. 14.

13 It is attractive to consider the possibility of examining Martí's national project for Cuba in light of his experience of exile. In this regard, exile exerts a number of influences on its subject (e.g., cosmopolitism, reconstruction of traditions, formulas of solidarity) that could have found expression in Martí's thinking about national formation; this possibility was suggested to me by Donald Pease. Said sees the relation between nationalism and exiles from a different angle. Following the tradition of Frantz Fanon and Aimé Césaire, Said notes that "although there is inestimable value to what an intellectual does to ensure the community's survival during periods of extreme national emergency, loyalty to the group's fight for survival cannot draw in the intellectual so far as to narcotize the critical sense." This is followed by a surprising allusion to Martí (surprising because of the reference to a Latin American, but also because of the dubious pertinence of identifying Martí with Tagore): "[G]reat intellectuals like

Tagore of India or José Martí of Cuba were exemplary in this regard, never abating their criticism because of nationalism, even though they remained nationalists themselves" (*Representations of the Intellectual,* p. 41).

14 George Steiner, "Extraterritorial," in Steiner, *Extraterritorial: Papers on Literature and the Language Revolution* (New York: Atheneum, 1971), pp. 3–11.

15 Eric Auerbach, *Mimesis* [1942], trans. I. Villanueva and E. Imaz (Mexico City: Fondo de Cultura Económica, 1950).

16 See Said, "Secular Criticism."

17 Roland Barthes, "La extranjera," in Barthes, *El susurro del lenguaje. Mas allá de la palabra y la escritura,* trans. C. Fernández Moreno (Barcelona: Paidos, 1987), pp. 211–14.

18 Gilles Deleuze and Félix Guattari, *Kafka. Por una literatura menor,* trans. J. Aguilar Mora (Mexico City: Era, 1978).

19 Homi K. Bhabha, "The Other Question: The Stereotype and Colonial Discourse," *Screen* 24 (1983): 18–36.

20 The letter, dated New York, December 19, 1982, appears in vol. 9 of José Martí, *Obras completas,* 26 vols. (Havana: Editorial Nacional de Cuba, 1965–75). Subsequent references will be cited parenthetically in the text by volume and page.

21 See Fredric Jameson, *Modernisme et Imperialisme,* trans. Pierre Lurbe in *Modernisme et imperialisme,* ed. Sylviane Troadec, Ginette Emprin, Pierre Lurbe, and Jacqueline Genet (Lille: PU de Lille, 1994), pp. 43–67, Raymond Williams, *The Politics of Modernism* (London: Verso, 1989).

22 Gaston Bachelard, *The Poetics of Space,* trans. M. Jolan (Boston: Beacon Press, 1969).

23 Michael Seidel, *Exile and the Narrative Imagination* (New Haven: Yale University Press, 1986), p. 15.

24 Susana Rotker, *Fundación de una escritura: Las crónicas de José Martí* (Havana: Casa de las Américas, 1991).

25 For a detailed study of Martí's writing, see Manuel Pedro González, "José Martí: Jerarca del modernismo," in *Miscelánea de estudios dedicados al Doctor Fernando Ortiz por sus discípulos, colegas y amigos* (Havana: n.p., 1956), pp. 740–41, and Juan Marinello, "Sobre Martí escritor. Las españolidad litereria de José Martí," in Marinello, *Vida y pensamiento de Martí* (Havana: Municipio de la Habana, 1942), pp. 159–252.

26 Peter Cooper (New York, 1791–1883), philanthropist, inventor and

manufacturer, founder of the Cooper Union for the Advancement of Science and Art. In his final years, he summarized his philosophy with these words: "I have endeavored to remember that the object of life is to do good."

27 In order to understand the published reactions by U.S. intellectuals of the period to the trial of the Chicago anarchists, see Thomas Bender, *New York Intellect. A History of Intellectual Life in New York City. From 1750 to the Beginnings of Our Own Time* (Baltimore: Johns Hopkins University Press, 1987).

28 Quoted in *Crónicas, José Martí,* ed. Susana Rotker (Madrid: Alianza, 1993), p. 212.

29 Ibid.

30 Ibid., p. 227.

31 Ibid., p. 229; my emphasis.

32 Emmanuel Levinas, *Entre nosotros. Ensayos para pensar en el otro,* trans. J. L. Pardo (Valencia: Pre-textos, 1993).

33 Papastergiadis, *Modernity as Exile,* p. 15.

Doris Sommer

José Martí, Author of Walt Whitman

"Let us hear what this hardworking, contented people sings; let us hear Walt Whitman. Self-assertion raises this people to majesty, tolerance to justice, order to happiness" (8; 253).[1] José Martí's 1887 paean to Walt Whitman, written from New York and published in both Mexico and Buenos Aires, was in fact a pitch to his own countrymen, to the emerging citizenry of Latin American republics that should be engaged in constructing a bold, capacious, and unencumbered culture. The essay sent thrills up and down the Southern continent. Successive and cumulative responses would canonize Whitman as the bard of the Other America, "Our America" in Martí's famously defensive formulation of 1891. In the twentieth century, essayists and poets as commanding and as varied as Jorge Luis Borges, Pablo Neruda, Octavio Paz, and José Lezama Lima, among many others, would tease out different and competing Whitmans—left, right, and center—from the amorous stranglehold declared with the opening lines of "Song of Myself":

I celebrate myself,
And what I assume you shall assume.
For every atom belonging to me as good belongs to you.
(SOM 1)

What can anyone do, facing an irresistible Whitman who stares out between the covers held in your hand? Impossible to look away, the only self-defense is to look back, hard. To remind him that he may not be in the lead, and that his self-celebration can be translated into a competing pitch. In readerly terms, it is we who initiate the seduction by opening the book; and reading is bound to produce runaway supplements to gloss over his fixing glare. The poet whom we hold as long as we consent to read, his amorous glare lighting a one-way mirror meant to suspend judgment as it arouses desire, prepares unforeseen responses. As readers glare back, they provide complex images that re-vise the lover who wanted to see himself simply repeated and multiplied in the eyes of countless beloveds.

Whitman is complicated by the love (the dread and the jealousy) that he elicits.

José Martí was one such reflexive lover, probably the first Latin American to respond to Whitman's seductions with the kind of enthusiasm that feared its own gasping for breath. Strong readers who followed appreciated the promising shiftiness of pronouns which are so easily inverted once the listener dares to speak. The narcissistic "I" and the glassy "you" depend, of course, on positionality for meaning. And after Latin Americans set the grammatical shifters in motion, how can one be sure who occupies which position, for example, in the self-aggrandizing collapse of difference announced in Whitman's first lines?

The difference overcome is one hint of how readers can respond, after attracting Walt Whitman's lavish attention in "Song of Myself." It lightens the weight of wondering how any response could be worthy of his immeasurable appeal now focused on you, the reader. Whitman's concentration on those who pick him up, those whom he flatters by calling them his "equals," might perhaps fix us inside the contours of a page that our imputed equality can claim as belonging to us too. This readerly bind might, of course, repeat and return the objects of Whitman's attention in the shape of the bard himself. "He who looks at me looks at himself." And it shows his attention to be ideally self-reflexive, as if his partners were so many replaceable mirrors for the perfectly formed poet. "In the faces of men and women I see God, and in my own face in the glass" (SOM 48).

Latin Americans may sometimes have felt mesmerized by Whitman's seduction. But the written record of their spellbound readings shows them repeatedly breaking away. The repetition of successful escapes, if that is what they are, may be a symptom of some obsessive need to engage him, to look at the god's face and to live. He is so powerful and irresistible to other New World poets. But they evidently noticed that this attention to the reader is metaleptic; first we pick him up. His attention, in other words, is an effect of our move, rather than the cause of reading. Noticing that we are now cast as the initiators of the tangle with Whitman provides a glimmer of what has been done in the parodically "democratic" deadlock between an enthralling bard and an obedient listener, a glimmer that brightens the place of suture that Whitman had prepared between reader and text. His seduction depends in fact on our initiative, especially from our distance in time and from the spatial distance of readers, say, in Latin America. And this initiating willfulness on the part of his fans was an invitation to seduction that the idol had to accept; Whitman could not have dared to conquer that readerly will without losing all hope of his ultimate conquest. In his strongest readers that willfulness survives the first contact as the potential for further engagements.

The confusion between reading and writing here is very much to the point: it points to the title of this essay, which plays on Borges's joke in "Pierre Menard, Author of the *Quixote*." As with Borges's story about a modern reading that destabilizes and improves on a classic text, José Martí's early and astute reading of Whitman would necessarily challenge the very poet he vaunted as a model for the Americas. It would challenge him through the positioned interpretation from Latin America, a vulnerable position that was necessarily a blind spot for Whitman's equalizing insights. Compelling readings like Martí's unavoidably produce excesses, additions, and embellishments for the pre-text at hand; they produce arguments and emphases that demonstrate an availability for manipulation and even for substitution of the touted text. This jumble of writing and glossing also points to the project of American literatures now that they have been marked, as on a mystical writing pad, with the traces left by the kind of jealous and ardent admiration that challenges competitors as well as its very object. Writes Borges:

> Thinking, analyzing, inventing . . . are not anomalous acts; they are the normal respiration of the intelligence. . . . Menard (perhaps without wanting to) has enriched, by means of a new technique, the halting and rudimentary art of reading . . . that of the deliberate anachronism and the erroneous attribution. This technique, whose applications are infinite . . . fills the most placid works with adventure.

Given the years and books that have intervened between Cervantes and Menard, between Whitman and us, the adventure in reading is practically inevitable. Being the daring and experimental writer that Borges claimed Menard was, the undervalued "genius" knew very well that his novel was different in every respect from the far simpler book that Cervantes had written three centuries before. Although we might observe more simply that the new version is evidently and shamelessly plagiarized from the old, Borges rescues his readers from this patent but uninteresting point. Instead of comparing the books, Borges contrasts them by underlining the evident incongruity between Menard's modernity and the outdated text, and by alleging that the fit is so bad it must have been deliberate. How could it be otherwise? After so much time and so much writing, so many wars, fashions, technological developments, how could the verbally identical text mean the same to Menard as it did to Cervantes?

By the same anachronistic logic of readerly interventions, we can imagine, for example, that Whitman's celebration of America as synonymous with democracy means something rather different when Martí, or Darío, or Neruda repeats it. America, for the nineteenth-century Northerner, was a New World promise of individual liberty. It was so infinitely repeatable, so contagious and expansive that it dictated the country's manifest mission to liberate (forcibly when necessary) and to include the rest of the continent from Cuba to Canada. But by the time a Neruda repeats the paean to America and to democracy, the celebrated signifiers point elsewhere. This was after the United States' war on Mexico, when Mexico lost half its territory to the insatiable lover, after the equally ignominious Spanish-American War to annex Cuba and Puerto Rico, and after the continuing military and monetary intrusions throughout the area. For Neruda, America means first the Southern continent, where millennial and autonomous civilizations survive in new republics which resist Northern depredations as heroically as their ancestors had resisted Europe; and democracy describes the collective logic of national defense, rather than market-mediated liberty.

The "Other Americans" had more than one reason to stray from Whitman while they followed him. Besides the unavoidable originality that results from adapting models, Latin American adapters generally knew that they had to resist Whitman as they consented to his seduction. The problem for them was that his embrace predicts or invites so many backyard, and perhaps one-way, romances. It supplies that possessive and inclusive love which American expansionism imagines others to demand. And by extension into the classroom, Whitman's embraces also predict the flattering and troubling attention that some American studies teachers are beginning to lavish on Latin American texts. To read texts out of context, in translation, against their apparently original assumptions is, as we know from Menard's lesson, the inevitable (mis)adventure of reading. So it will not do to pursue frustrating and perhaps futile historicist reconstructions of authenticity. And taking into account the complexity of Latin America—where particular national traditions, languages, histories multiply the cultural area into twenty-one internally fragmented countries—particular works of one of these countries may be almost as exotic in another as they would be in the United States. Guatemala's sacred Popul Vuh, or even Guaman Poma de Ayala's revisionist chronicle of Peru, might be as foreign in Argentina or in Cuba as they are here. In any case, there would be little gained for Latin American writing from resisting the embrace of an expansive interest in the Americas. On the contrary, fresh (mis)readings promise to enrich those texts with adventurous interpretations. But if adventure is not to harden into colonizing appropriations, it will need the (pre)caution of establishing cross-cultural dialogues. Productive embraces tend to be mutual, even when they are not equally desired.

If contact seems entirely aggressive on one side, and submissive on the other, the play of the positions is not entirely predictable. For example, if our enthusiasm seems inspired by a partner, as Martí's enthusiasm seems inspired by Whitman, that partner may in fact be the pre-text for celebrating our own capacity for ardor. Martí's energizing passion for Whitman is strategic. "Perhaps without wanting to," Borges coyly wrote, Menard had something to teach about the destabilizing practice of sustained admiration, which can develop sycophants into creative plagiarists.

José Martí was a master of this move; he knew how to absorb news in New York in such a way as to send thrills throughout "Our" America. Martí celebrates an Anglo-American Whitman as the bard of "a new humanity, congregated into a fecund continent" (13; 259) (an incontinent continent where lovers "Dash me with amorous wet" [SOM 22]), perhaps in order to appropriate Whitman for the Other America. Because part of the area's incontinence, on Martí's linguistic turf, is the geographically expansive feature of the word *continente:* in Spanish it refers to the entire hemisphere, not merely to the North that the English would name. Whitman must have had even more aggressively expansive pretensions, given his shameful support of the midcentury war against Mexico that expropriated half of that country's territory. His admiring Latin American readers, tempted to forget about his editorial crusade against dark-skinned and demonized neighbors, may need to be reminded of that shame, writes a Mexican historian who collects and contextualizes the incendiary articles in a book called *Walt Whitman, Racista, imperialista, anti-mexicano.*[2]

A few decades after that war, Martí was pushing Whitman's poem slightly out of its self-aggrandizing Anglo-American bounds. Perhaps for Martí, Whitman's ideal American readers might be stretched to mean the *camaradas* who would most readily respond to that Spanish interpellation in his poetry. Martí literally underlines the word, and adds to it a list of border-crossed borrowings in Whitman's poetry. "At every step in his book, one finds *these words of ours* [a cada paso se hallan en su libro estas palabras nuestras]: viva, camarada, libertad, americanos" (my emphasis, 15; 261). It is as if Martí were saying, through a hemispheric and Hispanized appropriation of Whitman, that Americans already speak the same language.

A hundred years later, after so many inter-American misunderstandings, wars, and aggressions, continental continuity of language can hardly be taken for granted. And among those who make public spectacle of pursuing cross-cultural understanding, through sound waves that resonate throughout the hemisphere no less than did Martí's chronicles, is another Cuban living in this country. She is Gloria Estefan, whose hit song "Hablemos el mismo idioma" can be heard as an updated (Menardian and anachronistic) chorus to Martí's Whitmanian praise song.[3] Her tune is translated as "Let's Speak the Same Language" in the bilingual booklet that comes with the CD, an apparently ecumenical accompaniment to make good on the lyric's call for racial rainbows and musical mixes ("colores de un arco iris, acordes de un mismo son"). But universalism is not what it used to be during the heyday of Whitmanian liberalism,[4] because there is no denying that Estefan's monolingual appeal to get beyond differences is pitched to decidedly Latin locutors. After the title (which means, figuratively, "Let's get together") announces the undiscriminating plea of the first few lines, the song narrows its focus and disinterpellates some of us who may want to sing along. The "us" in the refrain turns out to be "nosotros hispanos."

Gloria Estefan rehearses here the pitch for Pan-Hispanic solidarity already intoned in this country by other recording stars, including the Puerto Rican Willie Colón, the Panamanian Rubén Blades, and the Cuban Celia Cruz. They too may be saying, with some relief for never having fit into the milky homogenization, that universalism is not what it used to be. But universality has a renewed hope, as Seyla Benhabib among others can remind us, in an America tuned in to the dissonance that Whitman would have wanted to melt down "with resistless heat."[5] It is precisely this dissonance that signals the political gaps that promise the kind of open space needed for negotiations.[6]

It happens that 1995 was auspicious for tuning in to the counterpoint of pitches that Our Americas sing.[7] The year commemorated two significant centennials. One marked the death of Jorge Isaacs, that universal but unhomogenized figure for Latin America. He was a fissured, mosaic star. A Colombian Jew, and the nineteenth century's only Latin American novelist to enthrall readers far beyond his own country, Isaacs's Hebraic habits made him almost unassimilable at home.[8] The other centennial marks a century since the death of José Martí himself, that poet and correspondent in New York who urged us to listen to the strains of the hemisphere. He not only tried to stretch jingoistic Whitman southward in order to consolidate a continent, as in the article of 1887, but he also tried to shore up the differences between North and South in his far more nervous celebration of "Our America" in 1891.

What "Our" means—in Martí's famous essay that exalts the indigenous and African strains of New World Hispanism, to distinguish it from the "European" America—is a promising problem, because the discriminating possessive pronoun is so shifty, so available for competing positionalities and equivocal meanings. It is the same pronoun that found *nuestras palabras* at home in Whitman's poetry only four years earlier. The same perfidious part of speech allows Whitman's strongest readers to shift the positions between "I" and "you" in the controlling coquetry of his opening lines. This is not to miss Martí's obvious meaning of danger to "Our America" 's politically and culturally enabling differences, the danger when one country threatens to override distinctions between "us" and "them." He was right, of course, to worry about "the descendants of the pilgrims . . . [who] are no longer humble, nor tread the snow of Cape Cod with workers' boots. Instead they now lace up their military boots aggressively and they see on one side Canada and on the other Mexico."[9] Even in the unstinting enthusiasm of the Whitman essay, one incitation to Martí's heightened passion has been the rub of real danger:

> Sometimes Whitman's language . . . sounds like a stolen kiss, like a rape, like the snapping of a dried-out parchment in the sun. . . . [H]is verses . . . gallop on devouring the land; at times they neigh eagerly like lustful stallions; at times covered with lather, they trample clouds with their hoofs. (13–14; 259–60)[10]

Worry can be a continuing border occupation almost anywhere. The problem is not only how to fix borders against aggression; it is also how to define the differentiated territories that the borders demarcate. And in a New World of either one continent or two, where commercial, cultural, and political border crossings define so many lives, boundary words like "here" and "there," "mine" and "yours," are hardly stable signposts. They are, as always, shifters. Merely to translate the possessive claim to "Nuestra América" as "Our America," for example, is to hear the claim deformed by the treachery of displacement. It is to move from a defensive position right into the enemy's camp.[11]

Strategists will know that mobility is not only a cause for worry; it is also an opportunity to gain ground. Perhaps "Nuestra América," in the genre of Estefan's solidarity song, has a future history here, up North. Translation, of course, literally means switching ground. And since Puerto Ricans have become quite expert at this—occupying the multiple positionalities that Martí explored between the Manhattan he shared with Whitman and another, Hispanic homeland—they can be our guides here. Following particular guides is an important precaution, if we hope to avoid the muddle of mistaking the category "Hispanics" in this America as an easily generalizable group. The very rhythm of repeated efforts in music and other media to promote solidarity, sometimes for particular political goals, is a cue to the division among constituencies usually identified by national origin.[12] Puerto Rico, as I said, can be our guide as the strong case of a nation that maneuvers along the faultline of grammatical shifters, in the space between here and there. Our America and theirs.

It is a case of an entire population that stays on the move, or potentially so, so much so that Luis Rafael Sánchez makes a hysterical joke about Puerto Rican national identity being grounded in the *guagua aérea* (air bus) shuttling across the Atlantic puddle.[13] Literally a nation of *Luftmenschen,* half are provisionally on the Caribbean island, and half are on and around the other mad-hatter island, which has become a homeland of sorts for new nationals. Tato Laviera calls them, and himself, "AmeRícan" in the title to his brilliantly bilingual book of poetry which adds a distinctive accent to Whitman's cosmos.[14] Laviera's genius is to read aloud the English sign "America" with an eye for Spanish. Anyone who reads Spanish properly can tell that the sign looks like "Americá"; because without a written accent mark on the "e" to give the word an irregular stress, "America" would use a default, unwritten accent on the "i." So Laviera's hyper-corrected reading of the arbitrary English name changes its stress by displacing the logic of diacritical marks from one language to another. The alleged omission of an accent mark then becomes an opportunity, an invitation to read the country with a facetious correction in order to pronounce AmeRíca, a new sound whose visible signs reform the look of the country too. With a foreign stroke if you read it in English (a mark which is just as superfluous and incorrect in even the most fastidious Spanish), and with an intrusive capital "R" that fissures and then fuses a conventional name into a convincing compound, Laviera's orthographic encroachments push both standard languages slightly out of bounds. The result is a practically providential metaphor: AmeRíca transforms what for English or Spanish is just a word into a mot juste in Spanglish. It proclaims doubly marked mainland Ricans as the most representative citizens we've got, just as Whitman's Spanish-speaking *camaradas* might have been his ideal readers.

Now, Puerto Rican independentists resent the doubling, as much as we might imagine a jingoist Whitman to resent it; and they resist being taken for endless rides in the *guagua aérea*. They have been saying "no" even before the 1917 U.S. decision to confer, or to force, "American" citizenship on the island. At that time, José de Diego published a protest simply and unequivocally titled "No." "Crisp, solid, decisive as a hammer blow, this is the virile word that should inflame our lips and save our honor in these sad days of anachronistic imperialism."[15] "Yes" may be useful for some things, he coyly admits after this first sentence, but

> in political evolution, in the struggle for freedom, it is . . . always deadly. . . . We must learn to say NO: arch the lips, relax the chest, tense up all the vocal muscles and powers of will, and shout out that O of the NO! It might resound through America and the world, and to the very heavens, more effectively than the roar of guns.[16]

De Diego had good reason to be confident; Puerto Ricans had in fact already armed themselves against one empire, successfully, simply by saying "no." I know this from Antonio S. Pedreira, a 1930s ideologue who otherwise deplored Puerto Ricans' "passivity" but who celebrates that passivity in two incidents when unaggressive patriots struck their unmovable pose: when Spain tried to draft them into its wars, first to stop the liberators of Venezuela and then to punish the patriots in Santo Domingo. The nationally legitimating effect of naysaying in both cases is reported in Pedreira's lapidary work *Insularismo,* where the incidents take up a chapter wisely and paradoxically called "Afirmación puertorriqueña."[17]

But I want to suggest another reason for so highly esteeming the simple slogan, an unspoken reason behind de Diego's reasoning about NO being the only word with real political purchase. It's that the value of "no" doesn't get lost in translation from Spanish to English. It seems so far from the Menardian supplements that occurred through movements in time and space. De Diego suggests as much by pausing to consider the alternative "sí," its brevity and harmony in Romance languages contrasting with the clumsier Latin equivalents,[18] and presumably with the cacophonic "yes" in English. You see, from Spanish to English the words of affirmation do not match up, and the asymmetry opens up a space, a trench like the one we might notice between NAFTA (North American Free-Trade Agreement) — sounding so explosive in European languages — and its Mexican counterpart, TLC (Tratado de Libre Comercio) — so misleadingly friendly in American English. When a Spanish speaker hears that English "yes," does s/he sometimes wonder at the insistent silibant "s" at the end, where it might have stayed discreetly underpronounced in Spanish, wonder if the word might be a hiss of disapproval or the totemic sound of a serpent stalking its prey? And is it possible that an English listener might hear in a Spanish "sí" not a simple endorsement but an invitation to look at something unsettling? "No," by contrast is as smooth and hard, as virile, as a bullet; it may in fact be the only politically significant word that is so firm in sound and substance, so impervious to interpretation, that it alone can safely be used. "No" is not vulnerable to ventriloquism, nor is it a traffic problem in the endless translations of Puerto Ricans from one place and language to another. Mercifully, one word, one possession at least, doesn't tarnish on the trips. NO remains intact and unambiguous.

Is it really so safe, though? The very coherence of the word, its traveler-friendly usage, is a kind of betrayal. The problem with "no" is precisely that it translates so easily, that it is as natural here as it is there, and floats effortlessly between its linguistic homes. It is as mobile and malleable as the *camarada* who cannot help but respond to America's "Song of Myself." The very word that refuses intimacy with empire produces that intimacy. For "no" is a weapon of self-defense that turns out to be a deconstructive trap, a roar of virile resistance that begins to sound like the moan of irresistible seduction. "No" treacherously turns around its supplementary message and, despite de Diego's painstakingly pronounced refusal to collaborate, is its own translatability, the essence of a supple and pragmatic war of positions. And the equivocal positions may not be a political disorder at all, but rather a strategy for staying afloat that de Diego's rival Luis Muñoz Marín was calling "posibilismo."[19]

To consider the possibilities of what "Our America" or AmeRíca may mean is first to hear where the accent falls. Does it name exceptionalism, in a paradoxically repeatable project from one American country to another, like the project that American studies celebrates for the USA, and the one José Vasconcelos consecrated in *La raza cósmica* (1925) as Mexico's synthetic mission to the world? Or is AmeRíca part of "La Raza Cómica," as the Puerto Rican scholar Rubén Ríos Avila suggests, a people whose hilarity shows up missions as madness?[20] And once we learn to hear local accents and sometimes purposeful mispronunciations, we may also want to notice that the tail end of America can sometimes turn up as a male signifier, an aggressive agency. Américo is the name, after all, of the father of Chicano studies, who in 1958 warned Texan readers, "with his pistol in his hand," that they were on shifty ground, a land alternately called the Southwest and El Norte.[21]

What then, are the boundaries of American belonging? How many histories does it evoke? Which America(s) can Whitman be said to have sung, once Martí published his Hispanized celebrations throughout the continent? Using Whitman to incite passion for "Our America" was a daring Menardian supplement to the bard's own monolingual monopolies on worth, an emblem of the dangerous doubling that monolingualism makes possible while it insists that we speak the same language. Translation produces excess, as in the possessive pronoun that shifts belonging from Nuestra América to Ours, and even the simplest NO of uncompromising refusal can get stuck in the slime of translation's surplus. But for English and Spanish speakers to avoid translation is, of course, simply to imagine a cultural emptiness on the other side of an imperial language, to mistake New York (Nous York, in an Air Canada advertisement) as unusably foreign. Ambiguous translation is not only a limit of understanding; it is also a beginning that stops squinting and starts winking at the enabling contradictions of AmeRícan negotiations.

Ambivalence keeps alive what the ethicist Emmanuel Levinas calls "the Saying," that is, the mystery and transcendence of social intercourse; it doesn't allow language to kill the desired Other by getting his meaning right. The ambivalence, for example, of hoping to speak the same (Latino) language and issuing a bilingual booklet suspends the copula between the speaker and her identity, so that "American" cannot yet "be" any essentialized, definitive, or dead thing. It remains a range of simultaneous belongings—desired, virtual, but wisely and prophylactically unconsummated connections—that safeguard Saying Our America, in all its accents, shifty attributions, and impossible refusals.

Notes

1 José Martí, "Walt Whitman" (1887), originally published in *El Partido Liberal* (Mexico City) and *La Nación* (Buenos Aires), in *Martí on the U.S.A.*, trans. Luis Baralt (Carbondale: Southern Illinois University Press, 1966), pp. 3–16. The Spanish-language version is to be found in *José Martí: En los Estados Unidos*, ed., prologue, and notes Andrés Sorel (Madrid: Editorial Alianza, 1968), pp. 247–62. Page references to both versions will appear parenthetically in the text.

2 Mauricio González de la Garza, *Walt Whitman, Racista, imperialista, anti-mexicano* (Mexico City: Colección Málaga, 1971).

3 "Hablemos el mismo idioma" is song no. 10 on Estefan's very successful CD *Mi tierra;* music and lyrics are by Gloria Estefan and Emilio Estefan Jr., and the 1993 copyright is by Foreign Imported Productions and Publications, Inc. I played the song during the first session of a course called "NAFTA Literatures" (co-taught with Werner Sollors and Marc Shell in the Fall of 1994) precisely in order to raise questions of inclusion and exclusion in language.

4 This was Werner Sollors's quip after hearing the song in the "NAFTA Literatures" course we co-taught with Marc Shell.

5 Walt Whitman, "Democratic Vistas," in *The Portable Walt Whitman*, ed. Mark Van Doren, enlarged by Malcolm Cowley (Middlesex, Eng.: Penguin Books, 1981), p. 324.

6 See Seyla Benhabib, *Situating the Self: Gender, Community and Postmodernism in Contemporary Ethics* (New York: Routledge, 1992).

7 The allusion is to Fernando Ortiz, *Contrapunteo cubano del tabaco y azúcar* (orig. Havana, 1941). Since then, the metaphor of counterpoint has been standard in discussions of cultural conflict and conflictual creativity in Latin America. A new translation of Ortiz's work, with an introduction by Fernando Coronil, is soon to appear from the University of Minnesota Press.

8 The classic novel by Jorge Isaacs is *María* (1867). It is the most widely read, pirated, and imitated novel of nineteenth-century Latin America. Required reading in Colombian high schools, it is also on standard syllabi in many other countries.

9 José Martí, *Obras completas,* vol. 9 (Havana: Editorial de Ciencias Sociales, 1965), pp. 205–6; quoted in, and translated by, José David Saldívar, *The Dialectics of Our America: Genealogy, Cultural Critique, and Literary History* (Durham: Duke University Press, 1991), p. 9n18.

10 "Walt Whitman habla en versículos, sin música aparente, aunque a poco de oírla se percibe que aquello suena como el casco de la tierra cuando vienen por él, descalzos y gloriosos, los ejércitos triunfantes. En ocasiones parece el lenguaje de Whitman el frente colgado de reses de una carnicería; otras parece un canto de patriarcas, sentados en coro, con la suave tristeza del mundo a la hora en que el humo se pierde en las nubes; suena otras veces como un beso brusco, como un forzamiento, como el chasquido del cuero reseco que revienta la piel; pero jamás pierde la frase su movimiento rítmico de ola . . . pero sus frases desligadas, flagelantes, incompletas, sueltas, mas que expresan, emiten" (Sorel ed., pp. 259–60).

11 Waldo Frank titled his book about the entire hemisphere *Our America* (New York: Boni & Liveright, 1919). Translated in references as *Nuestra América,* it was, for example, an inspiration and model for José Carlos Mariátegui, the eminent theorist of a particularized, Peruvian Marxism: "En Waldo Frank, como en todo gran intérprete de la historia, la intuición y el método colaboran. . . . Unamuno modificaría probablemente su juicio sobre el marxismo si estudiase el espíritu—no la letra—marxista en escritores como el autor de *Nuestra América.* . . . Diré de que modo Waldo Frank es para mí un hermano mayor" (Mariátegui, *El alma matinal y otras estaciones del*

hombre de hoy [Lima: Amauta, 1972], pp. 197, 192). Mariátegui was writing in 1929.

12 In "Do Latinos Exist?" *Contemporary Sociology* 23 (May 1994): 354–56, Jorge I. Domínguez reports this observation from two books under review: Rodolfo O. de la Garza et al., *Latino Voices: Mexican, Puerto Rican, and Cuban Perspectives on American Politics* (Boulder: Westview Press, 1992) and Rodney E. Hero, *Latinos and the U.S. Political System: Two-Tiered Pluralism* (Philadelphia: Temple University Press, 1992). "Very large majorities of Mexicans, Puerto Ricans, and Cubans," writes Domínguez, "identify themselves by their national origins, not as 'Latinos' or Hispanics" (p. 354).

13 Luis Rafael Sánchez, "La Guagua Aérea: The Air Bus," trans. Diana Vélez, *Village Voice,* January 24, 1984.

14 Tato Laviera, *AmeRícan* (Houston: Arte Público Press, 1985).

15 José de Diego, "No," in *Intellectual Roots of Independence,* ed. Iris Zavala and Rafael Rodríguez (New York and London: Monthly Review Press, 1980), pp. 131–33.

16 Ibid.

17 Antonio S. Pedreira, *Insularismo: Ensayos de interpretación puertorriqueña* (San Juan: Biblioteca de Autores Puertorriqueños, 1942, orig. 1936).

18 De Diego, "No," p. 131.

19 "Muñoz Rivera, el más moderado de los líderes unionistas, convenció a sus correligionarios de que no abandonaran la autonomía. Gracias a su intervención, el Partido aceptó dicha fórmula como medida de transición hacia la independencia.

"El principal partido puertorriqueño había dado de pronto con esta acción un giro hacia la izquierda. El resultado inmediato fue la división de las filas unionistas entre muñocistas y dieguistas. Muñoz Rivera seguía favoreciendo la reforma del régimen colonial, con o sin ciudadanía norteamericana. . . . El líder siempre pragmático combatía, por lo tanto, la resistencia a la ciudadanía estadounidense procedente del ala independentista del Partido dirigida por de Diego." Francisco Scarano, *Puerto Rico: Cinco siglos de historia* (San Juan: McGraw-Hill, 1993), p. 644.

20 Rubén Ríos Avila, "La raza Cómica: Identidad y cuerpo, Pedreira y Palés," *La Torre* nos. 27–28 (July–December 1993): 559–76.

21 I am, of course, talking about Américo Paredes and his classic book *With His Pistol in His Hand: A Border Ballad and Its Hero* (Austin: University of Texas Press, 1958).

Susan Gillman

Ramona in "Our America"

Harriet Beecher Stowe was known throughout the nineteenth century primarily as the author of *Uncle Tom's Cabin,* but José Martí's Stowe is something more. Rather than standing alone, for Martí she is always invoked in the same breath as Helen Hunt Jackson, author of *Ramona,* the 1884 romance of Indian reform, one of the five novels Martí translated into Spanish. Martí's Stowe has a twin, then, in Jackson. *Ramona,* Martí says in the introduction to his 1887 translation, speaks out in favor of the Indians as Harriet Beecher Stowe did for the Negroes; *Ramona* is an "otra *Cabaña,*" save, he notes, according to the "norteamericanos," the weaknesses of the book by "la Beecher."[1] It was, at the time of *Ramona*'s publication, a comparison common enough for Jackson herself to have made, in her case concluding, though, that she could never match Stowe. "If I could write a story that would do for the Indian a thousandth part that Uncle Tom's Cabin did for the negro . . . " but "I do not dare to think I have written a second Uncle Tom's Cabin."[2]

For Martí, however, the point of pairing Stowe with Jackson is less to rank the relative merits of the two reformist writers than to bring together the two oppressed groups for which they speak. To this end Martí begins a long article on the Lake Mohonk Indian reform movement in the United States (published in the December 4, 1885, *La Nación*) by invoking not only the well-known example of Jackson, as one would expect, but also the abolitionist tradition of Stowe. And it is Stowe who comes first: "In the United States," the lead paragraph asserts, "a woman opened men's hearts to compassion for the Negroes, and nobody did more to set them free than she. Harriet Beecher Stowe was her name, a woman passionately devoted to justice," and her book, a "prolific success," was *Uncle Tom's Cabin* — "a tear that has something to say!" Next Jackson: "It was also a woman who, with much good sense and sympathy, has worked year after year to alleviate the plight of the Indians. The recently deceased Helen Hunt Jackson, strongminded and with a loving heart, wrote a letter of thanks to President Cleveland for his determination to recognize the Indian's right to manhood and justice."[3] Martí's composite figure of Stowe-and-Jackson links the world-famous North American abolitionist with the nationally prominent spokeswoman for the Indian cause, bringing together what are in the United States the distinctly separate reform movements of the Negro and the Indian.

As a writer both of the abolitionist novel and the romance of Indian reform, Martí's Stowe-Jackson is greater than the sum of her parts: she becomes an interethnic, international figure capable of speaking to the limits as well as the possibilities of the multiple racial and national aspirations of Latin America and the Caribbean. This colonial world is "a vast zone," according to Roberto Fernández Retamar's influential essay "Caliban: Notes toward a Discussion of Culture in Our America," for which "*mestizaje* is not an accident but rather the essence"—and for which Martí's "our mestizo America" is, therefore, "the distinctive sign of our culture—a culture of descendants, both ethnically and culturally speaking, of aborigines, Africans, and Europeans."[4] The challenge of representing affirmatively this *mestizo* culture is central to Martí's "Our America." His famous essay of that title, known for asserting that "it was imperative to make common cause with the oppressed," devotes equal time to detailing the divisions, national and racial, that threaten and yet must constitute that common cause:

> We were a masquerader in English breeches, Parisian vest, North American jacket, and Spanish cap. The Indian hovered near us in silence, and went off to the hills to baptize his children. The Negro was seen pouring out the songs of his heart at night, alone and unrecognized among the rivers and wild animals. . . . As for us, we were nothing but epaulets and professors' gowns in countries that came into the world wearing hemp sandals and headbands. It would have been the mark of genius to couple the headband and the professors' gown with the founding fathers' generosity and courage, to rescue the Indian, to make a place for the competent Negro, to fit liberty to the body of those who rebelled and conquered for it.[5]

If Martí's new hemispheric, transnational nation, "our *mestizo* America," must not just be but must mark and represent itself, to itself, as a culture of descendants, both ethnically and culturally speaking, of aborigines, Africans, and Europeans, then Martí's Stowe points to the central challenges he faced in mobilizing and representing as a collectivity the descendants of the Africans, aborigines, and Europeans who are the *mestizo* inhabitants of "our America."

Associating the "Negro and Indian Questions" in ways virtually unheard of in the U.S. context, where those terms originate, Martí's Stowe—with her twin Jackson—represents his own remaking of the North American "woman's" tradition of sentimentalist reform and romantic racialism in the image of "our *mestizo* America." Just as the Indian context invariably frames Martí's comments on Stowe, Martí's *Ramona* is not the "Indian novel" that it is the United States, but rather the story of what he calls in his introduction "the arrogant *mestiza* who through persecution and death is knit to her Indian . . . until the conquering blond race casts them out" (204). To ascribe psychic and social characteristics to different races, as Martí does, is typical of the nineteenth-century European intellectual tradition of romantic racialism (originating with Herder and other German cultural nationalists) that underwrote Harriet Beecher Stowe's paradigmatic sentimental dichotomy between the submissive, emotional pure black and the intelligent, assertive mulatto. Moreover, Martí's *mestiza arrogante* represents a real departure from Jackson's Ramona, "the unsuspecting young girl with a taint of Indian blood in her veins," as the Reconstruction lawyer Albion Tourgée aptly describes her in his 1886 essay favorably reviewing *Ramona.*[6] Rather, Martí's Ramona owes her affirmative, mixed heritage to the Latin American ideal of *mestizaje,* or cultural mixing—a term for which there is, tellingly, no actual English equivalent but which is sometimes pejoratively translated as "miscegenation." She belongs among the "mestizoes" identified by Tourgée as "that new race which holds out a hand on either side to two great, but decaying civilizations," the Spanish and the Indian.[7] So much of an interethnic Pan-American is Martí's *mestiza arrogante* that his introduction repeatedly presents his *Ramona* as a work of and for Our America: "a work that in our countries of America could be a true resurrection"; a work with "all the serene clarity of our nights and the purple and blue of our sunsets" (203). "As Ticknor wrote the history of Spanish literature," Martí even speculates, near the end of the introduction, "Helen Hunt Jackson, with more fire and knowledge, has perhaps written in *Ramona* our novel" (204).

If Martí thus seems to rewrite Jackson's novel as a racial melodrama of Our America, Martí's Stowe speaks even more specifically to the nationalist, reformist tradition of the nineteenth-century Latin American woman writer. From the Cuban Gertrudis Gómez de Avellaneda's abolitionist *Sab* (1841) to the Peruvian Clorinda Matto de Turner's pro-*indigenista Aves sin nido* [Birds without a Nest] (1889), women intellectuals aligned themselves, and their national visions, with the racially oppressed. Stowe has always been the first lady dominating this American—hemispheric—feminist tradition, invoked by writers and critics in both Latin and North America since the mid-nineteenth century.[8] The editor's introduction to the 1904 English translation of Matto de Turner's novel, for example, praises "Mrs. Turner [who] was alone in her first effort," whereas "when Mrs. Harriet Beecher Stowe wrote her 'Uncle Tom's Cabin,' she had the faith and fervor of a great Christian nation behind her."[9] It is notable how such broadly Pan-American citations of Stowe's novel come largely from the Latin American side; in the U.S. context, as we have seen, Stowe is paired almost exclusively with her domestic ("Indianist") other, Helen Hunt Jackson. Stowe sets the standard for what has been seen by "Americanists" (i.e., critics specializing in the field of U.S. literatures) as the exclusively Anglo-American phenomenon of sentimentality.

From the cultural perspective of Our America, however, this transcultural woman's tradition is so striking that, as recently as 1978, in an essay marking the publication of a new Cuban edition of Martí's *Ramona,* Fernández Retamar urged Cuban readers toward "four estimable novels" that embody, "in our continent," the "struggle against the enslavement of blacks and against the brutal treatment of indigenous Americans," naming the sentimentalists Gómez de Avellaneda, Stowe, Jackson, and Matto de Turner.[10] With recent editions of all their work now available, Fernández Retamar says, Cuban readers will have examples of "how four singular American women from the past century, in differing ways, would denounce the most terrible aspects of the society in which they lived." Their gender is not incidental but central to their critique:

> One cannot stop calling attention to the fact that these novels were all written by women. . . . Shouldn't one conclude that these talented, energetic and valiant women—who knew that despite their virtues . . . they

would be situated in an inferior position to that of scores of mediocre men—were for that reason more likely to identify themselves in some way with other human beings unjustly ignored, and to express this sentiment above all through the indirect path of the imagination? (700)

Thus, although these novels may be labeled by "some hasty readers today . . . as sickly sweet or sentimental" [*lacrimosas;* literally, "tearful"], Fernández Retamar argues for "resituating the works in their age." To measure what *Ramona* represented then, we need only look at Martí's introduction to his translation of the novel, specifically where Martí speculates that "Helen Hunt Jackson . . . has perhaps written in *Ramona* our novel" (204). Although Martí's claim is historically suggestive, Fernández Retamar concludes, "today we know it was not so": it was the Peruvian Matto de Turner's 1889 *Birds without a Nest* that "approached the theme of the Indian and opened the path to the Hispanoamerican novel"; yet, still, Martí's *Ramona*—"a *thought-through* work" [una obra *transpensada*], "a work that we must consider as *also* his"—"contributed another important work to the development of the Hispanoamerican novel" (705; emphasis in original). According to Fernández Retamar, then, the genealogy of the Hispano-american novel must include the hybrid work *Ramona,* written by a North American sentimentalist and re-created in translation by a, perhaps *the,* Cuban nationalist.

Given the visibility of Latin American sentimentality, a tradition that Doris Sommer argues is associated with national romances all over Latin America, why would Martí, as Sommer puts it, choose to hide behind North American sentimentality?[11] Why would he, otherwise so attuned to the dangers of the monster's entrails, turn to a U.S. model, especially when "indigenous" ones, so to speak, were available? On the one hand, some would answer that Martí reframes the Latin American feminist tradition via North American sentimentality in order to make it more compatible with what may be called his masculinist discourse of nationalism. On the other hand, I would say that Martí works *within* a hemispheric tradition of sentimentality in order to work *through* the problematic terms of two Latin American traditions—the discourses of *mestizaje* and *indigenismo*—both emerging in Martí's time and destined to come to fruition in the twenties and thirties as active agents of a new Latin American national self-understanding.[12] The celebration of racial mixture encoded in the term *mestizaje* produced "the new Americans" of Martí's "our *mestizo* America," or what would come to be known in its most famous formulation as the "cosmic race" in the Mexican philosopher José Vasconcelos's influential work *La raza cósmica.*[13] Similarly, although *indigenismo* did not become a full-fledged literary movement until elite Latin American intellectuals, writing in the twenties and thirties, identified with indigenous traditions and adopted the "problema del indio" as the context in which to work out their new sense of national self-identification, Martí invariably invokes the Indian as a trope for "our *mestizo* America," calling for the telling of "the history of America, from the Incas to the present" ("Our America," 88).

In the late nineteenth century, that is to say, the most available discourses of modern Latin American national and hemispheric unity were already emerging with all their problematic colors flying. Just as Martí's rhetorical invocation of the Indian elides the role of the African in "our *mestizo* America," so too, more broadly, does *mestizaje* assimilate by whitening the peoples of America; so too does *indigenismo* celebrate a mythic Indianness while destroying actual Indians and displacing black Africans. Latin American racial theorists, from Argentina's Domingo Faustino Sarmiento to Brazil's Gilberto Freyre to the Cuban Fernando Ortiz, have argued for the national ideal of "whitening," whether achieved by intermarriage or by cultural assimilation.[14] And the celebration of the Indian past in the classic, nineteenth-century national novels of Brazil and the Dominican Republic, argues Doris Sommer, succeeds in replacing rebellious black populations with long-extinct natives who become putative ancestors for today's "Indian" masses—a sleight of hand that accounts for a dark population without mentioning blacks (*Foundational Fictions,* 21–22, 162). A fundamental contradiction thus emerges between race and *mestizaje* in its nineteenth-century formulations: the call for a new race of mixed beings is also a call for racelessness, for citizens defined by national rather than racial membership.

Fernández Retamar alludes to the problems with Latin American racial discourse in his essay "Caliban" when he closes a section on Martí's long-standing identification with and "passionate study" of indigenous peoples by asserting, somewhat defensively, that "naturally, Martí's approach to the Indian was also applied to the black." "Unfortunately," Fernández Retamar admits, the two approaches could not be truly equivalent since, in Martí's day, research in American aboriginal cultures (in which Martí was passionately interested) was far more advanced than similar studies in African cultures and their influence on "our mestizo America." Fernández Retamar's conclusion: "In any event, in his treatment of Indian culture and in his concrete behavior toward the black . . . [Martí] left a very clear outline of a 'battle plan' in this area" ("Caliban," 20). Notwithstanding Fernández Retamar's insistence, Martí's lifelong problem was to formulate a battle plan acknowledging colonial oppression of both the aborigine and the African, in order to forge the multiracial alliances, including the European, essential to the very conception of Our America.

This might be called more specifically the "race problem" of Martí's Cuban nationalism. Martí would have been confronted by the disjunction between the specific history of Cuban revolutionary and national discourse—deeply entwined with the issue of African slavery—and the history of most of the countries of Our America that were primarily engaged with the "problema del indio." In Cuba, where the Indian population had been virtually erased (through extermination and assimilation), the national independence movement throughout the nineteenth century periodically identified its cause with that of slave emancipation, producing temporary interracial alliances, ranging from the notorious "Conspiracy of La Escalera" (1842) to the first war of independence, the Ten Years' War (1868–78), in which slaves joined in an anticolonial insurgency that forced the issue of slavery. However, the process of emancipation in Cuba was, in the historian Rebecca Scott's words, "prolonged, ambiguous, and complex," a reflection of the shifting, highly unstable relationship between nationalism and race in Cuban politics, which has been brilliantly narrated by Scott, Aline Helg, and Ada Ferrer.[15] The positions most frequently elaborated by Cuban nationalists themselves (among them Martí), and later taken up, uncritically, by most Cuban historians, were that a vibrant national discourse, positing equality as the basis of unity and struggle against colonial and racial slavery, culminated in the first war of independence (marked by Afro-Cuban overrepresentation in the ranks of the military forces as well as the emergence of a powerful Afro-Cuban leadership) but disappeared by the late 1890s, when Cuba's "race problem" had been substantially eased, replaced by a discourse of "Cubanidad."

The Martí version of this complex unfolding is simultaneously to advocate interracial alliance and to assert that there are "no races" in Cuba. That is to say, Martí's revolutionary rhetoric allots equal time to the call for interracial cooperation, the inclusion of blacks in the movement, and to the nearly opposite claim that race is no longer part of the Cuban independence movement; indeed, that bringing up the question of race is unnecessary, and divisive, because the issue was resolved during the first war of independence. Martí's "no races" argument belongs to the history of the problematic silencing of race as a significant ideological category for the revolution. According to the historian Aline Helg, Martí's interpretation of the Ten Years' War, together with his vision of male racial fraternity in nationalist war, formed the principal foundation of Cuba's myth of racial equality, promulgated by white elites, as in other Latin American countries, along with the official ideology of white supremacy and the ideal of whitening through massive immigration (rather than intermarriage as elsewhere in Latin America). The Cuban discourses of racial equality and national fraternity, articulated so powerfully by Martí in several foundational essays, Helg concludes, made it impossible for Afro-Cubans to proclaim both their blackness and their patriotism.[16] Yet as Martí demonstrates, the claim that Cuba is race-neutral could be applied racially, to counter the whitening of traditional Latin American nationalist discourses, just as the language of Cuban patriotism allows both the elision of race and a challenge to racism.

The tension between race consciousness and race neutrality in Martí's construction of Cuban nationalism emerges graphically in the contradictory arguments on race, nation, and gender that form the trajectory of three of his best-known essays, from "Mother America" (1889) and "Our America" (1891) to "Mi Raza" (1893). As their titles indicate, the first two essays are devoted to constructing "America," a hemispheric, New World order dominated by mothers and Indians, whereas "Mi Raza" is more narrowly focused on Cuban nationalism and Cuban racism, both associated exclusively with black and white men. The essays, that is to say, mediate racial and national relations through gender: tracing a trajectory from Indianness to blackness, from mothers to brothers, from Our America to Cuba, the essays also move from arguing for national solidarity through integration of racial differences to calling for a nonracial society made up of "citizens of Cuba." If, in addition, we locate at the beginning of this trajectory Martí's 1887 introduction to *Ramona,* we will finally be in a position to return to the question of why he would make such Pan-American capital of—not to say hide behind—a novel written in the North American sentimental tradition.

"Mother America," Martí's speech before the Spanish-American Literary Society on December 19, 1889 (published a few months earlier in the Mexican newspaper *El Partido Liberal*) tells the history of independence movements all over Latin America as both racialized and gendered struggles. First, the representation of revolutionary alliances uniting the European, the aborigine, and the African: "The Mexican clergy are now talking to their Indians. . . . The battered Chileans march together, arm in arm with the halfbreeds from Peru. . . . The Negroes go singing behind their blue banner. Squads of *gauchos* . . . go galloping in triumph."[17] Second, the elimination of all differences under the tender influence of Mother America: even in the midst of her fight, "alone and as one people," Madre America knows that racial—cultural—differences will not matter in the future; indeed, are antagonistic to her own natural landscape.

> What does it matter if, when emerging as free nations . . . we saw that the government of a hybrid and primitive land (molded from a residue of Spaniards and some grim and frightened aborigines, in addition to a smattering of Africans . . .) should understand . . . all the elements that rose in a marvelous throng—by means of the greater politics inscribed in Nature—to establish that land? . . . What difference if the servile marquis felt a warlike disdain for the halfbreed workman? . . . Our capable and indefatigable America . . . conquers everything through the harmonious and artistic spirit of the land that emerged out of the beauty and music of our nature. . . . She conquers everything through the secular influence with which this encircling grandeur and order has compensated for the treacherous mixture and confusion of our beginnings; and through the expensive and humanitarian freedom, neither local nor racial nor sectarian, that came to our republics in their finest hour. (80)

The outcome of this tortured logic, which both affirms and denies the centrality of racial and cultural divisions, in part by consigning them to the continent's hoary past, is the emergence, "out of that troubled and sorely tried America," of "Our America of the present, at once hard-working and heroic, frank and vigilant, with

Bolívar on one arm and Herbert Spencer on the other" (81). If ever there was a syncretic vision, this is it, combining past and present, feminine and masculine, American nationalism and European social Darwinism, into the capacious "Mother America" of the last line. "Mother America, we found brothers there! Mother America, you have sons there!" (83). The twin myths of racial equality and fraternity are already emerging in the invocation of the brothers and sons, even as the founding racial and national groups are disappearing in the diminishing forms of "a residue of Spaniards," "some . . . aborigines," and "a smattering of Africans."

From here it is not very far to "Our America" (1891), in which the figure of the Indian—by standing in for, and displacing, the black—stands for the new America in which "there can be no racial animosity, because there are no races" (93–94). This triumphant conclusion of "Nuestra America," with its Whitmanian insistence on rejecting "the theorists . . . [of] the bookshelf races" in favor of "the justice of Nature where man's universal identity springs forth," is less well known than the essay's famous opening image of the mother of those born in America, wearing an "Indian apron," disowned and abandoned by her American sons (94, 85). She is a mute reminder of "the aboriginal race," the Indians who provide the model for all the new Americans: "In the Indian republics, the governors are learning Indian" (92). The figure of the Indian defines and dominates "Our America," reducing the black presence to a few formulaic references. Put another way: the list of the peoples of "our *mestizo* America" always follows the same order, starting with aborigines, ending with Africans and Europeans. More specifically, the Indian mother, enshrined in a mythic past that predates black slavery, enables the essay's contradictory embracing of "our mestizo America," the sign of racial mixing, and its ultimate rejection of racial animosity along with races themselves.

But Martí had by no means solved Cuba's race problem. The blacks who so nearly "disappeared" in Martí's Indianist/maternal vision of "Mother America" and "Our America" return in full force in "Mi Raza," the 1893 essay that Aline Helg identifies, somewhat too reductively, as one of the texts laying the foundations of the myth of Cuban racial equality. Focused specifically on the racial and class differences between blacks and whites in Cuba that threaten the independence movement, "Mi Raza" calls for—in the famous formulation "a Cuban is more than mulatto, black, or white"—a nonracial society made up of citizens of Cuba.[18] "Mi Raza" 's humanist ideal of citizenship fleshes out the denial of racial difference already emerging in "Madre America," through an implicit gendering that mediates the problematic racializing of national and social relations. If, according to Martí, the revolution is the mother—simultaneously a rescuing saint and a rape victim to be rescued—and if the Spaniard the father of a racially mixed family divided between black and white sons, then the nation of Cuba itself will become the fatherland, the *patria,* where racial differences no longer matter at all.

In "Mi Raza," published on April 16, 1893, not coincidentally in *Patria,* founded by Martí in New York as the mouthpiece of the recently created Partido Revolucionario Cubano, Cuban discourses of racial equality and male racial fraternity replace hemispheric myths of the Indian mother and the new *mestizo* America. The Cuban fear of "racial war," long associated with the specter of the victorious Haitian Revolution of 1791 and periodically revived in the form of alleged Afro-Cuban conspiracies to create a black republic—most recently associated with Martí's revolutionary compatriot, the mulatto general Antonio Maceo—replaces the threat of mere racial animosity supposedly laid to rest at the end of "Our America."[19] "Mi Raza" makes the claim that Cuba is race-neutral in order to counter the whitening of Latin American nationalist discourses of *mestizaje;* Martí thus invokes race neutrality to make a race-based argument about nationalism. He credits the first war of independence not only with abolishing slavery and granting racial equality, but also with eradicating all differences between blacks and whites. On the battlefields of the Ten Years' War, Cuban white men and Negroes fought as brothers and Cubans rather than as whites or blacks. The Cuban Negro, Martí insists, aspires to freedom not as a Negro, but as a Cuban:

> In Cuba there is no fear whatever of racial conflict. A man is more than white, black, or mulatto. A Cuban is more than mulatto, black, or white. Dying for Cuba on the battlefield, the souls of both Negroes and white men have risen together. In the daily life of defense, loyalty, brotherhood . . . there has always been a Negro standing beside every white man. . . . There will never be a racial war in Cuba. (313–14)

The masculine language of military and republican brotherhood overcoming racial differences vies here with the looming threat of racial war. So potent is the racial threat that even the gendered myth of male racial fraternity in a nationalist war cannot overcome it. Hence Martí's patriotism necessarily engages both the challenge to racism and the silencing of race.

And so, in another foundational text on Cuban racial equality, "The Cubans of Jamaica and the Revolutionaries of Haiti" (published in *Patria* in 1894), Martí directly counters Cuban fears, so often centered on the imagery of the "Haiti scare," that independence would bring race war. Here, in contrast to the masculinized racial discourse of "Mi Raza," his response is differently gendered. Countering what Martí characterizes as the Spanish government's effort to "stir up racial friction" by insinuating that Cuban revolutionaries were entering into secret agreements with Haiti, he asserts:

> There is an essential difference between the terrible and magnificent insurrection of the Haitian slaves, who had but recently left the African jungle . . . and the Cuban island where Negroes and white men in almost equal numbers are building a country for whose freedom they have been fighting together for so long. . . . Haiti is a strange and little-known land, with its smiling fields reminiscent of the solitude of golden flowers in maternal Africa.[20]

Haiti is still tied to Mother Africa, while Cuba, thanks to the racial fraternity forged on the battlefields of the Ten Years' War, has made a new nation which protects its guarantee of racial equality through an interracial, male force. "If a criminal hand, white or black, were raised against the heart of the country because of color, a thousand hands at once, both black and white, would force it down" (320).

Taken together, these essays by Martí convey how multiply problematic were the available discourses of racial and national unity, so often charged with an implicitly gendered substructure. The gendering of race and nation, or what Sommer calls the "erotics of national romance" in Latin America, is explicitly linked to the functions of sexuality in the context of racial and colonial domination. So, for example, Aline Helg argues that the Cuban myth of racial equality replaced the theme of sexual promiscuity, generally attributed to black men and women in the West, with that of male racial fraternity.[21] And yet, Martí shows us how the very notion of racial difference could be a liability in the arena of Cuban nationalist politics. In such a context, where the projects of Madre America, Nuestra America, and the Cuban *patria* were so often at odds, what could Martí's *Ramona* offer by way of a solution?

"The book," Martí concludes at the end of his introduction to *Ramona,* "gives us brothers and ideas."

> We enjoy a book that without offending the mind fires the soul, one of the few books that at once can take its place on the table of the thinker and in the hidden sewing box. All find in *Ramona* an exquisite pleasure: the lettered find merit, the artist finds color, the generous find courage, the politician finds a lesson, lovers find an example, and the tired find entertainment. (205)

For Martí, Jackson's novel of "the arrogant mestiza knit to her Indian" grafts onto the Latin American discourses of *indigenismo* and *mestizaje* the North American reformist tradition of sentimentality to produce a book that works through the subtle gendering of those racial and nationalist discourses. Martí's invocation of the stereotypically feminized and masculinist readers of this text reflects upon the multiple affective charges of sentimental reform literature in a way reminiscent of contemporary African American woman writers, who enlisted the exclusionary discourse of "true womanhood," encoded in popular sentimental fiction, to reveal the interplay of race and sexuality in dominant cultural representations. In this way Martí's *Ramona,* reconfigured as the sentimental romance of Indian reform of Our America, locates Martí somewhere between the high sentimentality of white feminists from Stowe to Matto de Turner and the critical adaptations of sentimentality practiced by African American writers from Harriet Jacobs to Pauline Hopkins.

Ironically, then, Martí may have been so drawn to *Ramona* because it was "the America which is not ours," in the form of the composite Stowe-Jackson figure, that provided a prototype at once for rescuing the Indian and making a place for the Negro. Still, though, the comments linking the Stowe and Jackson causes, not to mention Stowe and Jackson themselves, are actually few and far between in Martí's writing. So what is at stake in my foregrounding of "Our Stowe-Jackson"? First, the U.S. context. Martí's *mestiza* Stowe-Jackson brings together what are in the United States separate reform movements. If abolitionism preceded, and perhaps preempted, the emergence of a viable Indian reform movement, by the

1880s the increasing presence of the Indian Question—the disappearing Indian—on the national political and cultural agenda must be balanced against what amounts to a nearly opposite movement, supported by the law and by medico-scientific thinking, to erase—by legalized segregation or theories of black degeneracy and biological inferiority—the Negro Question from the national consciousness. In contrast, however, Martí's Stowe-Jackson insists on thinking of the two questions as one. Second, exported, or perhaps repatriated (since Gómez de Avellaneda and Matto de Turner are only two of the Latin American women writers working the "Stowe" vein), to Our America, Martí's composite figure breaks out of the various local critical categories and domestic U.S. debates—the sentimental versus the political, the artist versus the propagandist, the abolitionist versus the Indian reformer—that have heretofore isolated her. She thus complicates the nationalist and exceptionalist focus of American studies.

As a traveling figure, she points toward the possibility of a reoriented, triangulated U.S. history, viewed from the perspective of Spanish America as well as of the British empire. Looking toward the Southwest as well as the Atlantic seaboard, she would also locate a possible intersection between two important fields of geographical and cultural analysis, the (recently emerged) Black Atlantic and the (long-standing) Spanish Borderlands, both of which seek to disrupt the provincial focus and nationalist imperative of traditional American historical and literary studies. Paul Gilroy's Black Atlantic, the home of Martí's Stowe, takes as its unit of study the historical trajectory of the triangular trade, linking Canada, the Caribbean, Africa, Europe, and the United States as "geographical and/or figurative points of contact" in a transnational "narrative of involvement."[22] Gilroy's work both represents a new reinvigoration of geography in literary and cultural studies and acknowledges the long-standing role of geography within the historiography of slavery, informing such major studies as Philip Curtin's *The Atlantic Slave Trade* (1969) and *The Tropical Atlantic in the Age of the Slave Trade* (1991). Similarly, the Spanish Borderlands, an idea that originated in the twenties with Herbert Bolton's *The Spanish Borderlands: A Chronicle of Old Florida and the Southwest* (1921), defines its field of inquiry as comprising Spain's possessions in the continental United States, from northern Mexico and California to Louisiana and Florida, from the Gulf of Mexico to the

Atlantic—the locale of Helen Hunt Jackson. Martí's composite Stowe-Jackson, located within both of these contact zones, points to the possibility of putting them together in order to internationalize the study of "region" and nation in the United States.

Paul Gilroy and David J. Weber (the latter probably the most prominent of the Spanish Borderlands historians today) both stress the need for a dialectic between regional or national histories and the transnational. Models for, or perhaps rough equivalences of, such a dialectic already exist: in Martí's hemispheric nationalism; Fernández Retamar's Calibanic culture, which traverses numerous Indian, African, and European communities; and, finally, Frantz Fanon's well-known formulation that "national consciousness, which is not nationalism, is the only thing that will give us an international dimension." Paul Gilroy's "outer-national, transcultural reconceptualisation" defines a "diasporic, global perspective on the politics of racism" that is derived from his systematic account of the interconnections, rather than the one-way traffic, among Africa, Europe, and the Americas. David J. Weber, calling for a revitalization and expansion of Borderlands historiography, notes an apparent contradiction in Bolton's founding definition of the Borderland idea: "a place within the 'conventional framework' of US history that yet still transcends national boundaries, as 'the meeting place and fusing place of two streams of European civilization.' "[23] This contradiction should be embraced rather than rejected, Weber concludes, if Borderlands historiography is ever to contribute to the larger history of the hemisphere and thus fulfill Bolton's original vision of it as resting "on the borders rather than within the field of most other students' " (14). Marginal by definition, the Borderlands will remain peripheral to the core areas of both U.S. history and Latin American history, Weber argues, unless a broader definition emerges of a "Greater Borderlands," including perhaps the Central American, Caribbean, and Gulf regions (11). Such a Greater Borderlands certainly could be located at the intersection between the Black Atlantic and the traditional Spanish Borderlands.

How might the study of U.S. culture be affected if it were located at this intersection? Most prominently, a black-Indian connection, à la Martí, emerges to address (or even to reveal and formulate) the following puzzles and questions in late nineteenth-century American literary history: Why did the post-Reconstruction era witness the emergence of parallel, but unremarked, vogues for the "local color" of two regions, the Old South and the Southwest? Why would the influential *Century Magazine* publish Helen Hunt Jackson's California Mission Indian travel/ethnographic sketches alongside Mark Twain's and George Washington Cable's Southern essays and fiction? The historian Carey McWilliams has identified how the creation of a Spanish "fantasy heritage" for the Southwest, associated with the mission revival initiated in large part by the success of Jackson's novel, displaced the culture of Mexicanos and Chicanos with a constructed Spanishness. Similarly, the national visibility of both the Southwest and the South may be attributed to their differing constructions of a fantasy heritage, the nostalgic reinterpretation of the precapitalist, paternalist past, symbolized by the dominant regional symbols of the hacienda and the plantation. In the 1880s the myth of the Old South emerged in response to the economic and political threat of the "New Negro" and the "New South," just as the invention of a romantic, Spanish heritage (of aristocratic dons, saintly padres and contented Indians working the great ranchos of California; i.e., "the discovery of Spain-in-America" [Weber, 6]) coincided with the decline of the Californios (or Spanish-speaking peoples of the United States) as an economic and political power and with the need to maintain a racial-national dichotomy between the high-class "Spanish" and the low-class "Mexican-Indian"—the latter group constituting a growing social and economic threat to Anglo-American hegemony.[24]

Even more striking than this account of the parallel myths of the South and Southwest, crossing the perspectives of the Spanish Borderlands and the Black Atlantic might suggest an analogous explanation for what appear to be anomalous traces of "blackness" in U.S. literature. For Toni Morrison this racial trace is the "ghost in the machine," the American Africanism in texts ranging from Poe's *Narrative of Arthur Gordon Pym* to Hemingway's *To Have and Have Not,* that "through significant and underscored omissions, startling contradictions, heavily nuanced conflicts . . . was crucial to their sense of Americanness."[25] My examples, marked more specifically geographically, would include James Fenimore Cooper's Cora and William Faulkner's Charles Bon, both children of white fathers and black mothers born in the Caribbean. The Black Atlantic perspective encourages us to explore more broadly the question of the function of the Caribbean as displaced site and carrier of the "taint of blackness" in the Anglo-American national imaginary. (Both Charlotte Brontë's *Jane Eyre* and Jean Rhys's *Wide Sargasso Sea* come to mind.) Similarly, it takes the Spanish Borderlands perspective to remind us that the nineteenth-century Californio novel par excellence, María Ruiz de Burton's 1885 *The Squatter and the Don,*[26] is marked by its own traces of blackness: not only are the sectional stereotypes and national reconciliation of North and South superimposed on the different histories of struggle in Northern and Southern California against U.S. law and monopoly capitalism, but the declining Californios are ultimately lamented as "white slaves" doomed to wait for their redeemer—in a fascinatingly contradictory invocation, in the Spanish Borderlands context, of the dominant tropes of the Civil War, Emancipation, and the aftermath of Reconstruction.

Finally, to put together the systems of the Black Atlantic and the Spanish Borderlands as I am urging may provide a return to Martí as a new intersecting point for American studies: the two fields of study meet and overlap right at Cuba, strategically located at the outermost edge, geographically and chronologically, of the Spanish empire and at the center of the Black Atlantic. And this is not the Cuba whose history begins in 1898, a date that, I think it fair to say, marks for most literary and cultural types the beginning of U.S.-Cuban relations. Rather, this is also the Cuba of the triangular trade, the colonial Cuba that establishes the whole prehistory of nineteenth-century nationalism and abolitionism, of annexationism versus Africanization, of Cuban slave "conspiracies" versus U.S. slave "revolts" through which we might construct a comparative history of the multiple roles of "race" and "nation" in imagining the Americas. This is also the Cuban prehistory that leads to the second war of independence in 1895–98, the war in which Martí's revolutionary credentials were laid down once and for all, and the war all too often known here in the United States by collapsing it with the Spanish-American War. Although this is no secret to Cuban historians or to those who know Martí well, the recent (and ongoing) Martí revival in U.S. cultural studies would benefit from an awareness that Cuba–U.S. relations began long before the Spanish-American War.

Or as Fernández Retamar puts it: "ninety-eight" is not only a Spanish date (which gives its name to a complex generation of writers and thinkers in Spain); it is also a Latin American date (which should designate a no less complex group of writers, generally known as *modernistas*). It is " 'ninety-eight' — the visible presence of North American imperialism in Latin America — already foretold by Martí, which informs the later work of someone like Darío or Rodó" ("Caliban," 10). "Already foretold by Martí": the prerevolutionary, pre-emancipation Cuba in which Martí came of age, the Cuba which is not ours, will provide us (the us of "American studies"), at the very least, with a "situational-specific" reading of the Caribbean image in the American mind and, at the most, with a thoroughgoing Martían vision of the internationalism of national cultures.[27]

Notes

1 Introduction to Helen Hunt Jackson, *Ramona: Novela americana,* in José Martí, *Obras completas* (Havana: Editorial Nacional de Cuba, 1965), vol. 24, pp. 199–205. Subsequent references will be cited parenthetically in the text. For the translations of Martí's introduction and all of my other quotations from Martí's work not available in English-language editions, I am indebted to my graduate research assistant David Luis-Brown, to whom I am immeasurably grateful.

2 Quoted in Valerie Sherer Mathes, *Helen Hunt Jackson and Her Indian Reform Legacy* (Austin: University of Texas Press, 1990), pp. 77, 158.

3 José Martí, *Inside the Monster: Writings on the United States and American Imperialism,* ed. Philip S. Foner, trans. Elinor Randall et al. (New York: Monthly Review Press, 1975), pp. 216–17.

4 Roberto Fernández Retamar, "Caliban: Notes toward a Discussion of Culture in Our America," in Fernández R., *Caliban and Other Essays,* trans. Edward Baker, foreword by Fredric Jameson (Minneapolis: University of Minnesota Press, 1989), p. 4. Subsequent references to this essay will be cited parenthetically in the text.

5 José Martí, "Our America," in Martí, *Our America: Writings on Latin America and the Struggle for Cuban Independence,* ed. Philip S. Foner, trans. Elinor Randall et al. (New York: Monthly Review Press, 1977), p. 91. Subsequent references to this essay will be cited parenthetically in the text.

6 See Albion W. Tourgée, "A Study in Civilization," *North American Review* 143 (September 1886): 246–61.

7 Ibid., p. 256.

8 See Jean Franco, *Plotting Women* (New York: Columbia University Press, 1989), pp. 92–93, and Mary Louise Pratt, "Women, Literature, and National Brotherhood," in *Women, Culture, and Politics in Latin America: Seminar on Feminism and Culture in Latin America,* ed. Emilie Bergmann (Berkeley: University of California Press, 1990), pp. 48–73.

9 Clorinda Matto de Turner, *Birds without a Nest* (London: Charles J. Tynne, 1904), p. viii.

10 Roberto Fernández Retamar, "On *Ramona* by Helen Hunt Jackson and Jose Martí," in *Mélanges à la mémoire d'André Joucla-Ruau* (Provence: Editions de l'Université de Provence, 1978), vol. 2, pp. 699–705. Subsequent references to this essay will be cited parenthetically in the text.

11 I am deeply indebted to Sommer's published work as well as to her many provocative questions and comments at the University of California–Irvine Martí conference, January 27–28, 1995, among which was this critical question about Martí's relationship to sentimentality. See Doris Sommer, *Foundational Fictions: The National Romances of Latin America* (Berkeley: University of California Press, 1991). Subsequent references to this work will be cited parenthetically in the text.

12 On adapting to cultural criticism the psychological concept of "working through," see Carl Gutiérrez-Jones, *Rethinking the Borderlands: Between Chicano Culture and Legal Discourse* (Berkeley: University of California Press, 1995), p. 182n7.

13 José Vasconcelos, *La raza cósmica, misión de la raza iberoamericana* (Paris: Agencia Mundial de Librería, 1925).

14 On the problematics of racial theorizing in Latin America, see the essays by Thomas E. Skidmore (on Brazil), Aline Helg (on Argentina and Cuba), and Alan Knight (on Mexico) in *The Idea of Race in Latin America, 1870–1940,* ed. Richard Graham (Austin: University of Texas Press, 1990). See also Nancy Stepan, *The Hour of Eugenics: Race, Gender, and Nation in Latin America* (Ithaca: Cornell University Press, 1991).

15 Rebecca J. Scott initiated this enterprise with *Slave Emancipation in Cuba: The Transition to Free Labor, 1860–1899* (Princeton: Princeton University Press, 1985); Aline Helg picks up the phase after abolition in *Our Rightful Share: The Afro-Cuban Struggle for Equality, 1886–1912* (Chapel Hill: University of North Carolina Press, 1995). Finally, see Ada Ferrer's "Social Aspects of Cuban Nationalism: Race, Slavery, and the Guerra Chiquita, 1879–1880," *Cuban Studies/Estu-*

dios Cubanos 21 (1991): 37–56 and, in the present book, "The Silence of Patriots: Race and Nationalism in Martí's Cuba."

16 On Martí and the Cuban myth of racial equality, see Helg, *Our Rightful Share,* pp. 6–7, 16, 45–46.

17 "Mother America," in *Our America,* ed. Foner, p. 79. Subsequent references to "Mother America" will be cited parenthetically in the text.

18 "My Race," in *Our America,* ed. Foner, pp. 311–14. Subsequent references to "My Race" will be cited parenthetically in the text.

19 On the powerful imagery of Haiti, see Helg, *Our Rightful Share,* pp. 17, 47–54.

20 "The Cubans of Jamaica and the Revolutionaries of Haiti," in *Our America,* ed. Foner, p. 321. Subsequent references to this essay will be cited parenthetically in the text.

21 Helg, *Our Rightful Share,* pp. 7, 18.

22 Paul Gilroy, *The Black Atlantic: Modernism and Double Consciousness* (Cambridge: Harvard University Press, 1993). I take the notion of the slave trade as a figurative geography from Hortense Spillers, "Introduction: Who Cuts the Border?" in *Comparative American Identities: Race, Sex, and Nationalism in the Modern Text. Essays from the English Institute* (New York: Routledge, 1991), p. 9.

23 Frantz Fanon, *The Wretched of the Earth* (New York: Grove Press, 1963), p. 247; Gilroy, *The Black Atlantic,* pp. 17, 120–21; David J. Weber, "The Idea of the Spanish Borderlands," in *Columbian Consequences,* vol. 3: *The Spanish Borderlands in Pan-American Perspective,* ed. David H. Thomas (Washington, D.C.: Smithsonian Institution Press, 1991), pp. 13–14. Subsequent references to Weber's essay will be cited parenthetically in the text.

24 On the "Spanish fantasy," see Carey McWilliams, *North from Mexico: The Spanish-Speaking People of the US* (New York: Greenwood, 1990, orig. 1948), pp. 43–53. For an extended discussion of *Ramona*'s contributions to the "mainstream historical amnesia" about Mexicano and Chicano worldviews, see Gutiérrez-Jones, *Rethinking the Borderlands,* chap. 2, "Mission Denial: The Development of Historical Amnesia," pp. 50–69. Given Martí's admiration for Ramona as the *mestiza arrogante,* it is especially significant that Gutiérrez-Jones specifies that the "missing center" of the novel is "the mestiza within," just as a systematic historical amnesia denies "the rising mestizo class that Jackson must have walked among."

25 Toni Morrison, *Playing in the Dark: Whiteness and the Literary Imagination* (Cambridge: Harvard University Press, 1992), p. 6.

26 See the essays in the present book by José David Saldívar, Beatrice Pita, and Rosaura Sánchez.

27 See Fredric Jameson, "Foreword" to Fernández R., *Caliban and Other Essays,* pp. xi–xii; and Fanon, *The Wretched of the Earth,* p. 248.

II.

Annexationist Designs and the End(s) of Manifest Destiny

Rosaura Sánchez

Dismantling the Colossus: Martí and Ruiz de Burton on the Formulation of Anglo América

In 1998, a hundred years after the deaths of José Martí and María Amparo Ruiz de Burton, their words against U.S. imperialism continue to resonate in the concerns of present-day Latin Americans and U.S. Latinos. Their nineteenth-century deconstruction of U.S. policy statements, unmasking expansionist plans to annex and/or pillage the Americas south of the Rio Grande as far as the Strait of Magellan, is still relevant at the end of the twentieth century, despite global changes and discursive shifts that in some political and academic quarters have led to the disuse of the term "imperialism." Conditions of economic dependence, now masked by the more trendy terms "postcolonialism" and "postmodernity," are still much in evidence to those surveying the social, economic, and political advance of transnational capital in Latin America. The impact of NAFTA upon local and national Mexican industries, not to mention the possible consequences of other proposed trade agreements, draws attention not only to the deterioration of the nation-state but to the increased misery in urban and rural areas of Latin America resulting from debt crises, unemployment, underemployment, inflation, and imposed austerity measures.

Recent U.S. efforts to "bail out" Mexico as a result of the peso devaluation and rising inflation have led to cries from Mexican opposition-party members, and others, that Mexico is no longer free and sovereign but a "protectorate of the United States." As Noam Chomsky makes clear, what NAFTA protects are the interests of U.S. investors by ensuring that Mexico remains a source of cheap labor, "with industrial wages one-tenth of those in the U.S."[1] A hundred years ago projects for the outright annexation of Cuba, Puerto Rico, northwestern Mexico, part of Haiti, part of Colombia, the Isthmus of Tehuantepec, and Nicaragua, and their incorporation as states or "protectorates" of the United States, were common congressional and journalistic fare. In the midst of these discourses of expansionism it was imperative for both Martí and Ruiz de Burton not only to contest this neocolonialism from within the United States but to alert Latin America to what U.S. foreign policy discussions and aims augured for the continent. These imperialist "proclivities," then as now, went hand in hand with nativist and racist discourses and practices within the United States itself, practices that both Martí and Ruiz de Burton would condemn, especially when directed against Latinos and blacks, practices and discourses that are still very much with us today.

Dismantling the Colossus, unmasking the "giant with seven-league boots,"[2] took a discursive form in the case of both writers, and although neither one was a socialist revolutionary (far from it, in fact) and both were elitist to varying degrees in their writings, they do provide a forceful construct of the United States as a land-grabbing bully, hungry for regional resources and markets and willing to step on Latin American sovereignty to satisfy its needs and cravings. In the process of alerting the Latin American nations to the imperialist policies and practices of the Northern power, both writers also offer a strong critique of those aspects of U.S. monopoly capitalism which are detrimental to the citizenry within the United States itself and which demystify U.S. liberal democracy. Precisely because they are outsiders within the belly of the monster, both are able to view events from a critical distance and to disarticulate hegemonic constructions of "Anglo-Saxon America" by positing the Other America, Latin or Spanish America.

Their longtime residence in the United States and their class identity do, however, make both of them "insiders" as well, for clearly they share many of the assumptions and ideological discourses of dominant U.S. society. Their practice of disavowal and dismantling is thus commendable, especially considering the uncritical and at times servile admiration of other Latin American intellectuals. We also have to bear in mind that their deconstruction of U.S. myths comes after several years of acculturation; for by 1872, when Ruiz de Burton published her first novel, she had been in the United States for twenty-five years and was, as a result of the Treaty of Guadalupe Hidalgo, a U.S. citizen, while the Cuban Martí, who spent a good part of his life outside Cuba, would spend his last fourteen years in the United States.

For both writers, political struggle within this country necessarily took place at a cultural or discursive level, although of course Martí went beyond the discursive and had an active political praxis as well, including his founding, while in exile, of the Cuban Revolutionary Party and his later, if brief, participation in Cuba's armed struggle for independence. His political work, a good part of which involved planning and organizing the movement for independence, was also discursive, as Martí's copious correspondence and articles indicate. Ideological struggle was closely linked to writing and publishing in Latin American newspapers and journals. In his many essays, speeches, and articles, Martí focuses on the materiality and strategic role of mental productions, what he terms "weapons of the mind" and "barricades of ideas,"[3] and stresses especially the importance of the press. For Martí, the process called for analysis and reporting. "Pensar es servir" [To think is to serve], he says.[4] It also called for deconstructing discourses of "Pan-Americanism," discourses of continental unity under U.S. hegemony, enabling Latin America through this disarticulation to know "the truth about the United States"[5] and avoid being easily deceived by gestures of "friendship." In 1891 Martí was already alerting Latin America to the political implications of economic treaties with the United States. Only an alert and wary continent could prevent "the United States from spreading through the Antilles" and "from overpowering our lands of America."[6]

For Ruiz de Burton, who never published her novels under her own name—perhaps as much to conceal her gender as her Latina background—the field of discursive struggle was literary rather than journalistic, although it was epistolary as she was an avid letter writer. The space of fiction allowed the writer to address the rhetoric of liberal democracy and denounce not only imperialist practices abroad but colonialist, classist, racist, and nativist policies at home. Her struggle went beyond the politics of ethnic representation, but it too was important for Ruiz de Burton. By the 1870s, representation from a Californio perspective had become a crucial issue for her and for other Californios, like Mariano Guadalupe Vallejo, who considered that mediated representation through testimonials, even if tied to the Bancroft historiographic project, was better than no representation at all. Of course, once Bancroft's history was published, it became clear that their mediated narratives had been reduced to footnotes and derisive comments on the printed page.[7] The story of the Californios' dispossession and disempowerment, told from their own perspective, would not be in print until her publication of *The Squatter and the Don.*[8] Although Ruiz de Burton's novel represents an aggressive attempt to speak for the Californio and Mexicano collectivity, her struggle is more inclusive and her work seeks to speak for all "citizens," Californios as well as all those subject to domination by monopolies and to deception by corrupt legislatures and Congress. By the late 1880s Ruiz de Burton would be battling her own private war in the press and in the courts against a multinational corporation, in this case the British-American Colonization Company, which she sought to keep from developing and settling Mexican lands that she claimed in Baja California.

Both Martí and Ruiz de Burton offer a critique as well of the very notion of a united "American nation." As Martí makes clear in 1894: "It is supinely ignorant and slightly infantile and blameworthy to refer to the United States and to the real or apparent conquests of one or more of its territories as one total nation, equally free and definitively conquered. Such a United States is a fraud and a delusion."[9] The task was thus not merely to unmask expansionist interests but to demystify the myth of American uniqueness. For Latin Americans in general, especially leaders like Sarmiento[10] who tended to idealize the United States, and for Latinos and Cubans residing in the United States, whose support of the imminent war for Cuban independence was indispensable but who might be dazzled by fantasies about linkage to the United States, Martí wants to make very clear the illusion of transparency.[11] Up until the last six or seven years of his life, Martí too tends to be dazzled by the promises of this nation, a problem arising from "deception," from "taking nations at their word and accepting as a nation's realities what its Sunday sermons and its books tell us."[12] The task, as Martí sees it, is to uncover what lies concealed in religious and other hegemonic ideological discourses. Far from a melting pot, he explains, the United States is a divided nation, a place of conflict and hatred on the basis of region, class, and race/ethnicity;[13] here, freedom is not equally shared and democracy is constantly "being corrupted and diminished, not strengthened."[14] Instead of one big happy family, Martí sees division and fragmentation:

What the honest man should observe is precisely that it was not only impossible to fuse the elements of diverse tendency and origin out of which the United States was created, within a period of three centuries of life in common or of one century of political awareness, but that [in fact] a compulsory social intercourse exacerbates and accentuates their principal differences and turns the unnatural federation into a harsh state of violent conquest.[15]

Martí is certainly not positing a pluralistic model of diversity that blurs antagonisms of class and race. On the contrary, he stresses the domination and subordination forced upon particular elements within the nation-state. Only an informed "understanding of political reality in America" will enable Latin Americans to see that the United States is a place of "violence, discord, immorality and disorder"; it has, he says, all the traits generally ascribed to Latin America.[16] Far from an "imagined community" of diverse but united groups ruled by consensus, Martí sees social antagonisms and a sense of powerlessness among the colonized, marginalized, and oppressed.

The construction of the United States as empire would thus be closely linked, in Martí's deconstruction, to the United States as a nation of numerous internal contradictions. Unmasking these articulations, he explains, is the obligation of a responsible man whose sense of duty is to "know the truth and spread it,"[17] for only "in this way [can] a man form opinions, with a glimmer of reason, about the authoritarian and envious republic and the growing materialism of the United States."[18] In works by Ruiz de Burton, market discourses and consumerism are also reconstructed as indicators of a society totally dominated by corporate interests and corrupt monopolies, a capitalist society where only profit and the allegory of success matter.

Dismantling the myths of the Colossus is imperative for two writers alarmed at the blind admiration of the United States by many of Latin America's leading men, who, as a consequence, were all too willing to adopt U.S. paradigms. Those suffering from "Yankeemania," Martí warns, are lackeys given "to drink to the foreigners' breeches and ideas and to strut over the globe, proud as the pompom tail of the fondled lap dog."[19] Ruiz de Burton would share that opinion. By 1872 she sees Mexico already in good measure dominated politically by the United States. In her novel *Who Would Have Thought It?* two Mexican aristocrats, presented ironically as supporters of the Mexican Liberal government and involved in the fight against the French invaders, discuss the undue influence of the United States in determining Mexico's form of government. While opposed to the French invasion, they come to see in the liberal Maximilian, a Hapsburg and descendant of Isabel I and Ferdinand V, an opportunity to replace the weak republic with a constitutional monarchy chosen by the people and representative of their Latino culture. They recognize, however, that there is little likelihood of this political change, given "the influence of the United States" that, as one of the characters indicates,

> prevails with such despotic sway over the minds of the leading men of the Hispano-American republics. If it were not for this terrible, this fatal influence,—which will eventually destroy us,—the Mexicans, instead of seeing anything objectionable in the proposed change, would be proud to hail a prince who, after all, has some sort of a claim to this land, and who will cut us loose from the leading-strings of the United States.[20]

To this, the other character replies: "Half of our leading men love and kiss these leading-strings."[21] Written five years after the French withdrawal of troops, the defeat of the Conservative troops, and the execution of Maximilian, the novel reconstructs the divisions among the ruling classes of Mexico, not simply in terms of a monarchy-versus-republic dichotomy, but in terms of anti–U.S. imperialism and liberal-versus-conservative politics; in effect, Maximilian would prove to be far more liberal than anticipated by the Church and its conservative allies. Beyond the retrospective and aristocratic look at "what might have been," there is in this dialogue a strong denunciation of those willing to be dominated by the United States and a clear preference shown for a Latino culture and head of state. Martí too would see the placement of Maximilian in power in Mexico as an attempt to ward off Anglo domination; or, as he says, the Frenchman would be "brought there perhaps because of a desire to raise a barrier against Saxon power in the world's imbalance [of power]."[22]

Who Would Have Thought It? contains as well a strong critique of nativism in this country. Abolitionists in the North are shown to be nativist, xenophobic, and racist. Ruiz de Burton's 1872 novel begins with the reaction of a New England family toward a ten-year-old Mexican girl, Lola, brought into their home by James Norval, the returning geologist who has rescued her from Indians in the Southwest. Despite the family's abolitionist rhetoric, there is nothing but racism and classism on the part of Mrs. Norval toward what she considers a "black" child, and her immediate reaction is to send Lola to the kitchen and later to sleep with the servants, Irish in this case and also considered ethnically and religiously inferior in that community. Of course the child's "whitening" as her skin clears—this is, after all, a romance and the dye that her mother had used to protect her from the Indians does in time wear off—will change nothing; cultural racism against Catholics and Latinos will continue to keep the child marginalized.

Martí too is very much aware of U.S. nativism and wary of trusting Anglo-Saxon expressions of friendship. He, like Ruiz de Burton, frequently comments on the scorn with which Latin America is regarded in this country:[23]

> not a day passes when these ignorant and scornful newspapers do not treat us like trivial little nations lacking in transcendence, as farcical nations, as petty republics without knowledge or ability, as "nations with unsteady legs."[24]

This scorn he attributes to racism. In the United States, he says, they believe

> in the invincible superiority of the Anglo Saxon race over the Latin! They believe in the inferiority of the Negroes whom they enslaved yesterday and are criticizing today, and of the Indians whom they are exterminating. They believe that the Spanish American nations are formed principally of Indians and Negroes. As long as the U.S. knows no more about Spanish America, and respects it no more . . . can this country invite Spanish America to an alliance that would be honest and useful to our Spanish American nations?[25]

Like Ruiz de Burton, Martí is elitist enough himself to resent the Latino's classification as inferior on the basis of their presumed racial composition and here wants it to be known that Latin America consists of more than Indians and blacks. The issue, however, for Martí as for Ruiz de Burton, is not posed in terms of "whiteness" (both, after all, consider themselves "white" and of Spanish descent), but rather in terms of ethnic and cultural differences, then termed "racial" differences. For both, the important distinction is that between "nuestra raza" (i.e., the Latino race) and the Anglo-Saxon race. This "difference in origins, methods, and interests between the two halves of the continent"[26] is for Martí also a political and economic difference that makes it imperative that Latin America live "without unnecessary ties to an aggressive nation of another composition and purpose."[27] Thus, far from James Gillespie Blaine's assertions of "the solicitous goodwill of [the United States as] a common friend," Martí sees a tiger, a "thoroughly rapacious nation,"[28] ready to pounce upon Latin America with its seven-league boots and devour up these and other nations. The United States, he says, is "a country imbued with expansionist ideas,"[29] "a nation beginning to regard freedom . . . as its right and to invoke it for purposes of depriving other nations of it."[30] Martí, like Ruiz de Burton, is thus able to link transnational issues with domestic ethnic and cultural conflicts. He sees clearly the need to prevent the "annexing [of] our American nations to the brutal and turbulent North which despises them."[31] Martí, like Ruiz de Burton, knows this cultural racism firsthand: "I have lived in the monster and I know its entrails."[32]

The notion of the United States as a republic with a democratic, egalitarian core is also dismantled by both writers, at least partially; for their own critiques build on the very notions of equality and democracy that they criticize as failed promises. Both are writing during a period of social turmoil and frustrated expectations. The period of Congressional Reconstruction after the Civil War, which was touted as having generated the construction of a democratic nation, had by 1877, as Eric Foner indicates, led to a totally different outcome; in fact, the country had retreated from "the idea, born during the Civil War, of a powerful national state protecting the fundamental rights of all American citizens."[33] Women were still disenfranchised, and the national government, far from protecting the right of workers to strike, was sending out troops as strikebreakers[34] and sanctioning racial subordination and segregation. Democratic Southern "Redeemers" would reinstitute involuntary black labor in the South[35] and subject these new "citizens" to economic, political and social oppression. Martí reports not only on the lynching and persecution of blacks,[36] but also on police action against strikers and labor demonstrators.[37]

Discourses of rights and entitlement come under fire in the writings of both authors, especially the right to dissent. Ruiz de Burton's first novel, *Who Would Have Thought It?* in fact counters idealized and romantic conceptions of U.S. politics. If, as one critic explains, the celebration of dissent is central to romanticism and democracy,[38] then Ruiz de Burton's romance serves to unmask the farce of dissent through an allegory that traces the fall of "republican motherhood"; that is, the fall of the "moral authority" of a Yankee matron. What is transcoded is more than the fall of the nation, fractured during the Civil War; it is the fall of a romantic conception of politics and the unmasking of liberal/democratic ideologies. In *Who Would Have Thought It?* the geologist Norval will have to go into exile to avoid arrest for criticizing the suspension of the Habeas Corpus Act with the outbreak of the Civil War. His son, an officer in the Union Army, will face dismissal and loss of rank without a court-martial when his father's comments are attributed to him. He will be saved, not by constitutional guarantees and protections, but by the intervention of powerful political and financial supporters. For those with power and the right connections, the system works. Like Martí, who notes the facility with which "speculators make donations in exchange for legislation and assistance that furthers their interests,"[39] Ruiz de Burton in both her novels counters views idealizing the United States as a democratic nation. It is a place, she insists, where dissent is not tolerated, where justice works for the economically powerful, such as the railroad monopolies (the "hydra-headed monster" in *The Squatter and the Don*), and where the electoral system is for sale to the highest bidder.

While voicing strong antimonopoly and anticorporate views, Ruiz de Burton's 1872 novel is, however, ambiguous about egalitarianism. On the one hand it severely critiques the abrogation of individual rights, while on the other it derides the entire concept of representational democracy. This derision is evident in the likes of the Cackles, an opportunistic and conniving family of ignorant ex-farmers, who are able to gain political power and make great economic gains through corruption. Equality is also a problematic legal notion for Martí, who in striving to unite black and white Cubans in the struggle for independence, promises that race will not be allowed to divide them after independence. Equality will come in time, he asserts, on the basis of "merit, the manifest and continuous evidence of culture, and the constant process of trade [which will] eventually unite all men."[40] Here, of course, Martí betrays his assimilation of the discourses of economic liberalism, which, as C. B. Macpherson explains, is the politics of choice, of competition and the market, but not that of equality.[41]

Martí had a firsthand look as well at the system of justice operating in this country, particularly in the case of labor activists, blacks, and Italian immigrants. And although he prefers to think that the problems of labor can be solved through nonviolent means, Martí also sees the injustices and contradictions within this country. The workers, he says, were asked to "look to the law for righting [their] wrongs," but "as soon as the workers organized themselves into a party to look to the law for help, they were called anarchists and revolutionaries."[42] In the case of those accused in the Haymarket Square riot, he makes clear the plight of the accused and traces the social conditions that led to their labor protest, and he commiserates with those "who watch their wives and children rotting in those social evils."[43]

In this same article, however, Martí's own contradictions become apparent as he tries to present both sides of the case. Although recognizing the conditions of misery and poverty that led to these protests, he also assumes the viability of the system and blames the protestors by saying that "in this free nation the only obstacle to sincerely desired social change lies in the lack of agreement on the part of those who seek that change."[44] He favors remedying ills by peaceful and legal means and expresses his opposition to violence or subversive action, since he is against interfering "with the freedom and property of others";[45] in effect, he opposes anything that jeopardizes the property of the capitalists.

On the other hand, where labor negotiation is unproductive, Martí sees the problem as systemic—not individual—and notes that the "wretched" (not the exploited or oppressed) will find no solace until they change the system: "These wretched people fail to understand that they are merely cogs in the gears of society; if they are to change, all the gears must change."[46] It is however a system in need of reform rather than transformation. His liberal assumptions become evident when he lays the blame on labor leaders; that is, on recent immigrants who he says fail to understand the democratic system. They would "deprive their employers of the very dignity and human freedom which they claim for themselves."[47] Again Martí wants to have it both ways, to side both with capitalists and workers; what is evident is a bourgeois perspective that is unwilling to analyze or attack the economic and political structure, however much he might note the imperfections and contradictions of the system. Thus, even his critique of the treatment of the Indians in this country, their dispossession and marginalization, will lead to a call not for a restitution of stolen lands but for education of the Indians. Here too his class and ethnic biases are quite clear when he suggests that such education not be a textbook education but vocational education: "No details or fancy theories; only how to raise animals and plant fields, all the tasks that make the useful and self-possessed member of a community of workers."[48] Although critical of aspects of the system, then, Martí as a rule places his trust in the system and recommends abiding by it.

Like many theorists today, both Ruiz de Burton and Martí focus on struggle at a discursive level, providing an analysis that reveals a correlation within the United States between imperialist policies, on the one hand, and labor, racial, and ethnic strife on the other. The divisions and social contradictions that both see require a discursive dismantling of the "Colossus" to unveil the ideological "monstrosity" that has blinded Latin Americans and Anglo Americans alike. While their critique is in part structural, it does not call for a dismantling of the political and economic structure, but rather of its ideological tower. Ruiz de Burton challenges the populace to wake up to those practices which threaten juridical and political freedom and equality; but instead of proposing an end to exploitation, she suggests that a set of constraints be imposed on corporations and their power. She strongly denounces the domination of California by the railroad monopoly, but when she considers the plight of Mexico it is political domination that she decries and fears; she does not see the dangers of economic domination.

Martí, on the other hand, calls for an alert Latin American populace, aware of the expansionist interests of the United States and wise enough to develop strategies that can at least set up obstacles to such imperial designs. His discursive battles are of course much more productive than Ruiz de Burton's, as is evident in Martí's warnings to the Latin American nations about U.S. plans to have them all accept bimetalism and the equalization of silver and gold, a policy of benefit to the United States but not to Latin America. As he warns in a speech before the Monetary Congress of the American Republics, whoever says economic domination says political domination.[49] Representatives of the Latin American nations at that congress would ultimately reject the U.S. currency plan. Yet despite his analysis of imperialism, Martí nevertheless continues to find sufficient space within U.S. political and economic structures for working out internal problems. For he sees those problems as political rather than economic. He also fails to link imperialism and economic dependence on a global scale to capitalism itself.

Thus both writers dismantle the "Colossus" only to rearticulate it. This giant, then as now, is in fact an articulation of capitalism and liberal democracy, and both Ruiz de Burton and Martí were too invested in bourgeois society and too elitist to envision structural change. Both, however, do lay the foundation for a continental solidarity, a position from which U.S. hegemony can better be repudiated at home as well as globally. Their emphases on an inclusive, multiethnic, multiracial "Latinidad" as an international collectivity and on "Nuestra América"—both as a continental rather than a national sphere and as a construction standing in opposition to the racism and contempt of "Anglo America"—may well turn out to be strategically important in staking out a differentiated discursive space for political struggle that goes beyond the local.

Notes

1 Noam Chomsky, "Market Democracy in a Neoliberal Order: Doctrines and Reality," *Z Magazine* vol. 10, no. 11 (November 1997): 28.

2 José Martí, "Our America," in Martí, *Our America: Writings on Latin America and the Struggle for Cuban Independence,* ed. Philip S. Foner, trans. Elinor Randall et al. (New York: Monthly Review Press, 1977), p. 84.

3 Ibid.

4 José Martí, "Nuestra América," in Martí, *Política de Nuestra América* (Mexico City: Siglo Veintiuno, 1977), p. 44.

5 José Martí, "The Truth about the United States," in Martí, *Inside the Monster: Writings on the United States and American Imperialism,* ed. Philip S. Foner, trans. Elinor Randall et al. (New York: Monthly Review Press, 1975), p. 51.

6 José Martí, "Letter to Manuel Mercado," in *Our America,* p. 439.

7 See Rosaura Sánchez, *Telling Identities: The Californio Testimonios* (Minneapolis: University of Minnesota Press, 1995).

8 María Amparo Ruiz de Burton, *The Squatter and the Don,* eds. and intro. Rosaura Sánchez and Beatrice Pita (Houston: Arte Público Press, 1993, orig. 1885).

9 Martí, "TheTruth about the United States," p. 50.

10 Domingo F. Sarmiento, "Conflicto y armonías de las razas en América," in *Conciencia intelectual de América,* ed. Carlos Ripoll (New York: Las Américas Publishing Co., 1966), p. 100.
11 See Henri Lefebvre, *The Production of Space,* trans. Donald Nicholson-Smith (Cambridge: Basil Blackwell, 1991), p. 28.
12 José Martí, "To the Root," in *Our America,* p. 354.
13 Ibid., p. 355.
14 Martí, "The Truth about the United States," p. 51.
15 Ibid.
16 Ibid., p. 54.
17 Ibid., p. 51.
18 Ibid., p. 52.
19 Ibid.
20 María Amparo Ruiz de Burton, *Who Would Have Thought It?* ed. and intro. Rosaura Sánchez and Beatrice Pita (Houston: Arte Público Press, 1995, orig. 1872), p. 283.
21 Ibid.
22 José Martí, "The Washington Pan-American Congress," in *Inside the Monster,* p. 366.
23 José Martí, "Political Corruption," in *Inside the Monster,* p. 205.
24 José Martí, "The Argentine Republic as Viewed from the United States," in *Inside the Monster,* p. 329.
25 José Martí, "The Monetary Congress of the American Republics," in *Inside the Monster,* p. 372.
26 Martí, "Our America," p. 93.
27 Martí, "The Washington Pan-American Congress," p. 351.
28 Ibid., p. 344.
29 Ibid., p. 358.
30 Ibid., p. 351.
31 Martí, "Letter to Manuel Mercado," p. 440.
32 Ibid.
33 Eric Foner, *A Short History of Reconstruction* (New York: Harper & Row, 1990), p. 245.
34 Ibid., p. 246.
35 Ibid., p. 250.
36 José Martí, "The Negro Race in the United States," in *Inside the Monster,* p. 213.
37 José Martí, "A Terrible Drama: The Funeral of the Haymarket Martyrs," in *Inside the Monster,* p. 287.
38 Steven H. Shiffrin, *The First Amendment, Democracy and Romance* (Princeton: Princeton University Press, 1990), p. 142.

39 Martí, "Political Corruption," p. 201.

40 José Martí, "Mi raza," in Martí, *Cuba, Nuestra América, los Estados Unidos* (Mexico City: Siglo Veintiuno, 1973), p. 314.

41 C. B. Macpherson, *The Real World of Democracy* (New York: Oxford University Press, 1981), pp. 6–7.

42 José Martí, "The Schism of the Catholics in New York," in *Inside the Monster,* p. 281.

43 Martí, "A Terrible Drama," p. 294.

44 Ibid., p. 295.

45 José Martí, "An Epidemic of Strikes," in *Inside the Monster,* p. 260.

46 Martí, "A Terrible Drama," p. 295.

47 José Martí, "The Labor Problem in the United States," in *Inside the Monster,* p. 263.

48 José Martí, "The Indians in the United States," in *Inside the Monster,* p. 225.

49 Martí, "The Monetary Congress of the American Republics," p. 372.

Beatrice Pita

Engendering Critique: Race, Class, and Gender in Ruiz de Burton and Martí

Yes, the mind had to be prepared—slowly, educated first. Now it has been.—María Amparo Ruiz de Burton, *The Squatter and the Don*[1]

Y no cumple con su deber quien lo calla, sino quien lo dice . . . Es preciso que se sepa en nuestra América la verdad de los Estados Unidos.—José Martí, "La verdad sobre los Estados Unidos"[2]

Beyond the fact that both would die in the year 1895, the circumstances and the places—in the widest sense—from which Ruiz de Burton and Martí write could not be more dissimilar: she an acculturated member of the dispossessed Californio elite who at the time she wrote her novels was the widow of a Yankee army general, an always enterprising woman who, while ultimately failing, attempted to "make it" as a capitalist; he a poet, a journalist, a freedom fighter (in the good sense of the word), a Cuban intellectual fighting for independence from Spain who would live the last fourteen years of his short, forty-two-year life in exile in the United States, and who would return to the island and die there in battle against Spanish troops.

Both Ruiz de Burton and Martí came to have intimate intercourse with the United States—she more so than he perhaps—and from that close contact both came to share in a disenchantment with the "promise" of the United States. Both would come to share an intense sense of betrayal, both would engage in a detailed dissection of the United States—a vivisection, rather, since for both the "monster" was all too alive and robust—and, most important, both would feel compelled to display the entrails of the monster and exhort their respective readers to react, to take proactive action so as not to be trampled by what Martí and Ruiz de Burton both interestingly figure as the destructive juggernaut cart of U.S. monopoly capitalism and imperialism. We shall return to this image in my concluding paragraphs.

What interests me in juxtaposing these two writers (who in different ways identify first and foremost as Latinos and as sons/daughters of "our America") is to trace how their respective texts chronicle for us the early constitution of what will increasingly be in the twentieth century, in Latin America specifically, a contestatory and critical stance vis-à-vis the United States. My purpose will be to investigate how and why and to what degree the two coincide, what correspondences can be found in their textualizations of the *espejismo* (mirage) of the United States and, more telling perhaps, in what ways their assessments are discontinuous. It will be necessary, of course, to deal with the "holy trinity" of race, class, and gender as these factors are at the very core of both Martí's and Ruiz de Burton's work. Noting how each, in their writings, deals specifically with these three points of articulation is crucial for a reading of the political and ideological shifts taking place on a continental level with respect to the United States (and to discourses on the United States) as the nineteenth century approached its close, discourses that we know were to have long-standing resonance.

1

In both Ruiz de Burton and Martí one finds that disenchantment and resentment are deployed as discursive strategies from which acerbic critiques and warnings issue. In their works this shared *desengaño* (disillusion) increasingly takes the form of lucid denunciations, disavowals, and a commitment to be rid of false ideas as to the "nature" of the "American Way." The "New World Order" that they see consolidating itself economically and politically in the last quarter of the nineteenth century is the ideology of American expansionism. Despite its early potential and promise, both Martí and Ruiz de Burton come to see the United States as what Martí terms a "civilización dañada," a damaged civilization, arguing that it is dangerous, in fact hazardous to one's political and economic health (both within the United States as well as without), to admire uncritically or to continue to idealize a nation in decay, full of flaws that both writers come to see as "constitutional."

Both Martí and Ruiz de Burton held an early admiration and affinity for the United States. Ruiz de Burton, we should recall, although she was an adolescent at the time, was among those who cast their lot with the invading U.S. forces at the onset of the U.S.-Mexican War and would at war's end be "boat-lifted" out of Baja California, coming to live in Upper California, where she would marry one of the officers of the invading army. The "seductiveness" of the United States, which boasted of being a more advanced, more enterprising, less "backward" nation, undoubtedly played a role in Ruiz de Burton's willing acculturation into U.S. society, despite the fact that she would always and forever hold onto a Latino cultural specificity and make it a point in her writings to counter the prevailing derogatory portrayals of Mexicans and Latinos. Resentment of the racism directed at Californios-Mexicanos, and their mistreatment and betrayal both by individuals and official U.S. policy, clearly fueled the critiques in both her novels: *Who Would Have Thought It?* (1872)[3] and *The Squatter and the Don* (1885). Ruiz de Burton makes good use of her intimate knowledge of the American scene—she did, after all, spend many years living on the East Coast and, as a result of her husband's position, was privy to high political and military workings in the nation's capital. Both her novels thus focus pointedly on matters of race and ethnicity, but go beyond a culturalist perspective as she widens the scope of her denunciations by taking to task the ostensible "superiority" of the Anglo, the ignominious state of internal U.S. politics, and the travesties of justice taking place in the halls of Congress, in the prisons and hospitals of the Civil War, in the boardrooms of the railroad monopolies, and in the bedrooms of New York's elite. Such contemptible conditions all hold sway in the very nation that with self-congratulatory hubris prides itself on having what her characters call "the greatest and the best government on Earth" and whose people claim "righteousness" in all they do (whether despoiling Californios of their land, willfully refusing to exchange Civil War prisoners in order to further starve the South, or using deceitful legal machinations to claim that which they have no right to).

Martí's trajectory of disillusionment and denunciation of the United States needs no review here. By the late 1880s, and especially in the 1890s, Martí's disenchantment with the United States has given way to a clear compulsion to warn, to issue the alarm about what lies down the road—this especially to any Latin Americans still enthralled by the "genius and presence" [genio y figura] of the U.S. "Colossus." To carry out his denunciations he calls for "clear-eyed sentinels" vis-à-vis a United States that is internally fraught with inequality and violence and yet positioning itself as heir to an imperial and despotic rule over Latin America. Martí states:

> This republic, because of excessive devotion to money, has fallen, without any of the ties of tradition, into the inequality, injustice, and violence of the monarchical countries. [Esta república por el culto desmedido a la riqueza, ha caído, sin ninguna de las trabas de la tradición, en la desigualdad, injusticia y violencia de los países monárquicos.][4]

That is to say, the United States is presenting precisely those traits — seen as "inherently European" — from which Latin America wished to disassociate. How different from the image of the United States as a land full of promise found in his 1881 piece "Impresiones de América" ("At last I am in a country where everyone seems to be his own master. Here one can be proud to be of the species" etc., etc.) where he goes on to say "everybody works, everybody reads" etc., etc., admiring a country where the individual can develop fully.[5]

It bears recalling, of course, that despite the loathing — and at times the fear — demonstrated toward Latin America, the United States was more often than not admired and held up as a model and point of comparison. In Martí, as in Ruiz de Burton, there is in evidence a certain degree of resentment for having been taken-in early on, for having been too quick in admiring the "skin" without having tasted the bitter fruit beneath. In both cases it is useful to trace the process and specific benchmarks of this "disenchantment" which discursively takes the shape of a jeremiad on the part of one who was once blind to the truth but who now knows better and is compelled to spread the word. This powerful trope of blindness or naiveté is invoked often in Martí to rail against what he comes to term the "yanquimanía" of all too many:

> That kind of blind admiration, whether it be a result of the novice's zeal or a lack of close study, is the greatest force on which a certain sort of politics in America can depend; this politics invokes, in order to dominate in America, a dogma which among the American nations needs no outside invocation. [Eso de la admiración ciega, por pasión de novicio o por falta de estudio, es la fuerza mayor con que cuenta en América la política que invoca, para dominar en ella, un dogma que no necesita en los pueblos americanos de ajena invocación.][6]

Martí points out that a surface acquaintance with the United States is not enough to know its inner workings:

In others, Yankeemania is the innocent product of the occasional pleasure jaunt, as a person who judges the inner workings of a house, and the souls who in it entreat or expire, by the smile and the luxury of the front parlor. . . . Let him suffer, let him go without, let him work, let him love . . . let him cry with the wretched, let him hate the brutality of wealth, let him live in the palace and in the slum . . . and thus will he be able, with a hint of reason, to have an opinion about the authoritarian and covetous republic and the sensibility of the United States. [En otros, la yanquimanía es inocente fruto de uno y otro saltito de placer, como quien juzga las entrañas de una casa, y de las almas que en ella ruegan o fallecen, por la sonrisa y lujo del salón de recibir. . . . [P]adézcase, carézcase, trabájese, ámese . . . llórese con los miserables, ódiese la brutalidad de la riqueza, vívase en el palacio y en la ciudadela . . . y así se podrá opinar, con asomos de razón, sobre la república autoritaria y codiciosa, y la sensibilidad de los Estados Unidos.][7]

In both Martí and Ruiz de Burton this early, nearsighted admiration for the United States comes soon to be replaced by distrust and fear; their texts denounce the "special interests" impelling U.S. policies internally and abroad as an adversarial force "which takes advantage of its power and of its standing to create despotism in a new form" [que se sirve de su poder y de su crédito para crear en forma nueva el despotismo].[8] Both writers attempt to compel their readers to action against this adversarial force, going so far as to impugn their readers' intelligence (or, as we shall see, their "virility") in their exhortations regarding "the giants with seven-league boots" [los gigantes que llevan siete leguas en las botas].[9] Martí, for example, asks rhetorically: "Or are the nations of America statues of blindness and marvels of decay?" [¿O son los pueblos de América estatuas de ceguedad, y pasmos de inmundicia?][10] Ruiz de Burton, too, ponders whether Americans have become so pusillanimous that they are "ready and willing to kiss the foot that tramples them."[11]

Martí especially becomes keenly aware of the danger facing Latin America — and Cuba more immediately — of being revisited, all too soon, by a second imperialism. His political work, his journalistic writings, and in the end his life itself are consumed by the struggle against the impending threat of back-to-back imperialisms. By virtue of age if nothing else, and perhaps by virtue of living for a longer period "in the belly of the monster," Ruiz de Burton came to an earlier disenchantment with the United States than Martí. For her part, already in her first novel (*Who Would Have Thought It?*), Ruiz de Burton works out through the genre of the romance her denunciation of the collusion of a corrupt government and moneyed interests (i.e., between public policy and profit); she gives a name to the culprit responsible for that moral and political decay within the United States which victimizes its own citizens: racism and monopoly capitalism. In *The Squatter and the Don,* written thirteen years later, she again rails against the ever more powerful monopolies. She anticipates Martí's later critique of U.S. imperialist designs, decrying a U.S. expansion buttressed by a racist "rationale," saying: "they have set up within our borders an *imperium in imperio* . . . [and are] building railroads in Guatemala and British America."[12] This she asserts in her exposé on corporate loopholes and tax dollars being misspent. Thus, both Martí and Ruiz de Burton examine the "nature" of imperialism and its ideological corollaries, which in the name of "progress and civilization" are set to trample not only "barbarous" peoples abroad but, as Ruiz de Burton sarcastically states in mock shock, "even, its fellow-citizens, *free-born Americans*."[13]

Both writers are therefore engaged in a process of diagnosis very much in keeping with the positivist bent of the period to employ clinical metaphors for the analysis and representation of the sociohistorical processes taking place on the continent. As in the work of their Peruvian contemporary Manuel González Prada, in both Martí and Ruiz de Burton there is an abundance of medical tropes that draw on images such as "national health," "robust moral fiber," "worm-ridden blood and corroded entrails"; of references to handicaps or conditions such as "impotence," "paralysis," and "blindness." While powerful critiques can issue from the discursive positioning of the writer as clinician, as is evident in the work of these two writers, it bears remembering that these tropes have been (and still are, as the debates surrounding California Propositions 187 and 209 demonstrate) consistently deployed by conservatives as well, who place blame on the "patient" and fail to address the causative agents of the condition, or who buttress their racist and/or classist policies on the need for "saneamiento," a cleansing of the social body.

Although they both inveigh against cultural racism directed

against Latinos, neither Ruiz de Burton nor Martí is devoid of deeply held and not easily overcome class, racial, and patriarchal prejudices; both for example are less than generous in their assessment of the Chinese and other "rabble" immigrants, and both on occasion fall back upon stereotypical portrayals of Jews, Indians, blacks, and other groups. And while admittedly acting strategically to counter anti-Latino cultural biases, both argue for an essentialist Latin "difference" seen as culturally and morally superior. Still, with their respective cultural and ideological baggage in hand, through different but not entirely unrelated struggles, both Martí and Ruiz de Burton arrive at contestatory and denunciatory stances vis-à-vis the United States, and both attempt to articulate and propel strategies that seek to forestall or resist what Ruiz de Burton terms "the hydra-headed monster"[14] in both its economic and cultural manifestations.

But lest one risk reading more into their critiques than is in the texts, one must remember, for example, that Ruiz de Burton attacks corporate monopolies and government collusion, but not the capitalist system per se; in effect, underlying her critiques is a defense of earlier entrepreneurial competitive capitalism, seen in jeopardy owing to the onslaught of monopoly capitalism and its political power. Ruiz de Burton rails against corruption and collusion, but her stance is ultimately reformist. She has no fundamental problems with capitalism (or patriarchy for that matter), calling for a "kinder and gentler," more principled capitalism, but she *is* nonetheless an astute-enough reader of her times to see that competitive capitalism's day will have gone forever if the "monster" is not checked by immediate political action. Consequently, while in her first novel she takes a caustic satirizing approach to point to the hypocrisy of U.S. society and the debasement of its government, in her second novel she exhorts her readers to act while there is still time, to take matters into their own hands, to divest monopoly of its stranglehold on a nation and a government ever less "of, by and for the people":

> It seems now that unless *the people of California take the law into their own hands,* and seize the property of those men and confiscate it, to reimburse the money due *the people,* the arrogant corporation will never pay. They are so accustomed to appropriate to themselves what rightfully belongs to others, and have so long stood before the world in defiant

attitude, that they have become utterly insensible to those sentiments of fairness animating law-abiding men of probity and sense of justice.[15]

While here referring specifically to the power of the railroad monopoly and its stranglehold on California transport, this statement of course configures all too clearly as well the deterritorialized and disenfranchised social and political position of the Californios in the period of postinvasion and annexation to the United States, a position with which she identifies and a resentment against the invader and usurper which she voices most clearly.

Ruiz de Burton, like Martí, looks at the systemic flaws, the underbelly, the very underpinnings of the system — both economic and political. Through contact at close quarters with the beast — Martí tells us: "I lived in the monster, and I know its entrails" [Viví en el monstruo, y le conozco las entrañas][16] — both Ruiz de Burton and Martí soon had their fill of the scorn, disdain, and anti-Latino racism of, according to Martí, a "disrespectful and rapacious" United States which, having already wrested half its territory from Mexico, was not yet sated.

Martí too, by the late 1880s and early 1890s, interacting of course more directly on a Latin American circuit, warns of a continued idealization of the United States. Writing in the period of accelerated capitalist development and consolidation of both monopoly capitalism and U.S. imperialism, Martí sees that the threat facing Latin America from the United States is no longer "simply" that of a land-hungry country with "growing-pains," but rather that threat arising from dominance accompanied by the military, economic, and political wherewithal to act upon its imperialist designs on Latin America. Martí, who had gone beyond Sarmiento's formulations to say in 1891 that "there is no battle between civilization and barbarism" [No hay batalla entre la civilización y la barbarie] and to speak instead of "Nuestra América mestiza," still had to deal with the legacy of "yanquimanía" which led Sarmiento, as late as 1883, to say:

Let us not halt the United States in its march; that is, in short, what some are proposing. Let us catch up to the United States. Let us be American the way the sea is the ocean. Let us be United States. [No detengamos a los Estados Unidos en su marcha; es lo que en definitiva proponen algunos. Alcancemos a los Estados Unidos. Seamos la América como el mar es el océano. Seamos Estados Unidos.][17]

Sarmiento's admiration for the "expansive wave" of the United States' extension of its borders was not, however, universally shared—definitely not by those dispossessed by it, like the Californios—nor did it go without criticism within the United States, despite a concerted campaign to represent the Latin American countries as black or Indian, as violent, as childlike, *and* as female. Martí would by 1894 cast the United States in an entirely different light vis-à-vis Latin America in speaking of

> the rude, unequal and decadent character of the United States, and the continual existence in [the United States] of all the violence and discord, immorality and disorder attributed to the peoples of Hispanic America. [el carácter rudo y desigual y decadente de los Estados Unidos y la existencia en ellos continua, de todas las violencias y discordias, immoralidades y desórdenes de que se culpa a los pueblos hispanoamericanos.][18]

Indeed, both Ruiz de Burton and Martí, for independent reasons, were uniquely situated to see and to respond to the transformations and dynamics being set in place and to question dominant discourses touting the American "model" as more just, more enlightened, and more liberating. Martí's realization that Cuba was at risk, in fact, led him to wish to accelerate independence from Spain, to better position it with respect to the "covetousness" of the United States for an island, only ninety miles away, from which by 1859 it was already purchasing 42 percent of its sugar.

2

In varying degrees both Martí and Ruiz de Burton factor in race, class, and gender issues into their critique of the United States, ultimately focusing more and more directly on the economic underpinnings of social stratification and political power in the United States as well as on the interconnected ideological discourses of class, ethnicity/nation, and gender. It is not so curious perhaps that both writers can only couch the uneven power relationships and desires of which they speak in gendered and sexualized terms. Martí, for example, renders the imperialist designs on Latin America via a "masculinization" of the Anglo-Saxon and the United States, and counters by asserting the equally "virile" qualities of Latin America:

The hour is near when a *enterprising* and *powerful* people, who do not know *her* [Our America] and who disdain *her,* will approach *her* demanding *intimate relations.* And since *virile peoples,* who have forged their way by means of the rifle and the law only love other virile peoples . . . [Es la hora próxima en que se le acerque demandando *relaciones íntimas* un pueblo *emprendedor y pujante* que *la* desconoce y *la* desdeña. Y como los *pueblos viriles,* que se han hecho de sí propios con la escopeta y la ley, aman y sólo aman a los pueblos viriles . . .][19]

Martí goes on in "Nuestra América" to exhort that there is still time to counter and forestall the effects of the United States' "covetousness":

The scorn of her *formidable neighbor* who doesn't know *her,* is Our America's greatest danger; and because the day of the visit is fast approaching, it is urgent that the neighbor meet her, that he come to know her soon so that he not disdain *her.* Because out of ignorance, perhaps, he might come to covet her. [El desdén del *vecino formidable,* que no *la* conoce, es el peligro mayor de Nuestra América, y urge, porque el día de la visita está próximo, que el vecino la conozca, la conozca pronto para que no *la* desdeñe. Por ignorancia, llegaría, tal vez, a poner en *ella* la *codicia.*][20]

The sexualized attributions, however, can be manipulated to cut both ways. Thus, Martí can invert the characterization, "feminize" the United States and impugn its "virility" just as dominant U.S. discourses have feminized Latin America into the role of subaltern female:

The North American character has gone into decline since independence, and today it is less humane and *manly;* while the Hispanic American [character] is today, by all rights, superior. [El carácter norteamericano ha descendido desde la independencia, y es hoy menos humano y *viril,* mientras en el hispanoamericano a todas luces es superior hoy.][21]

Already in 1889, in "Vindicación de Cuba," Martí had rebutted arguments that Cubans were an "effeminate race," not up to par for association with the United States, and that they were "unfit" to be citizens:

We have suffered impatiently under tyranny, we have fought like men, and at times like giants, to be free. . . . Can we be called, as *The Manufacturer* calls us, an effeminate people? [Hemos sufrido impacientes bajo la tiranía, hemos peleado como hombres y algunas veces como gigantes, para ser libres . . . ¿se nos puede llamar, como *The Manufacturer* nos llama, un pueblo afeminado?][22]

And, of course, we know a similar perspective was held generally in the United States in regard to Mexicans, seen as a "mongrel race."

Clearly Martí, here as elsewhere in his writings, is responding to a strictly delineated and highly romantic division of spheres for the feminine and the masculine—a dichotomy that extends as well to the literary. The following passage from Martí's introduction to his 1887 translation of Helen Hunt Jackson's *Ramona* is particularly revealing in this regard:

[Helen Hunt Jackson] paints in an American light landscapes, dramas and personalities . . . allowing *feminine* grace but to enhance, with new *allure,* constant literary *virility.* . . . One enjoys a book that, without offending reason, warms the soul, one of the few books that have a place on the *thinker's* table as well as in the *demure sewing room.* [Pinta (Helen Hunt Jackson) con luz americana paisajes, dramas y caracteres . . . sin que la gracia *femenina* haga más que realzar con *atractivo* nuevo la constante *virilidad* literaria. . . . Se disfruta de un libro que sin ofender la razón, calienta el alma, uno de los pocos libros que pueden estar sobre la mesa *del pensador* y en *el recatado costurero.*][23]

Writing is thus presented as a masculine enterprise that can nonetheless benefit from the "feminine touch." These gendered attributions will again come into play as Martí further dissects both the United States and the character of its people:

The greatest nation is not that which, with unequal and unrestrained wealth, produces *crude and petty men and corrupt and selfish women;* a great nation, of whatever size, is that which offers *generous men and chaste women.* [El pueblo más grande no es aquél que en una riqueza desigual y desenfrenada produce *hombres crudos y sórdidos y mujeres venales y egoistas;* pueblo grande, cualquier que sea su tamaño, es aquél que da *hombres generosos y mujeres puras.*][24]

In both her novels, Ruiz de Burton, although she has no basic quarrel with patriarchal values, creates representations of women that are markedly more nuanced and generous as regards women's roles and capacity for reasoning and agency. Where Martí recoils at the sight of "unfeminine gringas" and has numerous reservations about women in the public sphere, Ruiz de Burton will point in her texts to the subordinate and disenfranchised position of women—echoing U.S. feminist critiques of her period—while at the same time retaining, for her positively portrayed female characters, the traits of sensitivity, morality, and beauty so cherished by Martí in women. However, it will be through women characters—though not exclusively—that Ruiz de Burton voices her strongest critiques. It will be through Mary Moreneau and Doña Josefa in *The Squatter and the Don,* and through Lavvy and Lola in *Who Would Have Thought It?* that flaws and transgressions will be scrutinized and denunciations made.

Interestingly, in both novels Ruiz de Burton also carries out an operation in which she figures male agency as handicapped and/or truncated by the forces of decay and corruption. Thus the Californio men in *The Squatter and the Don* fall victim to accidents or debilitating illness in addition to suffering land loss and ignominy at the hand of squatters and the government; and in *Who Would Have Thought It?* the Norval men likewise suffer "compromised male agency," an "emasculation" of sorts, when they are "absented" from the scene as a result of the machinations of scoundrels—male and female—in collusion with the government and its policies.

3

In challenging their respective readers to see clearly and react before it is too late, both Martí and Ruiz de Burton look to the internal contradictions at work in the United States and consider as well the continental implications. Whether directed to those within the United States or to those living outside it, theirs is a disabusing project, a wake-up call and a warning that the United States isn't what it says (or even what it *thinks*) it is. Both reject the United States as a model to be emulated. As early as 1881 in his "Two Views on Coney Island" Martí begins to see beyond the veneer, and raises serious doubts in regard to the democratic foundations of the United States he once so admired.

During his prolonged stay in the United States, Martí develops a deepening understanding—more acutely than Ruiz de Burton perhaps—of the political as well as economic "causes of human misery." In this sense he goes beyond Ruiz de Burton, who still harbors a certain faith in the system, an expectation that "the people" can still bring their will to bear, that the problem is of a political nature and requires a political solution, that the state can be relegislated back to health; hers, then, is at bottom a call for a corrective, a purging of the system.

While there are numerous correspondences in Ruiz de Burton's and Martí's respective diagnoses and prescriptions, something needs to be said about the language chosen by each to carry out their respective denunciations, for language marks a clear break between the two and forces us to address the issue of intended audience. Clearly Martí, an exile, is voicing a wake-up call for a Latin American, Spanish-speaking audience. Ruiz de Burton, on the other hand, presents us with a more complicated scenario; for there is a marked split — not only in language choice but in terms of "cultural identification" — between her correspondence and the narrative personae adopted in her novels.

Yet despite their addressing different audiences, both advocate an awakening and a coming together of admittedly diverse groups in order to stand against the "hydra-headed monster" — an awakening both domestic *and* continental. In this sense Ruiz de Burton's and Martí's are complementary ideological projects that see a shared "Latinidad" as a useful construct to offset the preponderance of Anglo-Saxon influence on the continent. In Martí, as in the case of Ruiz de Burton, a flexible inclusivity allows for a transcendence of race, class, and nationality in opposition to what is constituted variously as a juggernaut, a hydra-headed monster, a soulless machine. While naming specific perpetrators, both writers' critiques go beyond seeing the problem as one of isolated cases of corrupt individuals; rather, they analyze the problems as systemic and point to the supraindividual forces at work, issuing their critique at the level of policy and politics, profit and propaganda.

4

To underscore again the correspondences to be found between Martí and Ruiz de Burton, I would like, in concluding, to return briefly to the image of the juggernaut cart. The reference is to the Indian festival for the deity Jagannatha (Lord of the World), whose massive cart often ran over pilgrims accompanying the procession in Jagannatha's honor, thus figuring a destructive force that requires blind devotion and cruel sacrifice, crushing all in its path. The central preoccupations of Martí and Ruiz de Burton come together as they call upon the image of the juggernaut cart, specifically in reference to the overwhelming and destructive force of corrupt governmental practices, U.S. monopoly capitalism, and attendant imperialist designs.

Ruiz de Burton ends *The Squatter and the Don* with allusions to a "firmly enthroned power that corrupts, ruins and debases [while] its citizens [seem] ready and willing to kiss the foot that tramples them," and she further develops the image in speaking of a debased citizenry of "white slaves"[25] now at the mercy of the "juggernaut" of the powerful railroad monopoly. In *Who Would Have Thought It?* she is even more explicit in invoking the juggernaut image to refer to capitulation to "the great monopolists":

> The Eastern worshipper saying to his idol "Crush me if thou wilt, to worship thee is my delight, my pride," is no more subservient than "the equal of kings," the *free-born* American before the *successful man,* before the millionaire, before the railroad king,—the great monopolists.[26]

We have a very close correspondence in Martí, who speaks of the less-than-disinterested maneuverings of the United States in its dealings with Latin America; that is, in its projects for annexations, construction of an interoceanic canal, and monetary agreements. In admonishing against an "unnatural alliance," Martí warns specifically of the risk of enslavement to a new master, given as a "disdainful juggernaut, who moves forward squashing his servants' heads" [Juggernaut desdeñoso que adelanta, aplastando cabezas de siervos]. Martí asks:

> Will Colombia pawn itself, will she sell her sovereignty? Will the free peoples who live in the isthmus clear it of obstacles for the juggernaut? And will they then get in his cart, as did the Mexicans in Texas? [¿Empeñará, venderá Colombia su soberanía? ¿Le limpiarán el itsmo de obstáculos al Juggernaut, los pueblos libres que moran en él, y se subirán en su carro, como se subieron los mexicanos de Texas?][27]

Martí again employs the juggernaut image as he recalls the fate of those Mexicans who colluded with the invader in Texas:

> The New York *Sun* said it yesterday: "Whoever doesn't want to be run over by the juggernaut should get into his cart." It would be better to

block the cart's path. . . . The Tejanos got into the cart, and with flames at their backs, like rabid foxes, or with their family's dead on the back of a horse, they had to flee, barefoot and hungry, from their homeland of Texas. [El *Sun* de Nueva York, lo dijo ayer: "El que no quiera que lo aplaste el Juggernaut, súbase en su carro." Mejor será cerrarle al carro el camino. . . . Al carro se subieron los tejanos, y con el incendio a la espalda, como zorros rabiosos, o con los muertos de la casa en la grupa, tuvieron que salir, descalzos y hambrientos, de su tierra de Texas.][28]

The complementarity of Ruiz de Burton's and Martí's projects is, I think, evident in this correspondence of both imagery and subject matter. The loss of the Southwest and the treatment of its people stands out in both Martí's and Ruiz de Burton's thinking as a watershed event, a caveat about the ominous consequences in store for those unwilling or unable to foresee and forestall the onslaught of the juggernaut cart.

Notes

1 María Amparo Ruiz de Burton, *The Squatter and the Don,* ed. and intro. Rosaura Sánchez and Beatrice Pita (Houston: Arte Público Press, 1993, orig. 1885), p. 172.

2 José Martí, "La verdad sobre los Estados Unidos" (1894), in Martí, *Cuba, Nuestra América, los Estados Unidos* (Mexico City: Siglo Veintiuno, 1973), p. 316. Unless otherwise indicated, all quotations of Martí are from this edition of his writings.

3 María Amparo Ruiz de Burton, *Who Would Have Thought It?* ed. and intro. Rosaura Sánchez and Beatrice Pita (Houston: Arte Público Press, 1995).

4 Martí, "La verdad sobre los Estados Unidos," p. 316. This and all subsequent translations into English (except the one cited in note 5 below) are by Karen Marie Belnap.

5 José Martí, "Impresiones de América" (1881), in Martí, *Inside the Monster: Writings on the United States and American Imperialism,* ed. Philip S. Foner, trans. Elinor Randall et al. (New York: Monthly Review Press, 1975), p. 31.

6 Martí, "El Congreso de Washington" (1889), p. 147.

7 Martí, "La verdad sobre los Estados Unidos," p. 317.

8 Martí, "El Congreso de Washington," p. 148.

9 Martí, "Nuestra América" (1891), p. 111.

10 Martí, "El Congreso de Washington," p. 148.
11 Ruiz de Burton, *The Squatter and the Don,* p. 365.
12 Ibid., p. 369.
13 Ibid., p. 365. Emphasis in original.
14 Ibid., p. 298.
15 Ibid., p. 366. Emphasis in original.
16 Martí, "Carta a Mercado" (1895), p. 105.
17 Domingo F. Sarmiento, "Conflicto y armonía de las razas en América" (1883), in Carlos Ripoll, *Conciencia intelectual de America: Antología del ensayo hispanoamericano 1836–1955* (New York: Las Américas Publishing Co., 1966), p. 100.
18 Martí, "La verdad sobre los Estados Unidos," p. 318.
19 Martí, "Nuestra América," p. 118. My emphasis.
20 Ibid., p. 119. My emphasis.
21 Martí, "La verdad sobre los Estados Unidos," p. 318. My emphasis.
22 Martí, "Vindicación de Cuba," 1889, p. 5.
23 See Martí's "Introducción" to his translation of Helen Hunt Jackson's *Ramona* (Havana: Ediciones Huracán, 1978, orig. 1887). My emphasis.
24 Martí, "Inmigración en América" (*Patria,* 1894), in Ripoll, *Conciencia intelectual de América,* p. 256. My emphasis.
25 Ruiz de Burton, *The Squatter and the Don,* p. 372.
26 Ruiz de Burton, *Who Would Have Thought It?* p. 119.
27 Martí, "El Congreso de Washington," p. 147.
28 Ibid., p. 139.

José David Saldívar

Nuestra América's Borders: Remapping American Cultural Studies

In the United States . . . the real [José] Martí is almost forgotten. . . . It is odd that there is no single book that explores Martí's ties with the United States. . . . And it is all the more surprising because, except for short intervals, the 15 years of his prime (1880–1895) were spent in exile in the United States, whose inner life he came to know profoundly. — Roberto Fernández Retamar, "Jose Martí: A Cuban for all Seasons"[1]

In the following pages, we shall consider how U.S.-Mexican border paradigms strive for comparative theoretical reach while remaining grounded in specific histories of what José Martí in 1891 called "Nuestra América" [Our America]. We shall also ask what such projects tell us about the cultures of U.S. imperialism and the cultures of displacement? Finally, we shall turn our attention to two late nineteenth-century articulations of an uneven and contradictory frontier modernism,[2] one situated along the banks of the Rio Grande in South Texas and the other located in the ranchos of Alta California: late *fin de siglo* quests for empire, politics, and subaltern difference.

Culturally, I write these days as a teacher and avid reader and consumer of U.S.-Mexico border texts, soundings, and visual cultural performances. Like many U.S. Latino/a intellectuals, I have lived both in the North and in the South, and the South in the North, as Rubén Martínez once dizzyingly and aptly put it.[3] While I now find myself located in what some hundred and fifty years ago was called the northern frontier of Alta California, I spent the first half of my life at the mouth of the Rio Grande in South Texas. My quest for a new mapping of American Cultural Studies necessarily worries about the politics of location.

When I first went to Yale to study American literature in 1973, I knew hardly anything about America. I had been nurtured in the rhetoric of the U.S.-Mexico Borderlands, what Américo Paredes called the liminal spaces of "Greater Mexico."[4] I was absorbed, moreover, in South Texas attitudes toward "El Norte"—a subalternity deepened by the pressures of economic, military, and cultural displacements. This interpretation of America, however, was not given to me in my provincial public school education in South Texas, where history began and ended with the master periodizing narratives of the Alamo. So I learned on my own all the hard facts about regional hegemony and global colonialism's cultures; for culture, my teachers believed, always lived somewhere else—never in our own backyard. I learned all the hard facts which were, of course, pejorative. But the symbology of the two Americas that José Martí mapped out for us in "Nuestra América" remained largely hidden from me.

Nothing in my background prepared me for my encounter with the Other America—a secular nation living like a dream on back of a tiger. With the sound tracks of my adolescence recirculating in me (hybrid *corrido* and *conjunto* soundings), I left South Texas to walk down the mean streets of New Haven to discover the rather different musics of America—from Walt Whitman's "I Hear America Singing" to the Funkadelics' "One Nation under a Groove" and Rubén Blades's *salsa* national anthem, "Buscando América."[5] Quickly I was immersed in the foundational myths of the Puritan Ur-fathers, evident everywhere all around me at the Old Campus, from its neo-Gothic buildings named after dissenters like Jonathan Edwards to the mainline American and British literature taught me in undergraduate seminars and tutorials. Beyond the walled-in panoptican of the Old Campus was something called the New England Way. To see this New England America as a phantasmatics was to historicize my identifications.[6]

The purpose of these brief personal remarks is not to demonstrate a Manichaean clash of identities and affiliations, but rather to begin mapping out the phantasmatics of Nuestra América's borders at our own complex *fin de siglo*. So what began in New England America with mainline American Studies became, years later, at an "Alta" California private university (founded by a prominent robber baron and member of the Gilded Age's "Big Four"), a trail into the intricate symbologies of American Cultural Studies.[7] Both in New England America and in California I encountered an imperial literary and cultural history: Perry Miller's garden variety errand into the wilderness; R. W. B. Lewis's constructions of the American Adam; Harold Bloom's Western canon based on elite

European and Euro-American isolatoes. Likewise, in California, I encountered Yvor Winters's and Wallace Stegner's constructions of the Western American literary frontier passages. The America they discovered (East Coast and West) seemingly (as Sacvan Bercovitch suggests) appeared out of nowhere, out of some Hegelian telos, respectively labeled Nature, the New England Mind, the Jeffersonian Way, and the American Frontier thesis, culminating in Newt Gingrich's all too familiar and tired "Contract with America."

American literary and cultural studies had developed, as Amy Kaplan suggests in "Left Alone with America," with a method designed *not* to explore its subject of empire, for "the study of American culture had traditionally been cut off from the study of foreign relations."[8] This was a simple lesson for someone like myself steeped in the U.S.-Mexico "contact zone," but it required (as they say) time, comparative study, and observation to absorb. My own view of American Studies fully formed (when I studied with Sacvan Bercovitch at the School of Criticism and Theory at Dartmouth College in 1987) was that mainline America was an "artifact" made foundational text by academics, Americanists, soldiers, anthropologists, and emergent traveling theorists. Occasionally, as in the work of a Gilded Age, frontier Americanist-ethnologist like Captain John Gregory Bourke—commissioned a first lieutenant at West Point in 1869, an Indian and Mexican hunter, and later a friend and colleague of the Smithsonian's Major John Wesley Powell and a follower of Franz Boas and Hubert Howe Bancroft—all of these force fields were embodied simultaneously.[9] Bourke's American Studies in the 1890s, I want to suggest, allow us to begin asking to what extent such disciplines as anthropology, ethnography, and travel writing legitimated the imperializing project of the U.S. government. (Parenthetically, was one of José Martí's major contributions as an anti-*letrado* in "Nuestra América" his critique of imperial governing and his artistic repositioning of what he called the consolidation of the arts of "buen gobierno" [governing well]?[10]

John Gregory Bourke's eminent career as a frontier "Americanist" requires a more precise exploration, which I will elaborate below, but even in modest outline form his project as a soldier-ethnologist is a rich and intricate thematization of the United States' famous frontier field-imaginary. As his biographer Joseph Porter put it, Bourke's "fascination with the land, the history and the peoples of the Southwest" not only "compelled [him] to keep extensive diaries"[11] but also obliged him to reproduce in the writing of his cultural poetics the paradoxes of Gilded Age imperialist formation.

After graduating from West Point, Bourke was ordered by the War Department to Fort Craig, New Mexico, where he began his military and ethnographic espionage, observation, and destruction of Pueblo Indian cultures. From March 1870 to August 1871, Bourke was continually in battle with the Apaches. It was "after hours" that he wrote his prodigious diary entries, "studied up" the Native American Indians of the region, and mastered the Spanish vernacular language of the Nuevo Mexicanos. According to Porter, a pattern developed in New Mexico: after Native American (and later Mexican) hunting, Bourke "stoically worked on his diary, recording incidents and details of that day's march, noting the natural scenery, and making cartographic and geological notes" (16).

Throughout much of the 1870s, Bourke was in battle against the Native American tribes of the Southwestern United States, and he was primarily responsible for what his biographer called "the only successful campaign against the Apaches since the acquisition of the Gadsden Purchase" (20). Now a fully developed "hero of the American frontier," as Porter characteristically phrased it, Bourke traveled from New Mexico to Omaha in 1875, where he was ordered to escort the U.S. Geological Expedition to the Black Hills. The soldier-ethnologist as well as a newly self-made "engineer officer" thus turned his attention to the Lakota and Cheyenne peoples and their native cultures. Typical of his diary entries during this period of ethnographic writing and military conquest is the following: "the sooner the manifest destiny of the race shall be accomplished and the Indian as an Indian cease to exist, the better" (quoted in Porter, 49).

Curiously enough, Bourke's destruction of "the Indian as Indian" occurred at the very same time that he was busy collecting notes, plants, animals, and pictographic artifacts of Native American and Mexican American cultures, items that he preserved by sending them off to the Smithsonian Institution in Washington, D.C. In other words, Bourke, together with Major John Wesley Powell, who in 1879 became the director of the Bureau of Ethnology at the Smithsonian, displayed almost *avant la lettre* what the ethnohistorian Renato Rosaldo calls "imperialist nostalgia," nostalgia "for the very forms of life they intentionally altered and destroyed."[12]

In 1881, Lieutenant General Philip Sheridan readily agreed to Bourke's personal request to be reassigned as an "ethnologist" with the Third United Cavalry, for he concurred with Bourke's assessment that there was institutional value in documenting what we now call the cultural poetics of, in Bourke's words, "the people whom we so often had to fight and always to manage" (quoted in Porter, 280). From Chicago, Bourke embarked on a late *fin de siglo* traveling tour that took him to Idaho, Texas, and New Mexico. In Santa Fe, he began his fieldwork at the Pine Ridge Agency, observing and writing an account in his diary of the sacred Oglala Sun Dance. As Porter writes, Bourke was "amazed, moved, and impressed by what he saw" (93). These and other extended military and ethnographic search-and-destroy missions allowed Bourke to write up his first ethnographic study of Native American peoples, *The Dance of the Moquis of Arizona* (1884). Later, after he crossed the present-day U.S.-Mexico border near Guaymas in pursuit of the Chiricahuas, he completed *An Apache Campaign in the Sierra Madre* (1886), a book largely chronicling his military travails and travels in the Western American frontier. For the remainder of his career as a soldier-ethnologist, Bourke traveled to and from Arizona, Texas, and Washington, D.C. Although many of his friends in Washington attempted to secure for him various positions in the War Department offices, Bourke eventually was ordered in 1891 to rejoin the Third Cavalry unit in South Texas.[13]

The dissident Chicano folklorist and cultural anthropologist José E. Limón offers us in his cogent and provocative *Dancing with the Devil* (1994) the first detailed metacommentary of Bourke's ethnographic writings about the South Texas–Mexico border. For Limón, Bourke's interests and his fascination with Mexicano border culture and folklore stem largely out of a "not too unconscious projection of [his] own uneasy and ambivalent ethnic identity onto the mexicanos."[14] In other words, Limón suggests, Bourke's double career as a "literal warrior turned anthropologist" (17) is not completely an example of colonialist desire; for, as a Catholic Irish-American, Bourke possessed the same ethnoracial contradictions of domination as his objects of study.

Some of Bourke's most engaging ethnographic writing about the U.S.-Mexico borderlands, Limón asserts, unconsciously represented the Mexicanos of South Texas as suffering from the very same hegemonic forces that his own Celtic forebears had earlier experienced at the hands of the Saxon and Danish invaders of Ireland. In thus "constructing [the cultural poetics of] mexicanos," Limón claims, "Bourke was also coping with his own repudiated and projected self-ambivalences" (33). Be that as it may, my own view of Bourke's writing U.S.-Mexico border culture, elaborated below, focuses more specifically on the molecular and molar dialectics of the cultures of U.S. imperialism.

If U.S. imperialism was also a cultural process, imagined and energized through recognizable signs, metaphors, tropes, and master narratives, Bourke's project of U.S. empire was expressive and (to use Raymond Williams's term) "constitutive" of imperial relations in themselves. Through his official military reportage and documents relating to the uneven modernizing process of governing well from Fort Ringold, Rio Grande City, Texas, Bourke situated hemispheric and global colonialism's cultures and narratives in terms of what he embodied—a military captain and agent of U.S. empire, a travel writer, and an ethnographer of South Texas border culture. Here in Bourke's frontier—not *frontera*—cultural work, my coordinates of travel, nativist modernity, anthropology, and cultures of U.S. imperialism can be seen as constitutive of one another.

Tracking the U.S.-Mexico Borderlands in the Gilded Age

Just three years after José Martí warned us in his magisterial "Nuestra América" of the profound gap between the two Américas, Bourke collected, gathered, and published his first so-called empirical studies of the U.S.-Mexico Borderlands. Part travel writer, and part participant-observer of the Rio Grande Valley from "Point Isabel to Roma," Texas, Bourke wanted his travel writing/ethnographic work to shed light (as he put it in his 1894 essay "Popular Medicine, Customs, and Superstitions of the Rio Grande") "upon the character of the Mexican population of our extreme southern border."[15] Like a latter-day Perry Miller in the African wilderness, Captain Bourke traveled up and down the Rio Grande into what must have been for him and his readers the American heart of darkness. This river project leads Bourke not to Perry Miller's displaced discovery of American studies, which Amy Kaplan has shown brilliantly,[16] but to the discoveries and trespasses of an imperial American border studies, a project overwhelmingly grounded in a rhetoric of "turbulence" and "ignorance," debasement and negation. Like many ethnographers, Bourke begins his project by traveling and looking: "As the Rio Grande is the main line of communication, a trip along its waters will be necessary for anyone who desires to become even fairly well acquainted with the general character of the country and that of the people living in it."[17]

Bourke's 1894 *Scribner's Magazine* essay, symptomatically entitled "The American Congo," demonstrates how U.S. culture in the Gilded Age was always already a global phenomenon, or at least already an extralocal and transregional project. While a good part of Bourke's essay is structured around the "being there" of travel writing and ethnographic thick description, it is also entirely underpinned with the theories of Franz Boas's anthropological project. Anthropology for Boas and his generation was, as Nicholas Thomas puts it, "a modern discourse that ha[d] subsumed humanity to the grand narratives and analogies of natural history."[18] Not surprisingly, "The American Congo" represents the U.S.-Mexico border zone exclusively in terms of its exoticized landscape, its unceasing *mesquites,* its noisy *urracas,* and its fantastic *javelinas* and *armadillos*—what the Cuban novelist and theorist Alejo Carpentier calls "lo barroco americano" [the American baroque].[19] A sympathetic reading of "The American Congo" might therefore stress how Bourke was merely following Boas's famous dictum that "cultures differ like so many species, perhaps genera, of animals" (quoted in Thomas, 89) and so on. In other words, in "The American Congo" there is not a simple, smoothed-over colonial discourse, but instead a highly ambiguous and ethnically fraught study of Mexican *pelados* and *peones* who are represented by a Catholic, Irish American gunfighter as if they were newly discovered species, as the bearers of particular characters, physiques, dispositions, political organizations, and juridical practices.

My own reading of Bourke's "The American Congo" is less idealist, though I hope not uncharitable. Bourke is to be congratulated for showing how two imperializing hemispheric events made the Rio Grande Borderlands and its local population what he called "a sealed book" (592). Two "ethnic storms," he writes, had erased for the rest of the United States the Greater Mexican population from the national imaginary. The first was Zachary Taylor's "march from Point Isabel, near the mouth of the Rio Grande to Camargo" and then to Saltillo (592); the second was "our own Civil War, when the needs of the Confederacy suggested the transportation of all available cotton . . . across the Rio Grande to the Mexican side, and then down to Matamoros, there to be placed on steamers to Nassau and Liverpool" (592). To his great credit Bourke shows, in decidedly spatial terms, how U.S. imperial culture is irrevocably local and global, for what makes the U.S.-Mexico Borderlands and its inhabitants "a sealed book" are the competing mappings of global capital, the multiple roots and routes of the Black Atlantic, and the submarine discourses of what Glissant calls Antillean discourses.[20] More locally, Fort Ringold, Fort McIntosh, and Fort Brown in South Texas were part and parcel of Zachary Taylor's military campaigns in the service of U.S. empire that resulted in what José Limón calls "the American incorporation of the Southwest" (22).

If the force field of American Border Studies in the United States was conceived by John Bourke, soldier-ethnographer, on the swirling, countercurrents of the Rio Grande in the 1890s, Chicano/a Cultural Studies—from Américo Paredes in the 1930s to John Rechy and Helena Viramontes in the 1990s—has had to challenge and undo Bourke's plethora of imperializing crude acts constituted in classic American frontier chronicles like "The American Congo," "Popular Medicine, Customs, and Superstitions of the Rio Grande" (both 1894), and "The Miracle Play of the Rio Grande" (1893). Bourke's title "The American Congo" immediately allows us metonymically and synecdochically to associate his brand of "American studies" with immediate acts such as conquest, underdevelopment, intervention, intrusion, and domination of the local *mestizo/a* Mexican inhabitants.

At the beginning of the essay, for example, Bourke recalls how a few years earlier from his military post at Fort Ringold, he had written about the Borderlands of Nuestra América to the War Department in Washington, D.C.: "I compared the Rio Grande to the Nile in the facts that, like its African prototype, the fierce River of the North had its legends as weird and improbable to be found in the pages of . . . Herodotus" (592). Almost in the very next sentence, however, Bourke corrects his rather baroque tropic comparison of the Rio Grande to the Nile by writing that the border zones between the United States and Mexico can be better "compared to the Congo than [to] the Nile the moment that the degraded, turbulent, ignorant, and superstitious character of its populations comes under examination" (594). One of the first constructions of the U.S.-Mexico Borderlands of Nuestra América is therefore cast in a literalized episode of rhetorical and anthropological war between the two shifting Américas, built upon what Jacques Derrida called "the violence of the letter"[21] by one culture upon the other. Culture in this light is the nimbus perceived by one group when it comes into contact with and observes another one. It is the objectification of everything alien and weird and exotic about the contact group.

Everything about "The American Congo" from this point on draws attention to Bourke's nativist, modernist, and politically unconscious representations and to the gross imperial inequities in the dominance of Nuestra América and Africa by the United States and by Europe's cultures of imperialism. While Bourke painstakingly surveys the landscape, flora, fauna, and zoology, from "the unvarying succession of the mesquite," the "nopal," "the chappro prieto," to the fabulous "jabalin," the "rasping noise of the urraca," and the "clumsy looking armadillos" (596, 597, 598), he remains oblivious to his project of imperial gazing—surveying, collecting, organizing, and aestheticizing the landscape, flora, and fauna. His work as a travel writer–ethnographer of the U.S.-Mexico Borderlands enabled and informed the imperial cultures of the United States to see the Mexicans of the Borderlands as ill-bred *pelados,* as lawless ("The Rio Grande Mexican has never known what law is") [606]), and as culturally inferior fatalists who indiscriminately practice what he calls a "weird pharmacy" and therapeutics of *curanderismo* (folk-healing medicine).

Bourke's "The American Congo" gives us a commonsense understanding of the emergent cultures of U.S. imperialism. His mirroring of the African jungle and the *frontera* of Nuestra América all but effaces the local inhabitants of both continents. The geopolitical border-contact zone, moreover, is all too like the underdeveloped continent of Africa for Bourke. The site-specific Borderland of the Rio Grande Valley is at once a "Dark Belt" grounded in "chocolate soils," marked by the unspoken signs of melancholy, the *agachado* (stooping) *mestizo,*" white man's burden, and the nativist, modernist dialectics of barbarism and savagery. "The American Congo," seen in this light, founds and enacts a paradigmatic "American Studies travel tale": the construction of an ethnoracial and male soldier–culture collector in the wilderness *frontera,* surrounded by exotic animals, plants, and human cultural practices of everyday life. Moreover, we can see Bourke embodying the desire for what Richard Slotkin calls "regeneration through violence."[22] The captain of Fort Ringold, after all, is in South Texas specifically to hunt down border-crossing revolutionaries like the journalist Catarino Garza, who, as José Limón writes, "attempted to bring down the US-supported autocratic dictatorship of Mexico's Porfirio Díaz in 1891" (29)—coincidentally the very same year José Martí published his incisive critique of the Díaz regime, among others, in "Nuestra América." As Martí sharply put it, "some of the sleeping republics are still beneath the sleeping octopus." Others, he angrily criticized, are "forgetting that [Benito] Juárez went about in a carriage drawn by mules, hitched their carriages to the wind, their coachmen to soap bubbles."[23]

By exploring John Bourke's "The American Congo," I have been attempting to supplement my provisional 1991 reading of José Martí's "Nuestra América" (see note 27 below) by now bringing Bourke, Martí and, as I will do below, María Amparo Ruiz de Burton spatially together in order to begin reconceptualizing American Cultural Studies. Here I am fully in agreement with Gayatri Chakravorty Spivak's challenge that "transnational Cultural Studies must put [transactions between the Americas] into an international frame."[24] The difficulties of such a project are almost insurmountable. How can we begin displacing what Donald Pease calls the old "field-Imaginary"[25] of American cultural and literary studies? How are we to begin remapping a field that is clearly no longer mappable by any of the traditional force fields I have touched on above. "If we are to benefit," as Carolyn Porter suggests in her splendid review of the emergent inter-American studies, from "trying to construct a new field imaginary, it seems crucial to pursue the logic"[26] of this comparative model. In what follows, I will briefly respond to Spivak's and Porter's enormous challenges by remapping the topo-spatial and temporal dynamics of the Alta California of 1848, turning to María Amparo Ruiz de Burton's ethnoracial historical romance *The Squatter and the Don* (1885).

María Amparo Ruiz de Burton and the Alta California of 1848

If Bourke's "The American Congo" initiates an empirical and imperializing project of U.S.-Mexico border studies, María Amparo

Ruiz de Burton's *The Squatter and the Don* begins to offer readers a subaltern literature of the U.S.-Mexico Borderlands. Like Martí, Ruiz de Burton is fascinated with travel and with the arts of governing well in the face of what she calls "the many-headed hydra" of monopoly capitalism. Born and reared in Baja California, María Amparo was the granddaughter of José Manuel Ruiz, commander of Mexico's Northern Borderlands. Very much a child of the "Inter-American Enlightenment," María Amparo would distinguish herself from the majority of her fellow Californios, however, by radically critiquing the monopoly capitalists of the Gilded Age, who she claims were "the Napoléons of this land."[27]

When President Polk sent U.S. forces to secure Baja California in July 1847, fifteen-year-old Doña "Amparito," with her friends and relatives, met Henry S. Burton and, in the journalist Winifred Davidson's words, "sneered at the proudly confident lieutenant-colonel of the First Regiment of New York Volunteers as he landed his small force and proceeded upon his errand of taking possession."[28] Like many others, Henry Burton had come west as part of the conquering U.S. military force. With the outbreak of the U.S.-Mexican War, Burton arrived from West Point (where he had been an artillery instructor) to begin his command at Monterey, Alta California. From Monterey, Burton was ordered to Santa Barbara and then transferred to La Paz, the capital of Baja California. It was in La Paz that Burton, in Davidson's words, "made the acquaintance of the prettiest young lady on the peninsula" (5).

Davidson's *Los Angeles Times Sunday Magazine* feature article, "Enemy Lovers," is fascinating not only for its biographical information but also for its 1932 marriage of eros and ethnoracial politics. "They were natural enemies," Davidson writes, "Henry by birth, breeding, tastes, and general appearance typically American [*sic*]"; "Amparo—'Amparito' for short—being typically Spanish" (5). The article becomes even more interesting as Davidson, a member of the San Diego Historical Society, expands on the galvanizing inter-ethnoracial romance in La Paz: "[Amparito] fell naturally and unconsciously into the role as pupil, eager to learn of a newly found teacher" (5).

When the outgunned Mexican forces in La Paz finally attacked the U.S. army post, Burton offered Amparito and her mother, Doña Isabel, transport on the USS *Lexington* north to Monterey. After four years of delays and postponements, Henry and Amparito were married. Like a real-life sentimental novel, Davidson writes, "The Burtons' was a successful union. In the very bloom of her young womanhood, Mrs. Burton went east with her husband; and there, particularly in Chicago, her beauty and grace won her a distinguished place in the best society" (5). In terms anticipating Davidson's feature story, Hubert Howe Bancroft had memorialized the marriage in *California Pastoral* in the following summary: "Captain H. S. Burton fell in love with the charming Californian, . . . born in Loreto, and aged sixteen. She promised to marry him."[29] Deemed by the conservative Catholic forces as a "heretical" (Catholic and Protestant) marriage, other local commentators referred to the love affair as the union of "natural enemies" (Californio and Anglo-American), points out Davidson (5).

After the death of her husband (who had contracted malaria while fighting in the South during the Civil War), María Amparo returned to Alta California. There, in San Diego, as Rosaura Sánchez and Beatrice Pita write, she "wrote and produced a five-act comedy of *Don Quixote*. Several years later, in 1872, her first novel *Who Would Have Thought It?* was published by J. B. Lippincott in Philadelphia."[30]

But it is with the publication of *The Squatter and the Don* that Ruiz de Burton fully writes against the grain of dominant U.S. historiography and represents the cultures of U.S. imperialism not only as territorial and economic fact but also inevitably as a subject-constituting project. While there is lots of room for debating Ruiz de Burton's politics of location as a subaltern subject, I want to suggest that in *The Squatter and the Don* her narrator is particularly well suited to begin describing for us the diversity of the Alta California Borderlands as a dispersed space of cultural and political displacement.

Additionally, I want to highlight how María Amparo engages in the fantasy work of transnational identity. In her own represented history, diverse kinds of memory and countermemory, knowledge, and discourse intermingle in the novel. What does it mean for our Alta California romancer to name herself "C. Loyal"—Loyal Citizen in 1848 America? How does she play out the complex regime of knowledge, power, and desire that transform her into being intimate with mass mediated culture and political culture? Does she perform in a ritual of consensus how it feels to be a loyal citizen by constructing Alta California as a domestic land and a place where the "actual" and the "imaginary" meet?

Admittedly, if the narrator is not a subaltern subject in the traditional Gramscian subordinate-class descriptive sense, the narrator can be seen as what I call a subaltern supplementary subject. In so doing, I want to argue for the subversive potential of the narrative subject as representative of what Gayatri Chakravorty Spivak calls the "marginal instance," for "the radical intellectual . . . is . . . caught in a deliberate choice of subalternity, granting to the oppressed either that very expressive subjectivity which s/he criticizes or, instead, a total unrepresentability."[31]

As a writer who painstakingly traces the juridical, political, and erotic activities of the Californios and Euro-Americans in the America of 1848 and beyond, Ruiz de Burton functions as a subaltern mediator who is simultaneously an insurgent critic of monopoly capitalism and a radical critic of Anglocentric historiography. Thus envisaged, *The Squatter and the Don,* written only some forty years after the Treaty of Guadalupe Hidalgo, is the author's strategy to bring the United States' hegemonic historiography to a crisis.

In suggesting that Ruiz de Burton does more than write a "local color" sentimental romance, I have in mind not only her cultural critique of the Alta California of 1848, but also her engagement with the manifold cultural anxieties of the Gilded Age moment in California—both Baja and Alta California. For present purposes, these cultural criticisms and anxieties may be described through two far-reaching projects and events—one internal, local, and literary-historical; the other external, worldly, and transnational, what Michael Rogin calls "the American 1848."[32] Both events are thematized in Ruiz de Burton's *The Squatter and the Don.*

Any reading of Ruiz de Burton's narrative would necessarily have to begin by recalling that scores of Alta Californios had not only written and dictated their own versions of the monumental historical past, but also, as the literary historian Rosaura Sánchez emphasizes, "had recognized and been driven by a perceived duty to counter hegemonic versions of the Spanish and Mexican periods of California history."[33] Moreover, through the splendid literary-historical scholarship of Rosaura Sánchez (*Telling Identities;* 1995) and Genaro Padilla (*My History, Not Yours;* 1993) we are now in a better position to see why Alta Californios such as Mariano Guadalupe Vallejo, Juan Bautista Alvarado, Antonio Franco Coronel, Eulalia Pérez, and María Inocenta Pico de Avila, among others, had readily agreed to document their *testimonios* about the Alta California experience to Hubert Howe Bancroft, a book dealer, culture collector, and Gilded Age historian. As Bancroft put it in *Literary Industries,* he and his assistants, Thomas Savage and Enrique Cerruti, collected more than "two hundred volumes of original narratives from memory by as many early Californios, native and pioneer, written by themselves or taken down from their lips . . . the vivid narratives of their experiences."[34]

María Amparo Ruiz de Burton, I believe, strategically aligns herself with the mediated-testimonial Alta Californio narratives collected by Bancroft. In the process, notes Sánchez, she generates in her own ethnoracial romance something characteristic of the Alta Californio narratives themselves: "new discourses of ethnicity, new constructs of identity as a marginalized, disempowered, and dispossessed ethnic minority."[35] Ruiz de Burton additionally supplements these testimonial collectivities by grounding herself in the rhetoric and structures-of-feeling of sentimentality and romance. If José Martí had translated Ruiz de Burton's *The Squatter and the Don* into Spanish—as he translated and wrote about Helen Hunt Jackson's *Ramona* (1884)—he would surely have written that the Alta Californio romance by Ruiz de Burton was, like *Ramona,* "our novel," a model full of "fire and knowledge," and a "tear that speaks."[36]

Throughout *The Squatter and the Don* Ruiz de Burton herself suggests the "American 1848" by focusing on Don Mariano Alamar, a character based largely on Mariano Guadalupe Vallejo, who years earlier, in November 1875, had given Bancroft his own five-volume *testimonio,* titled *Recuerdos históricos y personales tocante a la Alta California.* (Parenthetically, it is important to note that Ruiz de Burton was the only Alta California woman Vallejo had included in his "Prologue" as participating in the Alta California counterhegemonic project: "erudita de la honra y tradiciones de su patria. . . . ") As Genaro Padilla suggests, the very title of Vallejo's *testimonio* "establishes a reading position for the [text]: the narrator serves history by telling the story of Mexican California."[37] Thus, early in the novel, in a poignant chapter titled "The Don's Views of the Treaty of Guadalupe Hidalgo," Ruiz de Burton displays her close familiarity with Vallejo's strategic subaltern project by representing—in language reminiscent of Vallejo's and other Alta Californios—Don Mariano Alamar's critical responses upon first reading the treaty: "I felt a bitter resentment for the treaty said that our rights would be the same as those enjoyed by all other American citizens. But, you see, Congress takes very good care not to enact retroactive laws for Americans; laws to take away from American citizens the property which they hold now, with a recognized legal title" (67).

If the Treaty of Guadalupe Hidalgo did not completely create Don Mariano Alamar's land troubles in Alta California, Ruiz de Burton goes to great pains and length to show how Senator William Gwin, the originator of the Land Law of 1851, was also partly culpable for the Don's troubles. As the historian Leonard Pitt notes, Gwin "proposed a fine-tooth combing of all the titles without exception, for he believed them to be largely inchoate and fraudulent."[38] Not surprising, much of Ruiz de Burton's cultural critique of the "American 1848" is a local attack on the three-man commission (the Board of Land Commissioners) that sat in San Francisco and adjudicated the proofs of all the titleholders who came before them. Ruiz de Burton's strategy throughout the narrative is therefore to thematize the Don's engagement with the multiple constructions of legal authority: "By those laws any man can come to my land . . . plant ten acres of grain, without any fence, and catch my cattle which, seeing the green grass without a fence, will go to eat it" (66).

It may be helpful to distinguish Ruiz de Burton's historiographic strategy from other mainline positions, for the squatters in her romance are not mythologized as noble "settlers" and pioneers struggling quaintly in the frontier wilderness. Eight years before Frederick Jackson Turner, in "The Significance of the Frontier in American History," was to turn Western American history into his own chronicle of westward expansion, where the struggle with the edges and boundaries of "civilization" turned European immigrants into Americans, Ruiz de Burton quarreled with the folk democracy of the Western American frontier by giving full play to the hegemonic land laws, the railroads, and the institutions of commerce and financial monopoly capitalism. Chapters with such titles as "Pre-empting under the Law," "The Sins of Our Legislators!" and "The Fashion of Justice in San Diego" both provide extensive explorations of what the historian Patricia Limerick calls "the legacy of conquest" (1987) and take radical stances toward traditional understandings of what the legal scholar Carl Gutiérrez-Jones calls "consensual"[39] relations. By reconstructing the relationship between power and consent, Ruiz de Burton, we might say, following Gutiérrez-Jones's arguments about postcontemporary Chicano/a narratives, offers us a "vision of institutional power as a dialectic between coercion and hegemony[—]where outright material limits fail, or where they prove inefficient" (4).

Whereas "other writers defuse political violence," Anne Goldman writes, "by relocating it in a domestic space defined in opposition to the social domain, Ruiz de Burton politicizes the familial circle, so that home becomes the locus to articulate a sustained description of conflict in a [inter]national scale."[40] If the past speaks to us about our present as well as to our future, it is not entirely inappropriate, I believe, to read Ruiz de Burton's romance as foregrounding what the Chicana poet Lorna Dee Cervantes reterritorializes in her "Poema para los californios muertos" (1981) as memories "of silver buckles and dark rebozos . . . / and the pure scent of rage."[41]

Dialectically, love plots and political plots and familial plottings overlap in *The Squatter and the Don.* As a historical romance, the narrative, like subaltern writing, is seemingly written in reverse: it points backward to what Northrop Frye calls "medieval quest-romances where victory meant the restored fertility, the union of male and female heroes."[42] A would-be race melodrama or, better still, a future-looking *telenovela* with soap opera passions, *The Squatter and the Don* cooks up libidinal desire (eroticism and heterosexual passion) as well as patriotism throughout its pages for sexual consummation (binationalist passions for George Washington's tomb and for the Mexican national celebrations of Cinco de Mayo and 16 de Septiembre). If Ruiz de Burton's romance does not take us into its lovers' bedroom, it does play on (to paraphrase Sommer) inciting its readers' desire to be there (34).

In her remarkable *Foundational Fictions,* Sommer redefines romance as "a cross between our contemporary use of the word as a love story" (5), a genre in which readers (particularly women) leave behind their everyday lives and live out their secret desires and passionate phantasmatics, and a "nineteenth-century use that distinguished the genre as more boldly allegorical than the novel" (5).

Nathaniel Hawthorne's self-designation as a "romance writer" in *The Scarlet Letter* captures this generic distinction more spatially in "The Custom House" chapter as "a neutral territory, somewhere between the real world and fairyland, where the Actual and the Imaginary meet, and each imbue itself with the nature of the other" (5).

It is precisely this generic crossing of *The Squatter and the Don* as a popular love story and as a liminal narrative located between "the Actual and the Imaginary" that I want to explore below. Like other star-crossed lovers (Romeo and Juliet, Hester and Dimmesdale), the lovers in Ruiz de Burton's narrative undergo various travails and tragedies. But the lovers also represent, as Sommer puts it, "an erotics of politics" (6), thematizing specific ethnoracial formations, economic interests, and future idealized states. Put differently, *The Squatter and the Don* does not keep the dialectics of difference (race, ethnicity, class, and gender) pure, but—like other romances—in Sommer's words, "marr[ies] hero to heroine across former barriers" (123).

By grounding us in a variety of heterosexual unions between Euro-American Protestants and Californio Roman Catholics, Ruiz de Burton's novel provides us with a figure for future utopian unions in the "American 1848." Erotics and politics thus join forces exhorting idealized Euro-Americans and Californios to be fruitful and create the new national symbolic. Seen in this light, eroticism and nationalism (as Sommer theorizes) are master tropes for each other in modern and modernizing romance narratives. They function as allegories of each other.

From the very start of *The Squatter and the Don,* when Mercedes Alarmar stumbles all over Clarence Darrell at her father's rancho, Ruiz de Burton treats us to page after page of "burning blushes" and galvanized lovers' "eyes emit[ting] rays full of attractive, earnest" (99) forces. Clarence and Mercedes's "love at first sight" encounter spirals in a zigzag motion, seemingly out of control for most of the novel, but Ruiz de Burton subtly reminds her readers that she is perfectly self-reflexive about her genre: at one point, Elvira tells her sister Mercedes not to despair of the many obstacles that the older generation of Darrells and Alamares put in front of them, for it turns out Clarence is not a nefarious squatter and thus their "romance is spoiled" (141). "It would have been so fine—like a dime novel—" Elvira continues telling sad Mercedes, "to have carried you off bodily by order of infuriated, cruel parents, and . . . marry you, at the point of a loaded revolver to a bald-headed millionaire. Your midnight shrieks would have made the blood of passers-by curdle! Then Clarence would have rushed in and stabbed the millionaire, and you, falling across his prostrate body said: 'Tramp or not I am thine' " (141). By alluding to the mawkish and popular U.S. Western dime novel, Ruiz de Burton understands how (if her romance's political critique is to be widely read) *The Squatter and the Don* has to be aimed rhetorically to an American reading public hungry for gratuitous ethnoracial adventure.

As we follow the lovers' on-and-off-again wedding engagement, the love story of *The Squatter and the Don* produces a libidinal surplus value, allowing us — as Sommer suggests — to overcome the cultural, political, and ethnoracial roadblocks placed in front of them. Thus, after Mercedes and Clarence agree to marry on September 16 (the calendar date Miguel Hidalgo initiated Mexico's liberation from Spanish imperialism in 1821), the battles between Darrell and Mariano over "*honor*" and shame instill in the young lovers a socially symbolic and transcendent purpose. These obstacles, moreover, heighten the lovers' desire for a new national symbolic, which in Ruiz de Burton's words is "capable of emancipat[ing] the white slaves of California" (372).

The Squatter and the Don is dense with the emplotments of romance and filled with the cultures of sentiment — but with a Californio difference: *vaquero* cattle drives across mountains and rivers of blood, violent confrontations over cattle-raising versus farming etiquette. For example, when Don Mariano Alamar proposes that the Euro-American squatters raise cattle rather than aspire to being Jeffersonian farmers, a white supremacist squatter proclaims, "I Ain't no Vaquero to go busquering [*sic*] around" (94), suggesting that Californio *vaquero* labor is ethnoracially inferior to him. Cattle and things *vaquero,* I want to suggest, are the historical romance's political unconscious. They surround the Euro-American squatters and the Californios, and they are a continual focus of both energy (shooting and protecting) and attention through much of the narrative. Ruiz de Burton even gives her readers an extraordinary epic cattle drive, led by Don Mariano and his sons across mountains to get the cattle to market. The sacrifice of the cattle's lives, the paralyzing of Victoriano, and the Don's attack of pneumonia in the mountains constitute the text's economic and moral base. The sacrifice of the cattle's lives and the metaphorical crippling of the Don and his sons, in other words, underwrites almost everything that follows in the romance. Interestingly, within the cultural form of sentimentality (indulging in excessive structures of feeling), Ruiz de Burton's cattle drive teaches us how men (both squatters and Alta Californios) are enmeshed into taking pain and, of course, within the context of our emergent gunfighter national imaginary, giving it.

Ruiz de Burton, of course, critically "signifies" on this male *vaquero* imaginary when, late in the novel, she sets up a modern Hegelian-like battle on horseback between the supposed master (William Darrell) and his ethnoracialized slave (Don Mariano). Accusing Don Mariano of "parad[ing] [Mercedes] [like a pretty young filly for sale] before [his] son, to get his money," William, "livid with rage," induces a fight to the death with Don Mariano by beating him with his horsewhip. "Damn you!" Darrell screams out. "Can't make you fight. Won't you be insulted, you coward?" The more sophisticated and able *vaqueros,* Victoriano and Everett, "dash their horses" between Darrell and Mariano, "the blow" falling on their backs (248). When Darrell again "lift[s] his whip to strike" Don Mariano, Gabriel lassos the master into submission. Darrell, the author writes, "instantaneously felt as if he had been struck by lightning. . . . His arms fell powerless by his side, and the iron hoop seemed to encircle him . . . [for] the coil of the reata held him in an iron grip, and he could not move" (249). If *The Squatter and the Don* juxtaposes the ritualized Roman Catholic "marriage lasso" (which ties the inter-ethnoracial couple Clarence and Mercedes) with that of Gabriel's dramatic "iron-hooped" homosocial "lassoing" of Darrell, this scene also alludes (through the images of the *reata* and rope) to the historical lynching of a Mexican woman, Josefa, who allegedly stabbed to death a man by the name of Cannon in the summer of 1851 in the Gold Rush town of Downieville.[43]

As a dizzying double-voiced text, the narrative also thematizes cultural conflicts over land, racial status, class positionings, and ethnicity as discursive excess—all within the framework of Californio-centered ideas of what the historian Ramón Gutiérrez calls in a related context "*honor y vergüenza.*"[44] In other words, if naming is at once the setting of a boundary and also the repeated inculcation of a norm, Ruiz de Burton's text is excessively overdetermined by shifty and shifting multiple interpellations. Don Mariano, for example, refers to the Alta Californios as "we, the Spaniards" (66) and, in more Latin American frames of reference, as "Spano-Americans" (67). At other times, however, the Don takes on a more local appellation, as in "I am afraid there is no help for us native Californians"; or, as when reading the Treaty of Guadalupe Hidalgo, he casts himself as a dispossessed child of Mexico. The Don's shifting interpellation as a "Spano-American" or as a native Alta Californio is both reiterated and, of course, challenged by various authorities reinforcing or contesting this apparently naturalized naming. Thus, throughout the narrative, white squatters refer to the Don as well as to other Alta Californios as "inferior" (222), "lazy" (222), and "ignorant" (222) or as *vaquero* "greasers" (249).

At times, the historical romance veers uncontrollably toward passionate Hispanophilia—perhaps an apology for the Spanish conquest of the Americas, as is clearly the case when Don Mariano sees the colonialist founding of the California missions and their defense as "not a foolish extravagance" (176). Most of the time, though, the narrative subaltern subject puts the U.S. government on trial (the novel ends with a stirring chapter, "Out with the Invader," calling for the nation's removal of the railroad monopolists Leland Stanford, Collis Huntington, Mark Hopkins, and Charles Crocker, who are "the Napoléons of this land" [365]).

Although *The Squatter and the Don* relies on the mythic time of medieval romance to tell its love story, Ruiz de Burton uses her own authorial time of 1846–84 to ground her readers in the rhetoric of U.S. imperial temporality (Rogin's "American 1848"). Rogin's brilliant reperiodizing makes a telling parallel between the year in which President Polk signed the Treaty of Guadalupe Hidalgo, securing Texas as U.S. territory, and the European revolutions of the same year. "There was a crisis over slavery from the Mexican peace treaty in 1848 through the passage of the 1850 compromise and the enforcement of its fugitive slave provisions in 1851," Rogin writes, and these same dates, 1848–51, also mark the triumph of the revolution in France and its final defeat by Napoléon III (103). If the promises of the French Revolution were destroyed by the class war that followed February with the June Days in Paris, the promises of the American Revolution were contradicted and negated by the U.S.-Mexican war (103). Rogin's "American 1848," in other words, creates a startling historical resonance between the

United States and France, and allows him to construct one of the most significant ideological readings of Melville's *Moby-Dick*.

What would happen, though, to Rogin's "American 1848" if it were to be "Alta Californiaized"? What might happen if we viewed 1848 not merely as an episode in the violent history of the Borderlands of Nuestra América? What if U.S. imperialism were displaced from its location in a national imaginary to its proto-imperial role in the Americas and the rest of the world? This is precisely what María Amparo Ruiz de Burton wishes to map out—spatially and hermeneutically—in *The Squatter and the Don.* For the U.S. war with Mexico not only casts the "shadow of the Civil War" but, more significantly, opens up the Americas to the Big Four and its government's incorporation of the geopolitical arena. The point isn't to make Martí's Cuba, Ruiz de Burton's Baja and Alta California the new protagonists, but rather to see paratactically one story in relation to another, to note the new politics of location and respatialize the cultures of displacement. *The Squatter and the Don* thus embodies the historical and ethnoracial conflict of the time, explores its sources, and manufactures through its erotics of politics conciliatory gestures with which to utopianly escape it.

But before the subaltern narrative subject begins to emplot her tale of romance (both as love story and as national allegory of land loss), she tells us in chapter one about the multiple roots of the New England Way farmer, William Darrell (Clarence's father), a recent immigrant to Alta California. Although William is presumably well-off in his "Alameda farm house," the historical romance begins with him sitting up late with his wife, Mary, attempting to persuade her of his grand design "to locate somewhere in a desirable neighborhood" (55). Relocate he does, building a "casa grande" on the rancho of Don Mariano Alamar, an Alta Californio cattle rancher. We then move from the immediate authorial present of 1884 to the American 1846–48, when William and his family "had crossed the plains . . . in [a] caravan of four wagons, followed by . . . five horses and choice Durham cows" (56).

Some twenty-four years later, William tells his wife that he is still poor in Alameda, and that all he has "earned is the name of squatter" (56). Believing that the Alamar rancho's land-grant title has been "rejected," and encouraged by crude nativists and fellow 1846 immigrant travelers (Gasbang, Miller, Hughes, and Matthews) that "San Diego is sure to have a railroad direct to the

Eastern States," William Darrell travels south to the Alta California Borderlands and occupies 640 acres belonging to Don Mariano Alamar. Unbeknownst to William, however, his son Clarence, on his mother Mary's wise counsel, purchases these lands from the Don, falls hopelessly in love with the Don's sixteen-year-old, blushing, Cinderella-like, and *vergüenza*-driven daughter, Mercedes, and by investing in the stock market and Arizona mines earns more than a million dollars.

By focusing on Clarence's mining interests, Ruiz de Burton subtly moves her romance out of the myth and symbol of Western American historiography which represented life in the American West, as one eminent New Western American historian put it, as "labor free."[45] Clarence's engagement with mining thus takes precedence over the Don's cattle and the squatter's farming enterprises. As Limerick emphasizes, "no industry had a greater impact on Western history than mining" (99). Mining, Ruiz de Burton's romance shows, not only brings thousands to Alta California but also places what Limerick calls "settlements of white people where none had been before" (99). As a result of Clarence's investments in mines, he not only becomes incredibly wealthy but, ironically, helps displace from cattle production the very Alta Californio family he will eventually marry into.

The remainder of the (trans)national romance becomes a tale of star-crossed lovers, particular regionalisms, economic interests, and competing cultural values—all wonderfully chronicled through the chronotope of what Ruiz de Burton lyrically calls "sentimental twilight" (169). The soap opera passions of the squatter's son and the Don's daughter for conjugal and sexual union spill over to Ruiz de Burton's sentimental readership in a move by the author to win what Doris Sommer, writing about romances in general, calls "partisan minds and hearts" (4). All of this makes for a coherent plot; the narrative moves through dizzying "reconciliations" and "amalgamations" as one reimagines the Alta Californio of 1848. When Clarence and Mercedes (after years of delays and fantastic tragedies) are eventually reunited and marry, Doña Josefa and her daughters can only weep "all the time," teaching us the mass-mediated lessons of what the most popular Univision *telenovela* of all time announced in its title: *Los ricos también lloran* [The Rich Also Cry].[46]

Put in more cultural-materialist terms, Ruiz de Burton's *The*

Squatter and the Don ends by dramatically illustrating the proleterianization (notwithstanding Mercedes Darrell) of most of the Alta Californios. This is allegorized for us in the scene where Gabriel Alamar falls from a roof in San Francisco—"carrying," the author writes, "his hod full of bricks up a steep ladder" (352). "In that hod of bricks," Ruiz de Burton continues, "not only his sad experience was represented, but *the entire history* of the native Californians . . . was epitomized. The natives . . . having lost all their property, must be hod carriers" (352; emphasis in original). Curiously enough, about a hundred years later, the Chicano novelist Alejandro Morales in his California chronicles *Reto en paraíso* (1983) and *The Brick People* (1988) would explore in magic-realist detail how Mexicano and Chicano/a "hod carriers" were largely instrumental(ized) in the construction of Anglocentric utopias, paradises that were also monuments of barbarism.[47]

Let us recall the scene I began with, in the chapter where Don Mariano reflects on his reading the Treaty of Guadalupe Hidalgo, especially the treaty's articles that promised to deal fairly with the Californio/Mexicano people who became U.S. residents by default:

> I remember, calmly said Don Mariano, that when I first read the text of the treaty of Guadalupe Hidalgo, I felt bitter resentment . . . against Mexico, the mother country, who abandoned us—her children—with so slight a provision of obligatory stipulations for protection. But afterwards, upon mature reflection, I saw that Mexico did as much as could have been reasonably expected at the time. . . . How could Mexico have foreseen that when scarcely half a dozen years should have eclipsed the conquerors would, "In Congress Assembled," passed laws which were to be retroactive upon the defenseless, conquered people, in order to despoil them? (66–67)

It is worth stressing that in Ruiz de Burton's hands, the U.S.-Mexico border contact zone outlined in the Treaty of Guadalupe Hidalgo is a signifier not simply of discrepant movements but, more significantly, of political struggles to define the local as a distinctive community in historical contexts of displacement.

If *The Squatter and the Don* puts the U.S. government on trial, it also challenges hegemonic U.S. history (cultural and literary) by bringing it to a crisis. Official U.S. history, as we know, did not exist as a profession until the late nineteenth century, as David Weber argues in *The Spanish Frontier in North America*, for only a few

Englishmen and Anglo Americans wrote histories about Californios, Tejanos, Nuevo Mexicanos, and so on. From their English forebears, Weber explains, Anglo-American historians "had inherited the view that Spaniards [and, later, Mexicans and Chicanos] were cruel, avaricious, treacherous, fanatical, superstitious, cowardly, corrupt . . . decadent, indolent and authoritarian, a unique complex of pejoratives."[48] Thus, as one of the squatters routinely says, "Those greasers aren't half crushed yet. We have to tame them like they do their mustangs, or shoot them" (73).

Throughout *The Squatter and the Don* Ruiz de Burton counters this intense Hispano/Californio-phobia by strategically representing the Don and his clan as subaltern ironists. As Don Mariano puts it, "The settlers want the lands of the lazy, the thriftless Spaniards. Such good-for-nothing, helpless wretches are not fit to own lordly tracts of land. It was wicked to tolerate the waste, the extravagance of the Mexican government. The American Government never could have been, or ever could be, guilty of such thing. But, behold! . . . [T]his far-seeing Congress . . . goes to work and gives to railroad companies millions upon millions of acres of land" (175). If theory, in the words of William Spanos, "has taught us . . . that the institutional production and consumption of literary texts constitutes one of the most important and powerful means of legitimating and reproducing the dominant cultural and sociopolitical formation,"[49] it is hardly surprising that Ruiz de Burton's romance received nary a review or an extended interpretative essay from the local San Francisco news media and literary establishment. The emergent U.S. literary national canon formation and its multiple institutional machinery (English departments, presses, journals, accrediting agencies, etc.) largely succeeded in burying Ruiz de Burton's ethnoracial romance, just as Hubert Howe Bancroft censored the *testimonios* of Alta California, thus paving the way for what Spanos calls the U.S. "*Pax Anthropologica*" (12).

Briefly, Ruiz de Burton shows how the interracial love between Mercedes Alamar and Clarence Darrell sets the limits of the national imagined community, and simultaneously deromanticizes the traditional plot of the U.S. Western romance. With unrelenting cultural critique and literary grace, the author shows how followers of the New England Way (Darrell and his cronies) set out systematically to exploit the Californios. Moreover, she moves beyond the binary opposition of white squatters versus Alta Californios by demonstrating how both the Alta Californios and the squatters are pawns ruled by Leland Stanford and the railroad robber barons. Late in the novel, Don Mariano visits Governor Stanford and tries to convince him of the benefits of allowing the Texas Pacific to come into San Diego. The author's portrait of Stanford's ruthlessness is nothing short of devastating (316): "You don't seem to think of business principles," Stanford tells Mariano Alamar. "You forget that in business every one is for himself. If it is to our interest to prevent the construction of the Texas Pacific, do you suppose we will stop to consider that we might inconvenience the San Diego people?" Leland Stanford's railroads function in this historical romance as a great symbol of national and capitalist unity. It is a complex and industrial phenomenon that transforms California into a state, and joins it to the U.S. nation and to América Latina by linking commerce and communication among widely dispersed local communities, both North and South. As the New Western American historian George Sánchez explains, "Railroads development in Mexico occurred almost entirely during the *Porfiriato*—the reign of dictator Porfirio Díaz from 1876 to 1910." Not surprisingly, "the same financial magnates that controlled the Southern Pacific, Santa Fe, and other railroads . . . became the major shareholders in Mexican railroads. Financiers J. Pierpoint Morgan, Jay Gould, Collis P. Huntington, Thomas Nickerson, and Thomas Scott dominated investment in railroads on both sides of [the U.S.-Mexico] border."[50] Díaz thus underdeveloped Mexico through the development of the monopoly capitalists. It is therefore understandable that the inter-American anti-imperialist José Martí, in his "Prologue to the Niagara Poem," could in a dialectically modernist, bombastic rhetoric write: "Una tempestad es más bella que una locomotora" [A tempest is more beautiful than a locomotive].[51]

The Squatter and the Don is an interpreter's guide to the late nineteenth century's emergence at the stage of capitalism social theorists call monopoly capitalism.[52] Virtually every scene near the ending of this romance is a socially symbolic commentary on Leland Stanford, Mark Hopkins, Collis Huntington, and Charles Crocker—the Big Four—who paid for the construction of the Central Pacific railroad, thereby consolidating a monopoly that controlled state and individual alike. Ruiz de Burton comes down hard on the Big Four for contributing to her Alta Californios' demise and for the ruination of communities like San Diego which was once a "fresh and rosy" town (171). According to the Don's son-in-law, San Diego's fall began when "the managers of the Central Pacific railroad" bribed congressman and committed "open fraud" (297). Stanford, Hopkins, Huntington, and Crocker are represented as wanting to "grab every cent that might be me made out of the traffic between the Atlantic and Pacific Oceans," hardly caring if "people are ruined" or if towns "are made desolate" in California (298).

Ruiz de Burton's critique of the monopolists has both a molecular and a molar logic driving it, for the destruction of the Alta Californios foretells the larger demise of the American nation-state and its citizens. In the conclusion, "Out with the Invader," Ruiz de Burton alludes to the idea that the monopolists were contributing to a new stage of capitalism. The Big Four's momentum knows no borders, for their monopoly is characterized by the development of mechanisms to absorb economic surpluses. Straightforwardly, the romance warns, like Martí's "Nuestra América," of the monopolists' power to "take the money earned [through plunder] to go and build railroads in Guatemala and British America" (370).

What is the point in juxtaposing Bourke's imperialist and Martí's and Ruiz de Burton's anti-imperialist chronicles of the Borderlands of Nuestra América? In the dispersed archives of "The American Congo," *The Squatter and the Don,* and "Nuestra América," we can track the almost forgotten histories of the cultures of U.S. imperialism. These narratives shed light on the late nineteenth-century world, on everyday life in advanced capitalism and how *letrado* and anti-*letrado* intellectuals write for and against the uneven development of modernization and modernity. These chronicles help us remember the world systems that catalyzed the rise of what Edward Said has described as the United States' truncated century of empire.[53] "The American Congo," "Nuestra América," and *The Squatter and the Don* maintain a clear awareness of the obstacles to "outing the invader," as Ruiz de Burton put it about a hundred years ago. Yet, these chronicles, too, express a great hope for an alternative chronicle of the Gilded Age—what José Martí proposed as a total rejection of the monumentalist European university for the American: "The European university must yield to the American. . . . The history of America, from the Incas to the present, must be taught letter perfect, even if the Argonauts of Greece are never taught."[54] These alternative archives are indispensable for perusing crucial political visions: worlds after "The American Congo" and American empire, after Contracts with America, after nativist Proposition 187s and so-called illegal aliens.

Notes

1 *Washington Post Book World* (May 14, 1995): 8.

2 My use of the term "frontier modernism" is meant to suggest in part the distinctive nature of modernism along the extended U.S.-Mexico border from, say, the 1840s to the 1940s. I am also using it to describe a set of issues as a chronological as well as a qualitative concept. Of relevance here are the following works: Jürgen Habermas, *The Philosophical Discourse of Modernity: Twelve Lectures,* trans. Frederick G. Lawrence (Cambridge: MIT Press, 1987); Zygmunt Bauman, *Modernity and the Holocaust* (Ithaca: Cornell University Press, 1989); Julio Ramos, *Desencuentros de la modernidad en América Latina: Literatura y política en el siglo XIX* (Mexico City: Fondo de Cultura Económica, 1989); Roberto Fernández Retamar, *"Nuestra América": Cien años y otros acercamientos a Martí* (Havana: Editorial Si-Mar, 1995); and Fernando Coronil, *The Magical State: Nature, Money, and Modernity in Venezuela* (Chicago: University of Chicago Press, 1997).

3 See Rubén Martínez's *The Other Side: Fault Lines, Guerrilla Saints, and the True Heart of Rock'n'Roll* (New York: Verso, 1992), p. 1.

4 Américo Paredes, *Folklore and Culture on the Texas-Mexican Border* (Austin: CMAS and University of Texas Press, 1993), p. 84.

5 In contrast to my dialogical views of the varied music of America, see Ronald Reagan's second inaugural address, delivered on January 21, 1985. Using Frederick Jackson Turner's frontier rhetoric, Reagan declared that "a settler pushes west and sings a song, and the song echoes out forever and fulfills the unknowing air. It is the American sound. It is hopeful, big-hearted, idealistic, daring, decent and fair. That's our heritage, that's our song. We still sing it." See *Public Papers of the Presidents: Ronald Reagan, 1985* (Washington, D.C.: Government Printing Office, 1985), vol. 1, p. 58.

6 For more on phantasmatic identification, see Judith Butler's *Bodies That Matter: On the Discursive Limits of "Sex"* (New York: Routledge, 1993), esp. pp. 93–120.

7 José David Saldívar, "Chicano Border Narratives as Cultural Critique," in *Criticism in the Borderlands: Studies in Chicano Literature,*

Culture, and Ideology, ed. Héctor Calderón and José David Saldívar (Durham: Duke University Press, 1991), pp. 167–80.

8 Amy Kaplan, "Left Alone with America: The Absence of Empire in the Study of American Culture," in *Cultures of U.S. Imperialism,* ed. Donald Pease and Amy Kaplan (Durham: Duke University Press, 1993), p. 11.

9 My discussion here makes use of Joseph C. Porter's *Paper Medicine: John Gregory Bourke and His American West* (Norman: University of Oklahoma Press, 1986) and José E. Limón's *Dancing with the Devil: Society and Cultural Poetics in Mexican-American South Texas* (Madison: University of Wisconsin Press, 1994).

10 See José Martí's "Our America," in *The Heath Anthology of American Literature,* ed. Paul Lauter (Lexington, Mass.: D. C. Heath & Co., 1994), pp. 821–27. My present view of Martí as an "anti-*letrado*" intellectual is much indebted to Julio Ramos's superb *Desencuentros de la modernidad en América Latina: Literatura y política en el siglo XIX* (Mexico City: Fondo de Cultura Económica, 1989); see esp. chap. 9, "Nuestra América: Arte del buen gobierno," pp. 229–43.

11 Porter, *Paper Medicine,* p. 4. All subsequent references to this book will be cited parenthetically in the text.

12 Renato Rosaldo, *Culture and Truth: The Remaking of Social Analysis* (Boston: Beacon Press, 1989), p. 69.

13 Between 1886 and 1891, Bourke wrote the following books: *On the Border with Crook* (New York: Charles Scribner's Sons, 1891); *Scatologic Rites of All Nations: A Dissertation upon the Employment of Excretious Remedial Agents in Religion, Therapeutics, Divination, Witchcraft, Love Philters, etc., in All Parts of the Globe* (Washington, D.C.: W. H. Lowermilk, 1891); and *The Medicine Men of the Apache: Ninth Annual Report of the Bureau of Ethnology, 1887–1888* (Washington, D.C.: Government Printing Office, 1892).

14 Limón, *Dancing with the Devil,* p. 4. All subsequent references to this book will be cited parenthetically in the text.

15 John Gregory Bourke, "Popular Medicine, Customs, and Superstitions of the Rio Grande," *Journal of American Folk-lore* 7 (April–June 1894): 119.

16 See Kaplan, "Left Alone with America," pp. 3–21.

17 John Gregory Bourke, "The American Congo," *Scribner's Magazine* 15 (May 1894): 590–610. All subsequent references to this essay will be cited parenthetically in the text.

18 See Nicholas Thomas's *Colonialism's Culture: Anthropology, Travel, and Government* (Princeton: Princeton University Press, 1994), p. 89.

All subsequent references to this book will be cited parenthetically in the text.

19 Alejo Carpentier, "The (American) Baroque and the Marvelous Real," in *Magical Realism: Theory, History, Community,* ed. Wendy Faris and Lois P. Zamora (Durham: Duke University Press, 1995), pp. 89–108.

20 See Paul Gilroy's *The Black Atlantic: Modernity and Double Consciousness* (Cambridge: Harvard University Press, 1993) and Edouard Glissant's *Caribbean Discourses: Selected Essays,* trans. and intro. J. Michael Dash (Charlottesville: University Press of Virginia, 1992).

21 Jacques Derrida, *Of Grammatology,* trans. Gayatri Chakravorty Spivak (Baltimore: Johns Hopkins University Press, 1976), p. 107.

22 Richard Slotkin, *Regeneration through Violence: The Mythology of the American Frontier, 1600–1860* (Middletown, Conn.: Wesleyan University Press, 1973). Slotkin explores how warfare on the colonial frontier was transformed into a body of narrative lore, which was in turn codified in myth and symbol by mainline U.S. writers.

23 Martí, "Our America," p. 826.

24 Gayatri Chakravorty Spivak, *Outside in the Teaching Machine* (New York: Routledge, 1993), p. 262.

25 See Donald Pease's "New Americanists: Revisionist Interventions into the Canon," in a special issue of *boundary 2* 17 (Spring 1990): 1–37. "By the term field-Imaginary," Pease claims, "I mean to designate a location for the disciplinary unconscious. . . . Here abides the field's fundamental syntax—its tacit assumptions, convictions, primal words, and the charged relations binding them together" (pp. 11–12).

26 Carolyn Porter, "What We Know That We Don't Know," *American Literary History* 2, no. 4 (1994): 507.

27 María Amparo Ruiz de Burton, *The Squatter and the Don,* ed. Rosaura Sánchez and Beatrice Pita (Houston: Arte Público Press, 1992, orig. 1885), p. 365. All subsequent references to this book will be cited parenthetically in the text.

28 Winifred Davidson, "Enemy Lovers," *Los Angeles Times Sunday Magazine* (October 16, 1932): 5. All subsequent references to this article will be cited parenthetically in the text.

29 Hubert Howe Bancroft, *California Pastoral* (San Francisco: The History Company, 1888), pp. 330–31.

30 See Rosaura Sánchez and Beatrice Pita's introduction to María Amparo Ruiz de Burton, *The Squatter and the Don,* p. 11.

31 Gayatri Chakravorty Spivak, "Subaltern Studies: Deconstructing Historiography," in *Selected Subaltern Studies,* ed. Ranajit Guha and Gayatri Chakravorty Spivak (New York: Oxford University Press, 1988), p. 17.

32 Michael Paul Rogin, *Subversive Genealogy: The Politics and Art of Herman Melville* (New York: Knopf, 1983). All subsequent references to this book will be cited parenthetically in the text.

33 Rosaura Sánchez, "Nineteenth-Century Californio Narratives: The Hubert H. Bancroft Collection," in *Recovering the U.S. Hispanic Literary Heritage,* ed. Ramón Gutiérrez and Genaro Padilla (Houston: Arte Público Press, 1993), p. 279.

34 Hubert Howe Bancroft, *Literary Industries* (San Francisco: The History Company, 1890), p. 282.

35 Rosaura Sánchez, *Telling Identities: The Californio Testimonio* (Minneapolis: University of Minnesota Press, 1995), p. xiii.

36 See José Martí's introduction to *Ramona: Novela americana,* in Martí, *Obras completas* (Havana: Editorial Nacional de Cuba, 1965), vol. 24, pp. 203–5.

37 Genaro Padilla, *My History, Not Yours: The Formation of Mexican American Autobiography* (Madison: University of Wisconsin Press, 1993), p. 85.

38 Leonard Pitt, *The Decline of the Californios: A Social History of the Spanish-Speaking Californians, 1846–1890* (Berkeley: University of California Press, 1966), p. 85.

39 Carl Gutiérrez-Jones, *Rethinking the Borderlands: Between Chicano Culture and Legal Discourse* (Berkeley: University of California Press, 1995), p. 4. Subsequent references to this book will be cited parenthetically in the text.

40 Anne E. Goldman, "Review of Ruiz de Burton's *The Squatter and the Don,*" *MELUS* 9 (Fall 1994): 130.

41 Lorna Dee Cervantes, "Poema para los californios muertos," in Cervantes, *Emplumada* (Pittsburgh: University of Pittsburgh Press, 1981), pp. 42–43.

42 Doris Sommer, *Foundational Fictions: The National Romances of Latin America* (Berkeley: University of California Press, 1991), p. 49. All subsequent references to this book will be cited parenthetically in the text.

43 In an unpublished essay, "I Ain't No Vaquero: Reconfiguring Whiteness in *The Squatter and the Don,*" David Luis Brown splendidly reads the ritualized marriage lasso in the romance against Gabriel's lassoing of William Darrell. Ruiz de Burton, he argues, "counterposes

the reata of violent conflict with the feminizing alternative, the double loop of marital unions" (p. 6). For an analysis of the history of the lynching of Josefa, the only woman ever lynched in California, see William B. Secrest's *Juanita* (Fresno, Calif.: Saga-West Publishing Co., 1967).

44 Ramón Gutiérrez, *When Jesus Came, the Corn Mothers Went Away: Marriage, Sexuality, and Power in New Mexico, 1500–1846* (Stanford: Stanford University Press, 1991). According to Gutiérrez, "*honor* was strictly a male attribute while shame (*vergüenza*) was intrinsic to females. Infractions of behavioral norms by males were dishonoring, in females they were a sign of shamelessness" (p. 209). Ruiz de Burton's romance thematizes the Don's *honor* and his daughter Mercedes's *vergüenza* almost ad nauseam.

45 Patricia Nelson Limerick, *The Legacy of Conquest: The Unbroken Past of the American West* (New York: W. W. Norton & Co., 1987), p. 99. All subsequent references to this book will be cited parenthetically in the text.

46 *Los ricos también lloran,* originally aired on Univision in 1989, is now televised in reruns all over the world, from Brazil to Russia.

47 Alejandro Morales, *Reto en el paraíso* (Ypsilanti, Mich.: Bilingual Press/Editorial Bilingüe, 1983) and *The Brick People* (Houston: Arte Público Press, 1988). For an incisive reading of Morales's fiction, see Gutiérrez-Jones, *Rethinking the Borderlands,* pp. 80–102.

48 David J. Weber, *The Spanish Frontier in North America* (New Haven: Yale University Press, 1992), p. 336.

49 William V. Spanos, *The Errant Art of Moby-Dick: The Canon, the Cold War, and the Struggle for American Studies* (Durham: Duke University Press, 1995), p. 12. All subsequent references to this book will be cited parenthetically in the text.

50 George J. Sánchez, *Becoming Mexican American: Ethnicity, Culture and Identity in Chicano Los Angeles, 1900–1945* (New York: Oxford University Press, 1993), p. 22.

51 José Martí, "Prólogo al Poema del Niágara," in Martí, *Obra literaria* (Caracas: Biblioteca Ayacucho, 1978), p. 214.

52 See Keith Cowling's *Monopoly Capitalism* (London: Macmillan, 1982) and Paul Baran and Paul Sweezy's *Monopoly Capitalism* (New York: Monthly Review Press, 1966).

53 Edward W. Said, *Culture and Imperialism* (New York: Knopf, 1993).

54 Martí, "Our America," p. 823.

III.

Martí's Prescriptive Map of Our America

Enrico Mario Santí

"Our America," the Gilded Age, and the Crisis of Latinamericanism

for Carlos Ripoll

I begin this essay by considering the following passage from Martí's May 3, 1890, chronicle of the Washington Pan-American Conference. By the time Martí writes and publishes his piece in *La Nación,* the eight-month conference is effectively over and the delegates from Latin America are each returning to their respective countries. But Martí chronicles what appears to have been their last gathering in New York City, a celebration of the Latin American defeat of the U.S. proposal of a continental customs agreement and a parallel arbitration agency. During their last New York bash, the gathered delegates toasted to the health of Manuel Quintana, a young and from all signs aggressive Argentine delegate, whom the delegates proceeded to hail with no less than the epic epithet of "Bayardo de la conferencia" for his heroic, eloquent defense of the so-called Latin American position during the proceedings. Martí quotes Quintana's response to the toast of his fellow delegates: "¡Para mi patria acepto estos cariños! ¡Nada más que un pueblo somos todos nosotros en América!" [I accept this kindness on behalf of my country! We in America are but one single people!] To which Martí, in turn, adds in his chronicle:

> Un americano sin patria, hijo infeliz de una tierra que no ha sabido aún inspirar compasión a las repúblicas de que es centinela natural; y parte indispensable, veía, acaso con lágrimas, aquel arrebato de nobleza. Las repúblicas, compadecidas, se volvieron al rincón del hombre infeliz, y brindaron por el americano sin patria. Lo que tomaron unos a piedad y otros a profecía (OC, 6:106–11).[1] [One American without a country, unfortunate son of a land that has not yet learned to inspire the compassion of republics of which it is its natural sentinel as well as an indispensable component, was contemplating, perhaps teary-eyed, that rapture of nobility. The republics, taking pity, turned to the unfortunate man's corner, and they all toasted to the American without a country. What some of them saw as pity, others saw as prophecy.]

My remarks are based on the idea that sustains this particular passage from Martí's chronicle, and they are also circumscribed by it. I am interested in documenting and analyzing Martí's, and by extension Cuba's, isolation within the "rapture of nobility" of Pan-Americanism or, as I shall call it, Latinamericanism: the pious fiction of continental unity that both motivated the U.S. invitation to the 1889–90 conference and justified the Latin American delegates' defeat of U.S. proposals within it. While in the one case Latinamericanism is the pious fiction that serves the United States to keep at bay European interests, in the other case it is the fiction that keeps at bay U.S. interests against those of postindependence Latin America.[2]

Martí's critique of imperialism, as witnessed by the conference "'Our America' and the Gilded Age: José Martí's Chronicles of Imperial Critique," (University of California, Irvine, January 27–28, 1995) has been the one theme most exhausted by the critical and ideological canon—beginning perhaps with Julio Antonio Mella and continuing up to Fidel Castro. But little if any attention has been paid to Martí's parallel critique, bordering on sheer anxiety, of the exclusion of Cuban interests by her so-called sister republics. That Martí's critique of Latinamericanism has been overlooked should not surprise us perhaps. Thanks in part to the rhetorical uses to which Martí's own Latinamericanist position has been put since his death—the defense of "our America"—all his other concerns on the subject have been put aside.

Even more decisive is the fact that Martí's own repeated critical statements, in the passage above and elsewhere, are dispersed, oblique, and ultimately ambivalent: they sound more like jabs at a good friend than stabs at an enemy. And while Martí's obliqueness regarding this critique may have been justified by political pressures and by his own strategic concerns for the imminent struggle for Cuban independence, our own historical distance dictates, or at least should dictate, a different judgment altogether. Least justified of all perhaps is the blindness, moral and otherwise, of the Martí canon regarding this particular subject—although this, too, can be explained by the pervasive effects of Latinamericanism as discourse and ideology. It matters little, finally, that historical reality might show that Martí was indeed not counted among the Latin American delegates during their last celebration. From Martí's perspective at least, Cuba was, as he himself says, "an indispensable component" of "our America," and his sense of exclusion is what urged him to speak in those very terms. And yet, a close reading of the historical context out of which Martí wrote the essay "Nuestra América" demonstrates that his rhetoric is tainted by a sharp ambivalence before the entire project of Latinamericanism, to the point that it ends up questioning the very "rapture of nobility" that sustains it. To paraphrase the well-known essay by Angel Augier, it could be said that Martí propounds an "anti-Latinamericanist thesis within the very cradle of Pan-Americanism." Thus my contention: the critique of Latinamericanism not only constitutes the rhetoric of "our America" but also helps explain Martí's motivation in writing the famous essay of the same name.[3]

1

As we begin this particular reading, we need to recall first the issue that for Martí lurks in the background of the Pan-American Conference: namely, the threat of annexation of Cuba by the United States. Martí's chronicles allude at times to the issue, but his correspondence with Gonzalo de Quesada, who was the assistant to Roque Sáenz Peña, the chief Argentine delegate, shows fully his anxiety over it. The anxiety came from three immediate sources. First, there was the rumor of visits at the time to both Cuba and Madrid by State Department officers exploring the purchase of Cuba from Spain; then there was the actual proposal, initiated by the Cuban annexationist José Ignacio Rodríguez, to have the U.S. government purchase Cuba's independence, a proposal that Martí viewed with open suspicion; and, finally, news had reached Martí that a chronicle datelined Washington and bearing his own initials had been spuriously published in *La Discusión,* a Havana newspaper, describing Secretary of State James G. Blaine's commitment to the idea of annexation. It is clear that Martí viewed these events as a sinister conspiracy that was meant to coincide with the Pan-American Conference. Yet precisely because of that coincidence, he also saw fit to counter such a proposal by attempting to introduce the issue of Cuban independence in the conference proceedings while support from the Latin American delegates, the "sister republics," was still a possibility. Martí himself was not a delegate to the conference (even though he nominally did hold the diplomatic post of Uruguayan consul in New York), and so he acted indirectly by writing Gonzalo de Quesada on October 29, 1889:

Lo que del Congreso se había de obtener era, pues, una recomendación que llevase aparejado el conocimiento de nuestro derecho a la independencia y de nuestra capacidad para ella, de parte del gobierno norteamericano. . . . De quien necesitamos saber es de los Estados Unidos, que está a nuestra puerta como un enigma, por lo menos. Y un pueblo en la angustia del nuestro necesita despejar el enigma (OC, 1:249). [What we ought to obtain from the Conference is, then, a recommendation that would join an acknowledgment of our right to independence and the U.S. government's acknowledgment of our capacity for it. . . . About whom we need to know is the United States, which is at our door like a question mark, at least.]

The following month, at the further news of talk among the Latin American delegates of the U.S. annexation of Cuba, he writes Gonzalo de Quesada more pointedly:

Para todo hay ciegos, y cada empleo tiene en el mundo su hombre. Pero el Sr. Sáenz Peña sabe pensar por sí y es de tierra independiente y decorosa. El verá y sabrá lo que hace. Trabájele bien, que este noviciado le va a ser a Ud. muy provechoso, y de utilidad acaso decisiva (OC, 6:121). [There are blind men for everything, and each job has his own man. But Sáenz Peña knows how to think for himself, and he comes from an independent and proud land. He will see and will know what to do. Work on him well, for this novitiate will be very good for you and will be decidedly useful.]

That Martí was hoping for a conference resolution on the Cuban question along the lines outlined in his October letter and introduced by a Latin American delegation (preferably Argentina, arguably the most powerful among the Latins) is therefore clear from these statements. No such resolution ever came, however, and already in the next letter to Gonzalo de Quesada, dated November 16, Martí expresses his disillusionment:

Son algunos los vendidos, y muchos más los venales; pero de un bufido de honor puede echarse atrás a los que, por hábitos de rebaño, o el apetito de las lentejas, se salen de las filas en cuanto oyen el látigo que los convoca o el plato puesto (OC, 6:122). [A few have sold out, and many are corrupt; but a single blow of honor will push back those who, acting like part of a herd or hungry for a plate of beans, break lines as soon as the whip summons them or hear that dinner is served.]

The same day that Martí wrote this he also wrote to Serafín Bello, another Cuban exile then living in Key West, about such annexationist designs. Then he added:

En la soledad en que me veo — porque cuál más cuál menos espero lo que abomino — lo que he de impedir, he de implorar, estoy implorando, pongo al servicio de mi patria; en el silencio todo el crédito que he podido darle dando en esas tierras hermanas mi nombre (OC, 1:254). [In the loneliness in which I see myself — because sooner or later I await what I despise — I shall prevent it, I shall implore, I am imploring, I place at the service of my silent country all the credit to my name that I can give those sister lands.]

Finally, in another letter to Sáenz Peña, on April 10, 1990, as the conference was closing, Martí announced a future trip to Washington in order to give him "una súplica cauta y muy privada por mi patria" (OC, 7:398) [a careful and very private request on behalf of my country].

At the heart of Martí's position, then, was a burning conflict: the America to which he was so devoted had done or would do nothing to assist the one sister land, Cuba, that he loved most. Martí may have considered it politically wise to preserve and even exacerbate his Latinamericanist allegiances, but his resignation to this circumstance does not eliminate or even lessen the moral gravity of the conflict. Indeed, the conflict, which goes unstated by Martí but is, or should be, nevertheless evident to his readers, is what determines his aggressive Latinamericanism as well as the frequent remarks that serve to temper it, or that at least show his own reservations toward its ideology. Proof of this appears in Martí's well-known speech on José María Heredia, the Cuban romantic poet, which Martí delivered in New York City in the same month of November 1889, at what was perhaps his first face-to-face encounter with the Latin American delegates to the Pan-American Conference. In the middle of that speech, as Martí is describing Heredia's life in Mexico, he chooses to allude to the Congress of American Republics, which Simón Bolívar had gathered in Panama in 1826 and at which it was decided that the Latin American independence movement could not reach the island of Cuba:

Por su patria había querido él [Heredia], y por la patria mayor de nuestra América, que las repúblicas libres echaran los brazos al único pueblo de la familia emancipada que besaba aún los pies del dueño enfurecido. ¡Vaya, decía, la América libre a rescatar la isla que la naturaleza le puso de pórtico y guarda! . . . Ya ponía Bolívar el pie en el estribo cuando un hombre que hablaba inglés y que venía del Norte con papeles de gobierno, le asió el caballo de la brida, y le habló así: "Yo soy libre, tú eres libre; pero ese pueblo que ha de ser mío, porque lo quiero para mí, no puede ser libre" (OC, 5:136). [On behalf of his country, and of his greater country Our America, (Heredia) had wanted the free republics to lend their arms to the only people of the emancipated family that still kissed the feet of the angry owner. He said: let free America rescue the island that Nature gave it as gate and guardian. . . . Bolívar himself was set to go when an English-speaking man, who came from the North with government papers, grabbed his horse by the bridle and said: "I am free and so are you; but that people which must be mine, because I want it, cannot be free.]

It would not be an exaggeration to describe Martí's labors during this time as walking a tightrope between praise for Our America along with blame of U.S. imperialism, on the one hand, and a critique of Latinamericanism, on the other. In this sense, Bolívar in this passage is no less to blame for the continued enslavement of Cuba as the "English-speaking man" who persuades him to give up the fight. But this proposition can only be gathered by implication, given the delicate balance between political expediency and historical conscience that Martí was forced to preserve in order to facilitate an eventual independence of Cuba from Spain by means of an equally possible (though ultimately unreal) helping hand from the rest of Latin America.

What in the Heredia speech is a historical jab at the delegates regarding their lack of action at the Pan-American Conference with respect to the Cuba issue, in "Madre América" (the other major speech that Martí, the following month, gave before the same delegates) will become a vindication of the Latin American experience. In it, Martí not only justifies the delegates in their resistance to U.S. proposals during the conference; he also appeals to a continental sympathy for his own status as an exile, making repeated references, particularly toward the end of the speech, to the life of Latin American immigrants in the United States. And yet, in September 1890, once the conference is over and the delegates are gone, in an essay on the Cuban poet Francisco Sellén, Martí will describe the poet in the following ambivalent terms: "Hijo de Cuba, a cuyos héroes novicios dió tiempo para errar la indiferencia de un continente sordo" (OC, 5:187) [Son of Cuba, to whose novel heroes he gave time in order to correct the indifference of a deaf continent].

The passage from the May 3, 1890, chronicle with which I began this essay, where Martí describes the toast of the Latin American republics to Manuel Quintana and from which he found himself excluded, finds its fullest meaning (perhaps even as its source) in another significant passage, not so much from Martí but from Alexis de Tocqueville's *Democracy in America.* "When ranks are almost equal among a people," writes Tocqueville in part 3, chapter 1 of his liberal classic, then

> as all men think and feel in nearly the same manner, each instantaneously can judge the feelings of all the others; he just casts a glance at himself and that is enough. So there is no misery that he cannot readily understand, and a secret instinct tell him its extent. It makes no difference if friends or enemies are in question; his imagination at once puts him in their place. Something of personal feeling is mingled with his pity and that makes him suffer himself when another body is torn.[4]

It is precisely because Martí viewed himself as a paradoxical "American without a country," suspended midway between the factual pity of his peers and the necessity of historical prophecy, that he sought refuge in "our America": "tendiendo la mano, sin que se nos canse de estar tendida a los mismos que nos niegan la suya" (OC, 4:247) [holding out our hand, without its getting tired of being held out to the same ones who deny us theirs], he wrote on October 10, 1890, barely five months after the conference was over and all the delegates had gone home. All, of course, except Martí himself.

2

One searches in vain, in the reams of scholarship devoted to José Martí over the years, for any discussion of his ambivalence toward so-called Latin America. The most prevalent view is rather the opposite, to the extreme that the portrait of Martí as a militant Latinamericanist — in the sense of an ideologist of Latin American cultural and political union — erases any complexity from his ideology or personality. The monographs by Florencia Peñate and Graciella Chailloux, devoted respectively to studies of the First Pan-American Conference and Martí's economic anti-imperialism, to take two recent examples, make no mention of ambivalent comments such as the ones I have highlighted. Their omission could perhaps be excused given their thematic and methodological limits.[5] But what is one to say of such compendious studies as Ricaurte Soler's *Idea y cuestión nacional latinoamericanas* or perhaps Jean Lamore's *José Martí et l'Amérique?*[6] The former sticks closely to a reading of Martí's anti-imperialist canon but chooses not to problematize his views on Latin America. The case of the latter, however, is particularly pathetic given its stated subject. Originally a multivolume thesis at the University of Toulouse and later a book, nowhere does it so much as gloss over Martí's double-edged view of his cultural peers; instead, it invests heavily in Martí's portrait as a blind if faithful Latinamericanist. We can perhaps wonder endlessly at such critical blindness, but the reason for it is simple: over the years Martí, hero and martyr on behalf of Cuban independence that he was, has been co-opted by the ideology of Latinamericanism in order to justify petty regional-economic interests, particularly before U.S. administrations. And this co-option has taken place, tragically and unfortunately, in ways parallel to those in which successive Cuban political regimes, beginning with Tomás Estrada Palma and up to and including the present government, have enlisted the image of Martí in order to justify themselves.[7]

It is with this background in mind that I believe we should revisit one important document of the Martí canon: the essay "Nuestra América." While there is no arguing that this essay is an extension of Martí's defense of the Latin American experience, as opposed to its North American versions, it should also be clear that "Nuestra América" condemns the adulteration of that experience and places blame squarely on the shoulders of Latin Americans themselves, whose laziness at knowing their own culture—what Martí himself calls "el desdén inicuo e impolítico de la raza aborigen" (OC, 6:6) [the iniquitous and impolitic disdain of aboriginal culture]—was exceeded only by their political opportunism. From the very title the essay is addressed to Latin Americans, among whom Martí includes himself, and no amount of negative reference to European and U.S. cultures—what Martí elsewhere called "la América europea"—can replace its object. It was precisely in "Nuestra América" that Martí gave vent to his pent-up critique of neocolonial behavior, which must have been evident to him in the actions of the Latin American delegates to the previous year's conference, a behavior particularly evident in their lack of solidarity with the cause of Cuban independence, foremost in Martí's mind.

It is particularly deplorable that most ideological readings of "Nuestra América," most of which have taken place during the past thirty or so years, choose to frame the text as Martí's belated response to U.S. actions at the First Pan-American Conference, rather than as a reformist critique of mores that were prevalent then among Latin Americans, particularly among its so-called cultured classes.[8] Thus Cintio Vitier, in what could be called the canonical framing of "Nuestra América"—namely, his presentation to the oversize critical edition done by the Centro de Estudios Martianos jointly with Casa de las Américas in 1992—states that the problems Martí addresses in his text

> llegan hasta nuestros días, dramáticamente agravados, en el contexto de lo que hoy llamamos Tercer Mundo, por la creciente codicia, prepotencia y agresividad del imperialismo norteamericano. [come all the way to our own times, dramatically worsened, in the context of what today we call the Third World because of the growing greed, power, and aggression of American imperialism.][9]

Were it not for the fact that Vitier fails to mention anything else about the contents of "Nuestra América"—not even the critique of colonial alienation to which Martí devotes the greater part of his essay—it would not be difficult to agree with at least part of that statement. On the other hand, ignoring that important aspect of Martí's essay simply reduces it to an anti-imperialist pamphlet that plays into the hands of Latinamericanism—one more turn of the screw of imperialism. And so, it would not be farfetched to see "Nuestra América" as Martí's defiant assertion of a Latin American cultural identity that those delegates, representatives of free Latin American countries, resisted while he, "American without a country," was eager to embrace it.

This particular corrective of the canonical representation of the contents of "Nuestra América" is borne out in part by another well-known document of the times, the preface to *Versos sencillos*, where Martí reveals that the Pan-American Conference took a toll on his health:

> y la agonía en que viví, hasta que pude confirmar la cautela y el brío de nuestros pueblos; y el horror y vergüenza en que me tuvo el temor legítimo

que pudiéramos los cubanos, con manos parricidas, ayudar al plan insensato de apartar a Cuba, para bien único de su amo disimulado, de la patria que la reclama y en ella se completa" (OC, 16:142). [the agony in which I lived, until I was able to confirm the caution and pride of our peoples; and the horror and shame of my legitimate fear that we Cubans, with parricidal hands, might help in the senseless plan to draw Cuba . . . away from the fatherland that claims it and in which it is completed, the Spanish American fatherland.]

Notice, once again, that the blame is placed not solely on North Americans or Europeans but on Latin Americans themselves, including Cubans, whose annexationist attempts in time were to prove much more persistent than those of ambitious U.S. government officers (like Secretary of State Blaine).

3

It is a commonplace of the Martí canon that he had an ambivalent attitude toward the United States: he admired its democratic institutions and the way that North American society embraced modernity, but he despised its imperial practices, particularly its condescension toward Latin America. Philip Foner has aptly referred to this attitude as Martí's perception of "the two faces of the United States." We should also be aware, however, that just as Martí saw two faces up north, he also saw two faces down south. He both loved what he called "Our America" and also felt pity toward it, but his devotion was tempered by a tragic knowledge of the petty interests that prevented the so-called sister republics from acting as a political block—a reluctance, one should add, that he knew would seal, as it did, the fate of his country of origin. Martí's representation of this dilemma, this burning conflict, is that of an outsider; he writes from a position of extreme marginality and isolation. The figure for this representation is that of the orphan and, by implication, his imagining of an absent mother: "Madre América." If Martí was isolated, it was not so much because, as the canon has insisted, he felt alienated from an imperial power like the United States, with which he ultimately had little in common. Martí's alienation, rather, stemmed from the very people for whom he wrote and worked: the other Latin Americans who he wished would regard him not as a foreigner but as a peer; not as an Other but as an equal Self.

The fact that Martí's Latin American peers never exerted themselves to acknowledge his political right to his own country does not make the matter any more justified, rational, or palatable. In fact, many descendants of those same peers deny, even today, the right of Cuban exiles, Martí's descendants, to a land that has never ceased to be theirs. But such a fact only makes Martí's original insight that much sadder, that much more tragic, that much more pathetic.

Notes

1 All quotations from Martí's works, except where noted otherwise, are taken from *Obras completas,* 26 vols. to date (Havana: Editorial Nacional de Cuba, 1964–) and are my translations. For a useful gathering of the texts that Martí wrote around the two Pan-American Conferences of 1889–90 and 1891–92, see *Dos congresos. Las razones ocultas,* ed. Centro de Estudios Martianos (Havana: Editorial de Ciencias Sociales, 1985).

2 I develop this concept in my essay "Latinoamericanismo," *Vuelta* 210 (May 1994): 62–64 [partly translated in "Latinamericanism and Restitution," *Latin American Literary Review* 20 (July–December 1992): 88–96]. The Spanish-language version has been reprinted in my book *Por una politeratura. Literatura hispanoamericana e imaginación política* (Mexico City: Ediciones del Equilibrista/UNAM, 1995).

3 For Augier's essay, "Martí: Tesis antiimperialista en la cuna del panamericanismo," see *Dos congresos,* pp. 185–210.

4 Alexis de Tocqueville, *Democracy in America,* ed. J. P. Mayer, trans. G. Lawrence (New York: Harper Perennial, 1988), p. 564.

5 See Florencia Peñate, *José Martí y la Primera Conferencia Panamericana* (Havana: Editorial Arte y Literatura, 1977) and Graciella Chailloux, *Estrategia y pensamiento económico de José Martí frente al imperialismo norteamericano* (Havana: CESEU/Universidad de la Habana, 1989).

6 See Ricaurte Soler, *Idea y cuestión nacional latinoamericanas de la independencia a la emergencia del imperialismo* (Mexico City: Siglo XXI, 1980) and Jean Lamore, *José Martí et l'Amérique,* 2 vols. (Paris: L'Harmattan, 1986 and 1988).

7 On this theme, see my essay "José Martí and the Cuban Revolution," in *Cuban Studies* 16 (1986): 139–50.

8 Perhaps the best illustration of Martí's intent is his brief essay "Pueblos nuevos" [New Countries], where he says: "Por nuestra América abundan, de pura flojera de carácter, de puro carácter inepto y segundón, de pura impaciencia y carácter imitativo, los iberófilos, los galófilos, los yankófilos, los que no conocen el placer profundo de amasar la grandeza con las propias manos, los que no tienen fe en la semilla del país, y se mandan a hacer el alma fuera, como los trajes y los zapatos" [In our America there abound, out of pure spinelessness, out of pure ineptness and second-handedness, out of pure impatience and imitation, many iberophiles, galophiles, yankeephiles, those who know not the deep pleasure of softening greatness, with their own hands, those who don't have faith in the country's own seed, and design their souls abroad, like their shoes and suits]. See *Escritos desconocidos de José Martí,* ed. Carlos Ripoll (New York: Eliseo Torres & Sons), p. 211.

9 See Cintio Vitier, "Presentación," in *Nuestra América. Edición Crítica* (Havana: Centro de Estudios Martianos/Casa de las Américas, 1992), p. 12.

Jeffrey Belnap

Headbands, Hemp Sandals, and Headdresses: The Dialectics of Dress and Self-Conception in Martí's "Our America"

There can be no racial animosity, because there are no races. . . . The soul, equal and eternal, emanates from bodies of various shapes and colors. —José Martí, "Our America," 1891[1]

The American intelligence is an Indian headdress. —José Martí, "Aboriginal American Authors," 1884[2]

Like the work of many key anti-imperial colonial intellectuals constrained to spend large portions of their lives in exile, José Martí's writing is characterized by constant shifts in perspective, shifts that shuttle abruptly between concern with his own nation's independence and interest in other, more "cosmopolitan" matters. On the one hand, Martí struggled to complete the "final stanza of the poem of 1810" (71), the liberation of Cuba from the Spanish metropole; this activism compelled him to produce hundreds of pamphlets, articles, and letters dedicated to the Cuban cause. On the other hand, Martí's extended exile in the United States gave him access to the inner workings of a relatively new imperial system, the growing economic and military authority that had come to claim the status of being the region's de facto metropolitan center. And while his first concern was always Cuba, the fact that Martí made his living by dispatching journalistic interpretations of the culture and politics of the United States to Latin America's capital cities makes his thought singularly important. For in simultaneously orchestrating the Cuban revolution against Spain and interpreting the United States for Latin America's newspaper-reading public, he was persistently required—as a thinker—to frame and reconfigure the national struggle at the center of his personal concern within a regional and even global perspective.

This perpetual process of framing and reconfiguration, dictated by the shifting exigencies of nationalist activism and transnational journalism, taught Martí to read the difficulties facing both the Cuban independence struggle and the relations among the various American states as parts of the same elaborate geopolitical puzzle. Indeed, it is precisely this nationalist/transnational take on American geopolitics that produces the incisive lucidity of Martí's most influential piece of newspaper prose, "Our America" (1891), an essay that, after a century, still serves as a necessary touchstone for any analysis of inter-American cultural politics.[3] Written in the aftermath of a set of inter-American conferences in which Martí had been instrumental in convincing the Latin American representatives to reject U.S. proposals antithetical to their interests,[4] the essay is in one sense an articulation of the threat that Anglo America poses to Our America's sovereignty. But the necessary corollary to the essay's conceptualization of Our America as a single community of nations united by a common enemy is its articulation of the Latin American bodies politic as societies plagued by similar social pathologies. In other words, the exterior threat is coupled with an interior analogue. Siblings produced by the same processes of imperial miscegenation, Our America's nation-states are composed of kindred hierarchical arrangements in which predominantly *criollo* ruling classes (with their supporting intelligentsias) rule over disenfranchised Native American, African, and mixed-race peoples. At the same time, then, that "Our America" addresses itself to the Latin American intelligentsia in order to awaken it to the external danger posed by the United States, the essay carefully confronts this same class with an articulation of its own internal enemy: the intellectual orientation that turns the ruling class toward Europe and away from its own peoples. Martí thematizes this turning away as a pathological misapprehension of the elite subject's place in the world.

My objective in this essay is to tease out the logic of Martí's critique of this pathology, a critique that includes both an articulation of the intelligentsia's Eurocentric cosmopolitanism and a program for transforming into a positive tool the polydiscursivity that cosmopolitanism makes possible. First, I follow Martí's account of the way that elite culture, reproduced within the educational system bequeathed to the former colonies by imperialism, transfixes the "independent" ruling elite within a Eurocentric mimetic gaze, alienating it from its own people and rendering Our America's postimperial cultural systems unintelligible. Of particular interest is how metaphors of artificiality, effeminacy, and unnaturalness scattered throughout Martí's discourse emplot the male intelligentsia's pathology in a family romance of perverse lust and maternal abandonment; in this tale, the miseducated son is led by a lust for Europe to try to pass as European at the same time that he abandons his Native American mother. Next, I tease out the counternarrative that constitutes Martí's prescriptive program for rewriting this romance, a counternarrative that metaphorically charts the intelligentsia's rehabilitation as a rejection of the artificiality associated with Europe and a return to the "nature" associated with America. As a result of a reformed American university in which the curricula rest on principles dictated by America's natural landscape, the new American intellectual who learns to "see nature" will at the same time learn to nurse Mother America on her sickbed. Because he has both assimilated Europe's culture and become nature's oracle, he is simultaneously able to evaluate the relevance of foreign ideas and to translate the message of American Nature into the civic life Our America's nation-states. In a striking example of the teleological naturalism that identifies the nation-state with the completion of natural history, the mind of what Martí explicitly calls the Natural Statesman becomes (*pace* Hegel) *the* site of mediation that makes possible the synthesizing triumph of nature within modernity.

One of the features of Martí's narrative of alienation and return to which I pay particularly close attention is the way that the difference between the "artificial" and "natural" elite is marked by metaphors of dress and bodily adornment. Taking a suggestion from Sylvia Molloy's assertion that images of clothing constitute a ubiquitous and yet largely unexamined feature of Martí's work,[5] I am particularly interested in how Martí's use of metonyms of mismatched and incongruous costume enables him to give plasticity to the processes of formation that produce the intellectual's social identity. By "dressing up" his alienated objects of analysis in mismatched and culturally incongruous costumes, Martí thematizes the tension between the intelligentsia's subjective conception of itself as an extension of the European bourgeoisie and its objective inscription within societies that are complex amalgamations of Native American, African, and European influences. Moreover, Martí likewise scripts the intellectual's reintegration into Our America's natural landscape in terms of a metaphoric identification with Native American costume. By replacing the Eurocentric education that deforms the intellectual's historical self-conception, Martí's program for an Our American humanism teaches the intelligentsia that it must learn to cross-identify with the "natural" historical cultures produced by Native America's classical civilizations—regardless of the intellectual's particular "racial" identity. In one text, which I will read in conjunction with "Our America," Martí even goes so far as to equate this act of affective cross-identification with the forging of a fiction of kinship, an act of cross-identification in which the intelligentsia learns to don an "Indian headdress" and imagine itself as descended from Native American peoples "by blood."

The alienated intellectual who forms the object of Martí's critique makes his first appearance within the context of the call to arms sounded in "Our America" 's opening two sections. In these opening sections of his essay, Martí (*a*) calls upon Latin America's ruling class to awake from the parochial slumber that keeps it oblivious to the threat of the United States and (*b*) undertakes an analysis of the negative effects of the intelligentsia's inadequate educational preparation on Our America's social and political life. Set against an allegorical tableau in which Our America is represented as a blossom-filled wood and the United States as a menacing giant, the cosmopolitan is figured as an ineffectual weakling unable to help prevent the United States from invading. Invoking the tropes of American pastoralism, Martí asserts that he and his fellow Latin Americans ought no longer remain inactive before the forces of history, spreading their branches passively in the air like a "people of leaves." Because their peace is threatened by the United States, their blossom-laden trees must be transformed into a protomilitary barricade in order to prevent the giant from marching all over them:

> We can no longer be the people of leaves living in the air, our foliage heavy with blooms and crackling or humming at the whim of the light's caress, or buffeted and tossed by the storms. The trees must form ranks to keep the giant with the seven-league boots from passing. (85; translation altered)

Although Martí quickly moves on to other metaphors (a characteristic of his style), the rest of the essay might nevertheless be read as an articulation of the cultural politics that will make possible the militarization of Our America's pastoral grove.

The specific relationship of the cosmopolitan intellectual to this wood emerges at the beginning of the second section. Before setting aside entirely the allegory of the pastoral wood, Martí alludes to it once again as one of a string of negatively inflected metaphors used to describe the elite subject who is unable to contribute to the anti-imperial struggle:

> Those without faith in their country are seven-month weaklings. Because they have no courage, they deny it to others. *Their puny arms of bracelets and hands of painted nails, arms of Paris or Madrid*—can hardly reach the difficult limb, and they claim the tall tree to be un-climbable. The ships should be loaded with those harmful insects that gnaw at the bone of the country that nourishes them. *If they are Parisians or from Madrid, let them go to the Prado under lamplight, or to Tortoni's for a sherbet.* (86; my emphasis)

This baroque string of interlocking metaphors characterizes the cosmopolitan as a feminized, premature infant incapable of contributing to the nationalist construction project; his nail-painted hand and braceleted arm are barely strong enough to reach the tree's first branch, let alone able to cut down the tree and build it into a barricade. Furthermore, this weak *criollo* is plagued by skepticism. Lacking the strength and courage to labor himself, he insists that the task is impossible. And like a harmful insect, this skeptical attitude eats away into the marrow of the nationalist resolve, causing decay in the strength of others. Martí's response to these kinds of people? If emotionally they are from Paris or Madrid, load them onto boats and send them off to the metropolitan centers with which they identify.

Much could be said about the gender ideology that connects physical weakness, moral decay, and a lack of nationalist commitment to braceleted arms and painted nails. In representing the intellectual's corruptive attraction to European cafés by way of his bracelets and nail polish, his moral decay has been identified with his dressing like a woman. But in the following passage the plot thickens, for Martí suggests that the crime of Eurocentric desire necessarily produces a second violation of gender norms—the expatriate son's shameless abandonment of his Native American mother.

> Those born in America who are ashamed, *because they wear the Indian loincloth of the mother who reared them,* and who disown their sick mother, the scoundrels, leaving her alone on her sickbed! Then *who is a man?* He who stays with his mother and nurses her in her illness, or he who works out of sight, and lives at her expense in decadent lands, sporting fancy neckties, cursing the breast that sustained him, *displaying the sign of the traitor* on the back of his paper frockcoat? (85; translation altered, my emphasis)

Once again the cosmopolitan's pathology is thematized in terms of a failed masculinity. But this time the desire for the European café has simultaneously corrupted his natural affect for his maternal/geographical origins, leading him to disavow the Native American mother whose loincloth he wears. By abandoning his sick mother, whose labor supports him while he travels through Europe's "decadent lands," he ceases being a "man."

What is particularly compelling about this account of how the cosmopolitan's yearning for Europe leads to simultaneous violations of the norms of gender and nationality is Martí's marking of the tension between the mutable and immutable components of identity by using metaphors of dress. Clothing can and cannot be changed. Convinced that the frock coat and the necktie are enough, the weakling of braceleted arms and painted nails tries to pass as European. At the same time, however, he is unable to rid himself of the loincloth that identifies him to the objective gaze as a *mestizo,* and this article of clothing simultaneously marks his treachery to Mother America. Although a certain component of his identity may be mutable, in the sense that he may manipulate the external markers that mobilize the matrices of gender, ethnicity, and nation, he is not free to perform any identity *convincingly.* And while the construction of subjective desire may drive him to try to "pass" (or to cross-dress), the effects of sociocultural origins cannot be shed definitively. The legibility of the loincloth will always remain.

The rhetorical tenor of Martí's manifesto-like style allows him to dispatch the cosmopolitan skeptic and his negative influence off to the European cafés where he belongs. But as I have already indicated, the body of Martí's essay might be read productively as a critique of the educational institutions that make such drastic dismissals necessary. Using the cosmopolitan's violation of natural affect as a metonym for setting up his general problematic, Martí proceeds in the heart of the essay's second section to articulate the complex cause-and-effect relationship between the misguided educational curricula that produce this kind of person and nineteenth-century Latin America's general social and political difficulties. Because the educational curricula bequeathed to Our America are structured by the tyranny of the "imported book," those students who read only in this foreign book "go out in the world wearing Yankee or French spectacles." Furthermore, when these miseducated students opt to stay at home and become political leaders (rather than travel the world as exotic expatriates), they go out into their own countries "hoping to govern a people they do not know" (87). In other words, not only does this foreign curriculum schematize the hierarchies of knowledge so that the intelligentsia's desire plays itself out in (real or imaginary) European cafés, it also simultaneously blinds would-be leaders to the realities of their own lands. Peering obscurely through misplaced French or Yankee maxims, suffering from what Martí at one point calls "too much imitation" (92), the intelligentsia sets up governments that are fundamentally unstable. Because *miseducated* leaders have not governed "in accordance with the obvious needs of the country" (88), *uneducated* leaders capable of manipulating popular forces overthrow the legal governments and lead the nations into tyranny.[6]

The question of the miseducated leader alluded to in "Our America" 's second section becomes one of the central focuses of the essay's third and fourth sections, passages that analyze (*a*) the history of imperial violence that produced Our America's societies and (*b*) the failures and potential greatness of her governmental institutions. In the fourth section, the effect of the French or Yankee spectacles on the history of the Latin American intelligentsia is articulated once again in terms of a costume, this time one made up of a mismatched assemblage of fragments collected from various European and North American sources—clothing from everywhere, it seems, save from the leader's native land. At the same time that Martí burlesques this endemic disjuncture between the traditional leadership's subjective understanding and its objective appearance, he also specifically implicates himself and the class to which he and his readers belong by using the pronoun "we" to begin his description of this historical tradition of "masquerade":

We were a phenomenon with the chest of an athlete, the hands of a dandy, and the brain of a child. We were a masquerader in English breeches, Parisian vest, North American jacket, and Spanish cap. The Indian hovered near us in silence, and went off to the hills to baptize his children. The Black was seen pouring out the songs of his heart at night, alone and recognized among the rivers and wild animals. The peasant, the creator, turned in blind indignation against the disdainful city, against his own child. As for us, we wear nothing but epaulets and professors' gowns in countries that came into the world wearing hemp sandals and headbands. (91; translation altered)

At the individual level, Martí once again articulates the effects of miseducation in terms of the interplay between misapprehended self-conception and incongruous appearance. The misconceived educational system that installs a mélange of foreign ideas as eyeglasses in the leaders' minds leaves them largely blind to their objective circumstances. At the same time, the leaders who misimagine themselves as *au courant* actually appear to the objective gaze as an absurdly dressed assemblage of incongruity. Thinking themselves to be the height of fashion, they dress up their malformed bodies in a mismatched patchwork of fragments from Spain, England, the United States, and France — forgetting all the while the most important garments, the sandals and headbands that pertain to the cultures of their native lands. Most significant, though, are the negative social effects of this farcical masquerade, for the miseducated leader's misrule produces social dissolution that fragments along ethnic lines. While the *criollo* leader claims the authority of the professor's gown and the general's epaulet, the Native Americans remain hovering in silence, nearby and yet unrepresented. Although Africans might be seen and heard through the influence of their music, they likewise remain marginalized and alone. At the same time, the *mestizo* peasants, the synthesizing class of Our America's society, turn in anger against the urban centers and their Eurocentric, *criollo* culture. The result, of course, is perpetual social instability.

Following the logic of Martí's program for renovating Our America's intelligentsia requires that we grasp his conception of the New American University, especially his articulation of the mediating role that the humanistic imagination produced within this institution should play in Our America's national life. He calls for the restructuring of the university curriculum so that education will center on the actual condition of Our America's societies, a recentering that will disenthrall the intelligentsia from its mimetic dependence on Europe and productively integrate it into its own social context. Since a good leader for Martí is one who "sees things as they are" and who brings the "elements" of a nation together according to the "methods and institutions originating in the country" (86), it necessarily follows that the objective of education should be to teach the leadership "to see" these elements—that is, to understand the makeup of Our America's societies and the histories of their "methods" and "institutions." In other words, the New American University is an institution where the "French or Yankee spectacles" left behind by colonial education are replaced with correctly prescribed indigenous lenses.

But in addition to articulating his program for reclaiming Our America's intelligentsia through the metaphor of "learning to see," Martí further thematizes the abandonment of its characteristic artificiality in terms of a "return to nature." Although only implied at first, the call for a renovation of university curricula in the name of nature is hinted at in one of the essay's most often quoted passages, the sentences in which Martí insists that in the New America the "foreign book" is conquered by the "natural man," and that this same natural being will overcome "learned and artificial men" (87):

> [T]he foreign book has been conquered . . . by the natural man. The natural men have vanquished the artificial lettered men. The native-born *mestizo* has vanquished the exotic Creole. The struggle is not between barbarity and civilization, but between false erudition and nature. (87)

Casting the struggle between exogenous schemata and indigenous contexts in metaphors of ethnicity that revisit and rewrite the melodrama of perverse lust and maternal abandonment in a European café, Martí asserts that in the New America the "native-born *mestizo*" conquers the "exotic Creole" and that "nature" triumphs over "false erudition." In other words, the same exotic *criollo* whose dress and desire had been oriented by the foreign book's false erudition has been triumphantly overcome by a native *mestizo* who now functions as Nature's agent. (Indeed, the "natural" *mestizo* may actually be the being that lives *in potentia* within the exotic *criollo,* the partially hidden offspring of the forces of hybridization that the traveling *criollo* had unsuccessfully tried to disavow when attempting to pass as European.)

In Martí's next paragraph the relationship between this "natural man" and his triumph over false erudition is explicitly related to the hierarchy of values that will govern the new university curriculum. This "natural man" is not some purely intuitional being who has managed to slough off the alienating effects of formal education, but rather a "natural statesman" whose education has taught him to strike a balance between an indigenous perspective and a synthesizing project. By means of such a balance, he is able to integrate foreign ideas productively into the struggling republics:

> The European university must bow to the American university. The history of America, from the Incas to the present, must be taught in clear detail and to the letter, even if the archons of Greece are overlooked. Our Greece must take priority over the Greece that is not ours. We need it more. Nationalist statesmen must replace exotic statesmen. Let the world be grafted into our republics, but the trunk must be our own. And let the vanquished pedant hold his tongue. (88; translation modified)

In this passage, Martí marks the fundamental distinction between the ability to healthily assimilate foreign ideas and the dogmatic insistence on these foreign ideas' universal validity. Because the Natural Statesman's mind is steeped in Our America's newly classicized cultures, he is able to determine which ideas should be "grafted" into the republican "trunk" and which should, because of their irrelevance, be left to wither and die. Moreover, because his education has prepared him to judge between the relevant and the irrelevant, his "natural" erudition also enables him to reduce the ideologically co-opted pedant—who wears only French or Yankee spectacles—to silence.

In the final paragraph of the essay's fourth (and penultimate) section, Martí moves from a micrological sketch of the university's effect on the formation of the intellectual to a macrological vision of this intellectual's integration into Our America's newly resilient social life. And, once again, nature triumphs over artificiality. In sharp contrast to the images of misdressed incongruity and social alienation, we have here a Whitmanesque enumeration of a resilient community of leaders, urban workers, artists, and Indian nations. Because it has been grounded in the "direct study of Nature," the intelligentsia has been transformed from a class of parasitic buffoons into productive intellectual workers who facilitate transnational and intranational communication.

The new Americans are on their feet saluting each other from nation to nation, the eyes of the laborers shining with joy. The natural statesman arises, schooled in the direct study of Nature. He reads to apply his knowledge, not to imitate. Economists study the problems at their point of origin. Speakers begin a policy of moderation. Playwrights bring native characters to the stage. Academies discuss practical subjects. Poetry shears off its romantic locks and hangs its red vest on the glorious tree. Selective and sparkling prose is filled with ideas. In the Indian republics, the governors are learning Indian. (92)

The "direct study of Nature" functions as the transcendental key to the intelligentsia's transformation. Rather than reading to perpetuate the fancy-dress mirrorings of colonial mimesis, the Natural Statesman examines the foreign book only to test its relevance against the primacy of his own natural landscape. And at the same time that the playwright introduces Native American characters onto the urban stage and the poet forswears excessive subjectivism in order to become allied with the natural environment ("the glorious tree"), the governor of the Indian republic is able to test the relevancy of the foreign book precisely because he is "learning Indian." Successful negotiation with the discourses of the "outside" depends on a thorough fluency with those languages indigenous to the land.

Martí's reclamation of Our America's intelligentsia from the artificiality of its Eurocentric masquerade through a successful reintegration into American Nature certainly strikes a note of familiarity for students of U.S. culture. Nineteenth-century U.S. intellectuals who produced what have become the canonical texts of U.S. literary and historical writing utilized the same kind of artificial/natural binary in their understanding of the world-historical narrative that culminated in "America." These U.S. intellectuals (several of whom were, incidentally, the objects of Martí's commentaries)[7] read world history as a sequence of progressions from artificial to natural political formations, defining premodern arrangements like those of Catholic Europe as imaginary and artificial at the same time that they identified the "modern" nation-states of Northern Europe and (finally) America as the increasingly more advanced realizations of natural history. A particularly significant feature of this discourse in the United States is the singular importance that geography played as a legitimizing trope, for American space was the site where the teleological forces of historical progress realized themselves in their highest manifestation in the U.S. nation-state. Not only did this embodiment of the World Spirit in geography contribute to the doctrine of American exceptionalism, but it also reciprocally granted enormous aesthetic authority to the singularity of the (empty) American landscape. Like the rhetoric that penetrated the narratives of U.S. history and the celebration of the U.S. Constitution, the cultural life of the United States was represented as a "more perfect" embodiment of nature, indistinguishable from its landscape—there to be discovered and actualized, rather than merely created as some artificial product of the human imagination.

The essay by David Noble included in this collection summarizes for us the ways in which U.S. cultural self-consciousness has been caught up in the teleological narrative that sublated European artificiality within American Nature; Noble also reminds us of the processes of demystification that have led in past decades to a recognition that this nationalist discourse was itself a culturally overdetermined fiction. In this narrative of naturalistic inevitability, what was actually a transnational bourgeoisie was allowed to represent itself within its respective national formations as the privileged agent of history. For Noble, these processes of demystification which began in the 1960s reached a kind of denouement with the publication, in 1983, of Benedict Anderson's *Imagined Communities*. Anderson's text helped those who were interested in a critical understanding of U.S. culture to see the doctrine of American exceptionalism (as well as that doctrine's ideological repetition in the founding of American Studies) as a local variant of nationalist formations that took shape throughout the nineteenth and twentieth centuries in many places around the world. Not only was the doctrine of American exceptionalism not an exception, the logic of its claim to "natural" authority bore a strong family resemblance to the discourses of nation-states everywhere.

Noble's articulation of the aesthetisizing authority that the U.S. intelligentsia located in the natural landscape, as well as his account of how U.S. scholars have come to recognize in this trope a metaphor shared by the transnational bourgeoisie, are extremely significant for our understanding of the opposition between "artificiality" and "naturalness" implicit in Martí's reformation of Our America's intellectual class. At the analytical threshold, it helps us situate Martí's romance of expatriate lust, maternal abandonment, and reintegration into Our American nature within a comparative framework, underscoring the common use of "nature" as a legitimizing trope for bourgeois nationalism in both hemispheres. But as we move beyond this threshold, we find an important distinction between the U.S. version of this discourse and Martí's "Our Americanism." For while Anglo-Americans blinded themselves to the multiethnic complexities of their own nation by conceptualizing the natural landscape as an essentially empty space waiting to be taken up in history, Martí's version of naturalistic nationalism is based on a principle of inclusion rather than one of exclusion. Instead of some concept that renders the natural landscape prehistorical and precultural, American Nature for Martí is always already shot through with the history of Native American peoples whose descendants pertain to the postimperial commonwealth. Conflating America's natural landscape with its indigenous civilizations, the "artificial" intelligentsia's unwillingness to take up their national project is represented as an abandonment of their Native American mother and an unwillingness to acknowledge the loincloth, headband, and hemp sandals that pertain to her "natural" offspring. Conversely, the emotional return to nature is not only a return from Europe to America; it is concomitant with the development of a national imaginary rooted in Native American culture—the study of "our Greeks," the introduction of Native American characters onto the stage, and the acquisition of Native American languages. In other words, the key component of his project for "natural" national health is a thoroughgoing multicultural integration that teaches all Americans to invert the Eurocentric hierarchy bequeathed to them by imperialism. This inversion depends on Euroamericans' learning to conceive of themselves as the *cultural* kin of Native American civilizations, regardless of the particular "facts" of biological descent. And the specific function of the polydiscursive elite within the New America is to facilitate this cultural integration by engaging simultaneously in the "direct study of Nature" and the translation of Nature's languages into the discourses of multiethnic modernity.

Martí has provided us with an excellent text for supplementing "Our America"'s project to invert the cultural hierarchies that structure Our America's natural/historical imaginary. That text is to be found among a series of articles, dedicated to classical Native

American civilizations, that Martí published between June 1883 and June 1884.[8] Not only do these articles help us trace the development of the Native American component of Martí's thinking, but they also help us locate the special importance that Martí placed on literature and literary education as a tool for facilitating the development of healthy political life in a multicultural state. We shall focus on one of these articles, "Aboriginal American Authors" (April 1884), a review essay devoted to an edition of pre-Columbian literature published by Daniel G. Brinton, a North American scholar of Native American culture. Although ostensibly about Brinton's work, Martí's review serves as a pretext for more general comments on the cultures of the New World and on the processes of amalgamation that produce new kinds of American subjects. Discussing his own relationship as a Euroamerican reader to America's classical pre-Columbian cultures, Martí rejects a biologically based model of identity formation in the name of a cultural/geographical one. Incidental to this, he also suggests that Our America's anti-imperial cultural politics requires that Americans of European descent shift their primary sense of identity away from their European lineage and learn instead to think of themselves as offspring of American Nature and her natural peoples. Anticipating "Our America" 's call for a New American Humanism rooted in classical American civilizations ("Our Greeks"), Martí's review essay on Brinton's book suggests that, by reading the historical literatures of Native America, the *criollo* class should learn to construct for itself a fictive-kinship relationship in which they learn to "regard as their own" the blood of the warriors who died fighting the Spanish. And it is precisely in this ability to cross-identify with those who have lived within the same natural environment that Martí locates the essence of what he calls the "American intelligence." It is this intelligence which Martí represents as a reclamation of the "Indian headdress."

Martí articulates his rejection of the racial/biological model of identity formation in the name of a cultural/geographical one in terms of culture's primary dependence on its interaction with a natural landscape, a logic that links Martí's thought to naturalistic nationalism in the United States. We first see this logic at work near the beginning of the review essay, where Martí asserts that American "literature," like all cultural artifacts, is the "expression" of human interaction with the "American landscape":

> Literature is simply the expression, form and reflection of the vital spirit and natural setting of the people who create it. How, then, could our indigenous literature run counter to this universal law, and lack the beauty, harmony, and color of the American landscape? (194)

The "universal law," then, is that as a result of nature's coupling with the human spirit, the "beauty, harmony, and color of the American landscape" are continuously reproduced throughout the entire American tradition, from pre-Columbian times to the present.

But Martí distinguishes himself clearly from his North American counterparts when he turns specifically to the subject matter of Brinton's book. After listing some of the important themes, cultures, and events that Brinton brings together, Martí takes his argument concerning the maternity of the natural environment a step further, suggesting that landscape is more important than lineage in producing identity. One's kinship with those who live within the same geographical environment is stronger than any supposed relationship of race:

> The spirit of a people resides in the land in which they live and is drawn in with the air one breathes. One may descend from fathers of Valencia and mothers of the Canary Islands, yet one feels the blood of Tamanaco and Paracamoni run hot through one's veins and regards as one's own the blood of the heroic, naked Caracas warriors which stained the craggy ground . . . where they met the armored Spanish soldier. (195)

Using in this passage a barely veiled allusion to his own familial origins, Martí insists that geography takes priority over biology, a priority that he metaphorizes as a historically constructed blood relation. Although one's parents may be from Valencia and the Canary Islands (as Martí's parents were), the foundation of identity lies in the "spirit" of the "land" that has been "drawn in with the air one breathes." And since literature is an expression of the "spirit" of the "American landscape," it necessarily follows that the assimilation of literary traditions which have emanated from that landscape fortifies this natural relation. Indeed, by assimilating these narratives (the narratives analyzed in Brinton's book), one comes to regard "as one's own the blood of the naked . . . warriors" who died fighting the Spanish invaders.

In the review's closing passages, Martí makes an explicit connection between the construction of this fictive blood relation through the literary imagination and the health of Our America's modern societies. Not only does he assert that *criollos* like himself should learn to regard as their own the blood of anti-imperial Native Americans; he also anticipates one of "Our America" 's principal thematics by asserting that resistance to the dehumanization, materialism, and harshness of industrialization (qualities he comes to identify with the United States and its seven-league boots) depends on Our America's ability to maintain this sort of historical connection with the spirit of nature:

> It is good to open canals, to found schools, to build rail lines, to bring oneself up to date, to be on the beautiful vanguard of human progress; but it is also good, in order not to be overwhelmed by all this because of lack of spirit or a show of an artificial spirit, to nourish oneself—by memory and admiration, by accurate study and loving compassion—on the fervent spirit of the nature into which one was born, raised and enlivened and on that of the men of all races who emerged from it and who are buried in it. Only when they are direct do politics and literature prosper. The American intelligence is an Indian headdress.[9]

Although technological "progress" may have its beauties and advantages, the human spirit will be overwhelmed and rendered artificial by materialism unless it is nourished in the memory and admiration of those people "of all races" who have been instructed by the same natural environment. And because literary traditions—like political institutions—are meaningful only when they embody this natural environment, Our America's multicultural life will regain its health only when it reclaims a sense of its historical identity with that nature, a continuity marked in this passage by the headdress of the native peoples who first inhabited it.

Martí's assertion in 1884 that technological modernity needs to be mediated by the influence of America's natural landscape, as well as by the native peoples' historical narratives which embody that landscape's "spirit," evidences an important continuity in his conception (expressed in the last decade of his life) of the significance of the Native American component in Our America's national cultures. By articulating a model of collective "Our Americanism" that requires *criollos* (like him) to regard themselves as the "natural" offspring of the land, related "by blood" to the Native American peoples who fought the Spanish imperialists, Martí does not just help us understand the importance he attached to a thoroughgoing integration of America's multiple histories; he also suggests a way in which this multiperspectival assimilation of the history of the "Other" might reorder the *criollo*'s hierarchy of values, and thus reorient the dynamics of that class's sense of social identity. In "Our America," miseducation installs French or Yankee spectacles in the elite mind, compelling intellectuals to try to pass as Europeans. Because their education has taught them to conceive of themselves as extensions of the European bourgeoisie, dandified expatriates and mismatched politicians play out their incongruous self-conceptions with pathological social consequences. In Martí's review essay on Brinton's book, a parallel model of the relationship between educational curricula and the performative component of social identity is at work. Only in this text, instead of a *mestizo* trying to pass as European, a person of European descent learns—through pre-Columbian literature—to inscribe himself within a tradition of anti-imperial resistance by regarding himself as the "natural" descendent of anti-imperial Native Americans. Having learned to recognize the "American intelligence" by assimilating the "alternative history" represented by the Indian headdress, the Martí whose Valencian father and Canarian mother migrated to Cuba before he was born exchanges the mismatched fragments of the would-be cosmopolitan for the Indian apron, headband, and hemp sandals that pertain to his native land.

Martí's assertion that America's elite classes should learn to regard as their own the "blood" of Native Americans by studying the history of "Our Greeks" suggests that he recognized a profound connection between formal education and the way that one reads oneself in relation to the social environment. And in metaphorizing this connection in terms of loincloths and headdresses, Martí marks the way in which the inside/outside play that constitutes "identity" shuttles between self-conception and the complex cultural politics of social spectacle. When Martí insists that America's *criollo* elite should recognize the garments (on themselves and others) pertaining to their native land, he is only insisting that the largely Euroamerican ruling classes learn to read the world from the perspective of the natural/cultural environment to which both they and the people their ancestors brutalized pertain.

Although the notion of "playing Indian" may appear condescending when taken out of context, Martí's notion of returning to "nature" by identifying with the native peoples of America couples the nationalist rhetoric of his naturalistic age with a much more complex intuition as to what it might mean to reverse the negative sociocultural forces that govern racialized hierarchies in America's nation-states. In insisting that those who are most powerful in Our America need to unlearn their position of privilege by imagining themselves as children of the Native American mother upon whose labor their privileges depend, Martí points the way toward an important component of the project for social justice in America's multiethnic states. To remember, one hundred years after his death, Martí's attempts to translate his intuitions into politically useful fictions is to see his work as an early attempt to link a progressive pedagogy to the complex cultural realities of Our America's social life. And although the traces of naturalistic nationalism and a conventional gender ideology mark Martí clearly as a product of his times, his struggle to reimagine the institutions that reproduce the social imaginary serves as a powerful provocation for those who similarly struggle to reimagine the Americas in our own day.

Notes

1 In José Martí, *Our America: Writings on Latin America and the Struggle for Cuban Independence,* ed. Philip S. Foner, trans. Elinor Randall et al. (New York: Monthly Review Press, 1977), p. 71. Unless indicated otherwise, all subsequent citations of Martí's work are to this edition, and page numbers will be given parenthetically in the text.

2 José Martí, *Obras completas* (Havana: Editorial Nacional de Cuba, 1963), vol. 8, pp. 327–42.

3 For recent perspectives on the continued significance of "Our America" in Latin America's cultural and political discourses, see *Cuadernos Americanos* 32 (1992) a collection of articles commemorating the centenary of the essay's first appearance. The touchstone for consideration of the relationship between Martí's thought and Chicano/Latino cultural studies in the United States is, of course, José David Saldívar's *The Dialectics of Our America: Genealogy, Cultural Critique, and Literary History* (Durham: Duke University Press, 1991).

4 These two conferences were the First Pan-American Conference (1889–90) and the International Monetary Congress (1891), both of

which were convened by U.S. Secretary of State James G. Blaine in Washington, D.C.

5 In an endnote to a study of homophobic ideologies in Latin American fin-de-siècle culture, Sylvia Molloy comments on the ubiquity and complexity of Martí's use of dress. Expanding on her reading of Martí's journalistic commentary on Oscar Wilde's New York visit, Molloy suggests that "Martí's fetishization of dress (we are our clothing) is remarkable throughout his work and deserves further study" (p. 199). See Molloy, "Too Wilde for Comfort: Desire and Ideology in Fin-de-Siècle Spanish America," *Social-Text* 10, nos. 2–3 (1992): 187–201.

6 One of Martí's objectives in these passages is to account for nineteenth-century Latin America's political instability, an instability that was commonly cited in North America's racist discourses as "proof" of Latino inferiority.

7 Emerson is perhaps Martí's paradigmatic example of the intellectual who communes directly with Nature. In his 1882 essay written on the occasion of Emerson's death, Martí insists that Emerson was "one of those to whom Nature opens and reveals herself, extending her multiple arms as if to enfold within them the whole body of her son. . . . All Nature trembled before like a new bride" (p. 218). And again, "One came away from [Emerson] with the feeling of having seen a living monument, or a supreme being. There are men like mountains who level the land before and after them" (p. 219). And once again, "[Emerson] saw behind him the creative Spirit that spoke to Nature through him" (p. 220). See "Emerson," in *The America of José Martí*, ed. Federico de Onís, trans. Juan de Onís (New York: Noonday Press, 1953).

8 These articles were published in *La América* (a Spanish-language newspaper published in New York City). A final, related article appeared in 1887 in *El Economista Americano* (also published in New York City). See Martí, *Obras completas*, vol. 8, pp. 327–42. I will be quoting exclusively from one of these articles, "Aboriginal American Authors," and—with one exception—will use Juan de Onís's translation in *The America of José Martí*.

9 My translation. See Martí, *Obras completas*, vol. 8, p. 336.

Brenda Gayle Plummer

Firmin and Martí at the Intersection of Pan-Americanism and Pan-Africanism

This essay draws its inspiration from a momentary historical event: the single meeting in 1893 between José Martí of Cuba and Anténor Firmin of Haiti. Two years later, one would be dead and the other in exile. Yet that fugitive moment of collaboration reveals their collective vision for an earnestly desired and envisioned world that they did not succeed in creating. The rendezvous in Cap Haitien also illustrates how Caribbean nationalists in the late nineteenth century understood and addressed the dilemmas posed by racism and imperialism.

José Martí was born of peninsular parents in Havana in 1853. His father's career as a military officer assured him a measure of economic security. Martí's academic successes and literary precocity made him a useful partisan of a developing Cuban resistance. Still an adolescent at the time of the Ten Years' War, he joined the nationalist student movement. Arrested for revolutionary activities in 1869, Martí went briefly to prison and then, as was the custom, into Spanish exile.[1]

Once in Madrid, Martí launched a prolific career as a journalist and essayist while studying law. He contacted the revolutionary Cuban junta in New York City and, after receiving graduate degrees in law and letters in 1874, began a life of constant travel, clandestine missions, and polemics on behalf of the revolution. His journeys took him to Paris, where he met Victor Hugo, and to Mexico where he lived until the accession to power of Porfirio Díaz.

Permitted to return to Cuba at the end of the Ten Years' War, Martí's subversive activities led to his second deportation in 1879. He again made the circuit of Madrid, Paris, and New York. Apart from a brief interlude, Martí remained in the United States from 1881 to 1895, supporting himself through journalism and consulships offered by various Latin American republics. Using New York City as a base, he consolidated contacts with the Cuban exile communities in Florida and founded the journal *Patria* in 1892.

Martí also journeyed several times to the Caribbean before returning to Cuba to fight in the revolution. During one such visit, with help from the Puerto Rican revolutionist Dr. Ramón Emeterio Betances, he visited the noted Haitian intellectual and statesman Anténor Firmin in Cap Haitien on June 8, 1893.[2]

Firmin came from a working-class background in the northern city of Cap Haitien. His ability propelled him into a lower middle class whose penury made it expectantly support the palace revolutions of the age. Firmin's gifts, however, soon catapulted him beyond that social stratum. He studied the sciences, literature, and German philosophy; he edited the liberal *Messager du nord.* As a nationalist and polemicist, Firmin confronted the increasingly insistent sociobiological rationales for exploitation and the perverted Darwinist science characteristic of the era. His *De l'égalité des races humaines* (1885), a response to Count Gobineau's 1884 racist tract, *Essai sur l'inégalité des races humaines,* assailed the fundamental tenets of white supremacy. *L'effort dans le mal* took on Haitian politics. Another work, *Diplomates et diplomatie* (1899) was an account of certain leading statesmen of the late nineteenth century, some of whom he, as Haiti's representative, had been personally acquainted with.[3]

Firmin as a politician had little aversion to opportune alliances with the militarists who so thoroughly crippled Haitian national life. Like many before and after him, he thought it possible to subordinate them to an agenda of his own. Firmin believed in civilian government and a tempered capitalism enriched by foreign investment. His scholarship addressed the history and politics of the entire Caribbean region. Firmin dreamed of a West Indian federation, although he understood the practical difficulties such a body would confront.[4]

When President Florvil Hyppolite assumed the presidency in 1889 he vested Firmin with three portfolios: finance, commerce, and foreign relations. A steamship company with intimate ties to ranking U.S. navalists had bankrolled Hyppolite's campaign. In that era's enthusiasm for large navies, the U.S. State Department backed the aggressive demand by an admiral that Haiti cede a deep-water harbor to the United States. Hyppolite, after all, owed North Americans something. Firmin, as minister of foreign relations, turned aside the attempt to acquire part of the Haitian domain. He was assisted in this maneuver by the U.S. minister, the black, former abolitionist Frederick Douglass, who proved more open to Haiti's aspirations for sovereignty than to the threats and blandishments of fellow Republican Party politicos.[5]

At the end of Hyppolite's term, Firmin resigned the ministry and returned to Cap Haitien, where he briefly practiced law. The military establishment surrounding Hyppolite's successor perceived Firmin as dangerous and soon packed him off to Europe as a diplomat. This was no honor: at the time, presidents disposed of political rivals in this manner. Firmin could expect little income and few perquisites from his stints as minister to France, where he discovered the Latin American exile community, and later Britain.[6]

Martí, Firmin, and activists like them sought mutuality in struggle not only against the debilitating material effects of imperialist exploitation but also against the spiritual robbery that devalued the cultural vitality of the Antilles and drained it of its human resources. They needed to fashion a Pan-Americanism for West Indian circumstances. Their island states and territories were not continental giants like Brazil and Mexico. Small Caribbean polities faced particular challenges in an age that witnessed the apotheosis of the nation-state and the maturation of empire. A diminutive geography, however, did not necessarily mean diminutive thinking. Such countries had a political tradition rooted in at least three interrelated histories.

First was the ancient Amerindian base, with its own annals of revolt; second, the African foundation of rebellion and *marronage;* and third, the struggle of Creole planters and freemen against metropolitan domination. The Amerindian, African, and Creole bedrock underlay much of what was vital and unique about regional art and architecture, cuisine, maritime technology, and agriculture. In spite of significant linguistic, religious, and racial differences, Caribbean states and colonies could point to a host of similar customs, attitudes, and conventions. Likeness also inhered in structural commonalties of dependent commerce and agriculture, whatever the metropole.

Pan-Americanists sought to make these parallelisms an instrument for regional cooperation that would in turn abet modernizing projects and, on the cultural front, establish a positive politics of identity. The Caribbean represented potentiality: nationhood could emerge only from peoples firm in the belief in their own worth and optimistic about the future. In travels through the region, Pan-

Americanists learned how other territories compared with home. When they developed friendships with other like-minded colonials in the world's great cities, they found both their estrangement and their ambitions understood by persons who shared their optic. José Martí, for example, had been to Spain and British Honduras before he reached age twenty-one. Revolutionary activities would later take him to France, Mexico, Guatemala, the United States, Venezuela, Haiti, the Dominican Republic, Jamaica, Costa Rica, and Panama. Anténor Firmin, like Martí, simultaneously an exile and a diplomat, would ultimately live in England, France, Cuba, and Saint Thomas.

The Pan-Americanism discussed here differs from that articulated by U.S. Secretary of State James G. Blaine in the 1880s. Blaine's notion of hemispheric unity placed the United States at the center of a solar system in which other nations would revolve like planets. Only a Pax Norte-Americana could maximize peace and reciprocal commercial advantage. Caribbean Pan-Americanism had the ill-fortune of reaching great heights of articulation during an epoch of expanding U.S. influence in the region. Unlucky, because the United States soon came to apply its own understanding of republicanism to the historical experiences of its neighbors. U.S. policy makers did not accept politics that were not the product of orderly and gradual constitutional processes. The local governments they most readily tolerated were those that complied most completely with the U.S. agenda of market growth, strategic predominance, and racial chauvinism. In Washington's eyes, men like Martí and Firmin ran the gamut from eccentricity to criminality. Rarely was their creative genius acknowledged or respected.[7]

Caribbean Pan-Americanists instead envisioned the mutuality of egalitarian states, none so strong as to be able to dominate the others. This Pan-Americanist cultivation of fraternalism rested not only on the need for political solidarity in withstanding imperialist depredations; it also relied on the recognition of cultural commonalities and a shared history of imperialist domination. The colonial experience required a complex set of responses. Accordingly, the most ambitious and dedicated intellectuals among emerging peoples and developing countries cultivated what Jeffrey Belnap has called a "polydiscursivity."[8] They were simultaneously lawyers and poets, philosophers and guerrillas, scientists and artists. Their mastery across disciplines and esthetic genres did not stem solely from a need to compensate for the dearth of educated people in their struggling homelands. Just as important, they were driven by a desire to construct counterdiscourses to the ravaging racism and imperialism that continued to transform their world. This was the universe of Firmin and Martí. They understood this multitasking as fully engaged intellectual labor and, much like the contemporaneous Afro-American scholar W. E. B. Du Bois, saw themselves creating the foundations of a new science, philosophy, and literature. Whether as downtrodden colonials, subjects of a despotic power, or members of an oppressed national minority, they would accomplish this labor while facing the massive ideological assault mounted by all the cultural institutions serving racism and empire: the academies, learned societies, churches, and philanthropies.[9]

Scholarly and professional associations began to influence public policy in advanced nations in the late nineteenth century, when such organizations began to proliferate worldwide. At first, they were open to the membership and participation of a wide range of foreigners and nationals. By the last decade of the century, however, reactionary typologies of race and ethnicity and white supremacist agendas had made considerable inroads, not only in popular thought but also in the academy. The philanthropic assistance that cultural work and institution building might have attracted in another age did not exist for Caribbean intellectuals. Even had resources been available, it is doubtful that donors would have supported any initiative that did not endorse accommodation to authoritarianism and an unregulated market system.[10]

Martí and Firmin envisaged an America free of foreign domination, but their Pan-Americanism was suffused with metropolitan ideas. They had both lived in Paris, the nonpareil of world capitals. If Paris in the 1880s was the glittering nucleus of cosmopolitan culture, it was also the center of a state engaged in global expansion. At the beginning of the decade, France established control over Equatorial Africa; in 1883, Tunisia; between 1882 and 1896, Madagascar, and so on. Even as colonialism united the oceans in conquests from Tahiti to Dahomey, French artists, composers, and writers had begun to demolish the foundations of the *mission civilisatrice.* This heady atmosphere supported sizable expatriate colonies of Latin Americans and Eastern Europeans who found in Paris the necessary social and political space to think hard about, and plan practical agendas for, their countries of origin. Many of the

Latin Americans moved between Paris and Madrid, to which Martí was deported in 1879. In Madrid, cultural and linguistic compatibility brought exiles into the political community of Spanish republicanism.[11]

The cultural space inhabited by Martí and Firmin was thus a negotiated one where, at once cosmopolites and colonized intellectuals, their assimilation simultaneously threatened and appeased imperialists and disrupted conventional colonial discourses. Latin American exiles in Europe did not simply constitute a cerebral fraternity at odds with the authoritarian regimes they dreamed of toppling. These were also men of political action. As Firmin recalled in his collection of essays, *Lettres de Saint-Thomas* (1910), the Paris group centered on the Puerto Rican nationalist Dr. Ramón Emeterio Betances. Betances, chief organizer and veteran of the 1868 uprising remembered as the Grito de Lares, lived thirty years in exile. The dream of Betances and others, Firmin wrote, "was the intellectual and moral emancipation of all those whose growth is held back by whatever external force, national despotism or colonial exploitation. They hoped to establish an international connection which associated each one of the Latin American countries with the efforts and development of the others."[12]

The progressive leaders of Martí's generation could plainly see the correspondences and mutual resemblances in their societies, such as the prevalence of plantation agriculture or peasant subsistence economies, sometimes existing side by side. Cash poor and resource tight, the Caribbean islands had little surplus for building either the physical or the ideological foundations of reciprocal cooperation. Recognition of these common traits should not, however, permit understatement of the dissimilarities. Certain historical continuities traceable to conquest, displacement, the slave trade, and mercantilism linked the colonies. Yet, geography, demography, race, culture, and religion established distinctions that nationalism tended to amplify.

For José Martí, the principle of national sovereignty was emancipatory. "Everything that divides men, everything that separates or herds men together in categories, is a sin against humanity," he wrote. "The Cuban Negro does not aspire to true freedom, to the culture and happiness of men . . . as a Negro, but as a Cuban!"[13] Martí, reviewing the history of Cuba's efforts to liberate itself, saw how the slavery question had compromised revolutionary chances during the Ten Years' War. For Martí, a genuine Cuban nationalism, the recognition that slavery and independence could not coexist, would solve the problem of racism.[14] Although Martí insisted that there could never be a race war in Cuba, racial conflict simmered below the surface until it erupted in the Guerrita of 1912, an Afro-Cuban uprising that some maintained had Firminist roots.[15] In much of the Western world, a nationalism unreflectingly mixed with white supremacy caused extensive suffering among racial minorities and colonized subjects of color. How would Cuban nationalism be different? Martí believed that racism was an artifact of slavery and, holding a progressive view of history, that it would eventually decline as blacks achieved social equality through education. His Pan-Americanism lay rooted in a strong faith in the ability of nation-states, functioning as democratic and truly inclusive polities, to effect genuine change.

Improvement for Cuban blacks, however, rested firmly on their assumption of a Cuban identity. *Cubanidad* could have no color. "There can be no racial animosity," Martí insisted, "because there are no races." Nationalism required the submersion of all alternative ethnic identities, but *Cubanidad* was distinctly white and Creole. For the many who in the late nineteenth century routinely conflated statism, positivist science, and Christian ethics, this submersion could work only in the best interests of Africans. The fault was not Martí's alone. Few Westernized blacks in Africa or the diaspora ever interrogated their own complicity with the structures of domination. Christian communities of color opposed such obvious abuses as the slave trade but abetted great-power encroachments, often on their own territories, in the name of advancing Christianity, progress, and civilization.[16]

As a result, they could have but weak defenses against the wholesale destruction of small polities in Africa and Asia. The era when African sovereignty came under the broadest attack, when the machine gun appeared in world history as a weapon against the royalists of Ashanti and Benin, witnessed the most militant insistence on the essential savagery of African peoples. A few Europeans, such as Joseph Conrad, who skillfully illustrated it in his classic novella *Heart of Darkness,* understood this psychological projection.[17]

The turn of the century was also a fateful era for black people of the diaspora. The United States had effectively disfranchised black Americans in the South. The Supreme Court in *Plessy v. Ferguson* made complete social segregation the law of the land. An extralegal regime of terror, including lynching, bolstered these legal strictures. U.S. commercial expansion into the Caribbean, Central America, and the South Pacific after the Spanish-American War extended the domain of racist ideology.[18] In the independent republics of South America, infatuation with eugenics prescribed state policies that prohibited black immigration but fostered European settlement in the interests of "improving" native stock biologically and culturally. Industrial and commercial growth, planners hoped, would follow in the wake of these changes. Such interpretations of modernization in states like Brazil and Argentina accompanied—and dictated—deteriorating status for black and mixed-blood persons.[19]

The Pan-African Conference held in London in 1900 constituted an international black response to all these developments. Faced with the European military juggernaut, colonized blacks could not effectively resist what many people worldwide considered the inexorable tide of history. Many elites of color also subscribed to the belief that black, Indian, and mixed-blood societies must inevitably decline in a world dominated by powerful nation-states. They shared the West's faith that society naturally moves toward betterment, thus repudiating the values of indigenous communities less organized around triumphalist constructions of human history. The most liberal Westernized elites did not think Africans were innately inferior. They instead embraced the notion that enlightened tutelage, resulting in eventual self-rule, would deliver African countries from the darkness of timeless tribalism into modernity.[20]

The Pan-African movement would change its objectives, value system, and protagonists in the years to come. The world wars would so transfigure it as to make it unrecognizable to the Pan-Africanists of 1900. At the turn of the century, however, these racial ideologues sought to marshal the scattered common denominators of the black world into a voice powerful enough to exert moral pressure on the great powers. The Guadeloupian H.-Adolphe Lara articulated a Caribbean formulation in 1906, envisaging a Federation of Black West Indians. "We are French, English, Spanish, by right of conquest, but of common origin, enduring the same prejudices, we must unite to defend our interests," he wrote. "And such a movement, in our era of pacifism and internationalism," Lara opined rather too sanguinely, "would not disturb the metropoles at all. It would oblige them to be more just, and to treat us with less scorn."[21] A decade later, Lara's suggestion would materialize in the ideology and programs of the Jamaican Marcus Garvey's Universal Negro Improvement Association.

Pan-Africanism thus approached the world with a wholly different set of assumptions than the Pan-Americanism espoused by Martí and others. Its existence in the Western Hemisphere affirmed the failure of American nationalists to solve the problem of race. More optimistically, it testified to the continued vitality of subcultures thought to be doomed by modernization. Pan-Africanism furthermore was based on an essentially stateless model of political struggle. Pan-Africanists were typically colonial subjects or members of minority groups. Three sovereign black states did exist, but Haiti, Liberia, and Ethiopia were, in their way, closed societies for whom Pan-Africanism was hardly less menacing than imperialism. For entrenched elites, solidarity based on continent of origin unacceptably enlarged the playing field.[22] Struggling to maintain themselves in a world of powerful nation-states, they had only the most shallow affinity for a doctrine that opposed itself to conventional forms of political organization and embraced the widest interpretation of a civic community. Pan-African efforts to influence world affairs, then, could only take the form of moral suasion, economism, and cultural conservationism. No armed militants stood able and ready to challenge incumbency. Poised, if weakly, against the state, and against white Creole domination, Pan-Africanism could certainly have been portrayed as reactionary by the Whiggish Latin liberals of 1900.

Yet Pan-Africanism, like Pan-Americanism, sought to create a positive identity for people who would have crosscutting allegiances in any case. The challenge for both forms of organization was to negotiate the often vast differences among American peoples that imperial history frequently masked. Language was one of these, albeit a minor problem for many. Like citizens of the small states of Europe, many inhabitants of the Caribbean, especially outside the Spanish countries, tended toward polyglottism. The island of Saint Thomas, for example, long a maritime entrepôt and commercial emporium, was a virtual babel. Language nevertheless established specific sensibilities and thus ordered—and divided—consciousness. In this regard, Spanish served as an effective instrument of unification for Martí and other Hispanophones. French did less well, competing as it did with a powerful Creole vernacular. The activist intellectuals of Parisian and Madrileño exile fared well in multiple language contexts, but the nations they hoped to rule required a political order grounded in specific linguistic traditions and social realities. "The able governor in America is not the one who knows how to govern the Germans or the French," Martí instructed; "he must know the elements that compose his own country."[23]

Particular countries also had their unique histories. The political and social conditions that faced Firmin in Haiti differed substantially from those confronting Cuban nationalists, Pan-Africanists, or Pan-Americanists. Haiti was the experiment in nationalism par excellence. It had long since disposed of its colonial overlords, and Pan-Africanism did not interest the elites who replaced them. As in other Latin societies, perception of social status in Haiti had much to do not only with color but with class and ancestry. Culture colluded with this. Over time, Haiti produced a dual system of language, religion, and socialization. Creole and French elements were never mutually exclusive and together posed institutional barriers to education, political change, and social development. Firmin and other Haitian intellectuals recognized this problem, but almost all sought a solution in the suppression of Creole and the equation of the metropolitan culture with improvement.[24]

In this, they shared the optic of the Cuban bourgeoisie. Part of the failure of Caribbean national bourgeoisies to take a longer view of cultural emulation lay in the few examples of spectacular success they saw around them in the late nineteenth century. Could they repeat the achievements of Japan or, closer to home, of Brazil and Argentina? Perhaps imitating developed states and abandoning any defensive posture toward foreign investment and cultural influence was the answer to the dilemma of modernization. This was not Martí's position, but Firmin's. Firmin abandoned the traditional Haitian nationalist policy of opposing foreign ownership of land and advocated opening Haiti to foreign proprietorship and investment. Foreigners were circumventing the law anyway. In any case, Firmin argued, prohibition was obsolete and Haiti badly needed the additional capital that outsiders would bring.[25] Ultimately the parasitic nature of the bourgeoisie, the state it created, and the military that united the ensemble defeated Firmin personally and confounded Haitian development up to this moment.

In 1893 Martí, who traveled to Española to reconnoiter with Cuban insurgents in Santo Domingo, met Firmin in Cap Haitien, a city in northern Haiti not far from the revolutionists' Dominican stronghold at Monte Christi. Martí had made several trips to the island to confer with Máximo Gómez. The revolutionaries moved in and out of Haiti, shielded by local supporters. Martí was not positively impressed with what he saw of Haiti, a land he described as ravaged and dispirited, although he quickly sensed the Haitians' pride in their national independence. Martí recalled Firmin as a genial black man, a Pan-Americanist, who possessed rare insights on Caribbean politics, race, and culture. Martí was well aware of the Haitian belletristic tradition in French. He recognized the sophistication of the black republic's cultural-leadership class, and he knew of Firmin's book *De l'égalité des races humaines*. Firmin's ideas on equality accorded with his own. For his part, Firmin remembered conversations that "turned on the great question of Cuban independence and the possibility of a Caribbean federation. Apart from practical reservations, we were absolutely in agreement on principles. We felt for one another a compelling affinity." After their evanescent meeting, Martí was on the road again, to Costa Rica, New York, and Florida.[26]

Like many other visitors to Haiti, Martí was confounded by its mixture of "Parisians and primitives," but remained impressed by the elite's literary culture and the courageous revolutionists of a century before. Apart from collegial contacts and an appreciation of Haitian texts, however, Martí's interest in Haiti seems to have rested chiefly on probing the claim that Cuban independence would result in a state of anarchy and racial violence supposedly characteristic of the black republic. His visits to Española convinced him that Haiti and Cuba were very different and could never recapitulate each other's history. Martí did not describe, and perhaps was not fully aware of, one of the major elements that made this so: Haiti, no less than Cuba but more consciously so, had racially constructed its nationality.[27]

The racial construction of nationality raises the possibility that the nationalist mission in any given country can be misinterpreted. *Cubanidad* sought to displace blackness, but not whiteness. The conscious Haitian invention of *noir* as a political category sought to make normative what the colonialists had rendered monstrous. When Haitian governors surveyed the masses they indeed saw a population overwhelmingly black. When Cuban leaders did the same, a broad somatic spectrum confronted them. In Haiti's case, reversing the norm reversed the pattern of ascriptive domination. In Cuba's case, it reinforced it.

After a year's preparation, Martí and other Cuban revolutionaries launched the Plan de Fernandina in January 1895. The carefully coordinated general insurrection turned into a full-fledged war with Spain. Martí, a major-general in this conflict, died in action at Dos Ríos on May 19, 1895. The remainder of the century was not without difficulty for Cuban nationalists. Following the expulsion of Spain, they faced, with other peoples of the Americas and the Pacific, the power of a newly energized United States.

In Haiti, a reform movement coalesced around Firmin's charismatic personality. Numerous educated and reflective persons joined his ranks. They participated in the ongoing critique of Haitian society and institutions and in the political and military side of the Firminist movement. A strong reforming impulse developed in response to the harsh realities of Haitian life. Firmin as a historical figure and Firminism as a political creed represented the culmination of this process. The timing of the Firminist revolt was particularly significant. Since the early 1890s, Haitians had been preparing for the centennial celebration of their national independence. Steeped in historical lore, and imbued with a not altogether cheerful awareness of tradition, many felt a sense of urgency as 1904 approached.[28]

Firmin returned from exile in 1902 to mount a revolution against the national bourgeoisie and its military arm. Unlike Martí, Firmin was a reformer, not a revolutionary. Although his plans for Haiti reserved considerable economic power for foreigners and elites, these interest groups bitterly opposed even the most conservative innovations. After the failure of the revolution of 1902, Firmin returned to exile and wrote a number of books, tracts, and apologies. One of these was a lengthy history of Haiti and an exegesis of its foreign policy, entitled *M. Roosevelt, président des Etats-Unis et la République d'Haiti* (1905). In it, Firmin praised Roosevelt's forthright approach to regional diplomacy, a policy based on hemispheric security.[29] Washington feared European intervention in the Americas, Firmin reasoned, and could only benefit from the presence of a stable and autonomous Haiti. His "northern strategy," however, failed to impress the Yankees, who regarded him as a troublemaker and collaborated in the failure of his second insurgency in 1908. Firmin died in exile on Saint Thomas in 1911.[30]

Martí and Firmin shared elements of a milieu, a sensibility, and a single encounter, but the connection between them did not end there. After Cuban independence, Havana opinion makers linked the conservative and cautious Firmin, then in poor health and without resources, to the widespread unrest among Cuban blacks in the first decades of the twentieth century. In 1910 *La Prensa* charged the Haitian with plans to start a regional black uprising against whites. Fear of impending unrest led to the mobilization of rural police in some areas of Cuba. Havana authorities censored any intimation of racial conflict, and they suppressed newsreels showing the African American boxer Jack Johnson's defeat of the white fighter Jim Jeffries. Black Cubans had fought in the Revolutionary War only to find that they remained marginalized and deprived of opportunities that were available to others. Mounting racial tensions exploded in a full-fledged rebellion, the Guerrita of 1912, which centered in Oriente Province. The insurrection was put down within a year with the help of the U.S. military.[31]

Ironically, the Cuban government resurrected the old fear of Haiti as an instigator of underclass revolt. It also identified the growing numbers of Haitian and Jamaican migrant sugar workers as culprits. Black Cuban dissatisfaction had coincided with a wave of immigration and a xenophobic response. Martí's lessons on Haiti had been forgotten, his unconscious coupling of whiteness and *Cubanidad* all too quickly remembered.[32]

It is easier to analyze and pass judgment on the thought and behavior of people long dead than to suggest what they ought to have done from the perspective of their own time and place. Martí, Firmin, and others operated on two levels. One concerned revolutionary politics; the other had to do with consciousness-raising on an exalted plane. The audience for the politics did not always coincide with the attentive intellectual public. The *compañeros* of the battlefield were often not those of the lecture hall. This was perhaps a fatal flaw. These revolutionary scholars had networked across three continents and belonged to prestigious metropolitan academies and professional associations as well as to their own national counterparts to these institutions. They were not able, however, to make the national universities, learned societies, and other apparatus of high culture fulfill for their home countries the role such institutions played in the developed world.

In most Caribbean societies, intellectual work remained the leisure pastime of gentlemen, most particularly physicians and lawyers. The intellectual culture of Cuban cigar makers was an exception that proved the rule. Ideas were savored, but only a few, like Martí and Firmin, perhaps, expected them to have a vital impact on the interests of the powerful. There was no regional counterpart to Martí's New York–based Liga de Instrucción, which sought to give a liberal education to workers.[33] Polydiscursivity could not be an effective instrument for change if limited to a handful of individuals. Pan-Americanists would have had to use their skills as culture workers and opinion leaders to alter the perception of learning and the reward structures associated with it. They would have had to democratize learning, one of the prerequisites for the development of a Caribbean self that would be more resistant to demoralization and conquest, if they were to realize a genuine Pan-Americanism.

Martí and Firmin were also simultaneously imprisoned and emancipated by potentially totalizing iterations of nationalism. If Pan-Africanism was a way of stepping out of a discourse that did not privilege blackness, Pan-Americanism was a way of subordinating that and other particularisms in a manner that left the nation-state system intact. Throughout the Americas, with the exception of Haiti, that system was racially constructed as white. Haiti did not, therefore, fit the Pan-American mold in the same way as other states. Historically, the second-oldest American republic did not, in fact, participate in inter-American politics as did the others. This is often attributed to language difference, but race seems more central a cause.

As a nationalist in a black republic, Anténor Firmin could be no more comfortable with Pan-Africanism than José Martí. Haiti does not represent the nexus of Pan-Africanism and Pan-Americanism but, rather, a peculiar antithesis of both. That nexus lies instead in a revised conception of nationality that admits of pluralism, cultural and somatic. The seeds of that pluralism are embedded in Latin American thought. "Man's universal identity springs forth from triumphant love and the turbulent hunger for life," Martí wrote. "The soul, equal and eternal, emanates from bodies of various shapes and colors"[34] and, he might have added, embraces America such that it is.

Notes

1 Jean Lamore, *José Martí and l'Amérique* (Paris: l'Harmattan, 1986), pp. 9–10.

2 Anténor Firmin, *Lettres de Saint-Thomas* (Paris: V. Giard and E. Briere, 1910), pp. 115, 125, 128; José Martí to Sotero Figueroa, June 3, 1893, in *Obras completas* (Havana: Editorial Nacional de Cuba, 1963), vol. 2, pp. 353–54; Paul Estrade, *José Martí (1853–1895) ou des fondements de la democratie en Amérique Latine* (Lille: Editions Caribeennes, 1987), pp. 243, 739n216; Roberto Fernández Retamar, *Martí* (Montevideo: Biblioteca de Marcha, 1970), pp. 10–21.

3 Léonce Viaud, *La personnalité d'Anténor Firmin* (Port-au-Prince: V. Valcin, 1948), pp. 51–58; Furcy Chatelain, *Résumé des considerations sur la politique extérieure d'Haïti à propos du 15 janvier 1908* (Fort-de-France: L'Union Sociale, 1908), pp. 9–10; Brenda Gayle Plummer, *Haiti and the Great Powers* (Baton Rouge: Louisiana State University Press, 1988), pp. 26–28.

4 Plummer, *Haiti and the Great Powers,* p. 28; Anténor Firmin, *De l'égalité des races humaines* (Paris: F. Pichon, 1885); Anténor Firmin, *Diplomates et diplomatie* (Cap Haitien: Progrès, 1899); Firmin, *Lettres de Saint-Thomas.*

5 Roger Gaillard, "Firmin et les Etats-Unis à travers un document inédit," pt. 1, *Conjonction* (June 1975): 124; Viaud, *La personnalité d'Anténor Firmin,* pp. 15–16; Frederick Douglass, "Haiti and the United States: Inside Story of the Negotiations for the Môle St. Nicolas," *North American Review* 153 (1891): 337–45, 450, 459.

6 Emilio Rodríguez Demorizi, *Martí en Santo Domingo* (Havana: Impresores Ucar Garcia, 1953), pp. 597–99. One of Firmin's biographers has tried to turn this defeat into a success: Georges J. Benjamin, *La diplomatie d'Anténor Firmin* (Paris: A. Pedone, 1960).

7 Michael H. Hunt, *Ideology and U.S. Foreign Policy* (New Haven: Yale University Press, 1987); Dana G. Munro, *Intervention and Dollar Diplomacy in the Caribbean, 1900–1921* (Princeton: Princeton University Press, 1964).

8 See Jeffrey Belnap, "Headbands, Hemp Sandals, and Headdresses: The Dialectics of Dress and Self-Conception in Martí's 'Our America,'" in this book.

9 On the development of contemporaneous antiracist counterdiscourses, see Alfred A. Moss Jr., *The American Negro Academy* (Baton

Rouge: Louisiana State University Press, 1981) and Gordon K. Lewis, *Main Currents in Caribbean Thought* (Baltimore: Johns Hopkins University Press, 1983). On Du Bois, see David Levering Lewis, *Du Bois: The Biography of a Race* (New York: Henry Holt, 1994). The polymathic tendency among nineteenth-century Afro-American elites is evident in the biographical directory by William J. Simmons, *Men of Mark. Eminent, Progressive, and Rising* (Cleveland: G. M. Rewell, 1887).

10 Three useful works describe the triad of philanthropy, capitalism, and ideology as it affected Africans, black Americans, and Antilleans respectively: Kenneth King, *Pan-Africanism and Education: A Study of Race, Philanthropy and Education in the Southern States of America and East Africa* (Oxford: Clarendon, 1971); John H. Stanfield, *Philanthropy and Jim Crow in American Social Science* (Westport, Conn.: Greenwood Press, 1985); Thomas C. Holt, *The Problem of Freedom: Race, Labor, and Politics in Jamaica and Britain, 1832–1938* (Baltimore: Johns Hopkins University Press, 1992).

11 Koenrad W. Swart, *The Sense of Decadence in Nineteenth Century France* (The Hague: M. Nijhoff, 1964); Paul Estrade, *La colonia cubana de París, 1895–1898* (Havana: Editorial de Ciencias Sociales, 1984), pp. 5–8.

12 Firmin, *Lettres de Saint-Thomas*, pp. 109, 110, 112–18; Estrade, *La colonia cubana de París*, passim; Marc Péan, *L'illusion héroïque* (Port-au-Prince: Henri Deschamps, n.d.), p. 168. Betances lived for two years in exile in Haiti. See Ramón Emeterio Betances, *Las Antillas para los antillanos*, ed. Carlos M. Rama (San Juan: Instituto de Cultura Puertorriqueña, 1975), pp. xxxi–xxxiv, 11–69; Emilio Godínez Sosa, ed., *Cuba en Betances* (Havana: Editorial de Ciencias Sociales, 1985), pp. 16–17, 38–39.

13 José Martí, *Our America*, trans. Elinor Randall with additional translations by Juan de Onis and Roslyn Held Foner (New York and London: Monthly Review Press, 1977), p. 319.

14 For an original discussion of this matter, see Ada Ferrer, "The Silence of Patriots: Race and Nationalism in Martí's Cuba," in this book.

15 Works on the race war of 1912 include Rafael Fermoselle-López, *Política y color en Cuba: La guerrita de 1912* (Montevideo: Ediciones Geminis, 1974); Thomas Tondée Orum, "The Politics of Color: The Racial Dimension of Cuban Politics during the Early Republican Years, 1900–1912" (Ph.D. diss., New York University, 1975); Louis A. Pérez Jr., "Politics, Peasants, and People of Color: The 1912 'Race' War in Cuba Reconsidered," *Hispanic American Historical*

Review 56 (August 1986): 509–39; Armando Fernández Soriano, "El exilio cubano del expresidente de Haití Rosalvo Bobo," *Cimarron* 2 (Winter 1990): 20–27; Aline Helg, *Our Rightful Share: The Afro-Cuban Struggle for Equality, 1886–1912* (Chapel Hill: University of North Carolina Press, 1995).

16 Martí, *Our America*, pp. 93–94; Floyd Miller, *The Search for a Black Nationality* (Urbana: University of Illinois Press, 1975); Wilson J. Moses, *The Golden Age of Black Nationalism* (Hamden, Conn.: Archon Books, 1978); Wilson J. Moses, *The Wings of Ethiopia* (Ames: Iowa State University Press, 1990), pp. 85–86, 165.

17 On fin-de-siècle imperialism: Imanuel Geiss, *The Pan African Movement* (London: Methuen, 1974), pp. 174–75; Jacob U. Egharevba, *A Short History of Benin* (Ibadan: Ibadan University Press, 1960), R. J. Gavin and J. A. Betley, *The Scramble for Africa; Protocoles et acte général de la Conference de Berlin, 1884–1885* (Ibadan: Ibadan University Press, 1973); Jon Bridgman, *The Revolt of the Hereros* (Berkeley: University of California Press, 1981); Horst Drechsler, *Let Us Die Fighting: The Struggle of the Herero and Nama against German Imperialism (1884–1915)* (Berlin: Akademie-Verlag, 1986); E. D. Morel, *King Leopold's Rule in Africa* (London: W. Heinemann, 1904); E. D. Morel, *Red Rubber: The Story of the Rubber Slave Trade Flourishing on the Congo in the Year of Grace 1906*, 2d ed. (London: T. Fisher Unwin, 1907).

18 Rayford W. Logan, *The Betrayal of the Negro* (New York: Collier Books, 1970); Willard B. Gatewood Jr., *Black Americans and the White Man's Burden* (Urbana: University of Illinois Press, 1975). For examples of the new wave of imperialist writing on Central America and the Caribbean, see Archibald Colquhoun, *Greater America* (New York: Harper and Brothers, 1904); Sydney Brooks, "The Passing of the Black Republics," *Harper's Weekly* (May 16, 1908); Lothrop Stoddard, *The French Revolution in San Domingo* (Boston: Houghton Mifflin, 1914); and Lothrop Stoddard, *The Rising Tide of Color* (New York: Scribner, 1921).

19 Arthur F. Corwin, "Afro-Brazilians: Myths and Realities," in *Slavery and Race Relations in Latin America*, ed. Robert Brent Toplin (Westport, Conn.: Greenwood Press, 1974), pp. 385–437; Leslie Rout, *The African Experience in Spanish America* (London: Cambridge University Press, 1975), pp. 191–97.

20 Moses, *The Wings of Ethiopia*, pp. 141–58; Cedric J. Robinson, "Coming to Terms: The Third World and the Dialectic of Imperialism," *Race and Class* 22 (1981): 363–85. On declension: Brooks,

"The Passing of the Black Republics." On modernity: Talal Asad, "From the History of Colonial Anthropology to the Anthropology of Western Hegemony," in *Colonial Situations: Essays on the Contextualization of Ethnographic Knowledge,* ed. George W. Stocking Jr. (Madison: University of Wisconsin Press, 1991), pp. 314–24.

21 Lara quoted in Firmin, *Lettres de Saint-Thomas,* p. 129.

22 Benito Sylvain, *Du sort des indigenes dans les colonies d'exploitation* (Paris: L. Boyer, 1901); Antoine Bervin, *Benito Sylvain; Apôtre du relèvement social des noirs* (Port-au-Prince: La Phalange, 1969). Broad discussions of these issues are found in Cedric J. Robinson, *Black Marxism: The Making of the Black Radical Tradition* (London: Zed Press, 1983).

23 Martí, *Our America,* p. 86.

24 See the discussion in Lewis, *Main Currents in Caribbean Thought,* pp. 261–64.

25 Firmin, *Lettres de Saint-Thomas,* pp. 38–86.

26 Martí, *Our America,* p. 321; Martí to Gonazalo de Quesada, September 8, 1892, in Martí, *Obras completas,* vol. 2, pp. 159–60; Lewis, *Main Currents in Caribbean Thought,* pp. 261–64; Firmin, *Lettres de Saint-Thomas,* pp. 115–16.

27 Martí, *Our America,* pp. 320–21.

28 Hugh Thomas, *Cuba: The Pursuit of Freedom* (New York: Harper and Row, 1971), p. 316; Joseph Jérémie, *Haïti indépendante* (Port-au-Prince: Chéraquit, 1929), p. 37; Péan, *L'illusion héroïque,* pp. 168–69; Plummer, *Haiti and the Great Powers,* p. 26.

29 Anténor Firmin, M. *Roosevelt, président des Etats-Unis et la République d'Haïti* (New York: Hamilton Bank Note Company, 1905).

30 J. Hood to Bacon and appended note, November 16, 1908, State Department Numerical File, National Archives; *New York Herald,* June 12, 1908.

31 Orum, "The Politics of Color," p. 207; Louis A. Pérez Jr., *Cuba* (New York: Oxford University Press, 1988), pp. 210, 221–22.

32 Donna M. Wolf, "The Caribbean People of Color and the Cuban Independence Movement" (Ph.D. diss., University of Pittsburgh, 1963), pp. 18–66; Luis E. Aguilar, *Cuba 1933, Prologue to Revolution* (Ithaca: Cornell University Press, 1972), pp. 37, 42–43. See also Fermoselle-López, *Política y color en Cuba;* Pérez Jr., "Politics, Peasants, and People of Color."

33 Thomas, *Cuba: The Pursuit of Freedom,* p. 300.

34 Martí, *Our America,* p. 94.

Ada Ferrer

The Silence of Patriots: Race and Nationalism in Martí's Cuba

Individually and together, the essays collected in this book suggest that American Studies can learn something from the work of José Martí, the poet and activist who lived in the United States and organized for Cuban independence. The notion of an encounter between American Studies and Martí is not altogether surprising, for Martí wrote extensively about American life—about such topics as race relations and immigration, labor activism and electoral politics, about capitalism and consumption, about literary figures such as Whitman and Emerson, and about everyday life in Gilded Age New York. As he wrote about life within the borders of the United States, he spoke also about American expansion outward, warning, fearfully and defiantly, of a day soon approaching when the United States ("the giant with seven-league boots") would step out of its already expanding borders into the Caribbean, South America, and the world. Martí wrote of these American and imperial topics from an outsider's perspective and for audiences either beyond the nation's geographical borders or exiled within them. Martí's work, then, holds an understandable allure for a new, more critical and internationalized American Studies—one now eager (or at the very least willing) "to look inside with alien eyes."[1]

To make the encounter between Martí's work and American Studies productive—to allow oneself to see Martí the outsider seeing the United States—one must, however, allow Martí's vision to retain something of its geographical and temporal alienness. He wrote of American and other topics, but in ways shaped always by his past and by present political projects formed elsewhere in the world. Thus the project of bringing Martí into American culture is necessarily a project of apprehending the Latin America and, in particular, the Cuba that weighed so heavily on Martí's imagination and activism.

Nowhere is this need more apparent than in approaching Martí's writings on race, a key topic for Americans and Americanists. In those writings, penned mostly in the early 1890s, students will find passages that seem revolutionary. Writing in an age of racial theory and in a country that at that very moment sanctioned escalating racial violence and segregation, Martí denied the existence of what scientists and lay people called race. "There can be no racial animosity," he wrote, "because there are no races." He continued: "The theorists and feeble thinkers string together and warm over the bookshelf races which the well-disposed observer and the fair-minded traveler vainly seek in the justice of Nature where man's universal identity springs forth from triumphant love. . . . The soul, equal and eternal, emanates from bodies of various shapes and colors. Whoever foments and spreads antagonism and hate between the races sins against humanity."[2] But alongside such strident antiracist claims are conclusions that will perhaps ring familiar and troubling to American scholars in the 1990s, because for Martí the radical denials of biological race often devolved into arguments against race-based political action. As we shall see below, to speak and act on the basis of racial identification was, for Martí, to engage in racism, to erect barriers to national well-being, and to divide humanity. Even racial labels themselves were at best unnecessary and at worse divisive and racist. There was little room here not only for black political activism but perhaps also for black subjectivity in general.

There is thus much in Martí that could be used to support claims currently made in American scholarship (and in nonacademic writing) about race—claims about racial transcendence and universalism, as well as claims about identity politics. So, much in the same manner that Martí's words are invoked to bolster the authority of intransigent and competing positions on socialism, Fidel Castro, and the contemporary Cuban state, so too can Martí's words serve the purposes of contending academic factions on racial politics in the United States. To allow oneself to read Martí on race through the lens of contemporary American racial politics is, however, to forgo the challenge of writing a postnational American Studies. It is, in fact, to bypass an obvious and potentially fruitful opportunity to internationalize American Studies and to opt instead for a more pernicious, and in some ways familiar, tendency to Americanize the international.

To apprehend the seeming contradictions contained in Martí's writings on race, we must place those writings in the context of the movement and the place that produced the contradictions in the first place. For the inconsistencies in Martí's racial constructions were part of larger processes and, more specifically, part of a complicated struggle between racism and antiracism unfolding within the massive multiracial and anticolonial movements that transformed Cuban society between 1868 and 1898. That movement, brilliantly championed by Martí, produced three full-fledged insurgencies in three decades; mobilized an army which, by the final war in 1895, was said to be about 60 percent of color; and produced a new and vibrant nationalist discourse that posited the ideal of racial equality and the figure of the humble and heroic black insurgent as foundations of the new Cuban nation.[3] To understand Martí on race—or Martí at all—one must thus understand something of this ostensibly antiracist, anticolonial movement. And for American Studies to discover Martí requires that the field open itself up to Cuba, that a transnational American Studies consider seriously the question of Cuban nationalism.

Martí devoted his life to the labor of Cuban independence, championing and helping to consolidate those sectors of the movement that were most committed to a vision of antiracism. The independence movement, bolstered by a racially integrated army and by an explicit assault on racism, emerged from a colonial society where only decades earlier the most prominent intellectuals and anti-Spanish thinkers imagined a Cuban nationality "formed by the white race"—"the only [Cuban nationality] with which any sensible man would concern himself."[4] The movement emerged, moreover, from a society whose white minority had long rejected the path of independence taken by its South and Central American neighbors in order to protect a prosperous and expanding sugar industry built on the labor of African and Creole (Cuban-born) slaves. In fact, by the start of the final war in 1895, when the integrated army invaded the rich sugar regions of western Cuba under the leadership of the Dominican-born Máximo Gómez, the mulatto general Antonio Maceo, and the black officer and former bricklayer and boat worker Quintín Banderas, racial slavery had been abolished only nine years earlier. Thus, as the decade after slave emancipation in the U.S. South gave way to the racial reaction and violence of "Redemption," in postemancipation Cuba it saw the consolidation of a movement supported by former slaveowners and former slaves, led by white and nonwhite officers, and committed to a powerful vision of racial inclusion. José Martí was undoubtedly the most avid defender of that vision. In a characteristic article published in 1893, he made his famous assertion that "a Cuban [was] more than mulatto, black, or white. Dying for Cuba on the battlefield, the souls of both black and white men [had] risen together."[5] This interpretation was expressed by others as well, including Antonio Maceo, who similarly proclaimed that "there [were] no blacks or whites here, but only Cubans."[6]

By the start of the third and final insurrection against Spain (the one in which both Martí and Maceo would lose their lives), their claims appear to have been in a very literal sense quite accurate. In the sources generated by the independence fighters, people rarely uttered a word about blacks or whites. In fact, according to the authors of official insurgent documents, the movement was peopled not by members of racially categorized groups but simply by people identified as "Cuban citizens."[7] So in a society less than a decade removed from racial slavery, and in a rebel army that scholars and contemporaries agree was significantly—if not predominantly—black, the sources generated by the insurrection make scarcely a reference to race.

This absence of racial labels in the sources produced by the insurrection can be and has been interpreted as the natural outcome of a multiracial movement that had, over the course of thirty years, succeeded in transcending racial categorization and racial animosity. When this absence, however, is uncovered and tracked, it begins to appear as anything but natural. Instead it emerges as a conspicuous—and at times purposeful—silence produced at a particular moment in the history of Cuban nationalism. To understand this apparent silence of race—to name it, to analyze its origins, and to identify its creators and challengers—is to contest traditional interpretations of the relationship between race and nationalism and Cuba. This was not a silence indicative of a resolution of "the race problem," but a silence symptomatic of profound conflicts about the role of different social groups in a society undergoing the simultaneous transition from slave to free labor and from colonial to national status. The silence was active: it was an argument, a slogan, a fantasy.

Silence here, however, does not refer to a disjuncture between what one expects as a scholar to find and analyze in archival documents, on the one hand, and the language of nineteenth-century sources, on the other. For to use the notion of silence in that way would be to border on the ahistorical: it would be to assume the existence of meanings and categories that, when not found, then become silence and erasure. Rather, this essay speaks of the silence of race in the 1890s because the silence is so traceable, so audible: it developed over time as racial references disappeared; it emerged in particular contexts and not in others, in particular sources and, again, not in others. And it developed alongside and immediately following Martí's (and others') exhortations to dispense with racial ascriptions. Yet even as one sees (or hears) this silence evolve, it is clear that it was never absolute, never the product of consensus and control; and always—even as it emerged—it was fraught with tension. In fact, it echoed so loudly in part because it was so often tested, challenged, and broken. The silence then becomes evidence neither of a nationalist resolution of the racial division nor of elite efforts to preserve a racist status quo.[8] Rather, it was emblematic of the ways in which the struggles between racism and antiracism defined Cuban nationalism.

Sources of Silence

The silence of race in Cuban nationalism during the 1890s emerged out of a long attempt to reconcile the categories of race and nation—two categories that colonial discourse had constructed as irreconcilable for almost a century. Spanish authorities and Creole, slaveowning elites had long linked the preservation of social order in Cuba with the maintenance of colonial rule. Pointing to the numerical predominance of the nonwhite population and the economic significance of slavery, they argued for the necessity of maintaining a colonial bond with Spain. To challenge that bond, they said, was to imperil life and property. In this way, colonial and metropolitan elites used the "race problem" to provide an automatic and negative answer to the "national question." Dominant colonial discourse held simply that Cuba could not be a nation.

To attempt to overthrow Spanish rule, then, required that Cuban nationalists transform the ways in which colonial and elite discourse constructed the relationship between race and nation. This was the challenge facing the leaders of the first war of independence, the Ten Years' War (1868–78). The early leaders of that rebellion introduced very cautious measures for the gradual abolition of slavery within rebel territories. They also introduced a new language of national identity, which accorded the label of citizen to Cuban slaves and free people of color. Thus early rebel propaganda maintained that "every Cuban . . . without distinctions of color, age, or sex can serve their country and Liberty."[9] For the first time, the public encountered talk not only of "slaves" or "blacks" but also of "black Cubans" and "citizens of color." So, while advocates of colonialism had constructed the nonwhite population as an obstacle to independence, early nationalist insurgents explicitly rejected that contention by positing that slaves could become citizens and that a colonial slave society could become a free nation.

As the rebellion progressed, however, it became clear that the relationship between race and nation could not be transformed without dissent and conflict. Cautious abolitionist measures were soon superseded by the day-to-day practice of insurgency, as slaves abandoned plantations and found their way to rebel camps, and as local military figures freed or took slaves often without consent of central rebel authority.[10] These events then fed the opposition's claims about the imminence of slave rebellion and about the onset of economic and social chaos on the island. In response to widespread black and mulatto participation and to the emergence, by the end of the war, of a powerful nonwhite leadership, many white insurgents surrendered and condemned the rebellion as disastrous to Cuban interests. Insurgents surrendered in large numbers—invariably tired and hungry, but often also protesting the extent and character of black involvement in the independence struggle. In the region of Camagüey, for example, approximately 95 percent of the original insurgent forces had surrendered by the third year of the rebellion, many giving as their reason that "blacks were poised to take control of the situation."[11]

Thus while the early rebellion promised to overturn strictures about the impossibility of Cuban nationhood, the mobilization of slaves and the rise of black insurgents and leaders also reinforced those strictures, fanning old fears about the dangers of black ascendancy. These claims would reach their peak in the second Cuban insurrection (1879–80). Known as the Guerra Chiquita, or "Little War," this insurrection featured prominent black and mulatto leadership and eventually was publicly rejected by a majority of white insurgents, who classified the motives of its black leaders as racist and the insurrection itself as the prelude to a race war.[12] Spanish forces and Cuban factionalism defeated the rebellion in less than a year. By 1880, then, the independence project appeared to have failed. And it failed, in part, because its leadership had not been able to counter the pre-1868 construction of the relationship between race and nation. The lingering fear of race war and the manipulation of that fear by colonial interests were as rampant in 1880 as they had been before the first insurrection in 1868. The rise of black insurgents and the idea of black citizens operating in a public, political sphere were still powerful enough to compromise the success of a multiracial independence movement. So, by 1880, the nationalist movement had failed to reconcile the categories of race and nation.

It was from this failure that the silence of race in Cuban nationalism emerged by the start of the final war of independence in 1895. If opponents of independence spoke of race—of racial slavery, of the island's racial composition, and of race war—then to defeat those opponents, independence activists would have to strip race of its ideological hold. They would have to silence the issue of race.

The silencing of race was, at one level, a very literal absence of racial references in insurgent documentation. Writing in 1892, Martí had argued that the "constant allusion to a man's skin color should cease."[13] And by the start of the war in 1895, the allusions appear to have done just that. Official insurgent sources routinely failed to record any information regarding individuals' racial identification. Thus the list of roughly forty thousand members of the rebel army who survived the final war carefully recorded for each soldier his name, his parents' names, his age, place of birth, residence, occupation, level of literacy, the date he joined the rebel army, positions held, and duties performed. Nowhere, however, did the list record any information regarding racial categories.[14] In other routine documents of the insurrection, as well, authors tended to avoid all racial references. When these appeared, they did so as if by accident. For example, in lists of wounded and sick soldiers treated in a rebel hospital camp in Matanzas Province, the hospital staff never used racial terms to describe the patients. One such list, however, was the exception that proved the rule. Compiled by a newcomer to the hospital, this list ascribed racial categories to all patients; just under half were classified as of color. By the time the next list was prepared, the racial references had again disappeared.[15]

Besides this literal absence of racial references in official insurgent documents, however, there was another less literal silence of race found principally in essays published by pro-independence writers and ex-insurgents. Encouraged by the slackening of censorship laws after 1886, journalists, essayists, and insurgents from earlier insurrections advocated the cause of Cuban independence in writing. These authors, among whom Martí was most prominent, sought to invalidate traditional claims about the impossibility of Cuban nationhood. They entered into a conscious dialogue with Spanish portrayals of the Cuban rebellions as race wars; and, as part of this dialogue, they conducted a reevaluation of the role of the black insurgent within anticolonial insurgency. This reexamination involved, on the one hand, the telling of stories about everyday activities of unknown black soldiers. At the same time, it entailed the formulation of an ideal black insurgent, one who rose above others in acts of selfless and raceless patriotism. This reevaluation neutralized and transformed the figure of the black insurgent. Once a dreaded emblem of race war and a black republic, he now became an acceptable component in the struggle for Cuban nationhood.[16]

One beneficiary of this neutralization was a little-known black insurgent named José Antonio Legón, who was appropriated as the subject of numerous biographical portraits in the early 1890s. In one such biography, the journalist and ex-insurgent officer Ramón Roa explained that before the first war began Legón was a *negrito* and the slave of a Cuban who supported the cause of independence. Legón's master was killed by Spanish forces during the war, and shortly afterward Legón himself was captured. Given the opportunity to save his life by renouncing the Cuban cause, Legón declined, explaining to his captors: "Well, when my master—who raised me and who was good—passed away, he told me: 'Jose Antonio, never stop being Cuban.' And the poor man left this world for another. Now I comply by being Cuban until the end. . . . You can kill me if you want."[17] Kill him they did; but the insurgent the Spanish soldiers killed in war was not the slave who had lived in peace. For in the course of fighting the war, Legón had gone from being a *negrito* and a slave to being "Cuban." Even his black body, explained Roa, had been lightened by the scars that "everywhere interrupted the blackness of his skin." Legón, however, had not demanded this transformation from black slave to Cuban soldier and citizen for himself. Rather, he was freed by a benevolent master who upon his death expressed his wish that Legón be and remain Cuban. By resisting the authority of Spain, Legón merely consecrated the wishes and commands of his master. His rebelliousness was thus cast as an extension of his master's will and not as the result of personal initiative or political conviction.

Legón and other black insurgents portrayed in the prose of independence during the 1890s posed no social or political threat. Even with weapons in their hands, they respected the norms that relegated them to an inferior social and political status. They violated enough prescriptions of colonial society to help endanger the colonial state, but not enough of them to overturn traditional norms of racial etiquette, or to seduce or threaten a white woman, or to imagine—much less create—anything resembling a black republic.

Spanish authorities and their allies continued to point to black support for independence or to the perils of black rebellion, but pro-independence authors countered with claims about the insignificance of race. Black rebels, they argued, posed no particular danger. As Martí explained in 1894, "the black Cuban does not aspire to freedom . . . political justice, and independence as a black man, but as a Cuban."[18] Thus, the significant presence of black and mulatto soldiers in the rebel army was rendered less susceptible to accusations of race war because those soldiers were there not as black insurgents but as Cubans and, above all, as loyal and obedient patriots. To speak, then, of black insurgents and white insurgents was, as Martí claimed, "redundant"; the word "Cuban" sufficed. In fact, to persist in using racial labels and explanations was not only unnecessary, it was also anti-Cuban and antipatriotic; it was to align oneself with the enemies of independence who had long used racial labels, the island's racial composition, and the specter of racial warfare to keep Cuba a colony. In the words of Martí, "always to dwell on the divisions or differences between the races . . . was to raise barriers to the attainment of . . . national well-being."[19]

Breaking the Silence

As it emerged, however, this call for racial silence never completely cohered. Even before the start of the final war, it was challenged by journalists and activists of color who persisted in talking, writing, and organizing around race. Thus the new racial silence, as well as the portrayal of the passive and raceless black insurgent, coincided precisely with the emergence of their antithesis: the rise of black political activism. Following the abolition of slavery, black and mulatto leaders and their communities established mutual aid societies, recreational and instructional societies, schools, and newspapers. It was through the work of these institutions that a concerted campaign for black civil rights took off in 1892. Led by the mulatto journalist Juan Gualberto Gómez—a close friend of and collaborator with Martí—the campaign sought to secure changes in colonial legislation regarding access to public services and establishments, from restaurants to roads to schools. To win these rights, activists urged their constituents to organize, to vote, and occasionally even to boycott. The image of the silent and submissive black insurgent, then, clashed with the reality of black and mulatto activism. The clash resulted, in part, in disputes over how and whether to speak about race publicly. While some nationalist leaders insisted that the best way to promote unity was to not speak about or dwell on questions of race, journalists of color publicized an opposing view. Thus, J. G. Gómez, in an important article on the aims of the black newspaper *La Fraternidad,* wrote in 1890:

> I know well that some consider this problem [race] so dreadful, that they consider imprudent anyone who proclaims its existence, imagining with an incomparable naiveté (*candor*) that the best way to resolve certain questions is not to study or even to examine them. And I know as well that others, in bad faith, spread [the word] that those of us who propose to help arrive at a solution are bringing as the consequences of our efforts the separation of the Cuban races.[20]

Journalists of color were challenging the notion that national unity demanded reticence about racial justice or racial identification.

Just as black activists challenged the portrayal of their political behavior, so too did black insurgents challenge the silencing of race in official nationalist discourse. In fact, the ways in which official nationalist sources portrayed racial identification as insignificant stood in stark contrast to the ways in which race emerges in other sources. The significance of the comparison lies not only in that some sources are silent on the issue of race while others are not; it lies also in the realization that the silence, and the process of imposing and maintaining it, was perpetually confronted by those wanting or willing to break through it. So, while some sought to mute racial discussions, others challenged the silence of race and the resolution it implied.

This tension is captured perfectly in an episode recounted by Manuel Arbelo, a white, small landholder from the province of Matanzas who, upon joining the insurrection in January 1896, was given an officer's rank, a black assistant to cook and clean for him, and the job of managing a makeshift rebel hospital in the countryside. His duties at the hospital, he would later recall in his war memoirs, were made more difficult when "some officers began to arrive, almost all of these black and *mestizo,* men lacking any kind of education and made vain by the sudden change in their social position." The "accidents of war," he explained, "had removed them from the humblest of circumstances and placed them in positions of dominance that had filled them with pride and arrogance." The new arrivals regularly gathered in the evenings to speak of war and politics. They talked of a new social order in Cuba, one characterized by what they called "social equality." Often they went on to wonder aloud about whether that social equality would indeed be won with independence. Arbelo quoted one participant in the conversations as saying that "the race of color, which is the bone and sinew of this war, will have sacrificed itself so that white Cubans [can reap all the benefits]" of independence. Arbelo classified such ideas not only as "absurd," but also as dangerously prone to produce profound disagreements within the Cuban cause. In fact, Arbelo always tried to discourage these conversations and to banish these thoughts from his camp; such talk, he implied, was inappropriate for patriots. Here was race very literally being silenced.[21]

The tension between those who would speak of race and racial justice and those who would silence that talk may have been particularly acute in the province of Matanzas, where Arbelo's hospital was located. The province was dominated by large sugar plantations worked by slaves before abolition. Even by the period of the war, nine years after emancipation, the labor forces on these estates were composed largely of ex-slaves and their descendants. Little opportunity existed for these people outside the local sugar estates, and few persons of color were able to own or rent their own plots of land. Matanzas, then, may have been the province where emancipation brought the least change in the daily lives of rural black workers, in the expectations of their white employers, and in the patterns of class and race relations in the post-emancipation period.[22] According to the provincial governor in 1894, Matanzas, as the province with the largest number of slaves before emancipation, was now the most resistant when it came to any action that "tended towards the equality of the races."[23] This might help explain why so many black rural workers from local plantations were willing to go to war: freedom not gained with emancipation might be gained with independence.

One of the men operating in the region of Matanzas where Arbelo's hospital was located was a black soldier named Ricardo Batrell Oviedo. After the war, Batrell went on to publish one of the most interesting memoirs of that insurrection and, significantly, one that has been relatively little used by historians of Cuban independence. This memoir provides rich evidence of how the silence of race was challenged by Cubans of color in the rebel camp. While leaders maintained that to speak of race was to compromise the unity and success of a free Cuba, Batrell suggested to the contrary that not to speak of race and issues of racial justice was a greater affront to Cuban patriotism.

His memoir, titled *For History: Autobiographical Notes on the Life of Ricardo Batrell Oviedo,* is not an autobiography in the conventional sense of the term.[24] It is, rather, a war memoir filled with details of military maneuvers and encounters. Not one full paragraph is devoted to Batrell's life before the insurrection. Of the pre-1895 period, he informs us only that he was born in 1880 on the sugar mill "Trinidad," in Sabanilla del Encomendador, Matanzas, and that from the age of eight through his fifteenth birthday he worked in the cane fields of that mill. In telling the story of his life, Batrell carefully chose to begin with his decision to join the insurrection, defining it as the central experience of his life, and virtually erasing from the historical record his experience as a worker and resident on a sugar plantation.

Batrell gives only one explanation for his decision to join the independence rebellion. He joined, he wrote in the first pages of his memoir, because he "saw the symbol of my race in that grand endeavor: Mr. Juan Gualberto Gómez . . . the true personification of my race . . . that man-symbol."[25] Thus, we see that his decision to join the Cuban rebellion was made while he identified himself not just as a "Cuban" but as a Cuban of color—and as a member of "la raza de color." From the outset, then, Batrell distinguished himself from the standard chroniclers of Cuban independence by casting his participation in that movement in racial terms.

What Batrell expected to gain from that participation was also inextricably linked to his position as a black worker in a former slave society. There are no lengthy disquisitions on the meaning of independence or war, no explicit statements on how he envisioned the Cuba that he called his beloved, and no definitions of terms like "liberty" or "equality" or "fraternity." What he might have meant by or thought about any of these concepts is left for us to decipher in war story after war story. Batrell came closest to describing what he hoped to achieve in the struggle when he told the story of a white colonel and his black assistant. The insurgent colonel had received a serious wound in a battle against Spanish forces and found himself unable to walk. The colonel's assistant, "an individual of the race of color," placed the injured colonel over his shoulders and marched that way for miles, from the center of town to a sugar mill on its outskirts. There the assistant was himself shot by a Spanish soldier and was no longer able to carry the colonel. Because the assistant was more seriously wounded than the colonel, the colonel picked up the black assistant (twice his size), placed him over his shoulder, and continued the march, his leg now bleeding more profusely under the weight of the injured assistant. Batrell described the incident in detail and then concluded:

> Isn't it true, dear reader, that it would hearten us immensely to believe that at that particular moment humanity had been perfected? . . . Yes, we may believe it, because that *was* democracy, with all its most beautiful attributes, because at that moment there existed "human reciprocity"—a reciprocity that all civilized peoples, nations, and men struggle to attain.[26]

Democracy, for Batrell, was a form of reciprocity. And the highest form of reciprocity attainable in a society recently liberated from slavery was the reciprocity between ex-slave and ex-master, between black and white. In this moment of perfect equilibrium described and glorified by Batrell, black and white men (and it was always men) were capable of manifesting that reciprocity.

Batrell's vision of black and white combatants fighting together selflessly was, in fact, quite close to the images developed by pro-independence leaders such as Martí in the period immediately preceding the war. Just as Martí wrote of the blood and souls of black and white soldiers becoming one, so too did Batrell. But the mixing of blood and races that produced the nation was here not the product of miscegenation (as it would be in the writings of other Latin American writers such as José Vasconcelos and Gilberto Freyre). Rather, racial amalgamation occurred between men and in the masculine space of the battlefield. For both Martí and the fifteen-year-old sugar worker turned insurgent (who had probably never heard of Martí when he abandoned his workplace to join the rebels), the nation was born of the embrace of black and white men. Reflecting on that embrace and recalling episodes like the one discussed above, Batrell concluded nostalgically: "Those were the days of the true Cuban people; there was no prejudice, no race. All was joy and confraternity."[27]

But Batrell summoned more than nostalgia to write about an antiracism that he saw betrayed. He summoned, in fact, the legitimacy and authority of the nationalist movement itself. Nationalist discourse had clearly sanctioned the democracy to which Batrell aspired. Thus when Batrell saw that democracy or racial "confraternity" undermined by members of the rebel community, Batrell had a powerful ideological weapon in his hands.

Throughout his memoir Batrell argued that while a majority of the insurgents in Matanzas were people of color, when peace came it was the white insurgents who took the credit for liberating Cuba and consequently assumed most positions of power in the new republic. One victim of this process was Martín Duen, a man "as dark as ebony" who had led a rebel company for most of the war. When the armistice with Spain was signed, the white provincial leader of the movement stripped Duen of his title of captain and put in his place a white officer, Guillermo Schweyer. Schweyer, according to Batrell, had done little for the Cuban cause, spending most of his time sitting by a local river, with a rowboat handy in case things got rough and with regular supplies of corn bread arriving to him still warm from his family's oven in the town nearby. Yet this white insurgent, Batrell lamented, was to take the place of a dedicated, hardworking black rebel. For Batrell, the case of Schweyer and Duen was typical of what occurred in the rebel army at the end of the war. This sort of behavior, of which he gave numerous examples, he said was guided by "an antidemocratic spirit" and constituted a total disregard for "patriotic justice."[28]

At the end of his diary, Batrell concluded that if none of his valiant group, which had time and time again won battles of thirty versus hundreds, attained a rank higher than sergeant, that was because the billets they deserved, rightfully earned in the heat of battle, had been distributed among the growing number of "sons of distinguished families" who began appearing in the rebellion at the end of the war, and who were given these billets "only because of color." He concludes that these men were false stars and represented a kind of "mask that falsifies the history of the [true] Liberation Army."[29] What Batrell and others like him had earned had been unjustly taken, and Batrell identified the worthy and unworthy along racial lines.

Batrell's perspective on the final insurrection and on relations between white insurgents and insurgents of color is significant for several reasons. First, though written after the end of the war and from the vantage point of the early republic, it is one of the few remaining testimonies of a black insurgent during independence. Second, it demonstrates the ways in which the silencing of race within official Cuban nationalism was challenged by insurgents on the ground. Batrell continued to use racial categories to identify and describe himself and others around him. His fellow insurgents, white and black, appear to have done the same. Batrell further used racial categories to account for cause and motivation. Thus, he argued, it was racial pride that had led him to the Cuban insurrection, and it was racial hatred that had denied him proper credit and reward for his sacrifice.

Martí and others had tried to invalidate old claims of race war by arguing that black insurgents joined and fought not as "blacks" but as "Cubans." Batrell showed that he had fought as both. He constructed himself and felt himself to be simultaneously a member of "the race of color" and of the Cuban nation. These two identities were not mutually exclusive. The ways in which he fought for and imagined the Cuban nation were profoundly influenced by his sense of racial identity and racial justice. Leaders had further hoped that a new language of patriotism would replace earlier discourses of race. What Batrell demonstrated, though, was that nationalist discourse could lend itself well to exposing and condemning what he called "the preoccupation with race." Thus, when he condemned the racism of particular insurgents, he condemned it not only as racist but as antipatriotic, antidemocratic, and therefore anti-Cuban.

Batrell was not alone in this; others also realized that the independence movement had provided a language with which to attack behavior perceived as racist. Two similar incidents, one in 1876 during the first war and the other in 1895 during the final war, reveal the uses to which that language was put by the end of the independence period. One night in a rebel camp, a white woman rejected the overtures of an officer of color. The officer became furious, insisting that she refused him only because of his color. In anger, he then threatened her and anyone who dared court her in the future.[30] Twenty years and two wars later, at a dance at another rebel camp, another black officer tried to court a white woman. He asked her to dance and when she refused, the black officer again became angry and confronted the woman with a similar accusation. "You won't dance with me," he said, "because I am black." In this instance, however, the officer made no threats, but instead gave a long speech on valor, patriotism, and equality, condemning her refusal as antipatriotic.[31] Now, to be racist was to be anti-Cuban.

The language of nationalism had thus provided the means with which to challenge any behavior perceived as racist. The challenges made by black soldiers such as Batrell, or the men in Arbelo's hospital camp, were powerful precisely because they were sanctioned by nationalist discourse and directed against transgressors from within the nationalist camp. That discourse appealed to Batrell and other Cubans of color not because they felt little or no consciousness of race, but rather because nationalism, at least in theory, made racial equality a foundation of Cuban nationality and made possible the advancement of Cubans of color. Cuban nationalism, at least in theory, meant that a white man could carry a black one, that black and white soldiers could fight together, and that men of color could be justly rewarded for their labors. When practice did not conform to theory, then these insurgents could use the language of nationalism to acknowledge and attack that disparity and to chastize not their enemies but their allies, commanders, and compatriots.

Thus the pronouncements about racial transcendence made by Martí and other nationalists had no uniform and unchanging meaning; their patriotic assertions about racelessness were not abstract propositions about transcending race. Rather, they were statements made in a concrete historical context of forging an anticolonial movement in a former slave society. They were statements that expressed political aspirations but also political strategy. Martí and others claimed that race had been transcended, and they made that claim because making it helped make possible a future without colonial rule and because envisioning a future without colonial rule allowed them also to imagine a context in which such transcendence might become reality. What they might not have envisioned was that in speaking, writing, and imagining a raceless nation, they also gave voice to an ideal and a vocabulary that, by casting racism as an infraction against the Cuban nation, allowed insurgents of color to speak of that which should not be spoken. Thus the particular history of Cuban nationalism and its relationship to race at the end of the century meant that Cuban identity came to be defined simultaneously as a repudiation of racism that encouraged black political activity and as a rejection of the racial labels that allowed for that activity. For if Martí's words (and the language of Cuban nationalism in general) sanctioned the democracy to which Batrell and others aspired, and if it afforded legitimacy to their assaults on racism, it also provided the language with which their enemies could undermine those assaults and aspirations. "The Negro who proclaims his race, even if it may be his mistaken way of proclaiming the spiritual identity of all races," wrote Martí, "justifies and provokes the white racist."[32] And so, black demands for power—for recognition of the part they played in independence—were met by calls for patience and by accusations of black racism. While language of raceless nationalism served to bolster the claims of those who demanded greater rights for nonwhite citizens, it also authorized the claims of those unwilling to concede those rights. This doubleness was inherent in the patriotic language of Martí, but it was inherent as well in the nationalist movement as a whole—a movement defined by a powerful struggle between racism and antiracism, between revolution and reaction. Starting in 1898, that struggle would have to continue unfolding in the context of U.S. military intervention, which, of course, helped overdetermine the outcome.

Notes

Many thanks to the organizers of and participants in the January 1995 University of California–Irvine conference that served as the basis for this book, especially to Raúl Fernández, Silvia Pedraza,

Gerald Poyo, Doris Sommer, and Susan Gillman. I also thank audiences at Florida International University, Princeton University, and New York University and, for commenting on earlier versions of this essay, the following friends and colleagues: Alejandro de la Fuente, Martha Hodes, Winston James, Walter Johnson, Robin Kelley, Fernando Martínez, Louis Pérez, Marifeli Pérez-Stable, Rebecca Scott, and Michael Zueske.

1 The phrase is borrowed from Mauricio Tenorio, "History, Transnationalism, and the United States: Preliminary Notes," a paper presented at the conference "Internationalizing American History," cosponsored by New York University and the Organization of American Historians, Florence, July 6–7, 1997.

2 José Martí, "Our America," in Martí, *Our America: Writings on Latin America and the Struggle for Cuban Independence,* ed. Philip Foner, trans. Elinor Randall et al. (New York: Monthly Review Press, 1977), pp. 93–94.

3 On race and the independence movement, see Ada Ferrer, *Ambivalent Revolution: Race, Nation, and Anti-Colonial Insurgency* (Chapel Hill: University of North Carolina Press, forthcoming). The figure of 60 percent nonwhite army members is from Jorge Ibarra, *Cuba, 1898–1921: Política y clases sociales* (Havana: Editorial de Ciencias Sociales, 1992), p. 187. Another often quoted figure is that of 40 percent for nonwhite commissioned officers, posited by Louis A. Pérez Jr., in *Cuba between Empires, 1878–1902* (Pittsburgh: University of Pittsburgh Press, 1983), p. 106.

Attempts to estimate the percentage of Cuban soldiers who would have identified themselves (or been identified by others) as persons of color pose several problems. First, as we shall see, army rosters do not provide information on soldiers' racial identification. Thus, scholars who have tried to offer figures on the racial composition of the insurgent army have tended to rely on impressions recorded in war diaries and memoirs, in which individuals arriving at rebel camps to enlist describe the forces they are joining. Percentages provided in sources of this kind usually reflect the biases of the memoir writer—almost always white and literate, often urban, and occasionally foreign. One recent, and in many ways alarming, attempt to overcome impressionistic treatments of the army's racial composition is a study conducted by Cuban anthropologists, who, at the site of an 1896 insurgent attack, exhumed and analyzed the remains of thirty-three insurgent soldiers to conclude that all but six were "negroid" or "mestizo." See Sergio Luis Márquez Jaca, "Estudio antropológico de los mambises caidos en el combate de la Palma," in Centro de Estudios de Historia Militar, *Conferencia científica sobre historia militar. Resúmenes* (Havana: Fuerzas Armadas Revolucionarias, 1991), pp. 20–24.

By raising the question of the army's racial composition, I do not mean to imply that that army was composed of individuals belonging to distinct racial groups. Obviously, the ways in which a recruit was identified had everything to do with who did the identifying, the recruit's skin color, his manner of dress and speech, whether he arrived at a camp armed or unarmed, barefoot or not barefoot, and so on. However, even acknowledging the socially and historically contingent nature of racial thinking and classification, the question of the army's racial composition must still be addressed. I raise the issue in this paper as a way of calling attention to the generally multiracial character of the insurgent army. This characteristic is critical to understanding the social and political objectives of the rebellion and the range of responses they elicited. It is also critical because, as we shall see, the idea of a multiracial army became a central component of an emerging nationalist rhetoric which held that a unified and raceless Cuban nation had emerged precisely from the experience of multiracial insurgency.

4 Quoted in Jorge Ibarra, *Ideología mambisa* (Havana: Instituto Cubano del Libro, 1967), p. 25.

5 José Martí, "Mi raza" (April 16, 1893), in *Obras completas,* ed. Manuel Isidro Méndez (Havana: Editorial Lex, 1953), vol. 1, p. 486. All references to Martí's work are to this edition, unless otherwise noted.

6 Quoted in Ibarra, *Ideología,* p. 52. Maceo did not use the terms *blancos* or *negros,* but rather their diminutive forms *blanquitos* and *negritos.*

7 By official documents, I refer here to documents produced by the civilian and military wings of the rebel movement. These include company rosters, rebel judicial proceedings, and internal correspondence and reports regarding military maneuvers, provisions, recruitment, and so forth. Rather than referring to insurgents by means of racial labels, these documents generally identified people within or sympathetic to the movement as "C.C." (short for *ciudadano cubano,* or "Cuban citizen").

8 The first position—that nationalist struggle helped resolve and transcend racial division—is dominant in nationalist historiography, from before the 1959 revolution to the present. For compelling examples, see Emilio Roig de Leuchsenring, *La guerra libertadora cubana*

de los treinta años (Havana: Oficina del Historiador de la Ciudad de la Habana, 1958); Ibarra, *Ideología;* and Manuel Moreno Fraginals, *Cuba/España, España/Cuba: Historia común* (Barcelona: Crítica, 1995). The second position—that nationalism helped preserve a racist status quo—is more prevalent in North American revisionist scholarship. See especially Aline Helg, *Our Rightful Share: The Afro-Cuban Struggle for Equality, 1886–1912* (Chapel Hill: University of North Carolina Press, 1995).

9 Proclama del Comité Republicano, Havana, July 10, 1870, in Archivo Histórico Nacional, Sección de Ultramar (hereafter AHN, SU), leg. 6087.

10 On the effects of the war on the process of slave emancipation, see Rebecca J. Scott, *Slave Emancipation in Cuba: The Transition to Free Labor, 1865–1899* (Princeton: Princeton University Press, 1985), chap. 2.

11 The quotation is from a statement signed by surrendered insurgents, December 1871, in AHN, SU, leg. 4935, pt. 1, bk. 11, doc. no. 11. The percentage figure is from Ibarra, *Ideología,* p. 110.

12 On black participation in the Guerra Chiquita and the reactions of white separatists and colonial authorities, see Ada Ferrer, "Social Aspects of Cuban Nationalism: Race, Slavery, and the Guerra Chiquita, 1879–1880," *Cuban Studies* 21 (1991): 37–56.

13 José Martí, "Basta" (March 19, 1892), in *Obras completas,* vol. 1, p. 484.

14 The individual service records from which the final rosters were drawn may be found in Archivo Nacional de Cuba (hereafter ANC), Fondo Ejército Libertador, the index card catalogue for which contains much of the same information as the individual dossiers. Handwritten lists compiled for each brigade are located in ANC, Fondo Roloff. A final list, with significantly less information than was collected when the original lists were compiled, was published as Cuba, Inspección General del Ejército, *Indice alfabético y defunciones del Ejército Libertador de Cuba, Guerra de Independencia* (Havana: Rambla y Bouza, 1901). None of the lists or individual service records contain information on racial classifications.

15 See "Libro relacionado con el personal y asistencia de enfermos y heridos en los hospitales del 5° Cuerpo del Ejército Libertador," in ANC, Fondo Revolución de 1895, leg. 6, exp. 2357. (This collection has since been recatalogued, and the file number here is from the old classification system; researchers, however, in consultation with an archivist, should be able to locate the new number and document.)

16 On the ways in which the pro-independence writing of the 1890s appropriated the figure of the black insurgent, see Ferrer, *Ambivalent Revolution,* chap. 5.

17 Ramón Roa, "Los negros de la revolución," in *La Igualdad,* September 21, 1892, clipping in ANC, Donativos y Remisiones (hereafter DR), leg. 287, exp. 28. The article was later published in Ramón Roa, *Con la pluma y el machete* (Havana: Academia de la Historia de Cuba, 1950), vol. 1, pp. 248–51. Slightly different versions of Legón's story were also publicized by other pro-independence writers of the 1890s. Another veteran of the Ten Years' War, Serafin Sánchez, published a biography of Legón in his collection of biographies of lesser-known participants of the first war, *Héroes humildes,* published in New York in 1894. Manuel de la Cruz provided a briefer biography in his *Episodios de la revolución cubana,* first published in 1890. See Serafin Sánchez, *Héroes humildes y poetas de la guerra* (Havana: Editorial de Ciencias Sociales, 1981), pp. 41–50, and Manuel de la Cruz, *Episodios de la revolución cubana* (Havana: Miranda, López Seña y ca., 1911), pp. 126–27.

18 Jose Martí, "Plato de lentejas" (January 6, 1894), in *Obras completas,* vol. 1, p. 492.

19 Ibid.

20 Juan Gualberto Gómez, "Programa del diario *La Fraternidad,*" reprinted in Juan Gualberto Gómez, *Por Cuba libre,* ed. Emilio Roig de Leuchsenring (Havana: Editorial de Ciencias Sociales, 1974), p. 260.

21 Manuel Arbelo, *Recuerdos de la última guerra de independencia de Cuba* (Havana: Tipografía Moderna, 1918), pp. 54–56.

22 Scott, *Slave Emancipation,* pp. 261–63; Laird Bergad, *Cuban Rural Society: The Social and Economic Consequences of Monoculture in Matanzas* (Princeton: Princeton University Press, 1990), pp. 276–88.

23 Agustín Bravo, gobernador civil de Matanzas, to Antonio Maura, ministro de Ultramar, February 9, 1894, in Fundación Antonio Maura (Madrid), leg. 335-B, exp. 7.

24 Ricardo Batrell Oviedo, *Para la historia: Apuntes autobiográficos de la vida de Ricardo Batrell Oviedo* (Havana: Seoane y Alvarez, 1912). An incomplete manuscript version of the memoir (dated 1910) can be found in ANC, Fondo Adquisiciones, leg. 70, exp. 4242.

25 Batrell, *Para la historia,* pp. 3–4.

26 Ibid., p. 26.

27 Ibid., p. 166.

28 Ibid., pp. 170–71. See also "Diario de operaciones del Capitán Martín Duen y Richard," in ANC, DR, leg. 278, exp. 1.

29 Batrell, *Para la historia,* p. 171.

30 Antonio Rosal y Vásquez, *En la manigua: Diario de mi cautiverio* (Madrid: Bernardino y Cao, 1876), p. 92.

31 This episode was recounted by the insurgent doctor Guillermo Fernández Mascaró and is discussed in Tomás Savignon, *Quintín Banderas: El mambí sacrificado y escarnecido* (Havana: P. Fernández, 1948), pp. 10–11. The gender implications of this particular construction of Cuban nationhood are discussed in Ferrer, *Ambivalent Revolution,* chap. 5.

32 Martí, "Mi raza," in *Obras completas,* vol. 1, p. 486.

IV.

"Our Americanism" in the Age of "Globalization": Contemporary Frontiers

David W. Noble

The Anglo-Protestant Monopolization of "America"

It is important to relate Amy Kaplan's essay "Left Alone with America: The Absence of Empire in the Study of American Culture" to Jack Greene's recent book *The Intellectual Construction of America.*[1] Greene's purpose is to clarify the patterns used by Europeans from 1492 through the creation of the United States of America in 1789 in order to imagine the meaning of the Americas. In imagining a "New World" that was better than the European "Old World," the early-modern European middle classes created an "America" in which their modern values of limitless economic resources and individual political liberty could be fulfilled. Greene does not seem to be self-conscious, however, that his story begins with emphasis on Spanish, Portuguese, and French visions of a "New World" but becomes a European vision of the "New World" promise of the English colonies in North America. He does not seem aware that, when he writes about the United States of 1800, he gives to that particular American nation a monopoly of the words "American" and "New World."

Greene, writing in 1993, does not seem so different, therefore, from the Perry Miller of the 1950s presented by Kaplan. In her essay Kaplan sets up a contrast between Miller and William Appleman Williams, with whom I was in graduate school at the University of Wisconsin in the late 1940s. Miller, a founder of the Program in American Civilization at Harvard University in the 1930s, was by the 1940s a gigantic figure in the new fields of "American" intellectual history and "American" Studies. Kaplan analyzes Miller's collection of essays *Errand into the Wilderness* to call attention to his assumptions about the boundaries of "America."[2] Those assumed boundaries isolated the United States from Europe. One of Miller's major concerns was to prove that the "Old World" cultures brought by Europeans to North America dissolved in the "New World" environment. For Miller, then, Harvard's American Civilization program expressed the reality that there were two separate civilizations, European and "American." Miller and his Harvard colleagues, however, were not interested in comparing "American" civilization with Asian or African civilizations. And in their metaphorical geography, where Europe and "America" were the only spaces worthy of scholarly discussion, they were contrasting a European civilization composed of several nations with an "American" civilization that, for them, consisted of only one nation, the United States of America. This meant, I believe, that for Miller and his contemporaries, the other nations in North and South America were as unworthy of scholarly discussion as were the cultures of Africa and Asia. Like all the peoples of Asia and Africa, the inhabitants of the other American nations lived outside meaningful space. They were not part of the "New World."

In her essay, Kaplan is not directly concerned with the history of the concepts of space and time that informed the definitions of "America" presented by Miller and Williams. Her chief purpose is to call attention to how Miller's belief that "America" was separate from Europe made it possible for him to isolate imperialism as a European phenomenon. Miller's "America" was innocent of imperialism because, for him, power existed in Europe but liberty existed in "America." Kaplan's charge, then, is that, until recently, most American Studies scholarship has continued the tradition of Miller's generation, who were the founding fathers of American Studies. By continuing to imagine an "America" culturally separate from Europe, many recent scholars in the United States have been able to ignore the ways in which postcolonial cultural theory can be used to illuminate the imperialism of the dominant culture in the United States. Kaplan hopes to interest American Studies scholars in that cultural theory by demonstrating how Miller constructed a narrative that celebrated "American" exceptionalism. He did this by repressing, in his narrative, the institution of slavery in the English colonies and its centrality to the new nation of 1789. She demonstrates how Miller repressed, in his narrative, the Anglo-American use of power for hundreds of years to drive the Native Americans from their homelands. She demonstrates also how he repressed, in his narrative, the Anglo-Americans' use of power when they seized the northern half of Mexico in 1846.

I begin with Kaplan's powerful and persuasive essay because I want to explore in detail the history of the paradigms of space and time held by Miller's generation. I want to challenge the metaphor of "Two Worlds" expressed by the name of the Harvard Program in American Civilization. I will do this by tracing those paradigms of space and time back to the patterns of bourgeois nationalism identified by Benedict Anderson in his book *Imagined Communities.*[3] Anderson argued that, during the years from the 1770s to the 1830s, bourgeois elites on both sides of the Atlantic constructed the idea of the modern nation. I believe that when Miller, F. O. Matthiessen, Howard Mumford Jones, Henry Nash Smith, R. W. B. Lewis, and Leo Marx imagined the United States as an exceptional nation, their aesthetic authority for such a claim was based on the paradigms of space and time that were the foundation for the imagined bourgeois nations of the early nineteenth century. The paradigms of space and time used by Miller, Matthiessen, Jones, Smith, Lewis, and Marx were the same as those used by the Anglo-American historians George Bancroft, John L. Motley, William H. Prescott, and Francis Parkman in the mid-nineteenth century. But the most famous spokesman for these transatlantic paradigms of bourgeois nationalism was, of course, a Prussian: G. W. F. Hegel.[4]

Like most of our generation, William Appleman Williams and I were initiated into the conventions of bourgeois nationalism. Both of us came into the 1950s with an aesthetic authority that encouraged us to remove Native Americans, African Americans, Mexican Americans, as well as Anglo-American women from our picture of the national landscape. Both of us participated in an aesthetic authority that envisioned a European "Old World" and an "American New World." Neither of us imagined in 1955 that power had been used and was being used by Anglo-Americans against "red," "black," and "brown" people in the United States. But, then, like some of our generation, by the end of the 1950s we both began to lose the aesthetic authority of the particular form of bourgeois nationalism into which we had been initiated. We both began to doubt that the modern nation was the end toward which history was progressing. Once the idea of the nation began to lose its sanctity, once it was not seen as timeless and immutable, once its boundaries lost their metaphysical power, Williams moved dramatically, in his book *The Contours of American History,* to place "American" history within the patterns of imperialistic expansion developed in early-modern Europe.[5] This was no longer Miller's world of an "America" innocent of imperial power. For Williams, the history of the English colonies in North America, and of the United

States that grew out of those colonies, was one of constant use of power. Bourgeois culture in the United States, like that of the European nations, was, for Williams, a culture that could only imagine a future of imperial expansion.

When *The Contours of American History* was published, I had started to write *Historians against History*. For me, the major historians in the United States from George Bancroft to Daniel Boorstin were arguing that time as progress had culminated in the space that was the United States of America. Initiated into that system of belief, I, like Williams, was becoming a heretic. *Historians against History* coincided with Thomas Kuhn's *The Structure of Scientific Revolutions,* and I identified my experience as one of a dramatic change of paradigms.[6] As Kaplan reminds us in her essay, however, there are scholars two generations younger than I am who are still committed to "American" exceptionalism and "American" innocence; and, to this day, the only political discourse sanctioned by the establishment remains that of the consensus decade of the 1950s—the discourse of exceptionalism and innocence. But since the 1960s there has been a growing paradigmatic community of scholars who challenge the consensus paradigm. What I want to do now is share my understanding of how this adversarial community specifically rejects the concepts of space and time that characterized bourgeois nationalism in 1800 and that remained so hegemonic into the 1950s.

Meaningful time, for the bourgeois cultures of early modern Europe, began in the Renaissance and Reformation. Most human beings, from this perspective, had lived in meaningless time because their cultures were constructions of their own imagination. These artful and artificial cultures could not achieve permanence. As mere style they were ephemeral. They appeared in time and disappeared in time. Meaningful time, in contrast to meaningless time, was a movement away from the world of human construction, the inessential, toward the essential as timeless, immutable, external nature. Meaningful time was progress from the artificial to the natural.[7]

Anthony Kemp, in his book *The Estrangement from the Past,* has reminded us of the magnitude of the cultural crisis in Europe when the men of the Reformation and Renaissance declared that the thousand years between 400 and 1400 were an unusable past.[8] For Protestants, the truth of the original Church had been lost when the

Catholic Church replaced the timeless truths of the Bible with its artful and artificial traditions. For the men of the Renaissance the rationality of the classical world had been submerged by the irrational traditions of what they now named the "Dark Ages." The task, then, for mankind was to escape the flux of meaningless cultures and to discover a timeless space where one could enjoy stability.

For the bourgeois elites of Europe and the European colonies in North and South America, the supersession of the Dark Ages meant, at first, a return to a moment of preexisting perfection. But the imaginative construction of the modern nation made it possible for the bourgeois elites to conceive of the exodus from meaningless time, from the flux of ephemeral cultures, as a forward movement. Meaningful time was not a return to the primitive Church or to classical Rome. Meaningful time was progress forward from an "Old World" of subjects to a "New World" of citizens. Progress was a movement away from the political allegiance of local communities to a distant monarch. The new politics was one in which a national and homogeneous people was sovereign. Meaningful history as an exodus from the flux of meaningless history was to culminate in the nation. Imagining two earth-shaking moments of supersession, bourgeois elites were establishing a pattern of stages of history as progress. The years 400 to 1400 had been defined as an unusable past. Now one also defined the years from 1400 to the "American" and French Revolutions as an unusable past. But this more recent era was seen as a necessary stage for the exodus of progressive history moving to achieve its final culmination in the nation-state.

While the previous stage was necessary for the new stage, those who were participating in the exodus from an "Old World" to a "New World" had a responsibility to forget the cultural patterns of the stage that was being superseded. Memory of an unusable past made it difficult to be a citizen of the "New World" of the nation. Bourgeois elites since the Renaissance and Reformation had defined the unreal as the product of human imagination. Tradition was a major example of such unreality. But reality preexisted in nature: therefore, it could not be invented by human beings; it could only be discovered by human beings. The cultures of the new nations, it followed, were discovered, not invented. By the eighteenth century, nature was the principal source of the reality that bourgeois elites could discover. Now, in inventing the nation, they invented the national landscape as the source of national culture. One discovered one's cultural identity as a citizen by exploring one's national landscape. The nation's painting, music, architecture, poetry, and prose was inspired by the national landscape.[9]

In his book *Imagined Communities,* Benedict Anderson argued that the modern nation was imagined as having absolute boundaries that guaranteed its cultural as well as its political independence. A new man, the citizen, participated, as a member of the people, in this cultural and political sovereignty. The nation's art, as well as its politics, expressed the deep fraternity of the people. This was the perspective so eloquently expressed by F. O. Matthiessen in his epic book of 1941, *American Renaissance.*[10] Matthiessen and many of his generation of literary critics who came of age in the 1930s agreed with Ralph Waldo Emerson and many of his generation of the 1830s that "America" was finally achieving cultural independence, and they pledged that they would no longer live with the obstructive memories of the European past. Instead they would find inspiration for their various arts by turning to the national landscape.[11]

This explains the explosive quality of Anderson's book when it appeared in 1983. All the oppositional metaphors of "American" exceptionalism—"Old World versus New World," "power versus liberty," "subjects versus citizens," "hierarchy versus people"—were transnational metaphors of the bourgeois elites who were constructing nations on both sides of the Atlantic. I was confronted with the great irony that the metaphors of "American" nationalism that I had read as an undergraduate and graduate student in the works of Miller, Matthiessen, and Smith were transnational metaphors. Bourgeois nationalism as an art form necessarily repressed the memory that its vision of supersession was being shared and expressed simultaneously by bourgeois elites in many places in the Atlantic world. Like the individual bourgeois artist, the individual bourgeois nation, so the argument went, transcended community.

In this bourgeois synthesis of the Enlightenment and romanticism, of nature and nation, of rationality and a national people, Emerson's generation of Anglo-Protestant men shared Hegel's vision that only a particular nation could lead the exodus from a lower to a higher stage of civilization. Like Hegel they believed that such an exemplary nation would be Protestant. They shared

Hegel's view that Catholics refused to abandon their memories of their superseded world. They also shared Hegel's theory that there was a coincidence between Protestantism and the Germanic peoples. It was the Germanic peoples alone who had rejected the Catholic past and opted for the Protestant future. As Protestants, for Hegel, the Germanic peoples alone were capable of moving from the complex and overlapping political allegiances of the "Old World" to the unified and rational allegiance of citizens to the nation-state. Protestants could do this because they had rejected the corporate outlook of Catholicism. To be a Protestant was to be the autonomous individual who was capable of giving total loyalty to the nation-state.

Prescott, Motley, Parkman, and Bancroft constituted their narratives on the pattern of supersession. In two major histories by Prescott (1796–1859), *The Conquest of Mexico* and *The Conquest of Peru,* he identifies these two great indigenous civilizations with the civilizations of the Orient. Like those of the Orient, the politics of the Aztecs and the Incas were those of despotism. For Prescott, the Catholic Spanish were also despots, but their patterns of tyranny were better than those of the Aztecs and Incas: they were higher in the story of history as progress. The evils of the Oriental despotism of the Aztecs, Prescott wrote, "were the best apology for their conquest."[12]

For these Anglo-Protestant historians, as for Hegel, history as progress always linked time with space. Progress as the history of liberty was a movement from the space of the despotic Oriental civilizations westward. According to this story, a great battle between tyranny and liberty began in Western Europe when the Germanic peoples of the German states, Scandinavia, the Netherlands, and England chose Protestant liberty over Catholic tyranny. Motley (1814–1877) celebrates one of the major victories of Protestantism over Catholicism in his *The Rise of the Dutch Republic.* In this perspective, Southern and Eastern Europe are not part of that sacred space, the West, in which the history of liberty would reach its final destination. But, of course, for these men the North America occupied by the English colonies was part of that sacred space—the West. For them, as Spain and Portugal symbolized a profane space in which liberty could not fulfill its destiny, so that space from Mexico to the southern tip of South America was not part of the West. When Catholicism displaced the Oriental civilizations of the Aztecs and the Incas, one could not expect that Protestant liberty would supersede Catholic tyranny.[13]

But this was not true of the space northward in the English colonies. It was the manifest destiny of that space to be the home of Protestant liberty. This was the theme of *France and England in North America* by Parkman (1823–93). In contrast to Prescott, who portrays Spanish despotism as preferable to the despotism of the Aztecs and Incas, Parkman purposely describes the presence of the Catholic French in North America as equal in its antiprogressive tyranny to that of the Native Americans. For Parkman, "Lord and vassal and black-robed priest mingled with the wild forms of savage warriors, knit in close fellowship." Both of these lower stages of human history, French and Indian, were to be cleared from the Canadian landscape as well as from the landscape of the Ohio and Mississippi Valleys. All of North America above Mexico would become "the West," the space in which history as progress would culminate in Protestant liberty.[14]

Bancroft (1800–1891) agreed with Hegel that particular nations played a crucial role in the unfolding of history as progress. He also agreed with Hegel that one nation superseded another as the leader of progress. For Bancroft, then, England had played its role in the exodus from tyranny to liberty. England had driven Catholic France from North America. But England, in Bancroft's history, was not destined to achieve the highest stage of liberty, and neither was Hegel's Prussia. Prussia had played a necessary role in driving Catholicism out of northwestern Europe. But, according to Bancroft, neither England nor Prussia was able to abandon the institutions of organized power they had been forced to use in their victories over Catholicism. The United States of America was the beneficiary of the use of English and Prussian power. These Protestant nation-states, England and Prussia, had sacrificed their possibility of moving completely from the "Old World" of power to the "New World" of liberty.

When English leaders looked at the liberty enjoyed by the English colonists in the space of the "New World," they moved to use their institutional power to limit the liberty of the colonists. In the march of spirit in history this was an inevitable event that forced the colonists to engage in a revolution that would bring into being their nation-state. This new nation was destined to bring into being the final stage of history as progress, when liberty would completely transcend power. The United States would represent the perfect separation of liberty from power. Protestant England and Prussia, although they embodied a great deal of liberty within the spaces that were their national landscapes, had become an "Old World." The space of the nations of northwestern Europe was not destined to be the final home of liberty as it had moved from the east to west. The promised land, the West, where liberty would find her final home, was that space in North America populated by the descendants of English Protestants—the space destined to be the national landscape of the United States.

Bancroft, however, had the problem of writing a history of his nation in which the nation superseded the thirteen independent states of the Articles of Confederation—states that had emerged out of the long period of autonomy experienced by the colonies within the British empire. Bancroft argues that the spirit of the nation to come had been present in the Massachusetts of the Puritans. Here is an interesting parallel to Hegel's belief that the German nation-state destined to replace the long histories of the many German states was prefigured by Prussia as the first home of the spirit of German nationalism.

But Bancroft had an advantage over Hegel when it came to imagining the national landscape in which the histories of the local states would not be present. The national landscape that would provide a spatial home for the nation was already present in spirit in colonial Massachusetts. For Hegel, the German national landscape and the German national people, his "New World," could appear only as a Bavaria, Saxony, or Schleswig-Holstein disappeared into the dustbin of history. The Prussian vision must displace those local peoples and those local landscapes. Bancroft, however, could imagine one more exodus from east to west. West of the thirteen colonies and their long history intertwined with European power, across the Appalachians, was a "Virgin Land." The special role of the United States as a nation was to achieve democracy. This role was fulfilled when men from South Carolina, Maryland, New Jersey, or Connecticut crossed those mountains and became "Americans." They had left their local histories and local landscapes. West of the mountains they were a people born of that national landscape. This was the valley of democracy because "here, and here only, was a people prepared to act as the depository and carrier of all [democratic] political power."[15]

Bruce Greenfield has written about the aesthetic authority used by Lewis and Clark to remove from their accounts the many Native American peoples and their long local histories from the landscape. Like Myra Jehlen in her *American Incarnation,* Greenfield does not relate that aesthetic authority to the transatlantic patterns of nationalism discussed by Benedict Anderson.[16] But for Bancroft, as for Hegel, peoples and geographic areas had no meaning unless they were part of the nation-state. Bancroft had no problem in not seeing the Native Americans. In his eyes they were peoples without history and without meaningful space. His problem was to supersede the colonial past. And so he celebrated the birth of a national people and a national landscape where no one should remember the colonial peoples. "Everywhere," he rejoices, "an intrepid, hardy, and industrious population was moving westward through all the gates of the Alleghenies . . . accepting from nature their title deeds to the unoccupied wilderness." The ideal of a German nation appearing in Prussia would need the power of the Prussian army to persuade Bavarians and Hessians to forget their local histories. But, for Bancroft, the ideal of a national people first appearing in Massachusetts would achieve reality within the framework of innocence, and not power, when Americans discovered their national landscape in the last West.[17]

One can argue that all those aspects of Perry Miller's 1956 narrative which repressed the continental imperialism of Anglo-Protestants were central to the narrative of "American" innocence that Bancroft had begun to develop in the 1830s. But this latter narrative was in crisis between the 1880s and World War I. The argument of Karl Marx that the industrial revolution was a transnational phenomenon seemed irrefutable by the late nineteenth century. Bourgeois nationalists in the United States, like those of England, France, and Germany, feared that an international urban-industrial landscape was overwhelming their national landscapes. They began to fear that history had not culminated in the nation-state. They feared that a modern civilization based on this urban-industrial landscape was a higher stage in history as progress.[18]

This was the context in which Frederick Jackson Turner became the most famous historian in the United States from the 1890s to the 1920s. Turner achieved instant notoriety in 1893 when he delivered his paper "The Significance of the Frontier in American History" at the Chicago Columbian Exposition. At one level, Turner set himself apart from Bancroft. Turner was a member of the first generation of historians who identified themselves as professionals because they embodied the scientific method in their scholarship. This generation felt superior to that of Bancroft, identifying them as literary figures rather than scientists, subjective rather than objective. Turner, in contrast to Bancroft, did not identify progress as the will of God expressed through the agency of Protestantism. He also rejected Bancroft's explicit celebration of Anglo-Saxon racial superiority.

But Turner's narrative does embody Bancroft's thesis that American citizens were born in the final West beyond the Appalachian Mountains. Like Bancroft, Turner identified the "American" nation with this "valley of Democracy." He, too, believed that the particularism of the colonial past gave way to a homogeneous people. In affirming that unprogressive European cultural traditions could not enter this West, Turner, like Bancroft, did not imagine Native Americans, African Americans, or Mexican Americans as part of the deep fraternity of the American people—and, as for Bancroft, so for Turner, there was only one "American" nation that should be contrasted to Europe.

For Turner, however, the story of history as progress that culminated in the perfect liberty of the "American" nation was superseded by the story of an urban-industrial future born in Europe. According to Turner, the West was pronounced dead by the census of 1890. Now progressive history as the emergence of modern nations was being replaced by the youthful vigor of the transnational experience of the European-born urban-industrial future. Nature, as Turner understood it in the 1890s, was not exhausted by timeless national landscapes. A convert to an idea of evolution, Turner now argued that nature was both dynamic and universal. A transnational urban-industrial landscape, in his second narrative, was being produced by the dynamic laws of evolution.

Turner, however, unlike Karl Marx, was not able to identify liberty as the inevitable gift of the transnational urban-industrial landscape. Turner continued to identify liberty as the gift of the national landscape west of the Appalachians. Although he believed that the urban-industrial landscape was produced by nature, he still identified it with power. Coming from Europe, this landscape was characterized by hierarchal corporations. In this new world of corporate capitalism, a few men owned the means of production.

Established first in New England but inexorably pushing westward to the Pacific, hierarchal power was replacing the liberty and equality of the yeoman farmers who had lived in harmony with the national landscape. It was destroying the fraternity that should characterize the citizens of the modern nation.[19]

Turner, again unlike Marx, could not visualize evolution producing a higher stage of human civilization than that of corporate capitalism. But Turner's younger colleague, Charles Beard, did visualize such a higher stage. Going to England immediately after completing his undergraduate degree, Beard joined the Fabian socialists in predicting that the industrial landscape was the necessary environment for the emergence of political democracy. He rejected the identification of liberty, equality, and fraternity with the national landscape. Instead, he insisted that the new "American" nation of 1789 had been constructed by capitalists. For Beard, capitalists were men who placed self-interest above public interest. They were men who were corrupted by the power they exercised over the men who worked for them.

Accepting, like Turner, the categories of the English republican tradition of the eighteenth century, Beard also saw propertyless workers corrupted by their dependence on the owners of factories. For Beard, then, the census of 1890 did not symbolize the end of the United States as a democratic nation. Such a nation had never existed, because the nation always had been in the control of the capitalists who created it. But Beard, in his book of 1901, *The Industrial Revolution,* promises that evolution was bringing industrialism from England to the United States. In England, industrialism was already breaking the power of capitalism; it was beginning to produce democracy there. This was the future of the United States as it moved from the stage of world history that was international capitalism to the stage of international democracy. Unlike Marx, however, Beard saw this transition as peaceful. Part of his optimism came from his distinction between virtuous private property, used for rational production, and the corrupt private property of capitalism, used for irrational self-interest. Most of the "American" middle class, Beard believed, was committed to virtuous private property and would gladly participate in the peaceful overthrow of the capitalist elites and their self-centered world of profits-before-production.[20]

Beard's prophecy, one shared by such other influential academics as John Dewey and Thorstein Veblen, collapsed during World War I. During the 1920s and 1930s, therefore, Beard joined with many of his contemporaries in the United States in revitalizing the patterns of Bancroft's nationalism. With his wife, Mary, Beard wrote the four volumes of *The Rise of American Civilization* from the late 1920s to the early 1940s. There they explicitly reject the vision of a transnational history that would spread the industrial revolution from England to the whole world. They explicitly deny that nature should be equated with the universal laws of evolution. Instead they insist that there are only particular nations, each of which expresses the uniqueness of its national landscape.[21]

Bancroft's narrative implicitly became the Beards' narrative, one so popular that their first two volumes were distributed by the Book-of-the-Month Club. The West, for them, was the magic destination of human progress. And the final West, the national landscape of the United States, was the valley of democracy west of the Appalachians. Using Bancroft's aesthetic authority to remove the Native Americans from this virgin land, they shared Bancroft's view that all the other American nations were not real nations because their peoples existed outside progressive history. Without history and without meaningful space, the other American countries were mere impersonations of nations. The end of history as the perfect liberty of fraternal citizens existed, for them, only in the United States. They agreed with Bancroft that even the nations of Northern Europe could never experience such liberty and fraternity.

But, like Turner, they had to affirm that industry had spread from Europe to the United States. Nevertheless, they escaped Turner's contradictory two narratives by arguing that this urban-industrial landscape was absorbed by the more powerful national landscape. Within the boundaries of the United States, and only within those boundaries, the urban-industrial landscape took on the qualities of the national landscape. Only in the United States did the urban-industrial landscape become one that embodied the liberty, equality, and fraternity of that virgin land, the original pastoral landscape. This, for the Beards, was the American civilization that was so different from the civilization of Western Europe, one that could never transcend power. When the Beards demanded the isolation of "American" civilization in the 1930s from a Europe preparing for war, they, like Bancroft, imagined an "America" metaphysically distinct from the rest of the world. Guarding the boundaries of the sacred nation, the Beards were critics of international Marxism, international Catholicism, and international Judaism. But none of these alternatives to national autonomy was as dangerous as that of international capitalism. When the nation divided during the Civil War, capitalism seized the opportunity to cross the Atlantic. Committed to self-interest and the international marketplace, the capitalists, according to the Beards, imported an alien work force of Southern and Eastern Europeans. Because they were Catholics and Jews, the Beards argued that they were people who could not participate in the American nation as the culmination of human progress. They were people without history who had no place in that sacred West which was the national landscape.

The Beards also restored much of Bancroft's explicit linkage of "American" nationalism to Protestantism. In *The Rise of American Civilization,* they celebrate, therefore, the legislation in the 1920s that cut off most of the immigration of Catholics and Jews from Europe. They explicitly rejected the belief of Turner's generation in the 1880s that there could be no place for religion in a scholarly discipline that embraced scientific objectivity.[22]

The men who began the America Civilization Program at Harvard in the 1930s shared this aesthetic authority with the Beards. Then, like Charles and Mary Beard, they were shattered when "American" political and economic elites used World War II to force a revolution in the narrative of national identity. These capitalist elites wanted to destroy the tradition of their bourgeois nationalist ancestors which held that only the national landscape was a sacred space. The doctrine of the revolutionists of the 1940s was that the transnational marketplace was the sacred space of the future. The boundaries of the nation had to be lowered so that the national economy could flow into the international marketplace. By destroying the sanctity of the national landscape, these elites implicitly denied that this landscape was the environment from which the nation's people had sprung. But, calling themselves democrats, these elites wanted to separate the idea of democracy from the bourgeois nationalist vision of the people as a deep fraternity. Democracy was now to be associated only with the liberty of the individual as a consumer in the worldwide marketplace. Architecture, painting, music, and literature were no longer expected to express an organic relation to the national landscape. Rather, the arts were to express the universals of the international marketplace.

The first students of F. O. Matthiessen and Perry Miller at Harvard—Henry Nash Smith, R. W. B. Lewis, and Leo Marx—had the terrifying experience in the 1940s of having their narrative of an "American" civilization separate from Europe suddenly change from reality to myth. Yet they could not imagine writing about the role of the United States in the universal marketplace. They chose, therefore, to write elegies for the early nineteenth century, when history as progress had apparently culminated in the West as the national landscape of the United States. Smith in *Virgin Land: The American West as Symbol and Myth,* Lewis in *The American Adam,* and Marx in *The Machine in the Garden* all wrote as if, for a moment, time had stopped when the "American" nation appeared.[23] Ignoring the way elites had used power to construct the nation, they shared in Bancroft's theme of "innocence" which insisted that national identity was a gift from the national landscape. Like the Beards, they too had believed in the 1930s that the urban-industrial landscape coming from Europe had been incorporated within the national landscape. They, too, believed that it was capitalists who threatened the sacred boundaries of the nation. But, like the Beards, they defined the 1930s as the decade in which the American people would purge the nation of the presence of the un-American capitalists. Then, in 1945, they were no longer able to discern an "American" civilization in which the urban-industrial landscape was an organic outgrowth of the national landscape. Now they, like Turner, had two narratives. Like Turner, they chose to spend their scholarly energy and love on the narrative of the separation of the "American" nation from time, when progress culminated in the "West," the space of the national landscape. But, like Turner, they lamented in their second narrative that another pattern of progress had overtaken the national landscape. This newer and more powerful pattern of progress was leading from the nation to the international landscape of capitalism. And, again like Turner, they identified this landscape with power.[24] For them, the nation had been pushed back into time by the urban-industrial landscape coming from Europe. These men preferred to return imaginatively to the crisis of Frederick Jackson Turner and Charles Beard in the 1880s and 1890s rather than admit that the national landscape had been displaced by an international capitalist marketplace in the 1940s.[25]

While male Anglo-Protestant political and economic elites exercised their power by dominating the " One World" of the international marketplace, male Anglo-Protestant academic elites could no longer sustain their cultural hegemony within the nation. They could no longer claim to be the only Americans with a sacred history and a sacred space. Once upon a time they could claim that all women, as well as Native Americans, African Americans, Mexican Americans, Catholics, Jews, and Asian Americans, were people without meaningful history and without meaningful space. Now, these male academics retained only the memory of when their forefathers, around 1830, had had such a history and a space. They were experiencing a supersession that threatened to make them a people without history and without space.

Although a significant number of academics continue to choose to live with the memory of an "innocent America" free from European power, the academic landscape of the United States has, since the 1960s, become one in which Anglo-Protestant women, Native Americans, African Americans, Mexican Americans, Catholics, Jews, and Asian Americans mingle with male Anglo-Protestants. With this dramatic change in aesthetic authority, it has become increasingly difficult to look at that culturally diverse landscape and still fail to recognize the power that male Anglo-Protestants exercised from 1789 to the 1940s in monopolizing the academic presentation of the national landscape. The same logic applies to the exercise of power that monopolized the academic presentation of the United States as the only "American" nation. It was not only the logic of history as progress which had silenced the majority of Americans; rather, that idea of history was an instrument in the exercise of institutional power by Anglo-Protestant elites and their converts.

For some of my academic generation, and for even more of the subsequent generations, the narrative of bourgeois nationalism—that history was progressing from power to liberty—is no longer persuasive. When William Appleman Williams wrote *The Tragedy of American Diplomacy* (1955), he looked back to Charles Beard as a hero. I also had accepted Beard as a hero. Arthur Schlesinger Jr. had published *The Age of Jackson* in 1945 as a footnote to the Beards' *Rise of American Civilization.* This was the case also with

Richard Hofstadter's *Social Darwinism in American Thought* in 1945.[26] Like the Beards and Bancroft, we identified imperialism with the use of a nation's power outside its boundaries. Williams in 1955 did not see the English settlements on the Atlantic coast of North America as military beachheads that would be constantly expanded until Euroamericans had defeated every Native American community from the Atlantic to the Pacific and taken their lands. He (and I) in 1955 implicitly worked with the convention that these lands had no meaning until they became part of the nation called the "United States." He (and I) in 1955 implicitly worked within the convention of the "vanishing Indians," who had no real existence in the march of history that was culminating in the space of the nation. The tragedy of American diplomacy, for Williams, came when "Americans" were tempted to go beyond their continental innocence and used power outside their national boundaries. But Williams's generation was living in a revolutionary moment when we were being asked to rewrite history to demonstrate that the English colonies and the United States had always been part of the international marketplace expanding from Europe. Unlike most of his colleagues, Williams, when he converted to this narrative, could not place it within the progressive march of history toward liberty. He could not believe that the marketplace freed individuals from all power relationships. In his book *The Contours of American History,* then, he placed the English colonies and the United States within the patterns of imperial expansion that had begun in early-modern Europe. From this perspective, the manifest destiny of the United States was part of that use of power to coerce peoples everywhere to produce for the marketplace. Anglo-Protestant academic elites, when desanctified, could be denied their role as the vanguard of liberty within the United States. Losing their cultural hegemony, they could be identified as men of privilege who exercised power over their presumed "inferiors." Williams wanted to desanctify the United States and deny its international role as the vanguard of liberty. He wanted to call into doubt its role in uplifting the "inferior" nations of the "underprivileged" world.[27]

We live, then, in a time when the teleological narratives of bourgeois nationalism and of Marxism have lost much of their persuasiveness. The new teleological narrative of bourgeois liberty to be fulfilled in the universal marketplace does not seem to have the metaphysical power of the older metanarratives. The breaking of those metanarratives has called into question the categories of "progressive" and "unprogressive" nations, of "progressive" and "unprogressive" peoples.[28] For many of us it has become impossible to imagine any people's being without history, of humanity without variety, of any human culture without dignity and without the right to be free from external coercion. Many of us now know we need to listen to the voices of Americans who were once denied a hearing by the institutional authority of the Anglo-Protestant monopolization of "American" civilization. With the breaking of that monopoly, we gather together for the re-voicing of José Martí. Our air clearer now of that confounding code, more of us may at last be able to partake in Martí's invocation of Nuestra América.

For Martí, who was born in Cuba in 1853, Our America was composed of all the nations of North and South America. Having been exiled from Cuba by Spanish authorities because of his revolutionary activities, he came to New York in 1880. He left in 1895 to fight in Cuba, where he was killed in one of the first battles. During those fifteen years in the United States, he saw what my generation of scholars did not see until the 1960s. He became aware that the political and cultural leaders of the United States refused to recognize the other American nations because those leaders were racists. "They believe," Martí wrote, "in the invincible superiority of the Anglo-Saxon race over the Latin. They believe in the inferiority of the black race whom they enslaved yesterday and denigrate today, and of the Indians, whom they are exterminating. They believe that the Spanish American nations are made up principally of Indians and blacks."[29] When he came to the United States, Martí identified imperialism with Europe. When he left, he believed it was the United States that posed the greatest imperialist threat to the other American nations. It is fascinating to contemplate the many American teachers whom we scholars in the United States may discover as we are liberated from the aesthetic authority of the Anglo-Protestant narrative of "American" history. From Martí, whose poetry has been appreciated in many American countries, we may even learn just how extensive transnational and transracial cultural patterns have been and are throughout the Americas. Finally, we may learn to imagine American history as being more usefully told from the multiple perspectives of congruent and often allied objectors to the imperialism of the United

States — a critical multiculture to which Martí presciently belonged and, what is more, one that provides a context wherein the imperialism of the United States serves as text for scrutiny instead of the imperialism of the United States being the context that delimits the "subalterns" whom it oppressed.

Notes

1 Kaplan's essay is to be found in *Cultures of United States Imperialism*, ed. Amy Kaplan and Donald E. Pease (Durham: Duke University Press, 1993); also see Jack P. Greene, *The Intellectual Construction of America* (Chapel Hill: University of North Carolina Press, 1993).

2 Perry Miller, *Errand into the Wilderness* (Cambridge: Harvard University Press, 1956).

3 Benedict Anderson, *Imagined Communities* (London: Verso, 1983).

4 See Shlomo Avineri, *Hegel's Theory of the Modern State* (Cambridge: Cambridge University Press, 1972); Raymond Plant, *Hegel* (Oxford: Basil Blackwell, 1983); and Robert Wuthnow, *Communities of Discourse* (Cambridge: Harvard University Press, 1989).

5 William Appleman Williams, *The Contours of American History* (Cleveland: World Publishing Co., 1961).

6 David W. Noble, *Historians against History* (Minneapolis: University of Minnesota Press, 1965); Thomas Kuhn, *The Structure of Scientific Revolutions* (Chicago: University of Chicago Press, 1962).

7 See Roy Wagner, *The Invention of Culture* (Chicago: University of Chicago Press, 1981).

8 Anthony Kemp, *The Estrangement from the Past* (New York: Oxford University Press, 1991).

9 See Jonathan Boyarin, ed., *Remapping Memory: The Politics of Timespace* (Minneapolis: University of Minnesota Press, 1994), a powerful collection of essays dealing with these issues.

10 F. O. Matthiessen, *American Renaissance* (New York: Oxford University Press, 1941).

11 Books discussing how Emerson's generation believed it had achieved cultural independence by turning to nature include Benjamin Spencer, *The Quest for Nationality* (Syracuse: Syracuse University Press, 1957); Edwin Fussell, *Frontier: American Literature and the American West* (Princeton: Princeton University Press, 1965); and Emory Elliot, *Revolutionary Writers* (New York: Oxford University Press, 1982).

12 William Prescott, *The Conquest of Mexico* (Philadelphia: J. B. Lippincott, 1864), pp. 85–86. Quoted in David Levin, *History as Romantic Art* (Stanford: Stanford University Press, 1959), p. 159. Philip Wayne Powell also discusses Bancroft, Prescott, and Parkman in his *Tree of Hate: Propaganda and Prejudices Affecting United States Relations with the Hispanic World* (New York: Basic Books, 1971).

13 See the discussion of Motley in Levin, *History as Romantic Art.* Robert Young, in *White Mythologies: Writing History and the West* (New York: Routledge, 1990), relates the beginning of postcolonial cultural analysis in the United States with the publication of Edward Said's *Orientalism* (London: Routledge, 1978). Said implicated the work of European scholars in creating a representation of Asia and Africa that justified European imperialism as a necessary paternalistic role. Clearly the same argument can be applied to representations of "Latin" America by European and Anglo-Protestant scholars in the United States.

14 Francis Parkman, *The Jesuits in North America in the Seventeenth Century* (Boston: Little Brown, 1867), p. 135. Quoted in Levin, *History as Romantic Art,* p. 158.

15 George Bancroft, *History of the United States,* vol. 3 (Boston: Little Brown, 1837), p. 474.

16 Bruce Greenfield, "The Problems of the Discoverer's Authority in Lewis and Clark's History," in *Macropolitics of Nineteenth Century Literature,* ed. Jonathan Arac and Harriet Ritvo (Philadelphia: University of Pennsylvania Press, 1991); Myra Jehlen, *American Incarnation* (Cambridge: Harvard University Press, 1986).

17 George Bancroft, *Literary and Historical Miscellanies* (New York: Harper, 1855), p. 449.

18 See David W. Noble, *The End of American History* (Minneapolis: University of Minnesota Press, 1985) and Robert Breisach, *American Progressive History: An Experiment in Modernization* (Chicago: University of Chicago Press, 1993).

19 See Noble, *The End of American History,* chap. 2.

20 Charles Beard, *The Industrial Revolution* (London: Allen & Unwin, 1901).

21 Charles and Mary Beard, *The Rise of American Civilization,* vol. 1: *The Agricultural Era* (New York: Macmillan, 1927); vol. 2: *The Industrial Era* (New York: Macmillan, 1930); vol. 3: *America in Midpassage* (New York: Macmillan, 1939); vol. 4: *The American Spirit* (New York: Macmillan, 1942).

22 On Charles Beard's commitment to objectivity and universal history from 1900 to 1918, see David W. Noble, *The Progressive Mind* (Minneapolis: Burgess Publishing, 1981). On the Beards' rejection of objectivity and universal history after 1919, see Peter Novick, *That Noble Dream: The Objectivity Question and the American Historical Profession* (Cambridge: Cambridge University Press, 1988).

23 Henry Nash Smith, *Virgin Land: The American West as Symbol and Myth* (Cambridge: Harvard University Press, 1950); R. W. B. Lewis, *The American Adam* (Chicago: University of Chicago Press, 1954); Leo Marx, *The Machine in the Garden* (New York: Oxford University Press, 1964).

24 Smith, Lewis, and Marx shared the position taken by their teacher, F. O. Matthiessen in his book *American Renaissance:* namely, that "Old World" traditions had been transcended in the 1830s and "American" space had replaced European time. They equated space with liberty, time with power.

25 Unlike Turner, however, Smith, Lewis, and Marx accepted the Beards' post-1920 rejection of universal laws of evolution. When they lost the ability to see continuity in national tradition, they could not see a meaningful narrative in the future of the "American" nation. Gene Wise, in *American Historical Explanations* (Homewood, Ill.: Dorsey Press, 1973), focuses attention on this crisis of narrative in the 1940s. More recently, Thomas Schaub, in *American Fiction in the Cold War* (Madison: University of Wisconsin Press, 1991), has argued that this crisis of narrative found expression both among the literary critics of the 1940s and 1950s and among major novelists.

26 Arthur Schlesinger Jr., *The Age of Jackson* (Boston: Little, Brown, 1945); Richard Hofstadter, *Social Darwinism in American Thought* (Philadelphia: University of Pennsylvania Press, 1945). See also William A. Williams, *The Tragedy of American Diplomacy* (Cleveland: World Publishing, 1959).

27 See the discussion of Williams in Noble, *The End of American History.* See also the essays on Williams collected in *Redefining the Past: Essays in Diplomatic History in Honor of William Appleman Williams,* ed. Lloyd C. Gardner (Corvallis: Oregon State University Press, 1986).

28 A recent study of the profound role of racism in modern civilization, David Theo Goldberg's *Race and Culture* (Cambridge: Blackwell, 1994), helps explain the power of Anglo American racism in the United States. Andrew Janos, *Politics and Paradigms: Changing The-*

ories of Change in Social Science (Stanford: Stanford University Press, 1986) discusses the difficulties "American" social scientists had in establishing a theory of universal history immediately after World War II. Frederick Buell's *National Culture and the New Global System* (Baltimore: Johns Hopkins University Press, 1994) is an overview of the current confusion of narratives and the inability of any theory of universal history to establish its authority.

29 José Martí, "La conferencia monetaria de los repúblicas de América" (1891), in *Obras completas,* vol. 6 (Havana: Editorial Nacional de Cuba, 1963), p. 160.

Brook Thomas

Frederick Jackson Turner, José Martí, and Finding a Home on the Range

In an 1892 anonymous review in *Atlantic Monthly* entitled "The Figure of Columbus," the author remarks on how the series of centennial celebrations beginning in 1876 had generated important studies of American history. The four hundredth centenary of Columbus's voyage, he hopes, will extend those studies to "reëstablish our connection with Latin Christianity in all its forms." That connection would take us one step beyond studies that focused on how the institutions of the United States originated in Teutonic forests, were carried to England, and were then transplanted across the Atlantic. Expansion of studies beyond the "relation of the United States to England and Germany" was necessary because

> whether through war or through the more amiable ways of commerce and social intercourse, it is clear to most observers that the United States is to renew with Spain on this side of the Atlantic a connection which was broken off between England and Spain on the other side of the Atlantic more than three centuries ago, largely through the discovery and settlement of this continent. The era of industrial possession of our own domain has not closed, but the era of continental relations has opened, and this nation is destined to be affected strongly in its future development, not merely with the rest of America, but by the extension of its relations through this medium with contemporaneous Europe, and by contact in the realm of the spirit with ideas which are neither Anglican nor Teutonic.[1]

Although prophetic in sensing the possibility of war, the author is not accurate in his prediction of the direction of historical studies. To be sure, there is some subtle confirmation of his argument in the literature of the time. As early as Albion W. Tourgée's *A Fool's Errand* a protagonist journeys to Latin America at the end of a novel. In Henry Adams's *Democracy* the honorable Virginia lawyer about to marry Madeline Lee goes to Mexico to conduct business. Tom Corey at the end of William Dean Howells's *The Rise of Silas Lapham* is assigned to Latin America to open up markets for his paint company. Robert, Edna Pontellier's imagined lover in Kate Chopin's *The Awakening,* travels to Mexico on business. And then there is Henry James's remarkable *The Golden Bowl,* which reminds readers of the United States' Latin connection by having the daughter of a rich American who is intent on bringing imperial culture to American City marry Prince Amerigo, whose ancestors include not only the man who gave a continent a name, but also a pope.

But these confirmations are countercurrents. By far the most influential narrative about the history of the United States to come out of the late nineteenth-century celebration of Columbus is Frederick Jackson Turner's "The Significance of the Frontier in American History." Rather than call attention to the opening of an era of continental relations, Turner announces the end of an era with the closing of the frontier. Granted, Turner even more than the anonymous reviewer calls attention to problems with the Teutonic germ theory. Nonetheless, the trajectory that he establishes for U.S. history is quite different from what the reviewer hoped would be established.

Renewed North American interest in the work of José Martí helped to alter the course followed by "American" studies in the wake of Turner's frontier thesis. A Latin American who spent years of exile in the United States, Martí was the late nineteenth century's most important advocate for seeing American history as a relation between North and South America. The purpose of my essay is to compare the visions of America offered by Turner and Martí. That comparison confirms David Noble's argument that narratives of North American exceptionalism, like Turner's, are generated by certain senses of time and place. But the comparison does not simply champion Martí for offering an alternative to Turner's exceptionalism. It also suggests that Turner, despite his focus on North America, still has a contribution to make to Donald Pease's and Doris Sommer's fascinating explorations into the positive possibilities of displacement.[2] Indeed, I will argue that Turner's narrative of how people can remake themselves in a new land still has a role to play in any effort that "we" might want to make in redefining the "our" in Martí's "Our America."[3]

One reason why Turner's narrative has been so influential is that it fits the long-standing narrative of the westward course of empire. That narrative is so powerful that we sometimes forget that at the time when Turner delivered his address the history of the United States was for the most part not told according to an East/West axis, but as a conflict between North and South that culminated in civil war.

In drawing attention from the North/South axis, Turner's frontier thesis is part of a general project at the end of the nineteenth century by which historians dramatically revised accounts of the era of the Civil War and Reconstruction. Twice, for instance, Turner feels compelled to challenge Hermann Edward von Holst, the German institutional historian of the U.S. Constitution, who insisted that the dispute over slavery was the formative event in shaping national character. "When American history comes to be rightly viewed," Turner asserts, "it will be seen that the slavery question is an incident."[4] Still feeling the sectional conflict that a generation earlier had threatened to tear the country apart, Turner does not construct a narrative that focuses on the Mason-Dixon line separating North and South. Instead, he focuses on a frontier common to both. Not a fixed boundary like the one that created a division between free and slave states, the frontier, as defined by Turner, allowed for expansion rather than internal conflict. Indeed, "the economic and social characteristics of the frontier worked against sectionalism." A space of consensus, it produced people who "had closer resemblances to the Middle region than to either of the other sections" (27). To be sure, by 1893 the frontier was closed. But by evoking a history in which a "common danger" along it demanded "united action," Turner hopes once again to use it "as a consolidating agent in our history" (15).

Turner's transformation of the conflict between North and South into consolidation is typical of his narrative strategy. His narrative is punctuated by a series of conflicts that would seem to threaten the continuity of national progress. How those conflicts transform into progressive change rather than revolution, repetition, or decline is at the heart of Turner's progressive vision for the United States and helps to account for the most important conflict that his narrative constructs, that between America and Europe. For instance, just a few years earlier Henry Adams had described the early United States as a place with "no arts, a provincial literature, a cancerous disease of negro slavery, and differences of political theory fortified within geographic lines." "What," Adams asked, "could be hoped for such a country except to repeat the story of violence and brutality which the world already knew by heart, until repetition for thousands of years had wearied and sickened mankind?"[5]

Turner's answer to why that story was not repeated is the frontier. As such, the story he tells gives narrative form to a comment made by Hegel that the existence of free western land in the United States served as a safety valve to potential conflicts.[6] Providing a space of what we might call supplementation, the frontier made possible a narrative of American history in which conflicts could be endlessly deferred rather than dialectically resolved. Even if American history did not produce a classless society, it did, according to Turner, produce one in which class interests were complementary rather than oppositional. He quotes, for instance, a description of how three classes — pioneers, settlers, and men of capital and enterprise — lived off of and profited from one another by arriving in succession. "Like the waves of the ocean," these three "have rolled one after the other" (19). One after the other in diachronic sequence, not synchronic conflict. By providing a space in which synchronic conflicts could be avoided by transferring them into diachronic sequence, the frontier allowed for an organic synthesis of a diverse population without the need of a dialectical resolution. But it could do so only if Turner's notion of an ever expanding frontier could displace Adams's description of political differences "fortified within geographic lines." That displacement required a redefinition of "frontier."

"The American frontier," Turner asserts, "is sharply distinguished from the European frontier." The European frontier is "a fortified boundary line running through dense populations. The most significant thing about the American frontier is, that it lies at the hither edge of free land" (3). This distinction between American and European definitions of "frontier" is one of the most significant aspects of Turner's essay.

Turner is right to note that "frontier" took on a new meaning in the United States. That meaning did not develop, however, until the late nineteenth century; that is to say, about the time that Turner announced its closure. This philological detail is highly significant, for it means that, although Turner claimed to be using a peculiarly American notion of the frontier to account for the peculiar nature of American history, he was in fact, as John T. Juricek argues, "reading a late nineteenth-century world view back into the past."[7] Turner's use of the new definition of "frontier" suggests, in other words, that his compelling narrative of the nation's ability to reconstruct itself perpetually is itself an act of historical reconstruction. What, we might ask, is at stake in that act of reconstruction? As we shall see, quite a lot.

First of all, defining the frontier "to mean the edge of settlement, rather than, as in Europe, the political boundary"[8] allows Turner to shift the focus of previous interpretations of the frontier. Much has been written, Turner acknowledges, "about the frontier from the point of view of border warfare and the chase" (3). As we have seen, however, Turner is interested in how the United States avoids conflict, not how it perpetuates it. So long as the frontier was defined as a political boundary, any expansion of it immediately raised the possibility of "border warfare." Indeed, "frontier" derives from the later medieval Latin term *fronteria,* which means "line of battle," and an earlier meaning of the term in English is "a barrier against attack."[9] But if a frontier is no longer seen as between two political entities, its function can dramatically change. Rather than a site of conflict, it becomes, for Turner, a site in which conflicts and differences are overcome.

By creating a space where the United States can avoid the conflicts that have plagued European history, Turner's notion of the frontier allows him to exempt the United States from the repetitive cycles of European history. This opposition *between* the United States and Europe is possible, however, only because the United States is *between* Europe and the frontier. If Turner's image of the frontier lay in the East of Europe rather than in the West of the United States the narrative would move in the other direction. For instance, later historians, recognizing the power of Turner's thesis, tried to apply it to German and Russian history. But to do so they had to posit an Eastern frontier. Turner's narrative remains a document of American exceptionalism because it maintains a westward movement in which the United States, not Europe, becomes the site where history unfolds.

Let me repeat the point that I am making here, for it is crucial to my argument. If the United States' location between Europe and the frontier makes possible an opposition between Europe and America, it also establishes a link between them. Donald Pease has explored the existence of a similar link in Tocqueville.[10] In Turner the link occurs because the American frontier also serves as Europe's frontier. Even though the frontier does not affect Europe directly, it does affect it. Its effect generates a countermovement to the predominantly westward movement of Turner's narrative: "Steadily the frontier of settlement advanced and carried with it individualism, democracy, and nationalism, and powerfully affected the East and the Old World" (35).

Less noticeable than the opposition between the United States and Europe, this link between the two is important. If the presence of a frontier in the European sense of a political boundary inevitably raises the possibility of conflict, Americans had traditionally felt protected from a conflict with Europe because they were separated by the vast expanse of the Atlantic Ocean. By locating a new sort of frontier in the American West, Turner provides a somewhat different explanation for why the United States faced no threat from Europe. If, on the one hand, the frontier created an opposition between Europe and the United States by exempting the latter from the former's problems, on the other it transformed what seemed a clear-cut opposition into an interconnection. Although the presence of the ocean is important, even without it the boundary between Europe and the United States would be special because of the westward movement of Turner's narrative of progressive history. The major threat to the internal security of the United States in Turner's narrative had not been Europe but barriers to westward movement. As a result, the "common danger" to the country, according to Turner, was the "Indian frontier" (15). By 1893, of course, Indians no longer posed a threat. Appropriately, Turner's new definition of the frontier transforms the "Indian frontier" into simply "the frontier," a transformation that allows a former site of conflict to become a site of *communitas*.

In using the term *communitas* I evoke another Turner: Victor, the anthropologist. Indeed, the frontier for the historian operates as what the anthropologist would call a space of liminality. Liminality involves release from normal constraints: "In liminality what is mundanely bound in sociostructural form may be unbound and rebound." What needs emphasizing is that the frontier serves as a liminal space for Turner because it is a space of displacement. Removed from the lands of their birth, newly arrived immigrants could cast off their old cultures. But they cast them off in order to participate in the construction of a new, composite one. In a famous passage, Turner writes: "In the crucible of the frontier the immigrants were Americanized, liberated, and fused into a mixed race. English in neither nationality nor characteristics" (23). Allowing for a "rite of passage" in which the culture renews itself, the frontier shapes *communitas,* which "breaks in through the interstices of structure, in liminality; at the edges of structure, in marginality."[11]

To see the frontier as a liminal space is to understand its function as a space of cultural regeneration. It regenerates by transforming cultural difference into commonality and community. Whereas many of Frederick Jackson Turner's contemporaries linked race and culture as a way of stressing irreconcilable differences, Turner imagines a space in which people of different cultural backgrounds become one. Strangely enough, then, what is probably the most famous narrative of American exceptionalism is simultaneously a narrative about the universality of human nature. Relocated on the frontier, people from any culture could theoretically become Americans. Nonetheless, as much as Turner's narrative celebrates the potential commonality of all human beings, it locates the United States as the place where universal history can unfold. Indeed, Turner favorably quotes the Italian economist Loria, "America . . . has the key to the historical enigma which Europe has sought for centuries in vain, and the land which has no history reveals luminously the course of universal history" (11).

The United States may become the site in which universal history unfolds, but only because, as David Noble has demonstrated, narratives like Turner's deny non-European people a history. Furthermore, Turner renders non-Europeans, with the notable exception of Native Americans, invisible. Even though the march westward that he describes brought United States settlers in contact with what David Weber calls the "Spanish Frontier" and even though Chinese played such an important role in building the transcontinental railroad which helped spell an end to the frontier, Turner mentions neither.[12]

Of course, at this moment in the late twentieth century, to point out the invisibility of non-Europeans in our national narratives is a commonplace, if not an obligation. Their invisibility in Turner's narrative is certainly not surprising. A more interesting question is whether the structure of his progressive narrative inevitably excludes them. If it does, that is because neither Frederick Jackson Turner's notion of the frontier nor Victor Turner's notion of the liminal can accommodate what the later Turner calls "marginals." Marginals are "simultaneously (by ascription, optation, self-definition, or achievement) of two or more groups whose social definitions and cultural norms are distinct from, and often even opposed to, one another. . . . Marginals like liminars are also betwixt and between, but unlike ritual liminars they have no cultural assurance of a final stable resolution of their ambiguity."[13] Rather than achieve the synthetic, unified identity implied by Frederick Turner's metaphor of immigrants fusing into a "mixed race," the marginal is much closer to W. E. B. Du Bois's 1897 description of the African American's double consciousness: "this sense of always looking at one's self through the eyes of others, of measuring one's soul by the tape of a world that looks on in amused contempt and pity. One ever feels his twoness,—an American, a Negro; two souls, two thoughts, two unreconciled strivings; two warring ideals in one dark body, whose dogged strength alone keeps it from being torn asunder."[14] Rather than achieve an identity of organic synthesis, the African American is in a state of internal "border warfare."

As inclusive and regenerative as it promises to be, the liminal seems to have no place for the marginal. Its inability to accommodate or find a home for the marginal has opened it to attack by "border" anthropologists like Renato Rosaldo.[15] In this regard it is important to remember that one of the most important effects of Frederick Jackson Turner's use of a redefined notion of "frontier" was to efface the existence of Borderlands in American history. A liminal space on the "edge of settlement" rather than a political boundary around which a border can develop, Turner's frontier creates a community of inclusiveness only through a subtle process of repression.

That repression necessitates the paradigm shift in American studies alluded to by David Noble and undertaken by scholars like José David Saldívar.[16] Nonetheless, those participating in that shift cannot, I want to argue, completely dismiss Turner's narrative. A brief comparison with Martí's "Our America" can show why.

Whereas there are important differences between Turner and Martí, there are also some similarities. For instance, Martí does not indulge in Turner's narrative of *North* American exceptionalism, but he does offer his own version of American exceptionalism through his contrasts between Europe and America. Furthermore, like Turner, Martí rejects the major premise of the period's institutional histories: namely, that a nation's character is determined by its institutions. Indeed, more than Turner, Martí stresses that institutions should grow out of what he calls "elements peculiar to America."[17] "The government must originate within the country," Martí proclaims. "The spirit of the government must be that of the country. Its structure must conform to rules appropriate to the country. Good government is nothing more than the balance of the country's natural elements" (87).

This quotation reveals how much Martí is a child of his time, for it betrays what we can call his "naturalistic organicism." That organicism sheds light on the meaning of "our" in "Our America." Others have already suggested some of those meanings. Let me review a few of them. One is clearly performative. It is a call for a not-yet-existing collective identity. Bickering across national borders should stop: "Nations that do not know one another should quickly become acquainted, as men who are to fight a common enemy. Those who shake their fists, like jealous brothers coveting the same tract of land, or like the modest cottager who envies the squire his mansion, should clasp hands and become one" (84). The "our" also marks a joint claim to the title "America"; there is a Latin as well as an Anglo right to that name. But the "our," as it always does, also implies a "their." One "their" is that of the "other" America: especially the United States. Thus, "the scorn of our formidable neighbor who does not know us is Our America's greatest danger" (93). Another "their" is that of Europe or of neocolonialists who adhere to European notions: "Neither the European nor the Yankee could provide the key to the Spanish American riddle" (91).

Martí's voice, I need to emphasize, is not that of a border anthropologist. It is, as Enrico Mario Santí argues, that of an exile making a claim to return to his natural home, a home, to be sure, that he shares with others, but not with all.[18] America belongs to Americans, not to outsiders. But what, for Martí, makes an American?

To ask that question is to start to be able to distinguish Martí's exceptionalism from Turner's. Like Turner's, Martí's exceptionalism is based on universal premises. For him there are not races but "man's universal identity" (94). However, Martí's sense of American identity within a universal identity is not determined, as it is in Turner, by a westward-moving narrative. Further, he does not imagine an empty space of a Western frontier. What for Turner is a frontier in the new sense is for Martí a frontier in the old sense: a point of cultural contact.

One result is that the unacknowledged link between North America and Europe that we discovered in Turner helps Martí to distinguish "Our America" from the "Other America." Martí even differs from the anonymous reviewer with whom I began, because, unlike him, Martí is not interested in using a link between North and South America to reestablish a link with non-Protestant Europe. He instead wants to break relations with Spain by distinguishing those who are truly American from those whose ties are still with Europe. One way in which he makes that distinction is to focus on those who are denied a history in Turner. Thus, in a very important sense, Martí's account is more inclusive than Turner's.

But for all of Martí's inclusiveness, his naturalistic organicism risks generating exclusions of its own. For instance, at one point he claims that the "struggle is not between barbarity and civilization, but between false erudition (meaning European) and nature (meaning American)." And "the natural man," he immediately adds, "is good" (87). The natural, that which is rooted in the land, helps Martí define the "our" who have a claim to America.

To be sure, Martí's account of the making of an American is complicated. In "Mother America," he anticipates Turner's use of the metaphor of the crucible: "Never was there such a precocious, persevering, and generous people born out of so much opposition and unhappiness. We were a den of iniquity and we are beginning to be a crucible" (79). In the same talk, he defines Our America as "without jealousies or naive trust, fearlessly inviting all races to the fortunes of her home" (81). He especially stresses the importance of *criollos*. Furthermore, as Jeffrey Belnap points out, Martí describes how even those without Native American blood can make themselves Americans through an imaginative act of identification.[19] But even this act of imaginative inclusiveness betrays Martí's naturalistic organicism, since Native Americans help to define an authentic American because they are the original inhabitants of the continent. Thus, at the same time that he welcomes all races to Mother America, he also speaks of the importance of "cleansing our blood of the impurities bequeathed to us by our ancestors" (79), referring thereby to a corrupt Spanish inheritance. As important as it is to stress the corruption of that inheritance, nothing is to be gained by denying that, in order to unite people against the common enemy of Spain, Martí adopts a rhetoric implying that a legitimate claim to the land is rooted in nature. In contrast, Turner offers an account of the making of Americans through a dynamic, forward-looking process rather than one that looks backward toward natural origins.

As my discussion of Turner suggests, forward-looking narratives of process are not inherently superior. Nor are they all the same. For an example I can cite a work that had a much more immediate effect on the U.S. public than Turner's, a work that also might have contributed to Martí's choice of a title: Josiah Strong's *Our Country* (1885). A representative of a Protestant missionary society, Strong anticipated Turner in a chapter entitled "The Exhaustion of Public Lands." Also, like Turner, Strong adopts an evolutionary narrative that sees U.S. history in terms of forward-moving progress. Unlike Turner, though, he links national progress to the destiny of the Anglo-Saxon race, a destiny in part determined by natural origin. "There can be no reasonable doubt," Strong asserts, "that North America is to be the great home of the Anglo-Saxon, the principal seat of his power, the center of his life and influence." Furthermore, as the lack of open land around the globe leads to the "*final competition of races,*" "this powerful race will move down upon Mexico, down upon Central and South America, out upon the islands of the sea, over upon Africa and beyond." It does not take a "prophet's eye," Strong proclaims, "to see that the civilization of the *United States* is to be the civilization of America, and that the future of the continent is ours."[20]

If we want an imperial, racialist narrative of the time, Strong gives us one. Most important for my purposes, Strong's narrative is at odds with Turner's on the question of Americanization. Whereas for Turner Americanization is a process in which a brand-new identity is forged out of an almost ritual experience on the frontier, Strong proclaims that the United States—and by extension all of America—is destined to be a proper home only for those with biological links to the original Anglo-Saxons. To be sure, even for Strong the question of what constitutes an Anglo-Saxon is complicated since the race originated as a mixture. For him Tennyson's claim that "Saxon and Norman and Dane are we," must "be supplemented with Celt and Gaul, Welshman and Irishman, Frisian and Flamand, French Huguenot and German Palatine." Such racial mixing, he notes, is continuing in the United States: "What took place a thousand years ago and more in England again transpires today in the United States." Moreover, in the United States "strains of other bloods" are added to the mix. In the end, however, Strong absorbs this new mixture into an evolutionary narrative claiming superiority for the Anglo-Saxon race. The race may renew itself by mixing with other bloods, but those bloods must be closely related. To "preserve" the "general type" it is essential that "the largest injections of foreign blood are substantially the same elements that constituted the original Anglo-Saxon admixture." Such a new "amalgam" will "improve the stock" and "constitute the new Anglo-Saxon race of the New World" that is destined to rule the continent that contributed to its development.[21] Of course, if Strong's vision of Americanization is ultimately at odds with Turner's account of the frontier, his evangelical Protestant vision of "our country" taking over Latin America is even more at odds with Martí's account of "Our America." Nonetheless, Martí, like Strong, relies on metaphors of identity created through grafting upon an original stock.

My point in making these comparisons is by no means to champion Turner over Martí. On the contrary, I began by examining Turner's blindnesses. My point instead is twofold. First, I want to distinguish both Turner and Martí from alternative narratives of the time like Strong's. Second, I want to suggest that the two present us with powerful, though seemingly irreconcilable, narratives. Martí speaks poignantly for those who are displaced or threatened by displacement by European and North American imperialism. But he bases peoples' claims to a homeland on their relation to an original naturalness rooted in the soil. In contrast, Turner offers a narrative of process in which *voluntary* displacement can lead to the construction of a new identity and a new sense of home. What he fails to acknowledge is how the voluntary displacements leading to those new identities and homes involve the unwilling displacements of those championed by Martí. What generates Turner's blindness is his redefinition of the frontier. Turner, like Martí, assumes an organic relation between human beings and nature. But for him nature does not provide a foundation for claims to a homeland. Instead, it is an ahistorical space of blankness where people can construct a home. Nonetheless, because of the westward movement of his narrative—one that, as we have seen, establishes a connection between Europe and *North* America as well as a difference between them—Turner imagines that space primarily as a potential home for North American descendants from Europe.

Placing Turner next to Martí challenges us to imagine alternative narratives that, unlike Turner's, do not employ a narrative of progress to displace a history of oppression and that, nonetheless, retain the positive possibilities that Turner sees in displacement. As I have noted, both Donald Pease and Doris Sommer have taken up the challenge in fascinating ways. My focus on Turner offers a different perspective on those possibilities. For instance, if the reconstructive powers of Turner's narrative depend on the space of displacement that he designates "the frontier," the question I pose is whether there is a way of reimagining that space. An obvious way to do so is to return to the notion of frontier as a boundary around which a border space emerges. To understand the significance of the frontier in terms of borders is to construct narratives that dramatically alter Turner's spatial and temporal metaphors.

Efforts to redefine the frontier, I need to acknowledge, have been under way for quite sometime. In 1921 Herbert Eugene Bolton, though once a student of Turner, self-consciously titled his book in Yale's "The Chronicles of America" series *The Spanish Borderlands* and thus founded "Borderlands studies."[22] In 1968 Jack D. Forbes, following up on a provocative 1962 piece, pushed for a definition of the frontier as "an *inter-group contact situation,*" involving "such processes as acculturation, assimilation, miscegenation, race prejudice, conquest, imperialism, and colonialism."[23]

With today's ascendancy of border studies, alternative narratives are almost a commonplace. I will note just a few of their differences from Turner's. First of all, such narratives do not posit Europe as the origin of civilization. Rather, they assume the simultaneous existence of various civilizations with none at the center. Furthermore, they replace the linear movement of Turner's narrative with one of reciprocality. Instead of talking about the westward march of civilization, these speak about exchanges and conflicts—often uneven—among cultures. As we have seen, even Turner's narrative implies some such reciprocity. But he confines it to an exchange between Europe and America. The new narratives try to describe exchanges occurring in various directions across various borders around the globe.

As important as such work is, I shall end by offering a few warnings to those who are making border studies today's most exciting area of cultural analysis. First, as we imagine new narratives in which the frontier is reconstructed as a place of borders—spaces between, not spaces on the edge—we should not forget the military roots of the word "frontier." Borderlands are the sites of war as well as exchange, and narratives about cultural contact can be made in preparation for violent conflict, as in the case of Samuel Huntington's controversial thesis about the "clash of civilizations."[24] Our anonymous reviewer, after all, correctly predicted that it might take a war to draw the United States' attention to neglected connections with Latin America. Indeed, as much as we feel the need to reconstruct Turner's use of the frontier to displace a past history of violence, his narrative remains attractive if we view it not as a narrative about the past, but (like Martí's in part) as a vision for the future. For instance, given the horrendous problem of violence in U.S. society today and its clear link to issues of race and battles over turf, the vision of a nation regenerating itself, not through violence but by displacing violence, is as relevant at the end of the twentieth century as it was at the end of the nineteenth.

Second, whereas it is important to emphasize the historical contingency of how national boundaries are constructed, there might be times when they can still serve pragmatic functions. For instance, even though our anonymous reviewer is correct to note that commerce is more "amiable" than war, in a world of unequal economic power the breaking down of trade barriers rarely benefits all countries equally.

Third, we might consider whether border studies risk romanticizing the marginal. To be sure, it is important to point to historical conditions that led to the marginalization of numerous peoples around the globe. It is also important to note the incapacity of concepts like Victor Turner's "liminal" or Frederick Jackson Turner's "frontier" to accommodate the marginal. But the very word "accommodate" suggests problems with privileging the condition of marginalization. Can we criticize someone for not accommodating the marginal without assuming that the marginal has a claim to a home or some place of accommodation? Indeed, is it possible that various celebrations of border identities growing out of the physical displacement of people result from cultural critics imposing their self-image as free-floating intellectuals whose permanent mental displacement grants them a valuable space of independence? Are we guilty of conflating a metaphoric space of displacement with actual spaces of displacement and thus perpetuating the sense of homelessness felt by so many, like Martí, forced to live in a marginal state of exile? In other words, do we want to perpetuate a permanent feeling of displacement for marginalized people, or should we strive to create conditions in which those on the border can feel at home? Both Martí and Turner, it seems to me, remind us of the power generated by narratives that accommodate displaced peoples' desire to feel at home. Yet they do so in dramatically different ways. Displaced, Martí uses his condition of exile in the United States to mobilize forces for a return to claim Cuba as his home. Turner, in contrast, offers an account of how people can feel at home in a space of displacement.

These differences return me to my claim that placing Turner and Martí together is one way to take up the challenge posed by Doris Sommer to participate in a redefinition of the "our" in "Our America." An important part of that redefinition is, I have argued, the redefinition of Turner's notion of the frontier taking place in border studies. Nonetheless, I have also tried to suggest that any redefinition of "our" cannot be completely inclusive. It will inevitably generate its own exclusions. What we can work for, however, is a definition that allows for a dynamic process by which "our" is not a fixed category but one that is always open to redefinition. It is on this point that we still have something to learn from Turner's reconstructive use of history.

My point is not that Turner's description of the frontier gives an accurate account of the history of the United States. It is instead that, insofar as those intent on reconstructing our sense of history promise a more inclusive narrative of renewal through the displacement of that which comes before them, to a certain extent they continue to follow a path blazed most influentially by Turner. In this sense, the importance of the frontier in Turner's narrative is not its physical designation but the function that it serves as a metaphoric space of displacement. After all, to proclaim the end of the usefulness of the frontier as a concept for understanding American history is merely to repeat (with a difference) what Turner did more than a hundred years ago when, announcing the closing of the frontier, he challenged his readers to imagine new possibilities for America.

More often than not, those taking up the challenge have done so by displacing Turner's frontier with a series of metaphoric "new frontiers." Even Patricia Nelson Limerick, who has argued for the need to renew Western historiography by avoiding the "f-word," has recently recognized the virtual impossibility of escaping it. We may be undergoing a paradigm shift in American studies, but, as Limerick reminds us, before shifting paradigms we first have to engage the clutch.[25] To her insight I can add that because a paradigm shift is itself a metaphor of displacement, it is not inappropriate to call border studies the field's new frontier. Indeed, as much as our new narratives show—as to an extent mine does—that the frontier, as defined by Turner, was always at an end in American history, it is hard to imagine coming up with new narratives and new meanings of "Our America" without relying on some space of displacement that Turner in his narrative calls a no-longer-existing frontier.

Having made that point, I do not want to make the mistake that I earlier warned us against and conflate metaphoric displacements with the historical actuality of physical displacements. To be sure, the two should not be seen in simple opposition. Nonetheless, an important difference remains between the imaginative spaces opened up by *metaphoric* displacement and the *physical* displacement of people which almost always involves occupying land already occupied by others. If Turner offers a narrative in which newly arrived immigrants can imagine themselves at home on the range, Martí demands that we identify with those who are rendered homeless. How we meet the challenge of redefining the meaning of "Our America" a hundred years after Martí's death depends in part on how we can bring together these seemingly incompatible narratives.

Notes

1 "The Figure of Columbus," *Atlantic Monthly* 69 (1892): 409.

2 See Noble's, Pease's, and Sommer's essays in this book.

3 My argument about Turner (without the comparison with Martí) draws from my "Turner's Frontier Thesis as a Narrative of Reconstruction," in *Centuries' Ends, Narrative Means,* ed. Robert D. Newman (Stanford: Stanford University Press, 1996), pp. 117–37.

4 Frederick Jackson Turner, "The Significance of the Frontier in American History," in Turner, *The Frontier in American History* (New York: Henry Holt & Co., 1920), p. 24. Subsequent page references to this essay will be given parenthetically in the text.

5 Henry Adams, *History of the United States of America* (New York: Charles Scribner's Sons, 1891), vol. 1: *During the First Administration of Thomas Jefferson*, p. 156.

6 G. W. F. Hegel, *Lectures on the Philosophy of History*, trans. J. Sibree (New York: Colonial Press, 1900), pp. 85–87.

7 John T. Juricek, "American Usage of the Word 'Frontier' from Colonial Times to Frederick Jackson Turner," *Proceedings of the American Philosophical Society* 110 (1966): 33. The new use of "frontier" by no means completely drove out the old. In the same year that Turner presented the frontier thesis, Congressman Thomas J. Geary of California defended his 1892 bill (extending the exclusion of Chinese and severely punishing Chinese illegally caught in the United States) by detailing the expense needed to maintain "guards and inspectors upon our frontiers and at our different seaports, in order to prevent the infraction of our laws by a race of people who never have shown any respect for them." See Congressman Thomas J. Geary, "Should the Chinese Be Excluded?" *North American Review* 158 (1893): 61.

8 Frederick Jackson Turner, "The First Official Frontier of the Massachusetts Bay," in Turner, *The Frontier in American History*, p. 41.

9 Juricek, "American Usage of the Word 'Frontier,'" pp. 10–11.

10 See Pease's essay in this collection.

11 Victor Turner, *From Ritual to Theatre* (New York: Performing Arts Journal Publications, 1982), p. 84, and *The Ritual Process* (Chicago: Aldine Publishing Co., 1969), p. 128. Sacvan Bercovitch draws heavily on Turner's notion of liminality to describe how an American *communitas* is forged out of a "Ritual of Consensus." See Bercovitch, *The American Jeremiad* (Madison: University of Wisconsin Press, 1978), pp. 132–75 and 204n–205n.

12 David J. Weber, *The Spanish Frontier in North America* (New Haven: Yale University Press, 1992). Insofar as individualism was a sign of progressive democracy, Chinese were seen as a blocking force because they were linked to feudal-like forms of collectivity.

13 Victor Turner, *Dramas, Fields, and Metaphors* (Ithaca: Cornell University Press, 1974), pp. 232–33.

14 W. E. B. Du Bois, "Strivings of the Negro People," *Atlantic Monthly* 80 (1897): 195. On Du Bois and Turner, see William Toll, "W. E. B. Du Bois and Frederick Jackson Turner: The Unveiling and Preemption of America's Inner History," *Pacific Northwest Quarterly* 65 (1974): 66–78.

15 See Donald Weber, "From Limen to Border: A Meditation on the

Legacy of Victor Turner for American Cultural Studies," *American Quarterly* 47 (1995): 525–36.

16 José David Saldívar, *Border Matters: Remapping American Cultural Studies* (Berkeley: University of California Press, 1997).

17 José Martí, *Our America,* ed. Philip S. Foner (New York: Monthly Review Press, 1977), p. 87. Subsequent page references to this work will be given parenthetically in the text.

18 See Santí's essay in this collection.

19 See Belnap's essay in this collection.

20 Josiah Strong, *Our Country: Its Possible Future and Its Present Crisis* (New York: American Home Missionary Society, 1885), pp. 165, 175, and 167. Emphasis in original.

21 Ibid., pp. 171–72. It is worth noting that, as different as Strong is from a figure like Du Bois, the two rely on a common passage from "Locksley Hall," by Alfred, Lord Tennyson: "Till the war-drum throbs no longer, and the battle flags are furl'd / In the Parliament of man, the Federation of the world." Strong, however, imagines fulfillment of Tennyson's prophecy in "Anglo-Saxondom's extending its dominion and influence" (p. 179), whereas Du Bois cites the passage to warn the founders of the United Nations that the new world body needs to combat the tradition of colonialism perpetuated most notably by England. Indeed, Strong proclaims that a "marked characteristic of the Anglo-Saxon is what might be called an instinct or genius for colonizing" (p. 173). For Du Bois's citation of Tennyson, see W. E. B. Du Bois, *Color and Democracy: Colonies and Peace* (New York: Harcourt, Brace & Co., 1945), p. 16.

22 Herbert Eugene Bolton, *The Spanish Borderlands: A Chronicle of Old Florida and the Southwest* (New Haven: Yale University Press, 1921).

23 Jack D. Forbes, "Frontiers in American History and the Role of the Frontier Historian," *Ethnohistory* 15 (1968): 207, 205. Emphasis in original.

24 Samuel Huntington, *The Clash of Civilizations and the Remaking of the World Order* (New York: Simon & Schuster, 1996).

25 Patricia Nelson Limerick, "The Adventures of the Frontier in the Twentieth Century," in *The Frontier in American Culture,* ed. James R. Grossman (Berkeley: University of California Press, 1994), pp. 67–102. See also Limerick's "Turnerians All: The Dream of a Helpful History in an Intelligible World," *American Historical Review* 100 (1995): 697–716.

George Lipsitz

Their America and Ours: Intercultural Communication in the Context of "Our America"

Let us consider the world economy; it appears as nothing but a battlefield where businesses wage a pitiless war. No prisoners are taken. Whoever falls, dies. — François Mitterand, "Letter to the French," April 1988[1]

Well before the political fighting phase of the national movement, an attentive spectator can thus feel and see the manifestation of a new vigor and feel the approaching conflict. He will note unusual forms of expression and themes which are fresh and imbued with a power which is no longer that of an invocation, but rather of the assembling of the people, a summoning together for a precise purpose. Everything works together to awaken the native's sensibility and to make unreal and unacceptable the contemplative attitude or the acceptance of defeat. — Frantz Fanon, *The Wretched of the Earth*[2]

In "Theses on Historical Materialism," Walter Benjamin identifies the importance of "memories that flash up in a moment of danger."[3] Aspects of history that have been ignored, forgotten, or misrepresented can take on new meaning in the light of contemporary crises. Provoked by problems that seem new, we find ourselves rethinking parts of the past that previously may have seemed to be relatively insignificant but that take on great new meaning all of a sudden. For Benjamin, as for William Appleman Williams, we return to the past not to acknowledge its power over the present but, on the contrary, to break its hold on us and to develop new ways of acting and understanding.[4]

In response to the dangers of our time, many scholars in recent years have returned to the life and work of José Martí.[5] At a moment when the triumph of transnational capital has radically transformed relations between nation-states and citizens, between workers and employers, and between people and the places where they live and work, the memory of Martí serves subversive functions. The José Martí conjured up in contemporary criticism is both an intellectual and an activist, an artist and an agitator, a nationalist and an internationalist. His writings from a century ago resonate powerfully with what we see around us today. He condemned the oppressive materialism of North America, describing it as a place where "[achieving] a fortune is the only object of life. . . . Men, despite all appearances, are tied together here only by interests, by the cordial hatreds that exist between those who are bargaining for the same prize."[6] At a time when white supremacy increased and expanded in the United States, Martí turned in the opposite direction. Although his early writings expressed anxiety over how ethnic heterogeneity held back Latin America, he eventually came to a position celebrating *mestizaje* as an advantage that would hasten rather than retard the building of nations in Central America, the Caribbean, and South America. Furthermore, he wrote, "there can be no racial animosity, because there are no races. . . . The soul, equal and eternal, emanates from bodies of various shapes and colors. Whoever foments and spreads antagonism and hate between the races, sins against humanity."[7]

In our own time, when nation-states seem increasingly unable or unwilling to remedy social ills, Martí's insistence on linking nationalism with substantive social reform resonates powerfully with contemporary readers, reminding us of lost options still capable of being retrieved. The remembered José Martí of the late twentieth century offers radical alternatives to the kinds of internationalism advanced by the International Monetary Fund and the World Bank, to the terms of hemispheric unity prefigured by the North American Free-Trade Agreement and the General Agreement on Tariffs and Trade, and to the cultural uniformity and univocality engendered by the pervasive growth of mass-media monopolies, market-driven education, and neoconservative cultural repression.

The Chilean artist Alfredo Jaar (who now lives in New York) certainly evoked the tradition of Martí's "Nuestra América" in his 1987 work *A Logo for America.* Jaar used the Spectacolor light board in Times Square to display a map of the United States and the U.S. flag with the words "This is not America, This is not America's flag" superimposed on the images. He also used the 1974 Peters Map to show that the Southern Hemisphere countries are actually twice as large as the northern countries, rather than the same size as they appear on most maps.[8] Perhaps it is not surprising that a South American émigré would challenge the ways in which citizens of the United States confuse their country with the continent, but even in the United States Martí's emphasis on inter-American dialogue resonates powerfully because of the demographic and social changes of the past three decades. The United States now houses the fifth-largest Spanish-speaking population in the world; if current population trends in Colombia and Argentina continue, the United States will have the third-largest group of Spanish speakers by the year 2000.[9]

Los Angeles is the second-largest Mexican city, the second-largest Salvadoran city, and the second-largest Guatemalan city in the world. New York has a Caribbean population larger than the combined populations of Kingston (Jamaica), San Juan (Puerto Rico), and Port of Spain (Trinidad).[10] During the 1970s the number of people of Mexican origin in New York grew from 7,364 to 21,623; but by 1990 the city had more than 60,000 residents of Mexican origin, and current estimates range as high as 96,000.[11] More than one-third of all Puerto Ricans live in North American cities, and the Puerto Rican population in the continental United States has doubled since the 1950s.[12] Although the number of Puerto Ricans in New York increased tenfold between 1940 and 1970, by 1985 migration from the Dominican Republic, Mexico, Central America, and Colombia reached such heights that migrants from those places surpassed the Puerto Rican population in aggregate numbers.[13] Mary Waters claims that nearly one out of every four black people now in New York City is from the Caribbean.[14] Finally, more than 10 percent of the population of the Dominican Republic has moved to the United States since 1970, perhaps as many as 500,000 to New York City alone.[15]

Thus, there is a clear and coherent logic to the rediscovery of José Martí in recent years. But "memories that flash up in a moment of danger" can obscure as much as they reveal. Assessing the relevance of Martí's legacy for the problems that confront us today requires detailed investigation not only of the things that have changed during the past century but also of those things that seem to have remained the same. As the industrial era ends, we may gain a mature understanding of its accomplishments and failures; as the power of transnational corporations eclipses the power of the nation-state we may acquire in retrospect a more thorough understanding of nationalism. But we also run the risk of attempting to solve today's problems with yesterday's solutions, of resorting to a kind of reactionary nostalgia that continues to frame fundamentally new realities within the safe confines of categories from the past. Whatever conclusions we draw from the actions and words of José Martí for the transnational and postindustrial present must be tempered by an acknowledgment of the challenges posed by new patterns of capital accumulation to our traditional understandings of politics, nationalism, and culture.

It should be clear that ours is a time of dramatic and extreme change. Transnational corporations now control one-third of all the private-sector productive assets in the world. U.S. firms now employ more than 1.3 million workers in Latin America, 1.5 million workers in Asia, and 2 million workers in Europe.[16] The rise of these corporations has been made possible by new technologies and business practices, but also by the weakening of the state sector — by neoconservative tax policies and the evisceration of the welfare state in advanced industrialized countries, and by "structural adjustment policies" imposed on poorer nations through currency devaluation, trade liberalization, privatization of public enterprises, cutting wages, restricting credit, raising interest rates, and slashing social spending on education, health, housing, and transportation.[17] Structural adjustment policies have left 820 million workers (30 percent of the entire world labor force) either unemployed or working at less than subsistence wages.[18] As Dan Gallin points out in his important analysis of the transnational economy, "lower wages and reduced public spending mean less buying power, stagnation, recession, unemployment, and unendurable debt."[19]

During the 1980s, real wages in Mexico declined by more than 50 percent. The workers' share of national income in that country fell from nearly 50 percent in 1981 to less than 30 percent by 1990. More than 60 percent of the employed labor force in Mexico receive only the minimum wage, an amount capable of supplying a family of four with only 25 percent of its basic needs.[20] In Latin America, Africa, and Asia, an astounding number of children under five years of age have died each year since 1982 of hunger or disease.[21] The richest fifth of the world today receives 150 times as much income as the poorest fifth, and even in Third World countries the gap between rich and poor doubled during the 1980s.[22]

Structural adjustment policies have also produced massive displacement. In 1970, a United Nations commission counted 2 million refugees in the world; today the number exceeds 44 million. In 1992, the U.N. high commissioner for refugees announced that world refugee numbers were increasing by 10,000 people a day.[23] Walden Bello succinctly captures the overwhelming logic behind migration and flight for people from poor countries when he argues, "Perhaps it is the migrants who most clearly perceive the truth about structural adjustment: it was intended not as a transition to prosperity but as a permanent condition of economic suffering to ensure that the South would never rise again to challenge the North. If that is the case, flight is a rational solution. Migrants are not obsessed nomads seeking the emerald cities. . . . [T]hey are refugees fleeing the wasteland that has been created by the economic equivalent of a scorched earth strategy."[24]

Bello's eloquent formulation hides an even more sinister reality: the way in which elites in low-wage countries have come to rely upon labor out-migration as a means of securing foreign exchange, slowing population growth, and defusing pressures for job creation or income redistribution in their own countries. At the same time, the U.S. government manipulates immigration policies to relieve pressure on totalitarian governments friendly to transnational business interests like those in the Dominican Republic or South Korea, and encourages the mobility of capital to low-wage regions and the flight of desperate low-wage workers to previously industrialized and high-wage areas in order to drive down wages for all workers.[25]

New circumstances require new analyses. The social movements of José Martí's time operated in an age when capital could be trapped in one place. Under those conditions, revolutionary nationalism and socialism seemed like the forms of struggle best suited for controlling capital—taxing it, regulating it, or seizing it. Trade unions, political parties, and revolutionary movements sought physical control over factories, cities, and nations in order to extract concessions from capitalists or to take their place running things. Nation-states flourished during the era of industrialization; fixed capital used control of the state to protect its assets at home and to establish exploitative and extractive relations with the inhabitants of colonized areas abroad; reformers and revolutionaries saw that they had to get a share of state power in order to advance their own interests. Today, computer-generated automation, satellites, and fiber-optic technologies enable capitalists to separate management from production. No longer trapped in one factory, one city, or one nation, investors and managers move production all around the globe. They secure subsidies, tax breaks, control over production, and immunity from local laws in order to maximize short-term profits. The nation-state remains very important as a vehicle for capital accumulation and as an instrument of repression against popular movements, but it no longer seems to be in control of its own destiny. This is especially so in the Third World, where the International Monetary Fund and the World Bank have imposed austerity against even the most progressive nationalist regimes.[26] Taking control of state power turned out to be no solution for Salvador Allende's Socialists in Chile, Daniel Ortega's Sandinistas in Nicaragua, Maurice Bishop's New Jewel Movement in Grenada, or Michael Manley's People's National Party in Jamaica.

Strategies for social justice based solely on trapping capital in one place are now obsolete. Tomorrow's social movements will need to seek state power, to be sure, but they will also need to be local as well as global, mobile as well as situated, aimed at creating dynamic circuits and networks rather than at establishing "free spaces" or "liberated" zones. Thanks to the insurgency in Chiapas, we are starting to get a glimpse of what such movements will look like; but, so far, grass-roots cultural creation has responded to the transnational economy more visibly and more creatively than most political movements.

The transformation of capital's relationships with place and with the nation-state has had extensive cultural consequences. Transnational capital moves ideas and images as well as people and products with dazzling speed. Nations now recognize that large parts of their histories and their futures may happen somewhere else. The presence of 600,000 Central Americans in Los Angeles changes what it means to be a citizen of Guatemala or El Salvador, but also what it means to be "Latino," Chicano, black, Asian American, Anglo, or Native American in California. Los Angeles gang graffiti now appear in San Salvador. The importance of narco-trafficking to the economies of South America changes the price of drugs and exacerbates the violence that accompanies drug dealing in North American cities. Similar features mark the terrain of mass communication. In 1992 the single most popular radio station in Los Angeles (the biggest and most profitable radio market in the United States succeeded by programming *banda* music aimed at recent immigrants from Mexico.[27] Guatemalan expatriates in Washington, D.C., now watch Mexican variety shows on Spanish-language cable television stations run by Cuban Americans, while *merengue* music from the Dominican Republic has recently surpassed *salsa* (Afro-Cuban music played largely by Puerto Ricans) as the most popular music among Spanish speakers in New York and in Puerto Rico.[28]

The permutations of Dominican *merengue* music (Haitian *merengue* is somewhat different) over the past decades provide a particularly useful example of how commodity culture, migrant labor, exile, and return paradoxically reinforce *and* subvert traditional understandings of the nation. Few musical genres have been more fully fused with nationalism than the Dominican *merengue*. Characterized by lively 2/4 rhythms and a five-beat stroke at the end of every fourth bar, the *merengue* originated with small combos orchestrated for Hohner button accordion and a horizontally held double-headed *tambora* drum beaten by a gourd scraper (*güira*) on one side and by hand on the other. The presence of the accordion reveals the always international character of *merengue:* in the nineteenth century, tobacco farmers in Cibao conducted extensive trade with Germany and received accordions in exchange for tobacco.[29] A rural music originating as far back as the 1840s, *merengue* first became associated with national identity during the U.S. occupation of the country between 1916 and 1934, as nationalists embraced the Cibao region's form of the music as a distinctive marker of nationhood and as part of their program to mobilize Dominicans against the presence of the U.S. Marines. Their efforts led to the embrace of *merengue* as the quintessential expression of national identity during the dictatorship of Rafael Trujillo from 1930 to 1961.[30]

Trujillo came from a lower middle-class family in San Cristóbal on the south coast, but during his military service he became familiar with the *merengue* music played by light-skinned residents of Cibao, near the north coast. Trujillo put the power of the state behind *merengue* because he viewed it as an emblematic icon of the nation's white, Spanish, and Catholic traditions, a source of national unity that provided a sharp contrast with the Dominican

Republic's black, French, and Vodoun neighbors in Haiti. Anxious about what he perceived as a threat to "white" Dominican identity from adjacent Haiti (even though people of African descent have lived in what is now the Dominican Republic since 1502), and eager to obscure the existence of his own Haitian grandmother, Trujillo used *merengue* at all official state functions and personal appearances by the dictator. No one was allowed to leave a dance while the Orquesta Generalísimo Trujillo was playing until the dictator himself departed, which in at least one case meant more than twenty-four hours.[31] But government promotions of *merengue* went far beyond structuring ceremonial occasions of state. Trujillo used *merengue* songs as direct propaganda, commissioning lyrics supporting his policies, literally singing the praises of his regime in songs with titles like "Trujillo Is Great and Immortal," "Faith in Trujillo," and "We Venerate Trujillo."[32] Even more, Trujillo's brother, José Arismendi (known as Petán) founded the Orquesta San José to play *merengue* songs during the 1940s and 1950s in a luxurious ballroom inside the studios of his radio stations, La Voz del Yuna (1942–45) and La Voz Dominicana (1945–61), the most powerful broadcast outlets in the country. At the dictator's insistence, the latter station played only *merengue* music during its nearly two-decade-long existence. Moreover, Arismendi banned any recorded music from this station, insisting on live performances exclusively during the station's twelve-hour broadcasting day. Consequently, the Dominican government kept a stable of *merengue* musicians from ten different ensembles on retainer to play on La Voz Dominicana, further encouraging musicians in that impoverished country to master the genre.[33]

Merengue became an important frame for expressing Dominican national identity and for resituating imports from abroad. Dominican bands created *merengue* arrangements of popular Brazilian *sambas* and Mexican *rancheras*. In the 1950s Félix del Rosario's arrangement for Antonio Morel y Su Orquesta of a South African song, "Skokiaan," combined elements of *merengue* with U.S. big band jazz and South African *tsaba*.[34]

Like many other aspects of official and popular culture in the Dominican Republic, the visual performance and lyrics of *merengue* during the Trujillo years valorized "whiteness" in a way that exacerbated racial and class divisions within the country, marking as illegitimate those who did not conform to the idealized image. In

1937, Trujillo ordered his troops to kill Haitians in the Dominican Republic, and they murdered between 10,000 and 20,000 of them.[35] Trujillo's racial politics expressed and exacerbated the core contradictions of the country itself. As Paul Austerlitz notes in his astute analysis, "While Trujillo massacred Haitians and propagated an anti-Haitian Dominican identity, he was of partial Haitian descent himself; while he proscribed blatantly African-influenced magic-religious customs, he practiced them himself; and while he chose a national music associated with what is arguably the country's most European region, *merengue* itself has many African-derived characteristics. The music was an effective national symbol because it successfully articulated the contradictions of Dominican culture as well as of Trujillo's personality."[36]

People of African descent in the Dominican Republic learn to speak of themselves as *indio* rather than *negro,* and newspapers refer to light- and dark-skinned blacks as *indios claros* or *indios oscuros.*[37] Even as migration from the West Indies and Haiti has combined with intermarriage to gradually "blacken" the Dominican population, it's official culture has become all that much more defensive and emphatic about its "whiteness," although Dominicans considered *blanco* in their native country have often found themselves viewed as black elsewhere.[38] Trujillo prohibited any direct acknowledgment of folk traditions having Haitian or African origins.[39]

The assassination of Trujillo, his succession by a brief period of popular reform, and years of economic austerity and repressive rule by the dictator's former secretary Joaquín Balaguer (president for all but eight years between 1966 and 1996) have not diminished Dominicans' enthusiasm for *merengue.* In fact, because *merengue* received public support and secured market success during the Trujillo years, musicians from other genres, including the despised rural and lower-class *bachata,* often adopted the tempos and sounds of *merengue* to make themselves sound more respectable. In addition, *merengue* artists sometimes used the genre against the politics of its patron. During the 1965 U.S. military occupation of the island (aimed at overthrowing the popularly elected president Juan Bosch and installing a regime that would support Trujilloism without Trujillo), the *merengue* artist Johnny Ventura performed songs commenting on the crisis in order to raise the spirits of the followers of Bosch's Partido Revolucionario Dominicano. Similarly, Cuco Valoy's "No me empuje" [Don't Push Me] was widely viewed as a rebuke of the U.S. troops.[40] *Merengue* remained the national music, even though it had been associated with a tyrant who demanded total control over the country's cultural life.

The same structural adjustment policies that have gradually shifted the Dominican economy toward offshore manufacturing, tourism, and remittances from Dominican workers in the United States have also changed the content and form of *merengue* music. Dominican migration to the United States increased dramatically after the assassination of Trujillo in 1961, but especially after 1965 when U.S. Marines came to the island to suppress the popular uprising and support the coup d'état that deposed Juan Bosch. Almost 60,000 Dominicans came to the United States between 1965 and 1969.[41] The amount of money that enters the Dominican economy as remittances from workers in the United States amounts to anywhere from $500 million to $900 million—in either case, more than the Dominican Republic earns from the combined earnings of its ferronickel and sugar industries.[42] Within the Dominican Republic itself, consolidation of agricultural holdings by transnational corporations led to the displacement of rural residents to Dominican cities such as Santo Domingo, where the population doubled between 1961 and 1970. More than 50 percent of the population lived in urban areas by 1980.[43]

Displaced from rural areas and unable to secure employment in cities, Dominican workers arrived in New York in large numbers during the 1970s and 1980s. As many as 1 million Dominicans now live in the United States and Puerto Rico, some 400,000 of them in New York. So many Dominicans live in the Washington Heights section of Manhattan, in fact, that they refer to the neighborhood as Quisqueya Heights.[44] Just as political terror in El Salvador made low-wage work more feasible in the garment industry of Los Angeles because it provided an opportunity for employers to get around minimum-wage laws and fair labor practices by using refugees desperate for work, the Dominican presence in New York helped capitalists drive down wages. This decline played a role in New York's transition from a city where there were many high-wage jobs to one where janitors, domestics, child-care workers, security guards, garment workers, low-wage factory operatives, and personal-service workers became the fastest growing sectors of the labor force.[45]

Dominicans carried their national consciousness with them to New York, but the "Dominican Yorks" lived different lives than they had in their homeland. Interaction with dark-skinned Puerto Ricans, African Americans, and West Indians encouraged escape from the confining categories of Dominican racial hierarchy. In New York female immigrants found opportunities for employment, autonomy, and self-expression that had been denied them at home. The Dominican community experienced what Juan Flores (in reference to Puerto Ricans in New York) terms "branching out," which he defines as a move "toward those groups to whom they stand in closest proximity, not only spatially but also because of parallel cultural experience." Flores explains that this "growing together" is often misread as the "dissolution of national backgrounds and cultural histories" or as simple assimilation, but "the difference is obvious in that it is not directed toward incorporation into the dominant culture. For that reason, the 'pluralism' that results does not involve the dissolution of national backgrounds and histories but their continued affirmation and enforcement even as they are transformed."[46] As early as the 1960s, racist treatment on the U.S. mainland propelled some Dominicans to embrace philosophies of black power and black self-affirmation. Experience in subsequent decades, both as immigrant low-wage laborers and as subjects racialized by North American categories, further honed this racial consciousness.[47]

During the 1980s, New York–based *merengue* artists brought new experiences into their traditional music. In 1984, the *merengue* trumpet virtuoso (and former postal carrier) Wilfrido Vargas released "El africano," an international *merengue* hit featuring lyrics with a decidedly stereotypical depiction of "primitive" blackness. Yet Vargas also produced *merengue* versions of Haitian *konpa* including his 1985 hit "El jardinero," which blends *tambora* and *güira* with synthesizers, horns, and rap music.[48] At the same time, Juan Luis Guerra recorded tremendously popular *merengues* that rejected racist imagery about Haitians or dark-skinned Dominicans. Cuco Valoy and Wilfrido Vargas arranged *bachata* songs as *merengues,* a gesture that elevated the status of *bachata* and revealed how migration to New York transformed class hierarchies within the Dominican community. In 1987, Blas Durán introduced the solid-body electric guitar to the genre with his song "Consejo a las mujeres," bringing *merengue* closer to Anglo American rock and roll and African American dance music. In the early 1990s, a series of female performers including Millie Quezada and Alexandra Taveras achieved star status in what had previously been an exclusively male genre. Lyrics of *merengue* songs chronicled the experiences of workers and refugees. Certainly the desire to reach new audiences and secure greater exposure played a part in these changes, but even in strictly commercial terms, the avenues open to *merengue* artists depended upon the new life circumstances of Dominicans in the United States.

The popularity of Juan Luis Guerra and his group 4:40 (named after the 440-hertz vibrations emitted at the A pitch on a tuning fork) provides a particularly significant illustration of the ways in which commercial culture can combine with ethnic life and labor to refashion a national culture. The son of a Spanish mother and a Dominican father, Guerra studied literature in the Dominican Republic, where he was inspired by the poetry of Pablo Neruda and the music of the Beatles, Rolling Stones, and Pink Floyd. Sometimes he detected familiar things in this music from far away; he remembers hearing Paul McCartney and the Beatles' version of "Till There Was You" as "a kind of bolero, a *bachata* without bongos or maracas." After attending the Berklee School of Music in Boston where he specialized in jazz, Guerra brought a new dimension to the *merengue* by slowing down the beat, adding jazz harmonies, and writing lyrics on social issues in the spirit of the great Cuban *nueva canción* singer-songwriter Silvio Rodríguez.[49]

Guerra's 1990 album *Bachata Rosa* sold 3.5 million units, an astounding total for any Spanish-language singer, much less a Dominican. By faithfully "covering" the *bachata* sound, Guerra helped bring *bachata* and *merengue* closer together, securing new commercial viability for both.[50] His adventurous forays outside *merengue* traditions expressed the "branching out" of Dominicans in New York City and used them to reexamine race relations within the Dominican Republic and beyond. Guerra's song "Guavaberry" used calypso music and English lyrics to evoke the voices of black *cocolos* (workers from Jamaica, the Virgin Islands, Turks and Caicos, Saint Kitts–Nevis, and Anguilla) in the Dominican city of San Pedro de Macorís (just as the Nicaraguan group Soul Vibrations had accomplished for their nation's Anglophone black population along the Atlantic coast).[51] On his album *Areito,* Guerra called attention to the Taino Indians, the indigenous inhabitants of the Caribbean, especially on his *salsa/merengue* song "Si saliera petróleo" [If We Struck Oil], which refers to the Dominican Republic by its Taino name, Quisqueya.[52] Guerra employed Afro-Caribbean *zouk* rhythms from Martinique and Guadeloupe on "Rosalía," and he also recorded "A pedir su mano," a *merengue* version of the song "Dede Priscilla" by Lea Lignazi from the Central African Republic.[53] Guerra's song "El costo de la vida" [The Cost of Living] is based on a tune by the Zairean guitarist Diblo, whom Guerra first heard playing at the New York night spot SOB's.[54] On "Mal de amor" Guerra pays tribute to the Haitian songwriter Nemours Jen Baptiste, a significant gesture in a country with such a long history of opposition to all things Haitian.

Guerra's lyrics remind listeners that emigration has been a group experience rather than an individual decision; a product of global forces, not just of local realities. The lyrics of "Visa para un sueño" [Visa for a Dream] express the anguish of people desperate to leave the Dominican Republic, both those who secure visas through legal channels and those who try desperately to cross the seas in makeshift rafts to immigrate illegally. The song's up-tempo rhythms and swirling orchestration suggest determination, while the sounds of helicopter rotors remind listeners of the pain of those who are picked up by the INS off the coast of Puerto Rico and returned home, only to have to try sneaking through again. In 1990 alone, U.S. Coast Guard patrols intercepted almost 4,000 Dominicans in the waters near Puerto Rico, while authorities deported close to 15,000 Dominicans found to have entered Puerto Rico illegally. Perhaps as many as 80,000 Dominicans have become permanent residents of Puerto Rico, finding employment as domestic workers, street vendors, and other low-wage occupations.[55] In "Ojalá que llueva café" [I Hope It Rains Coffee], Guerra takes his lyrics from an anonymous poem that he discovered in a small Dominican village, Santiago de los Caballeros; he sings about the everyday experiences of *campesinos,* displaying powerful sympathy for their struggle to survive in the globalized economy.[56] *Merengue*'s emphasis on dance, its history as the country's national music, and the lyrics of many of the songs make this genre one of the places where the immigrant community comes into being as a distinctly new social entity formed out of common experiences, memories, and affective ties.

While *merengue* helps Dominicans in New York to draw selectively on their past to face the problems of the present, it also reflects the new opportunities available in the United States. Like Guerra, the New York Band brings an international flavor to the Dominican national music, singing songs in Spanish, English, and French—as a means of seeking a broader market to be sure, but in the process enhancing Pan-Caribbean and pan-hemispheric consciousness among Dominicans. Cuco Valoy draws brilliantly on Cuban musical influences, while Wilfrido Vargas mixes *zouk,* reggae, *konpa,* and rap music with *merengue* and *bachata* into an eclectic new sound.[57]

Differences between the United States and the Dominican Republic with respect to accepted gender roles have also influenced the course of *merengue.* Female migrants outnumber male migrants by at least a 3:2 ratio, and Dominican women find that the new economic opportunities open to them also allow for transformations in gender roles within the family. The community's music reflects these changes. Millie Quezada leads a very popular family band, Los Vecinos. She claims that her group had no conscious intention of challenging gender roles within Dominican culture, but her sister and fellow band member Jocelyn says emphatically that she thought of their efforts as a conscious assertion of gender equity. "We were making a statement," she explains, "because Dominican men are very male chauvinist; I mean, women stay home and cook. So, when we stood up in front of a band . . . women in the audience would identify with us. And the songs that we used to sing, we were attacking men: If you don't take care of your woman, you're going to lose her. So we had a lot of women fans, we still do."[58]

Similarly, the group Chantelle consists of three Puerto Rican women—Brenda Zoe Hernández, Annette Ramos Sosa, and Doreen Ann Zayas—produced by another, Bonnie Cepeda. Fefita La Grande brings a woman's perspective to *bachata* through her performances as a singer in working-class taverns in New York's heavily Dominican Washington Heights neighborhood.[59] Alexandra Taveras, lead singer for the New York Band, tries to incorporate a woman's point of view into her lyrics. "I tell the women we don't have to take everything that comes to us, and they love it," she explains. Las Chicas del Can provide a decidedly less feminist image, structuring their stage show and attire largely for the scopophilic pleasure of men, but the mere presence of women like the group's trumpet player and leader María Acosta and vocalists Miriam Cruz and Eunice Betances on stage in *merengue* challenges the hierarchies of the past.[60] *Merengue* and *bachata* are still decidedly male-oriented music celebrating the macho *tigerete* ideals of Dominican society, but the emergence in New York of female *merengue* and *bachata* artists signals at least the potential for change in the music's sex and gender coding.

Dominican *merengue* artists, of course, have not tampered with their national music and launched an attack on Dominican national identity because they are postmodern theorists. Their art owes more to Celia Cruz than to Gilles Deleuze.[61] Their new identities grow inexorably from the circumstances of their lives and labor. They have turned *merengue* into an immigrant music, one that records and reflects the changes in Dominican identity engendered by the conditions of life and labor created by the transnational economy.

Peruvian *chicha* music follows many of the same principles, even though its creators do not cross national borders but remain within one country. Displaced *mestizo* peasants created *chicha* in the squatter settlements and shantytowns of large Peruvian cities like Lima and Arequipa. More than 2 million people live in more than a thousand of these settlements in Lima alone. Centers of intense political mobilization for city services, these neighborhoods have also generated powerful new cultural expressions, including *chicha* music, that are neither wholly urban nor completely rural but, rather, are a fusion of the two experiences.[62] "It's a product of the migrations in the last few years," explains one *chicha* radio programmer: "this music didn't exist before, it's a mixture of *wayno* and [*cumbia*], of coast and highlands, resulting in the *cumbia andina,* it's a hybrid."[63]

Chicha does fuse Afro-Hispanic *cumbia, salsa,* rock and roll, and *huayno* into a new synthesis, but *huayno* itself is a hybrid that combines local Andean highland music with outside influences.[64] Within *chicha,* rock instruments dominate the orchestration, especially lead and rhythm electric guitars, electric bass, electric organ, and sometimes synthesizers. Taking its name from the genre's first commercial success, the song "La chichera" (a woman who sells the fermented-maize beer known as *chicha*) by Los Demonios de Mantaro (The Devils of Mantaro), *chicha* song lyrics deal with love and social issues. "El ambulante," written by Jaime Moreyra and performed by his group Los Shapis, recalls his experiences as a child selling things in the street as part of Peru's "underground economy." Starting with a connection between the rainbow colors of the Inca flag and the brightly colored ponchos that Andean *mestizos* wear and use for transporting goods, the lyrics of "El ambulante" detail the difficulties of selling shoes, jackets, or food on the street while trying to escape surveillance and incarceration by the police.[65] Los Shapis express their hybridity in their stage appearance, wearing white pants and shirts featuring Andean rainbow motifs across the knees and shoulders.[66] As Deborah Pacini Hernández observes, *chicha* "expressed the transition from rural to urban culture that *bachata,* juju, and other musics did in their countries of origin," and "politicians and businessmen astutely recognized *chicha*'s potential to serve as a Pan-Peruvian symbol that could be strategically used to attract the attention of migrants regardless of their region of origin."[67]

Like Dominican *merengue* in the 1980s, Peruvian *chicha* challenged racial hierarchies by celebrating *mestizaje* and claiming prestige from below. Massive unemployment exacerbated traditional racial tensions in Peruvian cities like Arequipa, where the Andean presence is often seen as a "threat" to whiteness.[68] But *chicha* affirmed *mestizo* identity proudly, and it provided great visibility for ensembles like Los Shapis, who sold more units in Peru during the 1980s than any other group. It also reflected, recorded, and processed changes in identity, in keeping with the new circumstances that Andean highlanders faced in the cities. *Chicha* helped break down divisions among Andean immigrants from different regions, and it gave children born in the cities a way to affirm their identity and to avoid having to make a mutually exclusive choice between highland or city culture.[69] Many middle-class Peruvians despise *chicha,* viewing it as too Andean and lower-class; at the same time, traditionalist migrants condemn it as too assimilated, as a degeneration of "authentic" Andean culture.[70]

More than an artistic reflection of an exterior social reality, *chicha* music enacted the social world it envisioned. Through Sunday-afternoon performances at crowded neighborhood music halls, musicians brought a community into being through performance. The rough lyrics and quotidian concerns of *chicha* songs registered the aggravations and aspirations of low-wage workers. Group singing provided an opportunity for ritualistic communion and somatic release. The highland past and the urban present blended together in aggressive festivity that imagined and instantiated new identities among Andean migrants. *Chicha* functioned as a node in a network of complicated social practices and relationships that includes some 6,000 social, cultural, and mutual-aid associations in Lima alone, but that also has started to take directly political forms such as the National People's Assembly which brought together 2,500 delegates from grass-roots organizations to coordinate strategy and share perspectives.[71] Although the popularity of *chicha* music has waned in the 1990s, the forms that succeeded it reflected equally dramatic instances of hybridity—*merengue, salsa,* and *saya*—a music that also blended Andean and African American elements.

Merengue and *chicha* music takes the cultural conflicts in the lives of immigrants and turns them into art. They create new alliances among people previously divided by race, region, gender, and class. They express collective experiences through music which serves as a stimulus for public congregation and celebration. They transform Dominican and Peruvian identities, and serve as psychic armor for unemployed and low-wage workers victimized by the transnational economy and despised for their nationality or ethnicity. Of course, one might see these "impure" and "mixed" genres as tragic betrayals of once coherent national cultures, but I think it would be more accurate to see them as cultural forms that help people cope with the present by strategically redeploying parts of their past. Certainly commercial considerations do lead *merengue* and *chicha* musicians to make their music more acceptable to Anglo-American audiences and to expand their markets by acknowledging other languages and musical styles. But the resulting hybridity represents more than an effort to reach fused markets. Rather, it signifies the dynamic nature of national and ethnic identity in an age of fast capital. Moreover, these musical genres are rooted in their listeners' lives in ways that place constraints on how much borrowing they can do from other musical styles, how far they can stray from their audiences' culture and consciousness.

Under these conditions, reliance on any single category of identity including nationalism, hemispheric solidarity, or even *mestizaje* will not suffice. Nationalism in Latin America has been an important vehicle for social change, but it has also enabled bourgeois elites to pursue their own self-interest in the name of the nation.

Hemispheric solidarity has been an important shield against U.S. imperialism, but it has also been a way for political leaders to be radical in their foreign policy pronouncements yet all that much more conservative at home. Celebrations of *mestizaje* have been important in building cross-class coalitions throughout the hemisphere, but they have also tended to glorify indigenous peoples in the abstract while forcing them to suffer terribly in real life. In some countries, the Indian past is celebrated specifically to divert attention away from African contributions to the nation's past and present.[72] No formal devices by themselves can ensure creative connection between cultural and concrete social realities; instead, new social relations give rise to corresponding cultural practices.

In our world, crossing borders and changing identities is the project of capital as well as the experience of labor. The question is not whether we will be transnational, but how? On whose terms? In what ways? For what ends? Here I think we can draw fruitfully on José Martí's legacy, on the author of "Nuestra América" who reminds us that "to govern well, one must see things as they are."[73] How do workers in the new transnational economy see themselves, how do they fashion meanings and identities out of the material conditions of their lives, how do they live with the apocalypse that global austerity has brought to their lives? *Merengue* and *chicha* are rarely overtly political in the way that New Song movements throughout Latin American have been, or even in the ways achieved by such "world music" stars as Rubén Blades in Panama, Boukman Eksperyans in Haiti, Mighty Sparrow in Trinidad, Fela Kuti in Nigeria, Thomas Mapfumo in Zimbabwe, and Mandawuy Yunipingu's Yothu Yindi in Australia. These two popular genres rarely address issues of state power directly, and they seek success within the apparatuses of commercial culture. But they reflect, store, and process the lives that people have open to them in an era of ever increasing austerity. Expressing anxiety and urgency, they are what Frantz Fanon called "unusual forms of expression and themes which are fresh and imbued with a power which is no longer that of an invocation, but rather of the assembling of the people, a summoning together for a precise purpose."[74] As political and economic crisis increasingly becomes the order of the day, commercial culture is one of the places from which new social movements may arise.

In the early 1990s, Bolivia, Argentina, and Ecuador experienced major riots and strikes.[75] Afro-Brazilians have mobilized for inclusion into a society that prizes their contributions to soccer and *samba* but excludes them from opportunities routinely granted to other Brazilians. Earthquake victims in Mexico and homeless squatters in Chile have organized themselves to secure goods and services that the state, as a result of privatization, has ceased to provide. Indigenous peoples throughout the hemisphere have demonstrated their ability to wage and sometimes win struggles against centralized state power and global capital.[76] The deployment of U.S. troops to Haiti in October 1994 in order to restore the credibility of transnational capital and that nation's local elite clearly dealt a deadly blow to popular democracy despite the restoration of Jean-Bertrand Aristide to the presidency, but the popular Lavalas movement which gave rise to Aristidism in the first place remains a force for land reform and moral uplift in the face of wholesale repression and terror.[77]

The transnational economy has provoked a new consciousness in North America as well. Rank-and-file members of UAW Local 879 in Saint Paul, Minnesota, take up shop-floor collections to support the Mexican Ford Workers Democratic Movement and to pay for an organizer at the Ford Assembly Plant in Cuatitlán, Mexico, despite their International leadership's total lack of interest in promoting these connections.[78] In a recent letter to *The Dispatcher,* the official publication of the ILWU, a rank-and-file longshoreman from Port Townsend, Washington, criticized his union's silence about the Mexican army's attacks on striking dockworkers in Veracruz. A church in Kansas City has rented buses so that assembly-line workers in that city can travel to Mexico and meet with their counterparts there. These transnational networks are at an early stage, but they offer important possibilities. New production systems in the auto industry, for example, depend on keeping inventories low. When demand is high, strikes can very quickly hurt the competitive status of the company, more so than in the Fordist days of high inventory. Channels of communication connecting workers and the things they know about production to one another could be an important strategic resource in fights for global work standards, wages, and welfare benefits. These new social relations challenge all of us to rethink the ways in which we are both connected to and divided from others throughout the hemisphere and throughout the world. We cannot merely be spectators of the changes that are taking place all around us; the things we teach, learn, read, and write — or play and sing — will make a difference. As José Martí asked a century ago, "What is . . . thinking without acting, saying without doing, desiring without loving. . . . What is the value of abhorring the tyrant, while living in his shadow and eating at his table? What is the value of preaching revolution, loudly or softly, without preparing the ill-ruled country for the revolution that is preached?"[79]

Notes

1 Quoted in Armand Mattelart, *Mapping World Communication: War, Progress, Culture* (Minneapolis: University of Minnesota Press, 1994), p. 207.

2 Frantz Fanon, *The Wretched of the Earth* (New York: Grove Press, 1968), p. 243.

3 Walter Benjamin, "Theses on Historical Materialism," in Benjamin, *Illuminations, 1892–1940* (New York: Harcourt, Brace & World, 1968).

4 See William Appleman Williams, *The Contours of American History* (Chicago: Quadrangle, 1966).

5 See, for example, José David Saldívar, "The Dialectics of Our America," in *Do the Americas Have a Common Literature?* ed. Gustavo Pérez Firmat (Durham: Duke University Press, 1990), pp. 62–84; José David Saldívar, *The Dialectics of Our America: Genealogy, Cultural Critique, and Literary History* (Durham: Duke University Press, 1991); Roberto Fernández Retamar, "The Modernity of Martí," in *José Martí: Revolutionary Democrat,* ed. Christopher Abel and Nissa Torrents (London: Athlone Press, 1986), pp. 1–15; Roberto Fernández Retamar, "Nuestra América y Occidente," *Casa de las Américas* 98 (1976): 36–57; and Julio Ramos, *Desencuentros de la modernidad en América Latina: Literatura y politica en el siglo XIX* (Mexico City: Fondo de Cultura Económica, 1989).

6 Martí quoted in Saldívar, "The Dialectics of Our America," p. 69.

7 José Martí, "Our America," in Martí, *Our America: Writings on Latin America and the Struggle for Cuban Independence,* ed. Philip S. Foner, trans. Elinor Randall et al. (New York: Monthly Review Press, 1977), pp. 93–94.

8 See Shifra M. Goldman, *Dimensions of the Americas: Art and Social Change in Latin America and the United States* (Chicago: University of Chicago Press, 1994), p. 251.

9 John Beverly, *Against Literature* (Minneapolis: University of Minnesota Press, 1993), pp. 121–22.

10 Winston James, "Migration, Racism, and Identity: The Caribbean Experience in Britain," *New Left Review,* no. 193 (May–June 1992): 36–37.

11 Robert Smith, "Mixteca in New York: New York in Mixteca," *NACLA Report on the Americas* 26 (July 1992): 39.

12 Jorge Duany, "Popular Music in Puerto Rico: Toward an Anthropology of Salsa," *Revista de Musica: Latino Americana* 5 (Fall/Winter 1985): 195.

13 Peter Manuel, "Latin Music in the U.S.: Salsa and the Mass Media," *Journal of Communication* 41 (Winter 1991): 108.

14 Mary Waters, oral presentation, San Diego, California, January 31, 1992.

15 Deborah Pacini [Hernández], "Social Identity and Class in *Bachata,* an Emerging Dominican Popular Identity," *Latin American Music Review* 10 (June 1989): 79; Jorge Duany, "Ethnicity, Identity, and Music: An Anthropological Analysis of Dominican *Merengue,*" in *Music and Ethnicity: The Caribbean and South America,* ed. Gerard H. Behague (New Brunswick and London: Transaction Publishers, 1994), p. 125.

16 Dan Gallin, "Inside the New World Order," *New Politics* 5, no. 1 (Summer 1994): 106.

17 Ibid., p. 113.

18 Masao Miyoshi, "Sites of Resistance in the Global Economy," Ms., statistics from the International Labor Organization.

19 Gallin, "Inside the New World Order," p. 114.

20 Davison Budhoo, "IMF/World Bank Wreak Havoc on Third World," and John Gershman, "The Free Trade Connection," in *50 Years Is Enough: The Case against the World Bank and the International Monetary Fund,* ed. Kevin Danaher (Boston: South End Press, 1994), pp. 21 and 26.

21 Walden Bello, *Dark Victory: The United States, Structural Adjustment and Global Poverty* (London: Pluto Press, 1994), p. 51.

22 Budhoo, "IMF/World Bank Wreak Havoc on Third World," p. 22.

23 See Gallin, "Inside the New World Order," p. 121.

24 Walden Bello, "Global Economic Counterrevolution: How Northern Economic Warfare Devastates the South," in *50 Years Is Enough* (see note 20 above), p. 19.

25 Sherrie L. Baver, "Including Migration in the Development Calculus: The Dominican Republic and other Caribbean Countries," *Latin American Research Review* 30, no. 1 (1995): 193.

26 This change is perhaps best expressed by the difference between Michael Manley's two terms of office in Jamaica. Of course, the experiences of Chile, Grenada, Panama, and Nicaragua show that the United States is still willing to use old-fashioned military force to preserve this order from nations seeking to follow another path.

27 Michael Quintanilla, "Que Cool!" *Los Angeles Times,* June 16, 1993; David E. Hayes-Bautista and Gregory Rodriguez, "Technobanda," *The New Republic* (April 11, 1994): 10.

28 See Duany, "Ethnicity, Identity, and Music," p. 75.

29 Paul Austerlitz, *Merengue: Dominican Music and Dominican Identity* (Philadelphia: Temple University Press, 1997), p. 25.

30 Duany, "Ethnicity, Identity, and Music," p. 66; Martha Davis, "Music and Black Ethnicity in the Dominican Republic," in *Music and Ethnicity* (see note 15 above), p. 135; Pacini [Hernández], "Social Identity and Class in *Bachata,*" p. 69; Mark Holston, "The Women of *Merengue,*" *Americas* (May–June 1990): 54; Austerlitz, *Merengue,* p. 31.

31 Deborah Pacini Hernández, *Bachata: A Social History of a Dominican Popular Music* (Philadelphia: Temple University Press, 1995), p. 40.

32 Ibid., p. 43; Austerlitz, *Merengue,* p. 60.

33 Austerlitz, *Merengue,* p. 71.

34 Ibid., p. 39.

35 James Ferguson, *Dominican Republic: Beyond the Lighthouse* (London: Latin America Bureau, 1992), p. 83.

36 Austerlitz, *Merengue,* p. 66.

37 Pacini Hernández, *Bachata,* p. 131.

38 Duany, "Ethnicity, Identity, and Music," pp. 66–69.

39 Pacini Hernández, *Bachata,* pp. 42, 130.

40 Ibid., pp. 82, 122.

41 Saskia Sassen, "Why Immigration?" *NACLA Report on the Americas* 26 (July 1992): 15; Sherri Grasmuck and Patricia R. Pessar, *Between Two Islands: Dominican International Migration* (Berkeley: University of California Press, 1991), pp. 19–23.

42 Ferguson, *Dominican Republic,* p. 77.

43 Pacini Hernández, *Bachata,* p. 63. In 1980, 77.6 percent of Dominicans in the United States resided in New York, 8.4 percent in New Jersey (Grasmuck and Pessar, *Between Two Islands,* p. 23). For information about the 1960s, see Peter Manuel, "The Soul of the Barrio," *NACLA Report on the Americas* 28 (September–October 1994): 28.

44 Ferguson, *Dominican Republic,* p. 75.

45 Grasmuck and Pessar, *Between Two Islands,* pp. 162–98.

46 Juan Flores, "Que Assimilated, Brother, Yo Soy Assimilao": The Structuring of Puerto Rican Identity in the U.S.," *Journal of Ethnic Studies* 13, no. 3 (1986): 11.

47 Austerlitz, *Merengue,* p. 130.

48 Ibid., p. 93.

49 Sue Steward and Jan Fairley, "*Merengue* Mania," in *World Music: The Rough Guide,* ed. Simon Broughton, Mark Ellingham, David Muddyman, and Richard Trillo (London: Rough Guides, 1994), pp. 496, 497; Philip Sweeny, *The Virgin Directory of World Music* (New York: Henry Holt & Co., 1991), p. 208.

50 Duany, "Ethnicity, Identity, and Music," p. 79; Pacini [Hernández], "Social Identity and Class in *Bachata,*" p. 83; Deborah Pacini Hernández, "*Bachata:* From the Margins to the Mainstream," *Popular Music* 11, no. 3 (1992): 359.

51 Ferguson, *Dominican Republic,* p. 82.

52 Neil Leonard III, "*Merengue* Messiah," *Rhythm Music Magazine* 3, no. 5 (May–June 1994): 21–23.

53 Pacini Hernández, "From the Margins to the Mainstream," pp. 359–60.

54 Steward and Fairley, "*Merengue* Mania," p. 497.

55 Ferguson, *Dominican Republic,* p. 79.

56 Duany, "Ethnicity, Identity, and Music," pp. 87–90.

57 Steward and Fairley, "*Merengue* Mania," p. 496.

58 See Austerlitz, *Merengue,* p. 117.

59 Daisann McLane, "*Bachata* in New York," oral presentation, New York University, February 25, 1995.

60 Holston, "The Women of *Merengue,*" pp. 54–55.

61 The musicologist Rob Walser deserves the credit, or blame, for this observation.

62 Carolina Carlessi, "The Reconquest," *NACLA Report on the Americas* 23 (November–December 1989): 14, 15.

63 Margaret Bullen, "Chicha in the Shanty Towns of Arequipa, Peru," *Popular Music* 12 (October 1993): 229, 230, 233; William Rowe and Vivian Schelling, *Memory and Modernity: Popular Culture in Latin America* (New York and London: Verso, 1991), pp. 121–22.

64 I thank Zoila Mendoza for her very helpful observations on an earlier draft of this essay which helped me clarify my understanding of *chicha* and *huayno* in important ways.

65 Charles B. Wolff, Jan Fairley, and Margaret Bullen, "Andean Music," in *World Music* (see note 49 above), p. 589.

66 Rowe and Schelling, *Memory and Modernity,* pp. 121–22; Bullen, "*chicha* in the Shanty Towns of Arequipa, Peru."

67 Pacini Hernández, *Bachata,* p. 233.

68 Bullen, "*chicha* in the Shanty Towns of Arequipa, Peru," p. 235.

69 Ana María Gazzolo, "Carta del Perú: El fenómeno '*chicha,*'" *Cuadernos Hispanoamericanos* no. 479 (May 1990): 110–11.

70 Pacini Hernández, *Bachata,* p. 233.

71 Carolina Carlessi, "The Reconquest," *NACLA Report on the Americas* 23 (November–December 1989): 14, 15, 21.

72 Duany, "Ethnicity, Identity, and Music," p. 69.

73 Martí, "Our America," p. 86.

74 Fanon, *The Wretched of the Earth,* p. 243.

75 Hannah Holm, "The Zapatistas Are Not Alone," in *Starting from Chiapas,* ed. Marc Cooper, Hannah Holm, Barbara Pillsbury, and the Zapatistas (Westfield, N.J.: Open Magazine, 1994), p. 19.

76 George Yudice, Jean Franco, and Juan Flores, "Introduction," in *On Edge: The Crisis of Contemporary Latin American Culture,* ed. George Yudice, Jean Franco, and Juan Flores (Minneapolis: University of Minnesota Press, 1993), p. viii; *Starting from Chiapas* (see note 75 above); Rowe and Schelling, *Memory and Modernity.*

77 Chris Tilly, "Haiti's Agony," in *Dollars and Sense,* no. 192 (March–April 1994).

78 Tom Laney, "UAW Local 879 Adopts Organizer," *Impact: The Rank and File Newsletter* 1 (February–March, 1994): 1, 12.

79 Quoted in John M. Kirk, "José Martí and His Concept of the *Intelectual Comprometido,*" in *José Martí: Revolutionary Democrat* (see note 5 above), p. 122.

Oscar R. Martí

José Martí and the Heroic Image

Heroes have a limited shelf life. They bud, bloom, and quickly wilt, withered by criticism from those who had before only admired. Why? Heroism is not something one does; it is an image, and images define, shape, bind—in life the individual, in death the memory. One becomes a hero not by dint of doing heroic actions but by the image acquired in doing them—by the spell cast by others. And others have a penchant for making and discarding heroes regardless of merit.

José Martí is the ideal *political hero:* an eloquent and charismatic revolutionary for the left, a soldier of freedom for the right, the apostle for all. He is also a *moral hero,* the embodiment of civic virtues, personal integrity, and patriotic fortitude in the face of adversity so beautifully expressed in *Versos sencillos.* Bolstering this heroic image is his status as a literary giant: a master of Spanish prose and poetry who authored plays, poems, novels, art criticism, essays, and translations; the editor of newpapers, of political and economic journals, and of a children's magazine. All these tasks he did well, except being a soldier; for he broke the rule that a soldier must always live to see the battle's end.

The centenary of Martí's death is marked with the usual eulogies praising often-contradictory features of his character and labor, an adulation typical of political and moral heroes. Yet, there was a time when he was relegated to the secondary role of one among many patriots, when his weaknesses and his faults were seen as larger than virtues, when no one would have him as a role model. In fact, Martí's image has undergone several transformations—from poet to revolutionary, to patriot, to martyr and apostle, and today to the politically correct hero of two opposing ideologies. These almost conflictual revisions of a public image can best be studied by examining the tension between his own activities as a poet and political leader and the transformation of his reputation in the public sphere, both before and after his death.

1

José Julián Martí y Pérez was born in Havana on January 28, 1853, to two loyal Spanish subjects, Mariano Martí and Leonor Pérez.[1] Don Mariano and Doña Leonor met and married in Cuba, where they had migrated seeking better economic conditions. Largely uneducated and honest, their financial situation was routinely precarious. Don Mariano had been a soldier in the Spanish army. Discharged because of asthma, he became a policeman but could not manage to get promoted, in part because of a bad temper and a refusal to bend to caste or corruption.[2]

A gifted child, Martí attracted the attention of his teachers for his intelligence, voracious reading habits, and ability to write. Among his mentors was José María de Mendive, a poet, a writer, a staunch independentist, and the director of the Escuela Municipal de Varones. Under his tutelage, Martí excelled, and by the age of sixteen he was writing articles and plays and publishing anti-Spanish student papers with his lifelong friend, Fermín Valdez Domínguez.[3]

Cuba, in the nineteenth century, was one of the last remnants of a once vast colonial empire that was now unraveling. A profitable possession, it was also an escape for excess population and a symbol of pride. Thus, Spain was determined to hold on to its overseas possessions in spite of growing resentment and a desire for independence on the part of those born in the colonies.

In 1868, an uprising in eastern Cuba opened the Ten Years' War between independentists and the colonial government. The immediate official reaction was intolerance of any display that could be taken as sympathetic to the rebels. What seemed to be youthful mockery at a military parade in 1869 thus caused the arrest of Martí and Valdez Domínguez. At the trial, Martí's pro-independence writings, a letter critical of the regime, and a fiery speech convinced a military jury to convict the seventeen-year-olds of disloyalty. Valdez Domínguez was sentenced to six months in prison and Martí to six years of hard labor in a stone quarry, chained waist and foot. Five months later, thanks to his father's efforts, this harsh sentence was commuted to metropolitan exile, and Martí was allowed to leave for Spain in January 1871.[4]

In Spain, Martí decided to finish his schooling and matriculated to study law at the Universidad Central de Madrid. Poverty and ill-health, however, repeatedly delayed his studies. He found work as a part-time teacher, and then had to undergo several groin operations to mend the injuries received while in prison. Seeking a healthier climate, he moved to Aragón and, in 1874, concluded his studies at the Real Universidad de Zaragoza, receiving degrees in both law and liberal arts.

The continuing Cuban struggle for independence also became a necessary distraction for Martí. In 1871, vandals had covered with graffiti the grave of a revered Spanish journalist. In reprisal, the colonial authorities rounded up thirty Cuban medical students, summarily tried them, and found them guilty of sedition. Eight were then chosen by lot and shot by a firing squad.[5] The savageness of the event stirred Martí to write a spirited defense in a pamphlet that was largely ignored.[6] In 1873, the rise of the liberal Spanish First Republic gave the Cuban cause some hope. In another pamphlet, Martí argued that in a truly republican and democratic government the rights of Spaniards in Spain should be given equally to Cubans in Cuba.[7] Again, Cubans were ignored or rebuked,[8] and Martí, witnessing the Zaragoza uprising and its ruthless repression by General Manuel Pavía, concluded that nothing could be gained from a dialogue with Spain.

In December 1874, Martí left Spain to join his family, who had migrated to Mexico to escape the deteriorating economic conditions of war-torn Cuba.[9] The trip took him and Valdez Domínguez (who had joined Martí in metropolitan exile) through France, where they met several important figures, among them Victor Hugo. Once in Mexico, Martí became a contributor to *La Revista Universal* and *El Federalista,* under the pseudonym "Orestes." He also wrote poetry and a play, which was successfully staged;[10] at Hugo's request, he translated *Mes fils* into Spanish.[11]

General Porfirio Díaz's bid for political power in 1876 persuaded Martí to leave Mexico, and for the next five years he was forced to travel in search of a stable base. A professorship of foreign literature and the history of philosophy opened at the Escuela Normal de Guatemala. On his way there, in January 1877, Martí visited Cuba, traveling with a Mexican passport as Julián Pérez, his maternal surname. That December, he went back to Mexico to marry the wealthy Carmen Zayas Bazán, returning to Guatemala to resume his teaching post. In July 1878, however, he resigned in protest over the government's dismissal of the school's director, left with his pregnant wife for Honduras, and continued on to Cuba in September 1878 to live under the general amnesty accorded by the Peace of Zanjón, which put an end to the Ten Years' War.

Once in Havana, Martí tried to practice law, but political strictures reduced him to clerical work and to teaching at the Liceo de Guanabacoa. He continued to advocate the cause of independence in public speeches and to foment another uprising in secret conspiracies. Notwithstanding the birth of a son, José Francisco, these political activities caused considerable marital friction. When, in September 1879, Martí was again arrested and deported to Spain for sedition, his wife, considering him "politically irremediable," chose to remain in Cuba.

This time, Martí quickly left Spain, again passing through Paris, and settled in New York City where his wife and child joined him in 1880 to attempt a marital reconciliation. That effort proved short-lived, and wife and child returned to Cuba later that year. Early in 1881, Martí moved to Caracas with the intention of taking up residence in Venezuela, but he fell afoul of the Guzmán Blanco government and had to leave that July for New York. Once there, Martí found a more stable companionship in the person of a Venezuelan widow, Carmen Mantilla, and settled down for the next fourteen years.

In New York, Martí's literary output became prodigious. Forced by economic need, he wrote articles in English on European art and culture for the *New York Sun* (1879) and *The Hour* (1880), and in Spanish for *La América* (1883)—all published in the United States. He continued writing perceptively on European and North American affairs, culture, and politics for several Latin American newspapers, including *El Federalista* (Mexico City), *La Opinión Nacional* (Caracas; 1881), *La Nación* (Buenos Aires; 1881), and *La Opinión Pública* (Montevideo; 1889). He collected his poems in two books,[12] wrote a novel,[13] and penned articles and pamphlets on Cuban affairs.[14] He became the editor of *La América* and of the children's magazine *La Edad de Oro* (1889), and he also translated into Spanish Stanley Jevons's *Logic* (1883) and Helen Hunt Jackson's *Ramona* (1887), among others, for the publishing house of Appleton & Company.

This intense literary labor earned him an international reputation as one of the best Latin American essayists and poets of his generation.[15] Reluctant praise came from Sarmiento[16] and unabashed admiration from Darío.[17] They cast him as a poet engaged in a political struggle in which words were mightier than swords, and his death on the battlefield brought only reproaches—"Oh Master! What have you done!"[18] Ironically, this was an image Martí himself felt uncomfortable with. For him, the writer had to take second place to the man of action: "One should not write with letters but with actions."[19]

2

Martí's political activities during this period were also prodigious. Although this activism had begun in his teens and was often the object of his literary output, in New York it intensified and focused on the political vision of a republican Cuba. He saw four alternatives: the status quo; autonomy or home rule for a colonial Cuba; annexation to the United States; or a war of independence. The first alternative was suicidal and, given the intransigence of the colonial government, the second was utopian. Annexation meant only changing masters and the loss of identity.[20] Only the last alternative seemed viable. But to one who believed in respect for others and the reconciliation of antagonisms, advocating war was almost a contradiction.[21] A war of independence had to be morally defensible—a just war—the last recourse after all other alternatives were exhausted. To avoid bloodshed, it had to be short and decisive; to avoid militarism, it had to be in civilian hands.[22] Its aim had to be the formation of a civilian republic, a nation for all, regardless of race, religion, or origin.

In the early 1880s, Martí hoped that his writings and literary reputation would help him gain access to the active and powerful Cuban-exile communities in the United States, without which no revolution could be carried out. He was admired enough that when Calixto García left for Cuba in 1880 to lead the brief and unsuccessful uprising known as the Guerra Chiquita, Martí was appointed interim president of the revolutionary council in New York. But the access Martí desired turned out to be difficult. Cuban circles in the United States were fragmented by political and personality clashes, and outsiders were regarded with suspicion, if not resentment. Dissent had already hampered previous insurgencies, particularly the Ten Years' War, when military and economic aid was constantly delayed by squabbles between military and civilian leaders, and between supporters of total independence, annexation, or autonomy. After the Peace of Zanjón, the Old Guard independentists had achieved a precarious balance and they did not want it upset by hotheads and outsiders. Thus, they closed ranks and relegated civilians or newcomers to minimal roles. Further, the Old Guard did not like Martí. He belonged to a younger generation; he lacked the necessary military credentials and battlefield experience; he advocated a civilian revolutionary movement rooted in general consensus; and he was a poet.

It took Martí four years to meet with Máximo Gómez and Antonio Maceo, the two most important and revered veterans of the Ten Years' War. Neither fully trusted Martí, regarding him as an opportunist with Machiavellian designs, a "Capitán Araña."[23] Although a friendship eventually developed between Martí and Maceo,[24] Gómez's abrasive personality struck Martí as authoritarian. A conflict ensued: Martí characterized Gómez as carrying out a private war, and Gómez saw Martí as an ineffectual man of words. The image of a poet—the image that had gained him access to the political world—now proved an obstacle to political recognition. Doors closed, and Martí the politician was marginalized to the world of literature, forced to wait and to endure bitter criticisms.

In 1887, Martí returned to political life. His strategy now was to forge new alliances from the ground up between the most dissimilar interest groups—alliances that stretched even across continents—as the New York consul for Uruguay (1884, 1887), for Argentina (1890), and for Paraguay (1890) and as Uruguay's delegate to the Inter-American Conference (1889–90) and to the International Monetary Conference (1891). In 1891, when it became evident that the Old Guard could not carry out a revolution, lift the independentist spirit, or even maintain a semblance of unity, Martí took the initiative. He made a direct approach to the émigré rank and file,[25] whether they were wealthy donors, New York City garment workers, or Florida cigar manufacturers, through speeches,[26] pamphlets,[27] newspapers.[28] He addressed the race question by promising blacks that there would be a Cuba for all and assuring whites that there would be no slave conflagration. He then united them under the Partido Revolucionario Cubano[29] and, in a brilliant if principled strategic move, invited Gómez and Maceo and the old leadership to participate in the new offensive as prominent figures.

From 1892 to 1895, Martí traveled through the United States, Central America, and the Caribbean, winning adherents, raising funds, inspiring fervor for independence, and creating a strong political consensus. He developed a new style of leadership and skillfully managed party funds to secretly finance and direct an invasion of Cuba.[30] This operation was so massive and complex that when, in 1894, the United States intercepted a huge shipment of arms to insurgents at Fernandina, Florida, the Spanish government was shocked and the Cuban independentists were pleased by its secrecy, size, and sophisticated logistics. Though in reality a major military setback, the seizure at Fernandina projected the image of a well-organized revolutionary plan in the capable hands not of an ineffectual poet but of a true political leader. War fever rose among Cuban exiles in the United States, and Martí was acknowledged as the leading political figure of the revolution. He had finally traded the image of the poet for that of the revolutionary leader.

Pressed to capitalize on this new image and carry on the struggle, Martí, as president of the republic-at-arms, and Gómez, as the general-in-chief, called the nation to war in the Manifiesto de Montecristi, and the revolution was proclaimed at Baire, Cuba, on February 24, 1895. Martí, Gómez, and Maceo slipped into Cuba in March of that year, meeting at La Mejorana in May to discuss strategy. The meeting, however, was marred by old disagreements that had to be ironed out through compromise.[31] With the civilian-control position tentatively prevailing, the talks broke on a cordial note, Martí and Gómez going on to meet with other revolutionary leaders already in the battlefield. A few days later, on May 19, 1895, they encountered a Spanish supply column at Dos Ríos; in the heat of the battle, Martí galloped into a crossfire and was killed.

3

Why did Martí have to go into battle? He did not need the military experience to be recognized as a leader, and he would have served the revolution better by continuing to work in the United States. Perhaps he wanted to put to rest the image of the ineffectual poet, perhaps to settle an inner conflict with external action. Perhaps he wanted to "give his life for Cuba."[32] Yet, pragmatic considerations required his presence at the battlefront: the war fever had to be kept up; the project of building a nation had to be completed;[33] a quick victory had to be pursued; squabbles had to be prevented; and, most important, civilian political control had to be asserted against the old warriors' temptation to remilitarize the campaign. Whatever the reasons, whatever the conflicts, his effectiveness ended at Dos Ríos.

Martí's death on the battlefield caused consternation among Cuban insurgents and expatriates alike. Many felt they had lost an effective leader who could inspire hope, give voice to an ideal of unity, even represent their interests.[34] They were proved right. With Martí gone, the revolution inevitably changed direction. The alliances he had so carefully forged broke apart; the goal of political consensus was forgotten; old factionalisms were reborn.[35] Despite Gómez's and Maceo's brilliant military strategy, momentum was lost. A stalemate would have resulted had it not been for the barbarous actions of the Spanish military, to which the insurgents responded with a scorched-earth policy.[36] The just war became a war of attrition.

Ominous events and larger forces came into play: the massive relocation of Cuban civilians to detention camps, the international outcry, the *Maine* incident, the "message to García," and Teddy Roosevelt's charge up San Juan Hill ended the war on a different note. American intervention, so feared by Martí, became a reality. "This is not the republic we fought for,"[37] complained Máximo Gómez when, in 1902, concessions to the United States allowed for the formation of a client republic.

Martí's death also marks the decline of his image as a revolutionary leader. He did not seem to fit the new circumstances. The new leaders of the revolution and of the emerging republic were confident of their destiny. Their fortunes were on the rise and they did not need heroes from the past. After all, they had won the war, and it was *their* vision of Cuba that was to be imposed. Further, Martí's warnings against the United States would not be popular with a government that depended on U.S. economic aid and that had acquiesced in the Platt Amendment.[38]

From 1902 to the 1930s, Martí's political, social, and moral influence were minimal.[39] True, commemorative speeches were made and events were held in his honor, but by 1902, in a newly independent Cuba, Martí was regarded as only one among many patriots who fought in the war. His image, when remembered, was that of a poet who had organized and helped found the republic. On public occasions, in speeches and memorials, when naming parks and buildings or dedicating statues, the names of Estrada Palma, Maceo, Máximo Gómez, and Calixto García stood on an equal footing with that of Martí.[40]

A Cuba without Martí? He is so much part of the culture today that such an idea seems almost inconceivable.[41] Yet, several reasons can be offered to explain the relative obscurity. Although Martí was well known in the United States and Latin America,[42] Spanish censorship had kept him in the shadows of colonial Cuba. After the establishment of the republic, poorly written biographical sketches and spurious biographical novels did not serve him well.[43] More important, Martí's words were no longer there.[44] True, his poetry was reprinted in newspapers and magazines, enhancing his image as a poet, but the prose was fragmented into "pensamientos," usually out of context, in popular collections such as *Flor y lava*[45] and *Granos de oro*.[46] No popular editions of his political writings—scattered throughout Latin American newspapers, letters, speeches—could be found.[47] For instance, "Nuestra América" and other important essays had been published only in newspapers abroad and were no longer available to either the Cuban or the Latin American reader.[48]

Historical circumstances were not propitious either. In an impoverished postrevolution Cuba, there were few editions of any author. Scarce resources allowed but the barest memory of the patriots. Even if there had been any major works published, their impact would have been minimal. During the first third of this century, Cuba had no sizable reading public to speak of—illiteracy, diaspora, and war are not fertile ground for intellectuals.[49]

4

In the decades that followed the late 1920s, Martí's image underwent an extraordinary metamorphosis. No definite date or event seems to mark the beginnings of this change but, as the literate population grew, so did interest in his writings and significance.[50] Moreover, there was a perceptible increase in the publication of his poetry and even his political essays.[51] Several commercial presses took advantage of Martí's increased popularity as a teacher of the young by publishing such magazines as the *Revista Martiana* (1921–27) and, from 1929 on, the *Revista Martí,* a children's magazine resembling *Edad de Oro.*

Efforts to prepare a definitive edition of Martí's writings began to bear fruit. Early in the century, Gonzalo de Quesada y Aróstegui had begun to collect and organize Martí's writings.[52] Others followed suit,[53] but the task proved formidable. Martí was a prolific writer of continental proportions. Articles, speeches, and letters kept on surfacing, and the number of volumes multiplied. In 1936, a careful project of collecting a complete corpus was funded, and by 1949 it had exceeded seventy volumes.[54] As the Martí scholarship grew, a series of studies appeared, among them an adequate biography: Jorge Mañach's *José Martí, El Apóstol* (1933). Most works were homages and commemorations, and a few dealt with Martí's literary effort, his poetry, his style, his labor as founder; but almost none critically analyzed the content of his writings.[55] The growth of scholarly interest in Martí continued, stimulating the publication of an academic journal, the *Archivo José Martí* (1940–52).[56]

In the public sector, groups and societies devoted to honoring Martí's name through events, social work, or charity also proliferated. Statues were erected, and in 1935 the Cuban Congress approved a national monument to Martí's memory.[57] The fiftieth anniversary of the founding of the Partido Revolucionario Cubano, in 1942, was used as an opportunity to bring out several works on Martí, as was the 1953 centenary of his birth. This time, the number of items printed was huge,[58] although quantity far exceeded quality.[59]

It is in Martí's political life, however, that interest was most pronounced. Martí's growing popularity in the 1940s and 1950s had caused politicians to take notice of the emotive significance his image had acquired. Martí was quoted, discussed, and revered. They seized on Martí as a symbol to defend their actions, support their policies, or criticize from a moral high ground. Such figures as Fulgencio Batista, Raúl Chivás, and Carlos Prío, even revolutionaries like Fidel Castro, cited Martí's "pensamientos" or claimed him as an intellectual mentor.

Martí had now become something larger and more perfect than

life. To the popular mind, he was an apostle, with all the emotion and charisma that image projects. What accounts for this popularity? For one thing, the past had failed. The memory of the patriots of 1898 was not sustained. Cronyism, corruption, squabbles, and old racism obliterated their memory. Those who died in the war lacked charisma, and those who survived the war honorably did not fare well in the peace. Martí filled a role-model vacuum. Second, the cult of political personality that started under Gerardo Machado as a solution to the need for a national identity also needed a hero.[60] These politicians needed a figure who could provide a mythology, a sense of direction and, perhaps also, a channel for discontent or, at the very least, a forum in which to vent anger. As a man intimately acquainted with adversity and with the perversity of men, as a man who held on to his beliefs, Martí was the perfect role model, the perfect cultural hero. Third, the growth of an incipient nationalism hostile to the United States found in Martí an ideal precursor, particularly in his warning about the enormous political and cultural power the northern neighbor wielded. Fourth, in the realm of ideas, changes in the philosophical climate validated Martí's writings. The positivist goal of scientific and pragmatic government, patterned on the model of the United States, had failed throughout Latin America. The immensely popular *arielismo* of José Enrique Rodó and the *idealismo* of José Ingenieros bolstered Martí's romantic idealism.

Finally, Cuba now had a growing readership of intelligent laymen, intellectuals, historians, and university students who discussed and appreciated Martí's ideas. And more likely than not, it was his reputation as a poet and essayist that stimulated interest. Here was a writer who said extraordinary things, close to the heart, who voiced disquiet, anxiety, anger. Popular dissatisfaction with the political establishment found in him a capable voice. People were drawn to his vision of a republic founded on a great consensus, without class or race divisions. In a way, politicians used Martí's writings as a political weapon to remind others of what they should do, to give others a model, to criticize others. They made an image, then deified it.[61]

The image of martyr and apostle became the standard for what was expected of Cuba's political figures and citizens in the face of a less than perfect government. Being ranked with Christ's disciples is a curious fate for a man who advocated views so much at odds with Catholicism. This comparison has seemed bombastic to many writers, who see it as perhaps a result of an exuberant Latin temperament. Such florid language might be just a customary form of speech, but it could also be an elliptical way for a Catholic mind to make a political point: if an impossible sainthood was the only quality that could keep a politician from becoming corrupt, then imitating Martí would lead toward national salvation.

There were detractors during Martí's apostleship as there had been during his lifetime. Good Catholics would balk at accepting the place Martí had in the national pantheon, pointing out that he was a Mason, that he had lived in carnal sin, and that he never went to Mass. Good communists also berated him for his utopian ideas, his mysticism, his disregard of the workers' cause, and his bourgeois aspirations. Paradoxically, by the 1950s, both groups cited Martí as an authority.

5

In 1959, the Cuban Revolution created a profound upheaval. Demanding a radical solution to old inequities, the Revolution brought fundamental changes not just to the structure of society but to ways of thinking. The past was compromised and everything related to it was tainted. Even Martí had to be reexamined and assessed in the context of new political dogmas. As in early independent Cuba, he did not seem to fit the new circumstances. The new leaders of the new revolution were confident of their destiny. Their fortunes were on the rise, and they did not need heroes from the past. After all, they had won this revolution, and it was their vision of Cuba that was to be imposed. This time, however, Martí's criticisms of the United States would not fall on unsympathetic ears.

Martí's prerevolutionary image had been that of an idealist, a dreamer, a poet, a mystic, an apostolic being above and beyond the daily struggle. He preached and taught magisterially. Portrayals of the hero had been flights of prose and emotive adulations, easier to produce than a critical examination of Martí's texts. Many scholars of the traditional left had doubted Martí's political and social value,[62] but the canon proved resilient and post-1959 Cuban scholarship undertook a thorough study of the old texts. Martí, reread, emerged as more than just a collection of quotable fragments. He was now perceived as a radical, a political activist, a revolutionary leader, and a trenchant critic of the United States who spoke and acted concretely on social questions and workers' causes.[63]

A new wave of Martí studies came out of Cuba. Some were serious critical analyses;[64] others, though without the supernatural or mystic qualities of former efforts, were still lofty flights of prose. Another academic journal appeared, the *Anuario del Centro de Estudios Martianos,* and the Casa de las Américas and the Centro de Estudios Martianos became centers for scholarly discussion of Martí's writings and thought. In addition, Cuban scholars continued the work of completing the Martí canon, contributing yet another critical edition of the *Obras completas.*[65]

As the Revolution continued its nation-rebuilding task, it alienated many intellectuals who chose or were forced into exile, usually to the United States, where they created of Martí an antithetical image, resembling but not identical to that of the apostolic Martí. They accused the Cuban government of using Martí for political ends, even of textual falsification or intentional misinterpretation, for instance of Martí's views of the United States.[66] They even produced their own version of the *Obras,* the *Enciclopedia martiana.*[67]

In the 1960s and 1970s, at least two politically "correct" images of Martí competed—coexisting because they were espoused by groups separated by geographic, political, and ideological borders. Much good work has been done by both camps, and under ideal circumstances a dialogue could have ensued, aimed at uncovering the hidden Martí behind the politically useful images: What really were his views on social movements? on the race question? on the United States? on mysticism? on capital and labor? and so on.

But other factors intruded to the detriment of such a dialogue. This competition turned out to be a race not for the discovery of an individual, but for the copyright of a myth. Hero brokers produced conflicting sets of complete works and interpretations that were used to keep antagonisms alive and to justify or criticize contemporary positions remote or tangential to Martí's original purpose. In the end, every political persuasion researched and produced a citation to show that Martí himself endorsed their particular position. Such is the fate of heroic images.

6

The question that remains open is, Why did Martí's image go through such changes? To say, at this point, that his image changed with historical circumstances would be trivial. If circumstances are beyond our control, it seems reasonable to argue that Martí's image is also beyond our control. But this kind of quietism misses the point. For if the heroic image is just a historical accident, one still can ask: Why *this* particular hero and not another? In other words, why Martí?

There are qualities in Martí that make him an ideal candidate for admiration, if not apostlehood. True, he had those qualities even when forgotten; but that is what makes the problem all the more interesting. Others have achieved heroic stature without redeeming qualities, but when they recede into oblivion the deficiencies explain why. Not so with Martí. Something sets him apart; something makes him heroic. What is it?

That something could not have been Martí's political actions, for although he was an indefatigable campaigner his actions failed to bear fruit. Of the military heroes, he was the weakest, and others had to carry the battle to a successful end. Martyrdom? He was one among many. His vision of a Cuba in which all could live harmoniously remains an ideal.

That something can be found in the power of his words. Whether they were in his *Versos sencillos* or in newspaper articles and political speeches, his words moved even those who did not share his views. They were the words of the poet, precise and subtle, fleeting though eternal, harsh but enchanting, sober yet emotional; the words of a lawyer, to the point, logical, citing relevant principles, making his case with devastating rhetoric; the words of a politician, persuasive, conciliatory, accessible, and memorable. And they were the words of a moralist who evokes lofty ideals that affect the conscience of a nation-to-be.

It is Martí the writer who rises above the politician and the apostle. He left a body of work that stood on its own merits even before the political hero was created. In these writings one can find the genesis of the hero and of the apostle. Their main purpose was to eloquently persuade his contemporaries to accept his vision of a future Cuba. Yet his eloquence transcended time and place and persuaded others who, outside his historical circumstances, reinterpreted his words to fit their own. Reading Martí, others saw merit and, seeking to protect him from the commonplace, endowed him with a heroic image. This process began in the late 1920s and early 1930s. The steps in the literary rediscovery went hand in hand with the stages of Martí's metamorphosis. His writings were collected, they became widely read, openly discussed, and were used to teach civic virtues. The writer's eloquence engendered the politician's zeal, the reformer's vision, and the apostle's mission. The political message became accessible through the literary identity and, whatever else, his apostlehood emerged at the intersection of his literary and political images. Apostlehood was a spell cast by those who read and reinterpreted him to protect him from the political changes so harmful to political heroes. Martí was remade to be safe from the drift of history.

Martí, however, is not completely immune to the fate of heroes. Spells can be broken. Others invested him with qualities they deemed desirable, albeit fitting different historical circumstances. Others used or reinterpreted his words and invented new images. And since there are many "others," there are many images of Martí; incompatible, inconsistent, trivial, empty of substance, and dependent on their creators. They can't all last. Thus, when we look to the future and ask ourselves which Martí will survive, the only answer possible is one that is framed in terms of the survival of the "others" who have invented him. Of heroes of the past, we have only images and reflections, perforce created by us. But we often change our minds, our tastes, our moral outlook. In this sense, even Martí the writer is at the mercy of history.

Notes

I thank Jeffrey Belnap and Raúl Fernández for their insightful comments and suggestions, and Dean Jorge García, College of Humanities, California State University–Northridge, for his encouragement and support.

1 There are few good biographies of Martí. The classic is Jorge Mañach, *Martí, El Apóstol,* available as *Martí, Apostle of Freedom,* with a

preface by Gabriela Mistral, trans. C. Taylor (New York: Devin Adair, 1950); reprinted as vol. 1 of *La gran enciclopedia martiana,* 14 vols., ed. Ramón Cernuda (Miami: Editorial Martiana, 1978). Carlos Márquez Sterling, *Martí, Ciudadano de América* (New York: Las Américas, 1965) is an update of Mañach's. Readily available and somewhat more acceptable is Félix Lizaso, *Martí: Martyr of Cuban Independence,* trans. E. E. Schuler (Albuquerque: University of New Mexico Press, 1953; reprint Westport, Conn.: Greenwood Press, 1974). All three lack the necessary scholarly apparatus present in the otherwise superficial and intransigent Richard B. Gray, *José Martí: Cuban Patriot* (Gainesville: University Press of Florida, 1962). More academically acceptable are two recent analytic studies: John M. Kirk, *José Martí, Mentor of the Cuban Nation* (Tampa: University of South Florida Press, 1982) and Peter Turton, *José Martí, Architect of Cuba's Freedom* (London: Zed Books, 1986).

2 For instance, in 1863, Don Mariano was detached to guard the village of La Hanabanilla, as a replacement for another policeman accused of corruption. He came across evidence of illegal slave trafficking and promptly notified his superiors, who immediately removed him and put back in charge the officer he was replacing. Young José, who was living with his father on this assignment, witnessed the horrors of slavery and his father's dismissal, and wrote about them in his poetry. See José Martí, *Versos sencillos* (New York: Louis Weiss, 1891), p. xxx.

3 In 1869, Martí and Valdez Domínguez took advantage of a short-lived lifting of political censorship to publish *El Diablo Cojuelo* and *La Patria Libre,* the newspaper in which Martí's play *Abdala* appeared. For the significance of these early works, see Ada María Teja's "El origen de la nacionalidad y su toma de conciencia en la obra juvenil de José Martí: Semantización de Cuba en España," *Revista Iberoamericana* (Madrid), nos. 152–53 (July–December 1990): 793–822.

4 Martí left a moving account of his experiences as political prisoner in the pamphlet *El presidio político en Cuba* (Madrid: Imprenta de Ramón Ramírez, 1871).

5 Among the accused medical students stood Valdez Domínguez who, luckily, was only deported to Spain.

6 José Martí, *¡27 de noviembre!* (Madrid: Asociación Protectora del Preso, 1872).

7 José Martí, *La República española ante la revolución cubana* (Madrid: Impresora de S. Martínez, 1873).

8 The colonial government's attitude toward Cuba was shown in the comment of a deputy to the Madrid Cortes, "What was a colony for, if not for exploitation?" Quoted in Turton, *José Martí,* p. 5.

9 See Alfonso Herrera Franyutti, *Martí en México: Recuerdos de una época* (Mexico City: Consejo Nacional para la Cultura y las Artes, 1996).

10 José Martí, *Amor con amor se paga* (Mexico City: n.p., 1876).

11 Victor Hugo, *Mis hijos,* trans. José Martí (Mexico City: Imprenta "La Revista Universal," 1875).

12 José Martí, *Ismaelillo* (New York: Thompson & Moreau, 1882), dedicated to his absent son, and the enchanting *Versos sencillos* finally published in 1891.

13 José Martí, *Amistad funesta,* serialized in *El Latinoamericano* (New York, 1885) under the pseudonym Adelaida Ral.

14 See, for instance, José Martí, *Politica de Nuestra América,* edited with a prologue by Roberto Fernández Retamar (Mexico: Siglo Ventiuno, 1977); and José Martí, *Nuevas caras de Nueva York,* ed. Ernesto Mejía (Mexico: Siglo Ventiuno, 1980).

15 Schulman and González point out that during the decade of 1882–92, Martí was probably the best-known Hispanic writer on the continent. See Iván Schulman and Manuel Pedro González, *Martí, Darío y el modernismo* (Madrid: Editorial Gredos, 1969), p. 60.

16 See Domingo Faustino Sarmiento, "La libertad huminando al mundo," *La Nación* (Buenos Aires), January 4, 1887, in Sarmiento, *Obras completas,* vol. 46 (Buenos Aires: Imprenta Mariano Moreno, 1900), pp. 166–73. For Martí's reaction to Sarmiento, see Martí to Valdez Domínguez, 7 April, 1887, reprinted in Fryda Schultz de Mantovani, *Genio y figura de José Martí* (Buenos Aires: EUDEBA, 1968), pp. 152–54.

17 Rubén Darío, "José Martí," in Darío, *Los raros* (Barcelona: Mauccis, 1905). For the intellectual relation between Darío and Martí, see Juan Marinello, "Martí y el modernismo" and "Un gran diálogo americano," in Marinello, *José Martí,* 2d ed., Colección "Los Poetas" (Madrid: Ediciones Júcar, 1976).

18 Rubén Darío, quoted in Roberto Fernández Retamar, "De *Calibán,*" in Roberto Fernández Retamar, *Lectura de Martí* (Mexico City: Editorial Nuestro Tiempo, 1972), p. 140.

19 José Martí, *La Nación* (Buenos Aires), April 29, 1888. See also Schultz, *Genio y figura de José Martí,* p. 20.

20 José Martí, "Letter," *New York Evening Post,* March 25, 1889. Reprinted in José Martí, *Vindicación de Cuba* (New York: El Avisador

Hispano-Americano, 1889). Facsimile Edition (Havana: Editorial de Ciencias Sociales, 1982).

21 For the influence of Krausism on Martí, see Turton, *José Martí,* pp. 66–68, 147–49.

22 Clearly, Martí's experiences with authoritarian regimes in Mexico, Guatemala, and Venezuela caused him to fear the war leadership's emphasis on militarism and to consider it as dangerous as any racial or class antagonism.

23 See Neale C. Roning, *José Martí and the Émigré Colony in Key West: Leadership and State Formation* (New York: Praeger, 1990), pp. 10–15.

24 Philip Foner, *Antonio Maceo* (New York: Monthly Review Press, 1977).

25 Roning, *José Martí,* pp. 33–37; Gerald E. Poyo, "José Martí: Architect of Social Unity in the Émigré Communities in the United States," in *José Martí, Revolutionary Democrat,* ed. Christopher Abel and Nissa Torrents (London: Athlone Press, 1986), pp. 16–31.

26 In "Con todos y para el bien de todos" (November 25, 1891) and "Los pinos nuevos" (November 27, 1891), Martí took advantage of the generation gap to ask for a break with old, ineffective politics.

27 Martí, *Cuba y los Estados Unidos* (1889).

29 *Patria* (New York: Partido Revolucionario Cubano, 1892).

29 José Martí, *Bases y estatutos secretos del Partido Revolucionario Cubano* (Cayo Hueso: Partido Revolucionario Cubano, 1892; Havana: Editora Política, 1978).

30 For an interesting discussion of Martí's political leadership style, see Roning, *José Martí,* pp. 126–45. See also Gray, *José Martí,* pp. 59–82.

31 "Maceo tiene otro pensamiento de gobierno . . . no puedo desenredarle la conversación. . . . Y me habla, cortándome las palabras, como si fuese yo la continuación del gobierno leguleyo" (José Martí, *Diario de campaña,* facsimile edition [Havana: Editorial de Ciencias Sociales and Centro de Estudios Martianos, 1985], p. 26). So sensitive were these issues that four pages were torn from the diary. See also Máximo Gómez, *Diario de campaña, 1868–1899* (Havana: Instituto del Libro, 1968) and Foner, *Antonio Maceo,* p. 168. Teja points to the importance of the *Diarios* for understanding Martí's developed political and personal views as well as his plans for nation building. See Ada María Teja, "El *Diario de campaña de José Martí* como discurso decolonizador y canto de vida," in *Actas del XXIX*

Congreso del Instituto Internacional de Literatura Iberoamericana (Barcelona: PPU, 1994), vol. 2, pp. 1156–58.

32 Assuming the literal truth of the assertion that Martí "gave his life" at Dos Ríos has led several scholars to speculate about such possible motives as suicide, or the desire for martyrdom, or the wish to fulfill Cuba's need of a national symbol. See, for instance, Schultz, *Genio y figura de José Martí,* p. 24; but cf. Turton, *José Martí,* p. 27.

33 This was to be achieved at the constitutional convention held at Jimagüayú during the summer of 1896. See Herminio Portell Vilá, *Historia de Cuba* (1939), 4 vols. (Miami: Mnemosyne, 1969), vol. 3, pp. 111–12.

34 Poyo, "José Martí," pp. 28–31.

35 Foner, *Antonio Maceo,* pp. 235, 243.

36 Louis A. Pérez Jr., *Cuba between Empires, 1878–1902* (Pittsburgh: University of Pittsburgh Press, 1983), p. 151ff; Foner, *Antonio Maceo,* pp. 228–30.

37 Pérez, *Cuba between Empires,* p. xv.

38 The Platt Amendment, a rider attached to the Cuban Constitution of 1902, stated that the United States could intervene if events in Cuba went against U.S. interests. A source of vitriolic criticism, the Platt Amendment was invoked in 1906 when American troops were sent to calm Cuban unrest. It was abolished in 1933.

39 Historians contemporary with this period, such as Charles E. Chapman (*A History of the Cuban Republic* [New York: Macmillan, 1927; reprint New York: Octagon Books, 1969]) and Herminio Portell Vila (see note 33 above) did not see much evidence of Martí's influence or popularity in republican Cuba. Even recent historians, such as Louis Pérez Jr., well acquainted with Martí's importance in the prior period (*Cuba between Empires*), can write of the subsequent period without mentioning Martí at all. See Louis A. Pérez Jr. *Cuba under the Platt Amendment, 1902–1934* (Pittsburgh: University of Pittsburgh Press, 1986).

40 Chapman, *A History of the Cuban Republic* p. 410.

41 Carlos Alberto Montaner, *El pensamiento de José Martí* (Madrid: Plaza Mayor, 1971), pp. 3–4; Kirk, *José Martí,* p. 3.

42 In 1913, volumes 11 and 12 of the Quesada y Aróstegui *Obras* (see note 52 below) collected all of Martí's then-known poetry. Darío, who was originally acquainted with only portions of *Ismaelillo* and *Versos sencillos,* devoted four articles in *La Nación* (Buenos Aires) to a study of the complete works. These articles are reprinted in Manuel

Pedro González's *Antología crítica de José Martí* (Mexico City: Editorial Cultura, 1960), pp. 267–95.

43 Richard Gray accounts for two such works. One was Ana María Barnes's *Martí: A Story of the Cuban War* (Chicago: D. C. Cook, 1899), which had little to do with Martí. Also, Erasmo Pella authored anonymously a pseudohistorical novel, *Martí, Novela histórica por un patriota* (Havana: Moderna Poesía, 1901), reissuing it as Franco Rander, *José Martí, Reseña histórica* (Havana: Imprenta de Juan A. de Cámara, 1915; reprint Industrias Gráficas, 1929; 3d ed. 1931). See Gray, *José Martí,* pp. 88–89.

44 See Manuel P. González, "Evolución de la estimativa martiana," in González, *Antología crítica,* p. xx.

45 José Martí, *Flor y lava,* ed. Américo Lugo (Paris: Sociedad de Ediciones Literarias y Artísticas, 1910).

46 José Martí, *Granos de oro,* ed. A. G. Argilagos (Havana: Cuba Contemporánea, 1918).

47 Fernández Retamar blames Martí's choice of medium for this relative obscurity ("De *Calibán,*" p. 107).

48 José Martí, "Nuestra América," *La Revista Ilustrada de Nueva York,* January 10, 1891, and *El Partido Liberal* (Mexico City), January 30, 1891.

49 In 1899, the total population having *some* instruction was 31 percent; by 1931 that figure had climbed to only 46 percent. By 1943, it rose to 50 percent but dropped to 49 percent in 1953, the Año Martiano. These figures are calculated from Susan Schroeder, *Cuba: A Handbook of Historical Statistics* (Boston: G. K. Hall, 1982), pp. 40–41, 125.

50 Manuel Pedro González, *Fuentes para el estudio de José Martí* (Havana: Dirección de Cultura, 1950); Fermín Peraza Sarausa, *Bibliografía martiana, 1853–1955,* 2d ed. (Havana: Anuario Bibliográfico Cubano, 1956); Celestino Blanch y Blanco, *Bibliografía martiana, 1954–63* (Havana: Biblioteca Nacional José Martí, 1966).

51 E.g., José Martí, *Vindicación de Cuba* (Havana: Presidencia de la República, 1926).

52 The first attempt to gather Martí's writings was Gonzalo de Quesada y Aróstegui, *Martí, Obras reunidas por Gonzalo de Quesada,* 15 vols: vol. 1 (Washington, D.C.: Gonzalo de Quesada, 1900); vols. 2–4 (Havana: Gonzalo de Quesada, 1900–1905); vol. 5 (Turin: Casa Editrice Nazionale, 1905); vols. 6–9 (Havana: Rambla y Bouza, 1906–10); vol. 10 (Berlin: Gonzalo de Quesada, 1911); vols. 11–15 (Havana: Imprenta de Rambla, Bouza y Ca, 1913–19).

53 *Obras completas de Martí,* 8 vols., ed. Nestor Carbonell (Havana: La Prensa, 1918–20); *Obras completas,* 8 vols., ed. Alberto Ghiraldo (Madrid: Atlántida), 1925–29); *Obras completas de Martí,* 2 vols., ed. Armando Godoy and Ventura García Calderón (Paris: Excelsior, 1925–26).

54 *Obras completas de Martí,* 74 vols., ed. Gonzalo de Quesada y Miranda (Havana: Editorial Trópico, 1936–53). A two-volume edition was printed on onionskin: *Obras completas,* with a prologue and biographical summary by M. Isidro Méndez, preliminary note and epilogue by M. Sánchez Roca (Havana: Lex, 1946).

55 See Kirk's criticisms in *José Martí,* pp. 3–18.

56 For an analysis of its contents, see Carlos Ripoll, *Archivo José Martí: Repertorio crítico* (New York: Eliseo Torres, 1972).

57 Clouded by controversy, however, it was not finished until the 1960s.

58 Gray, *José Martí,* pp. 100–101.

59 Kirk, *José Martí,* p. 3.

60 Kapcia sees Martí's surge in popularity during the 1930s and 1940s as resulting from an effort by the bourgeoisie to appropriate a popular image to legitimize its rule. See Antoni Kapcia, "Cuban Populism and the Birth of the Myth of Martí," in *José Martí,* ed. Abel and Torrents, p. 60. Unfortunately, he does not develop this interesting thesis.

61 The revivification of Martí's image is a very complex question and well beyond the scope of this essay. I lean toward the hypothesis that a contributing factor was the increased availability of Martí's works, satisfying the demands of a growing literate class interested in political issues. For a larger treatment of the question, see Ottma Ethe, *José Martí: Apóstol, poeta, revolucionario. Una historia de su recepción* (Mexico City: Universidad Nacional Autónoma de México, 1955).

62 See Carlos Ripoll, "José Martí and Socialism," in Ripoll, *José Martí, the United States, and the Marxist Interpretation of Cuban History* (New Brunswick: Transaction Books, 1984), pp. 61–74.

63 Roberto Fernández Retamar, "Noticia," in *Lectura de Martí,* pp. 13–17. See also John M. Kirk, "José Martí and His Concept of the Intelectual Comprometido," in *José Martí,* ed. Abel and Torrents, pp. 108–23.

64 E.g.: Ezequiel Martínez Estrada, *Martí revolucionario,* 2d ed. (Havana: Casa de las Américas, 1974); Ezequiel Martínez Estrada, *Martí, El héroe y su acción revolucionaria,* 3d ed. (Mexico City: Siglo XXI 1972); Jorge Ibarra, *José Martí, Dirigente político e ideólogo revolucionario* (Havana: Editorial de Ciencias Sociales, 1980); José Cantón

Navarro, *Algunas ideas de José Martí en relación con la clase obrera y el socialismo* (Havana: Editorial Política, 1980).

65 *Obras completas,* 28 vols. (Havana: Editorial Nacional de Cuba, 1963–73).

66 For example, the famous sentence from his letter to Manuel Mercado—"I have lived inside the monster, and I know its entrails" (May 18, 1895)—has given rise to at least two interpretations. See Kirk, *José Martí,* pp. 8–10; and Carlos Ripoll, " 'Inside the Monster': Martí and the United States," in Ripoll, *José Martí,* pp. 51–59.

67 A contradictory work, *La gran enciclopedia martiana* (see note 1 above) aims more at marketability or popular readership than at completeness or accuracy. Even its most valuable asset, the illustrations collected, suffer from very poor reproduction.

Index

Contributors

Jeffrey Belnap is Associate Professor of Humanities at Brigham Young University, Hawaii Campus where he teaches comparative arts and world humanities. He is presently at work on *Mediating Tehuantepec: Nationalism, Regionalism and Cosmopolitanism in Post-Revolutionary Mexico,* a project devoted to the relationships among Mexico's popular traditions, nation-building and the cosmopolitan avant garde from 1920–1950.

Raúl Fernández, Professor of Social Sciences at the University of California, Irvine, has written extensively on U.S.–Latin American economic and cultural relations. He is the author of *The United States–Mexico Border: A Politico-Economic Profile.* His current research focuses on latin jazz and salsa music.

Ada Ferrer is Assistant Professor of Latin American and Caribbean History at New York University. She is the author of *Ambivalent Revolution: Race, Nation, and Anticolonial Insurgency in Cuba, 1868–1898* (1999).

Susan Gillman, Professor of Literature and American Studies at the University of California, Santa Cruz, is currently completing a book entitled *American Race Melodramas, 1877–1915.*

George Lipsitz is Professor of Ethnic Studies at the University of California, San Diego. His publications include *The Possessive Investment in Whiteness, Dangerous Crossroads, Rainbow at Midnight, Time Passages, Sidewalks of St. Louis,* and *A Life in the Struggle: Ivory Perry and the Culture of Opposition.*

Oscar R. Martí specializes in Latin American Philosophy. He has taught philosophy and logic at the City College of New York, the University of California, Los Angeles, and the Universidad Autónoma de México. His writings on Latin American philosophy have appeared in *Metaphilosophy* and *Cuadernos Americanos.*

Beatrice Pita teaches in the Department of Literature at the University of California, San Diego. With Rosaura Sánchez, she has edited and introduced María Amparo Ruiz de Burton's two novels, *The Squatter and the Don* and *Who Would Have Thought It?*

David W. Noble is Professor of American Studies at the University of Minnesota. Among his several books are *Historians Against History, The End of American History,* and, with Peter Carroll, *The Free and the UnFree.*

Donald E. Pease is the Avalon Professor of the Humanities and American Studies at Dartmouth. He is the author of *Visionary Compacts: Renaissance Writings in Cultural Context,* and the editor of *The American Renaissance*

Reconsidered (with Walter Benn Michaels), *New Essays on the Rise of Silas Lapham, Cultures of U.S. Imperialism* (with Amy Kaplan), *New Americanists: Revisionist Interventions into the Canon,* and *National Identities and Post-American Narratives.*

Brenda Gayle Plummer is Professor of History at the University of Wisconsin, Madison. An expert on Caribbean history, Afro-American history, and the history of U.S. foreign relations, she is the author of *Haiti and the Great Powers, 1902–1915; Haiti and the United States;* and *Rising Wind: Black Americans and U.S. Foreign Affairs, 1935–1960.*

Rosaura Sánchez is a Professor in the Literature Department at the University of California, San Diego. She is the author of *Telling Identities,* and, with Beatrice Pita, she has edited two of Amparo Ruiz de Burton's novels.

Susana Rotker is Associate Professor of Spanish American Literature, Rutgers University, New Jersey. She is the author of several books including *Fundación de una escritura: las crónicas de José Martí,* Casa de las Américas Literary Prize for Best Essay 1991; *Los transgresores de la literatura venezolana* and *Ensayistas de Nuestra América.*

José David Saldívar is Professor of Comparative Ethnic Studies at the University of California, Berkeley, and Acting Director of the Center for the Teaching and Study of American Cultures. He is the author of *The Dialectics of Our America* and *Border Matters.*

Enrico Mario Santí is Professor of Spanish and Latin American Literature at Georgetown University in Washington, D.C. He is the author of several books including *Pensar a Martí: Notas para un centenario.* He is currently completing an intellectual biography of Octavio Paz.

Doris Sommer is Professor of Latin American Literature at Harvard University. She is author of *Foundational Fictions: The National Romances of Latin America* as well as the forthcoming *Proceed with Caution: A Rhetoric of Particularism.*

Brook Thomas is Chair of the Department of English and Comparative Literature at the University of California, Irvine. His books include *Cross-examinations of Law and Literature: Cooper, Hawthorne, Stowe, and Melville; The New Historicism and Other Old-Fashioned Topics* and *American Literary Realism and the Failed Promise of Contract.*